내신 및 시·도 교육청 영어듣기평가 완벽 대비

Listening

올리고

Level **3**

중학영어 듣기 모의고사

 DARAKWON

Structure & **F**eatures ┃ 구성과 특징

Listening Test

전국 16개 시·도 교육청 주관 영어듣기능력평가 및 내신 교과서 반영!

최신 기출 유형을 철저히 분석, 반영하여 실제 시험과 유사하게 구성한 모의고사로 실전 감각을 키울 수 있습니다. 또한 영어 교과서의 주요 표현 및 소재들을 활용하여 내신까지 효과적으로 대비할 수 있습니다.

Further Study

주요 지문 심화학습으로 내신 서술형 완벽 대비!

Listening Test의 주요 지문만을 모아 서술형 문제로 다시 풀어볼 수 있도록 구성하였습니다. 보다 심화된 듣기 문제로 내신 서술형 평가에 철저히 대비하고, 듣기 실력을 강화할 수 있습니다.

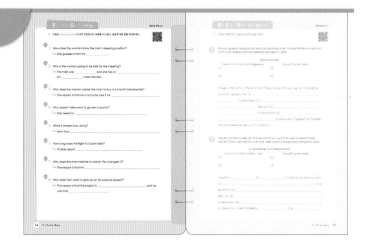

On Your Own

내신 말하기 수행평가 대비까지 한 번에!

Listening Test 및 기출 문제에서 출제된 주제와 소재를 응용한 다양한 연습 문제를 통해 별도로 준비하기 어려운 내신 말하기 수행평가까지 한 번에 대비할 수 있습니다.

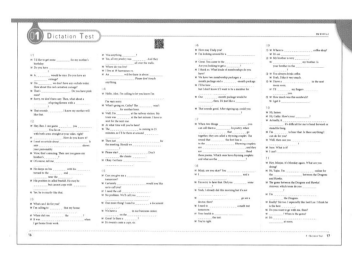

Dictation Test

전 지문 받아쓰기로 꼼꼼한 마무리 학습!

매회 전 지문 받아쓰기를 수록하여 놓친 부분을 빠짐없이 확인할 수 있습니다. 문제의 핵심이 되는 키워드, 중요 표현, 연음 등을 확인하며, 복습은 물론 자신의 취약점을 다시 한 번 확인할 수 있습니다.

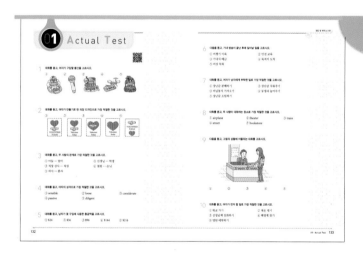

Actual Test

실전 모의고사로 최종 실력 점검!

실제 시험과 가장 유사한 모의고사로서 자신의 실력을 최종 점검해볼 수 있습니다. 시험에 자주 나오는 유형과 표현들을 100% 반영한 영어듣기능력평가 완벽 대비 모의고사입니다.

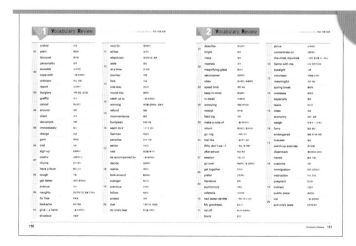

Vocabulary Review

중요 어휘 및 표현을 한눈에!

본문에 나오는 주요 어휘와 표현을 각 모의고사 회별로 한눈에 정리하여 단어 학습을 보다 효율적으로 할 수 있습니다.

Contents ㅣ 목차

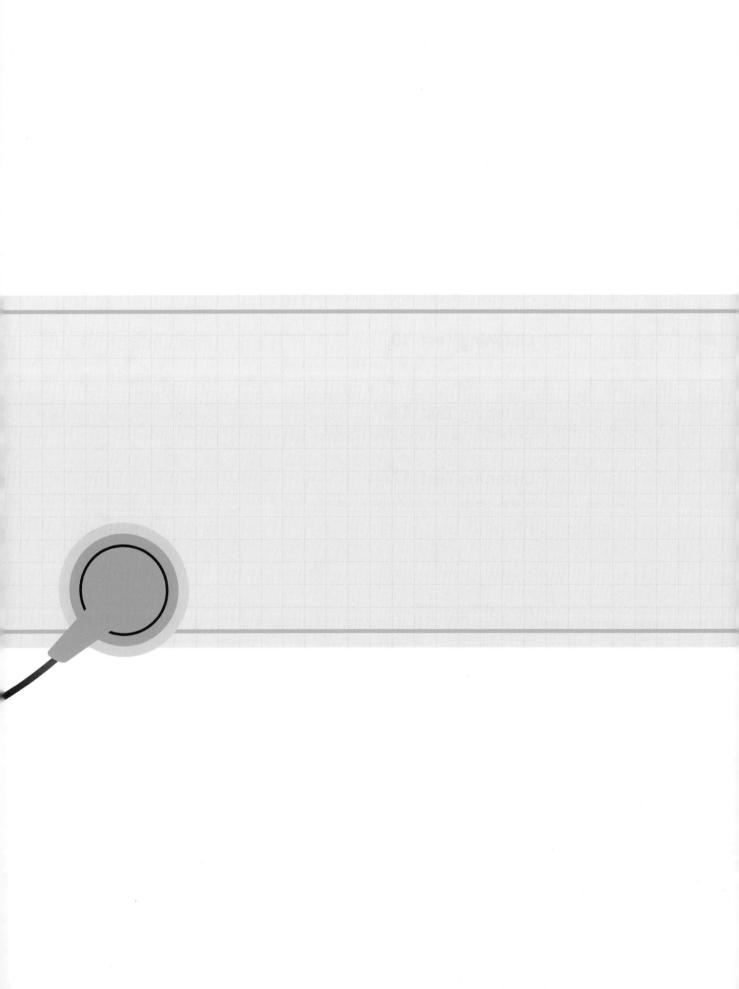

Listening Test
01~12회

01 대화를 듣고, 남자가 사려고 하는 것을 고르시오.

① ② ③  ④ ⑤

02 대화를 듣고, 남자의 형이 잠자는 자세로 알맞은 것을 고르시오.

①  ②  ③  ④  ⑤

03 대화를 듣고, 여자의 심정으로 가장 적절한 것을 고르시오.

① pleasant   ② shameful   ③ sorrowful
④ satisfied   ⑤ terrified

04 대화를 듣고, 두 사람이 참여할 회의 시간으로 가장 적절한 것을 고르시오.

① 11:00   ② 11:10   ③ 11:20   ④ 11:35   ⑤ 11:50

05 대화를 듣고, 여자의 직업으로 가장 적절한 것을 고르시오.

① 문방구 직원   ② 도서관 사서   ③ 전화 교환원
④ 복사기 판매원   ⑤ 호텔 접수원

06 대화를 듣고, 남자가 여자에게 요청한 일로 가장 적절한 것을 고르시오.

① 가입비 안내해주기　　　　② 가입 방법 안내해주기
③ 체육관 안내해주기　　　　④ 운동 방법 알려주기
⑤ 운동 효과 알려주기

07 다음을 듣고, 무엇에 관한 설명인지 고르시오.

① 시의 형식　　　　　　　② 단어들의 기원
③ 시 감상법　　　　　　　④ 시 외우는 방법
⑤ 친구 사귀는 방법

08 대화를 듣고, 여자가 할 일로 가장 적절한 것을 고르시오.

① 운동하러 가기　　　　　② 시험 공부 하기
③ 병원 가기　　　　　　　④ 약 먹기
⑤ 잠자기

09 다음을 듣고, 그림의 상황에 어울리는 대화를 고르시오.

①　　　　　②　　　　　③　　　　　④　　　　　⑤

10 대화를 듣고, 여자의 마지막 말에 담긴 의도로 가장 적절한 것을 고르시오.

① 감사　　　　　　② 요청　　　　　　③ 항의
④ 거절　　　　　　⑤ 충고

11 대화를 듣고, 두 사람이 축구 경기를 보기로 한 요일을 고르시오.

① 토요일　　　　　② 일요일　　　　　③ 월요일
④ 화요일　　　　　⑤ 수요일

12 대화를 듣고, 두 사람이 대화하는 장소로 가장 적절한 것을 고르시오.

① library　　　　　② bookstore　　　　　③ cafeteria
④ museum　　　　　⑤ art gallery

13 대화를 듣고, 대화 내용과 일치하지 <u>않는</u> 것을 고르시오.

Ticket Information			
Destination	① Guam	Date	② April 14th
Time	③ 10:10 a.m.	Hours	④ 8 hr. 40 min.
Ticket type	Round-trip	Fare	⑤ $1,800

14 다음을 듣고, 어떤 경기에 해당하는 내용인지 고르시오.

① table tennis　　　　　② baseball　　　　　③ volleyball
④ soccer　　　　　⑤ basketball

15 대화를 듣고, 여자가 환불을 요구한 이유를 고르시오.

① 사이즈가 안 맞아서　　　　　② 잘못된 가격으로 사서
③ 교환이 불가능해서　　　　　④ 지퍼가 고장 나서
⑤ 소매가 불편해서

16 다음을 듣고, 두 사람의 대화가 <u>어색한</u> 것을 고르시오.

①   ②   ③   ④   ⑤

17 대화를 듣고, Cinema Paradise Theater에 관해 언급되지 <u>않은</u> 것을 고르시오.

① 상영 중인 영화   ② 상영 시간
③ 관람표 가격   ④ 상영 영화의 등급
⑤ 웹사이트 주소

18 다음을 듣고, Tom이 가게 직원에게 할 말로 가장 적절한 것을 고르시오.

① Can I help you?
② Sorry, I don't know.
③ I want to buy the sneakers.
④ Can you order a pair for me?
⑤ I don't want these big shirts.

[19-20] 대화를 듣고, 남자의 마지막 말에 이어질 여자의 응답으로 가장 적절한 것을 고르시오.

19 ① A ticket is $8.50.
② The last show is at 11:30 p.m.
③ It's a fantasy adventure movie.
④ The movie begins at 4:30 p.m. and 7 p.m.
⑤ How about meeting at 3 o'clock in front of the theater?

20 ① I'm happy to hear that.
② Don't think like that. I'll help you.
③ Just give up and let's go watch a movie.
④ Can you give me a hand if you finish early?
⑤ You're working night and day to finish the project on time.

● 다음은 **Listening Test 01**의 주요 지문입니다. 녹음을 다시 듣고, 질문에 대한 답을 완성하세요.

Q2 1 How does the woman know the man's sleeping position?

    ⌐→ She guesses it from his _____.

Q4 2 Why is the woman going to be late for the meeting?

    ⌐→ The train was _____ and she has to _____

        for _____ more minutes.

Q6 3 Why does the woman advise the man to buy a 3-month membership?

    ⌐→ The reason is that he is not quite sure if he _____.

Q8 4 Why doesn't Minji want to go see a doctor?

    ⌐→ She needs to _____.

Q11 5 What is Minjae busy doing?

    ⌐→ He is busy _____.

Q13 6 How long does the flight to Guam take?

    ⌐→ It takes about _____.

Q19 7 Why does the man hesitate to watch *The Avengers 3*?

    ⌐→ The reason is that he _____.

Q20 8 Why does Tom want to give up on his science project?

    ⌐→ The reason is that the project is _____ and he

        only has _____.

● 자신의 상황에 맞게 내용을 완성하고 말해 보세요.

A Do you agree or disagree that schools should provide lunches? Write your opinion giving two reasons and a supporting example for each.

School Lunches

Reasons for agreeing/disagreeing	Supporting examples
(1)	(2)
(3)	(4)

I believe that schools (have to/don't have to) provide lunches for students for

two main reasons. First, (1)_____

_____. For example, (2)_____

_____. Second, (3)_____

_____. For example, (4)_____

_____. In conclusion, I (agree/don't agree)

that schools should have lunch programs.

B Novels are often made into movies. Would you prefer to read novels or to see movies? Write your opinion with two reasons and a supporting example for each.

To See Movies or to Read Novels?

Reasons I prefer movies/novels	Supporting examples
(1)	(2)
(3)	(4)

I prefer _____ to _____ for two main reasons. First,

(1)_____. For

example, (2)_____.

Second, (3)_____.

For example, (4)_____.

In conclusion, I think it is better _____ than _____.

01

M I'd like to get some _____ for my mother's birthday.

W Do you have _____ _____ _____ _____?

M A _____ would be nice. Do you have an _____ corsage?

W I'm _____ we don't have any orchids today. How about this red carnation corsage?

M That's _____ _____. Do you have pink ones?

W Sorry, we don't have any. Then, what about a _____ of spring flowers with a _____ _____?

M That sounds _____. I know my mother will like that.

02

W Hey, Ben. I can guess _____ you _____ _____. You lie on _____ _____ with both arms straight at your sides, right?

M _____ _____. How do you know it?

W I read an article about _____ _____. It says _____ _____ _____ shows your personality.

M Wow, that's amazing. Then can you guess my brother's _____?

W Of course, tell me _____ _____ _____.

M He sleeps on his _____ with his _____ turned to the _____ and _____ _____ near the _____.

W His position is called freefall. He may be _____ but cannot cope with _____ _____.

M Yes, he is exactly like that.

03

M What can I do for you?

W I'm calling to _____ that my house _____ _____ _____ _____.

M When did you _____ the _____?

W It was _____ _____ _____ when I got home from work.

M Was anything _____?

W Yes, all my jewelry was _____. And they _____ _____ all over the walls.

M Where do you live?

W I live at 19 Saemunan-ro.

M An _____ will be there in about _____ _____ _____. Please don't touch anything.

04

W Hello, Alex. I'm calling to let you know I'm _____ _____ _____ _____ _____. I'm very sorry.

M What's going on, Cathy? The _____ won't _____ for another hour.

W Well, I'm _____ at the railway station. My train was _____ at the last minute. I have to wait for the next one.

M At what time will you be here?

W The _____ _____ is coming in 25 minutes, so I'll be there at around _____ _____.

M Then just _____ _____ _____ for the meeting. Should we _____ _____ _____?

W Please start _____ _____. Don't _____ the clients _____.

M Okay. Get here _____ _____ _____ _____.

05

M Can you give me a _____ _____ tomorrow?

W Certainly. _____ _____ would you like us to call you?

M I need the call _____ _____.

W No problem. We'll call you _____ _____ _____ _____.

M One more thing! I need to _____ a document _____.

W We have a _____ in our business center, _____ on the _____ _____.

M Great! Is there a _____?

W It's twenty cents a copy, sir.

06

W How may I help you?

M I'm looking around for a _____ _____ _____.

W Great. You came to the _____ _____. Are you looking to get a _____?

M I think so. What kinds of memberships do you have?

W We have two membership packages: a _____-month package and a _____-month package.

M I'll be here _____ _____ _____ but I don't know if I want to be a member for _____ _____.

W Our _____-month package would be _____, then. It's just like a _____ _____.

M That sounds good. After signing up, could you _____ _____ _____?

07

M When two things _____ _____, you can call them a _____. In poetry, when _____ _____ that _____ go together, they are called a rhyming couplet. The sound that _____ the first line is _____ in the _____ _____. Rhyming couplets are _____ _____ _____, and they are _____ _____ _____. Read these poems. Which ones have rhyming couplets and what are the _____ _____?

08

M Minji, are you okay? You _____ _____.

W I _____ _____ _____ and a _____ _____.

M I'm sorry to hear that. Did you _____ some _____?

W Yeah, I already did this morning but it's not _____ _____.

M _____ _____ _____ go see a doctor, then?

W I need to _____ _____ a math test tomorrow.

M Your health is _____ _____ _____ the test.

W You're right.

09

① W Where is _____ _____ coffee shop?
   M It's on _____ _____.
② W My brother is very _____.
   M _____ _____ my brother. Is your brother in the _____ _____ _____?
③ W You always drink coffee.
   M Yeah, I like it very much.
④ W I have a _____ _____ in the next room soon.
   M I'll _____ my fingers _____ _____ you.
⑤ W How much was this sandwich?
   M I got it _____ _____.

10

W Hi, James.

M Hi, Cathy. How's your _____?

W Actually, it _____ _____ _____ _____. It's difficult for me to bend forward or stand for long.

M I'm _____ to hear that. Is there anything I can do for you?

W Well, then can you _____ _____ _____ _____?

M Sure. What is it?

W I can't _____ _____ _____.

11

W Hey, Minjae, it's Monday again. What are you doing?

M Hi, Yujin. I'm _____ _____ online for the _____ _____ between the Dragons and Hawks.

W The game between the Dragons and Hawks! Anyway, which team do you _____ _____?

M I'm _____ _____ _____ _____ the Dragons.

W Really? Me too. I especially like Jaeil Lee. I think he is the best _____.

M Do you want to go with me, then?

W _____! When is the game?

M It's _____ _____ _____ _____ at noon.

W Perfect.

12

M Excuse me, ma'am. Where can I find _____ about _____ _____ II?

W You can find them in _____ F. It's in the history section.

M Thank you. By the way, how many books can I _____ _____ _____ _____ _____?

W Five. And you can _____ them _____ _____ _____.

M Good. That's _____ _____ _____ me to write the report.

W If you have any _____ _____ a _____, please tell me.

M Alright. Thank you very much.

W _____ _____.

13

[Telephone rings.]

W Thank you for _____ ABC _____. How may I help you?

M Hi. Do you have a _____ _____ _____ tomorrow, _____ _____? I have urgent business.

W Yes, it leaves at 10:10 _____ _____ _____. Fortunately, we have four seats left.

M Good. _____ _____ does the trip _____ exactly?

W It will take about _____ _____ and _____ _____. It will be a long journey.

M I see. How much is the _____?

W A _____ _____ is $1,800, and a _____ _____ costs $2,200.

M Okay. I will _____ a round-trip ticket.

14

W The Sharks had a _____ _____ _____ this year. They _____ _____ _____ than any other team. And they won the _____. The final game was exciting. The Sharks were _____ _____ _____ in the _____ inning. The team had to _____ hard to _____ _____ _____ their opponent. Luckily, they did that. David Wilson _____

_____ _____ _____. He ran to home base with a big smile. He was very excited to _____ the _____ _____.

15

M Hello! How may I help you?

W I'd like to _____ _____ _____ for this jacket.

M _____ _____ with it?

W The jacket is nice, but the zipper _____ _____.

M Don't you want to _____ it for another one?

W OK. But let me check the _____ first.

M No problem. _____ _____ the _____.

W That's okay. I _____ _____ _____ it before I bought it.

16

① **M** Would you mind _____ _____ _____?

　　W Yes, of course. What is it about?

② **M** What are you _____?

　　W I'm reading a book _____ _____ _____ _____ _____.

③ **M** You look so happy.

　　W I just _____ _____ _____ _____.

④ **M** Have you ever met _____ _____ _____?

　　W Yes. I _____ met a _____ _____.

⑤ **M** What seems to be _____ _____?

　　W I have _____ _____ _____.

17

[Telephone rings.]

W _____ _____ for _____ the Cinema Paradise Theater. How may I help you?

M Hi. What movies _____ _____ _____?

W A new 007 _____, *The Virus*, and *Romantic Holiday* are now playing at the theater.

M How much is a ticket?

W A ticket is _____ dollars and _____ cents _____ _____ and _____ dollars _____ _____ up to _____ _____. A ticket for _____ is

_____ dollars.

M Does the movie *Romantic Holiday* have an age limit?

W That's an R-rated _____, so you must be at least _____ _____ _____ or be accompanied by _____ _____. For _____ _____, please visit our website at www.cinemaparadise.com.

M OK, thank you.

18

W Tom wants to buy _____ _____ _____ _____. He goes to _____ _____ and finds the style of sneakers he _____ _____ _____ buy. He asks _____ _____ to bring him the sneakers _____ _____ _____, but the clerk says that they _____ _____ _____ in his size. The sizes they do have are _____ too big _____ too small for him. Tom doesn't want to buy another style of sneakers. In this situation, what would Tom most likely say to the clerk?

19

W Would you like to see _____ _____ _____ _____?

M I'd like to. What would you like to see?

W How about *The Avengers 3*?

M *The Avengers 3*? I haven't watched _____ _____ _____ yet. Do you think it'll be okay?

W Yes. Don't worry. I heard that the movie is _____ _____ _____ and _____.

M _____ _____ of movie is it?

W It's a fantasy adventure movie.

20

W Hi, Tom. How's everything going?

M Amy, I'll _____ _____ on my _____ _____.

W Do you mean the project _____ _____?

M Yes. It's _____ _____ for me and I only have _____ _____ _____.

W Come on, just _____ _____ _____ and at least you won't _____.

M But I don't think I _____ _____ _____.

W Don't think like that. I'll help you.

01 대화를 듣고, 여자가 찾는 가방으로 알맞은 것을 고르시오.

①  ②  ③  ④ ⑤

02 대화를 듣고, 여자가 묘사하는 사진을 고르시오.

① ② ③  ④  ⑤

03 대화를 듣고, 남자의 직업으로 가장 적절한 것을 고르시오.

① 경찰관 　　　　② 환경미화원 　　　　③ 의사
④ 운전 강사 　　　⑤ 보험설계사

04 대화를 듣고, 여자의 심정으로 가장 적절한 것을 고르시오.

① jealous 　　　　② relieved 　　　　③ irritated
④ sorrowful 　　　⑤ miserable

05 대화를 듣고, 두 사람이 견학 갔다가 돌아오는 날짜를 고르시오.

① 9월 6일 　　　　② 9월 15일 　　　　③ 9월 16일
④ 9월 21일 　　　⑤ 9월 22일

06 대화를 듣고, 남자의 마지막 말에 담긴 의도로 가장 적절한 것을 고르시오.

① 수락　　② 조언　　③ 제안　　④ 거절　　⑤ 감사

07 대화를 듣고, 여자가 먼저 할 일로 가장 적절한 것을 고르시오.

① 수학 복습하기　　② 수학선생님과 상담하기
③ 수학 과제 제출하기　　④ 방과 후 수업 등록하기
⑤ 남자와 수학 공부하기

08 대화를 듣고, 두 사람이 선택한 영화 시작 시각을 고르시오.

① 1:50 p.m.　　② 2:30 p.m.　　③ 3:50 p.m.
④ 4:20 p.m.　　⑤ 4:50 p.m.

09 대화를 듣고, 남자에 대한 내용과 일치하지 <u>않는</u> 것을 고르시오.

Position	① Student teacher
Current Major	② English education
Current Year	③ Sophomore
Hobby	④ What it is – Horseback riding
	⑤ How often he does it – About twice a month

10 대화를 듣고, 남자가 할 일로 가장 적절한 것을 고르시오.

① go to the bookstore to buy a book
② go to the library to borrow a book
③ go to the classroom to have a class
④ go see the English teacher to ask a question
⑤ go to the cafeteria to look for his friends

11 다음을 듣고, 무엇에 관한 내용인지 고르시오.

① 수상 소감　　　② 기내 방송　　　③ 광고 방송
④ 취임 연설　　　⑤ 자기 소개

12 대화를 듣고, 남자가 화면이 큰 휴대전화를 선호하는 이유를 고르시오.

① 동영상을 많이 보므로　　　② 눈이 덜 피로해서
③ 디자인이 좋아서　　　④ 케이스가 다양해서
⑤ 사용하기 편해서

13 대화를 듣고, 두 사람이 대화하는 장소로 가장 적절한 것을 고르시오.

① travel agency　　　② restaurant
③ swimming pool　　　④ zoo
⑤ supermarket

14 대화를 듣고, 여자의 소망으로 가장 적절한 것을 고르시오.

① 성당 가기　　　② 비행기 타기　　　③ 긴 방학
④ 해외 여행　　　⑤ 바다 가기

15 대화를 듣고, 남자가 구입한 항공권과 일치하지 <u>않는</u> 것을 고르시오.

Flight Information	
① Ticket type	Round trip
② Departure	New York / 12-28-2013
③ Arrival	Seoul / 01-11-2015
④ Class	Economy
⑤ Fare	$1,986

16 다음을 듣고, giant panda에 관해 언급되지 않은 것을 고르시오.

① 생김새 ② 크기 ③ 개체 수
④ 종의 위기 ⑤ 보존 방법

17 다음을 듣고, 두 사람의 대화가 어색한 것을 고르시오.

① ② ③ ④ ⑤

18 대화를 듣고, 대화 내용과 일치하지 않는 것을 고르시오.

① 비행기는 곧 도쿄에 도착한다.
② 비행기는 지연 없이 순항 중이다.
③ 환승 승객들이 먼저 내려야 한다.
④ 환승 승객들은 세관과 입국 심사를 받지 않는다.
⑤ 런던행 환승객은 추가 안내를 받아야 한다.

19 다음을 듣고, 수지가 남자에게 할 말로 가장 적절한 것을 고르시오.

① That's too bad.
② How often do you smoke?
③ When did you first start smoking?
④ You are not allowed to smoke here.
⑤ You can smoke anywhere in this building.

20 대화를 듣고, 여자의 마지막 말에 이어질 남자의 응답으로 가장 적절한 것을 고르시오.

① I hope the food is nice.
② I'm not supposed to eat salty food.
③ Kimchi is a traditional Korean food.
④ The foods were fantastic and suited my taste.
⑤ Every time I eat spicy food, I have heartburn.

다음은 **Listening Test 02**의 주요 지문입니다. 녹음을 다시 듣고, 질문에 대한 답을 완성하세요.

Q2

1 Why do the woman's niece and nephew in the photo look serious?

⤷ The reason is that the girl is teaching the boy about _____ from the Earth.

Q4

2 What kind of trouble does the woman have with the earphones?

⤷ They make an _____ in the background, so the sound quality is _____.

Q8

3 What are the man and the woman going to do this Saturday?

⤷ They are going to _____.

Q9

4 How does the man feel now?

⤷ He feels _____ but _____.

Q12

5 What is the most important thing to Alison when she chooses a cell phone?

⤷ To her, _____ is most important.

Q13

6 Where does the man want to go for their vacation and why?

⤷ He wants to go to _____ because he thinks _____ _____ and they can _____.

Q15

7 How long does the man want to stay in Seoul?

⤷ The man wants to stay in Seoul for _____.

Q19

8 What makes Suji upset?

⤷ She is upset because a man _____ _____.

● 자신의 상황에 맞게 내용을 완성하고 말해 보세요.

A   Describe the following picture, answering the questions in the table below.

Describing a Picture

(1) What does the picture show?

(2) What do you think is happening now?

(3) Explain how you think the situation occurred.

This picture shows (1)_____.

It seems that (2)_____.

I think that (3)_____

_____.

B   Do you agree that everyone should dress according to the latest fashion trend? Write your opinion giving two reasons and a supporting example for each.

Following the Latest Fashion Trend

Reasons for agreeing/disagreeing	Supporting examples
(1)	(2)
(3)	(4)

I (agree/disagree) that everyone should dress according to the latest fashion trend for two reasons. First, (1)_____

_____. For example, (2)_____

_____.

Second, (3)_____

_____. For example, (4)_____

_____. In conclusion,

I (believe/don't believe) that everyone should dress according to the latest

fashion trend.

01

W Excuse me, could you please help me? I _____
_____ my _____.

M Oh, I'm sorry to hear that. Can you _____ it
to me?

W It is a _____ _____ bag with a
_____ on the front.

M Does it have a _____ _____ on it?

W Yes. Also it has a _____-_____
_____ attached to the handle.

M Okay, that helps a lot. Please wait _____
_____ _____.

W Thank you. I hope you can _____
_____ _____.

02

M That's a _____ _____. Did you take it?

W Yes. I took it last month and got it printed
yesterday.

M _____ are they in this _____?

W They are my seven-year-old _____ and five-
year-old _____.

M They are so _____ but they look really
_____. Why is she _____ _____
at the _____ _____?

W She has a _____ _____ in her hand.
She was explaining to her brother _____
_____ away the moon is from the earth.

M Wow, she will be an _____ someday.

03

W What do you usually do in your job?

M I _____ _____ _____ to people. I
mean to _____.

W What kind of drivers are they?

M They are the people who _____ _____
the _____ _____.

W What is the _____ _____ _____
of your job?

M Well, it is when people don't _____ the
_____ _____.

W Is there anything that you'd like to tell them?

M Well, they should _____ _____
_____ that following the _____

_____ is very important. _____
_____ when people don't follow them.

04

M Good afternoon, can I help you?

W I hope so. I bought these _____ here about
two months ago, but the _____ _____
is _____.

M Can you tell me the _____ with the
_____ _____ more _____?

W There is an _____ _____ sound in the
background, so I want a _____.

M Do you have your _____?

W No, I _____ it.

M I'm sorry but it _____ _____
_____ to give refunds without the receipt.

W I want to _____ _____ _____.

05

W What date will our field trip be on?

M It will be _____, _____ _____. It's
next Tuesday. Make a note of that in your calendar.

W Yes, I will write that down.

M We will leave at _____ _____
_____ _____. Be at school _____
_____ _____ _____ to get your
bags on the bus.

W When are we going to come back?

M We will _____ _____ _____
later and arrive at our school at 7 p.m. Any more
questions?

W No. I am really _____ _____
_____ the trip.

06

M Amy, you _____ _____ _____,
don't you?

W Yes, I do.

M Well, would you like to _____ _____
_____ today?

W Sorry, I don't _____ _____ it today.

M Then, what would you like to do?

W Why don't we _____ _____? Didn't
you say you'd like to _____ _____

_____ _____?

M OK. Let's go out now.

07

M What are you doing?

W I have been _____ _____ _____ this math problem for the last 20 minutes but I _____ _____ _____ _____ how to solve it.

M Is the homework for tomorrow?

W No, it is due at the end of next week.

M _____ _____ _____ get some after-school tutoring?

W Why haven't I thought of it? I'll _____ _____ for it tomorrow.

M Before going to the session, you _____ _____ _____ all the problems _____. Then you can _____ _____ _____ for the tutor.

W Thanks for your advice. I'll _____ _____ _____.

08

M Do you _____ _____ _____ this Saturday?

W Why?

M If you're free, let's _____ _____ and _____ _____ _____, Frozen.

W Frozen? I really want to see it. When is the movie showing?

M Do you prefer _____ _____ _____, _____, or _____?

W Well, let's go in the afternoon.

M Sure. There are _____ _____ in the afternoon; _____ at 2:30 and _____ _____ at 4:50.

W Let's go to the _____ one.

M No problem. I'll _____ _____ _____ at 4:20.

09

W Are you Seungyoon Lee, the new _____ _____? I'm the _____ of this school, Mary Jones. Nice to meet you.

M Hello. I'm _____ _____ _____ _____, too.

W How do you feel?

M I'm _____ about whether I can teach well or not. But _____ _____ _____ _____, I'm very _____ _____ _____ teaching.

W I know how you feel now because I had the same feeling when I was _____ _____ _____. _____, what's your major?

M I used to major in _____ _____ but now I'm majoring in _____ _____. I changed it two years ago when I was a _____.

W I see. What's your _____?

M I love _____ _____. I go to the horse-riding track _____ _____ _____ _____.

10

M Olivia, do you have the _____ _____ for our English class?

W I'm sorry. I _____ _____ _____ _____ because I don't have an English class today.

M Oh, no. I need to borrow that book before the class begins. _____ _____ _____ _____?

W _____ _____ _____ ask Tommy? He keeps all his books _____ _____ _____.

M Really? Thanks for the _____. Do you know where he is now?

W I saw him _____ _____ _____ a few minutes ago. He was with Rica.

M Good. I will ask Rica if I can't borrow Tommy's book.

W _____ _____ hurry up. The bell will ring in three minutes.

M _____ _____. Bye. See you.

11

M Good evening, _____ and _____. I'm very _____ to _____ this _____ for best actor this year. I can't begin to say how much I appreciate this honor. There are so many people I'd like to thank but I can't _____ _____ all of them. _____ _____ _____ I got on the stage, my _____ _____. I really appreciate their help. I will _____ _____ concentrate

on acting, so I will be worthy of getting this award.
_____ _____ again for _____
_____.

12

M Alison, what is _____ _____ to you
when choosing a cellular phone?

W To me, the _____ is most important.

M What else?

W Maybe the size of the screen. _____
_____ _____ _____.

M _____ _____ _____. Since I have
_____ _____, a small screen makes my
eyes easily tired.

W What about the color?

M I actually _____ _____ _____ it.

W I see. Anyway, we can change the color by changing
the _____ _____.

13

W Where shall we go for our _____ this year,
Luke?

M How about Busan? _____ _____ is
always good, and we can _____ _____
_____ _____.

W I'd rather do something _____ _____
this year, such as volunteering in a poor country.

M That's a good idea, but I want to have a _____
_____ during my vacation.

W By the way, _____ did we _____? It is
taking _____ _____.

M It's been _____ _____ _____
since we gave her the order.

W I'm _____ _____ that I could eat a horse.

14

M Sally, what are you going to do this _____
_____?

W I really want to _____ _____. I've never
been overseas because I'm too scared to fly.

M Are you serious?

W Yes. I can't get on a plane! _____ _____
_____ _____ abroad?

M Yeah, I traveled to Europe for 15 days last year with
my family.

W Sounds great. _____ _____ did you like
most?

M I _____ loved Italy. The Duomo in Milano
was very beautiful.

W I wish I could go to Italy.

M _____ _____ _____ _____
you. Every great _____ begins with a
_____ _____.

15

[Telephone rings.]

W ABC Airlines. How may I help you?

M I'd like to book _____ _____
_____ from _____ _____ to
_____.

W _____ _____ would you like to
_____?

M I'd like to _____ _____ _____
_____.

W _____ will you be _____?

M I'd like to _____ two weeks later, _____
_____ _____ of _____,
_____.

W _____ _____ would you like?

M _____ _____, please.

W That's _____ dollars, please.

16

W Let me tell you about giant pandas, today. Giant
pandas are large _____-and-_____
animals that look like _____ _____.
They grow to be about five feet tall and can weigh
up to 200 pounds. The _____ _____
_____ around their eyes _____
_____ _____ cute and cuddly.
However, they are _____ _____ that
only a _____ number still live in the world.
People fear that one day in the future, there will be
_____ _____ _____. We must
_____ these cute but endangered animals.

17

① M Do you know _____ _____
_____ around here?

W _____ _____ _____ 'Naples'
opened two weeks ago.

② M Where can I find _____ _____?

W They are _____ _____ _____
_____.

③ M Do you remember _____ _____
   _____ _____ ?
W I think it was _____ _____ .
④ M I'd like to buy _____ _____
   _____ _____ .
W She will probably like it.
⑤ M Be sure to do _____ _____ before
   you go in the water.
W I exercise _____ _____ _____ .

18

M Excuse me, could you let me know what the
   _____ said? I missed it listening to music
   with earphones.
W No problem. First of all, we are approaching Tokyo
   Narita _____ . Are you going to transfer to
   another plane in Tokyo?
M Yes.
W OK, when we arrive in _____ , passengers
   who are transferring like you should _____
   _____ .
M Should I _____ _____ _____ or
   _____ ?
W No. No transit passengers should _____
   _____ .
M Do you think I can catch my connecting flight,
   OZ837 _____ _____ _____ ?
W Oh, because of _____ _____ ,
   passengers who were to transfer to that flight
   should go to _____ _____ _____
   to receive _____ _____ .

19

W Suji is waiting for her friends _____
   _____ _____ . There's a _____
   _____ sign on the wall. However, she
   sees a man smoking _____ _____ a
   _____ _____ in the restaurant. That
   makes Suji _____ . She knows smoking,
   direct or indirect, is _____ for _____
   _____ , especially to _____ and
   _____ . She also knows that these days,
   smoking is not allowed in _____ _____ .
   In this situation, what would Suji most likely say to
   the man?

20

W Is this your first time _____ _____
   _____ ?
M Yes, it is. But I went to London _____
   _____ last year.
W _____ _____ will you be here this
   time?
M _____ _____ _____ .
W Have you ever tried any _____ _____ ?
M Sure. I have tried _____ , _____ and
   _____ .
W How did you like them?
M The foods were fantastic and suited my taste.

03 Listening Test

01 대화를 듣고, 여자가 구입할 선글라스를 고르시오.

①   ②   ③   ④   ⑤

02 대화를 듣고, 남자가 묘사하는 용의자를 고르시오.

①   ②   ③   ④   ⑤

03 대화를 듣고, 짐작할 수 있는 여자의 성격으로 가장 적절한 것을 고르시오.

① helpful   ② passionate   ③ lazy

④ humorous   ⑤ humble

04 다음을 듣고, 학교에서 열리고 있는 행사로 가장 적절한 것을 고르시오.

① 바자회   ② 진로 상담   ③ 미술 대회

④ 운동회   ⑤ 직업 체험

05 대화를 듣고, 남자가 지불할 금액을 고르시오.

① $28   ② $35   ③ $45   ④ $50   ⑤ $85

06 대화를 듣고, 두 사람이 대화하는 장소로 가장 적절한 것을 고르시오.

① police station   ② gym   ③ bus terminal
④ airport   ⑤ subway station

07 대화를 듣고, 여자가 할 일로 가장 적절한 것을 고르시오.

① 열쇠 복사하기   ② 열쇠 수리공에게 전화하기
③ 열쇠 찾아주기   ④ 잠긴 문 열어주기
⑤ 자물쇠 교체하기

08 대화를 듣고, 여자의 마지막 말에 담긴 의도로 가장 적절한 것을 고르시오.

① 충고   ② 동의   ③ 항의   ④ 감사   ⑤ 요청

09 다음을 듣고, 그림의 내용과 일치하지 <u>않는</u> 것을 고르시오.

①   ②   ③   ④   ⑤

10 대화를 듣고, 여자가 남자에게 미안하다고 말한 이유를 고르시오.

① 부당하게 화를 내서   ② 무면허 운전을 해서
③ 주차를 잘 못해서   ④ 남자의 차에 사고를 내서
⑤ 주차장 위치를 몰라서

11 다음을 듣고, 무엇에 관한 내용인지 고르시오.

① 마스크 광고　　　　　② 농학 강의
③ 관광 안내　　　　　　④ 날씨 안내
⑤ 의학 강의

12 대화를 듣고, 현재 시각으로 가장 적절한 것을 고르시오.

① 1:50　　　② 2:30　　　③ 2:40　　　④ 2:50　　　⑤ 3:00

13 대화를 듣고, 통화 내용과 일치하지 <u>않는</u> 것을 고르시오.

A Telephone Call
① From: Julie
② To: Jake
③ Purpose: To reschedule the appointment
④ What happened to the caller: Being hospitalized
⑤ When to meet: Two days later

14 대화를 듣고, 두 사람이 처음 만났던 장소를 고르시오.

① 도서관　　　　　　　② 학교 정문
③ 아이스크림 가게　　　④ 교실
⑤ 백화점

15 대화를 듣고, 남자가 할 일로 가장 적절한 것을 고르시오.

① 전시회 가기　　　　　② 포스터 붙이기
③ 입장권 예매하기　　　④ 그림 그리기
⑤ 모네 작품집 사기

16 다음을 듣고, 두 사람의 대화가 <u>어색한</u> 것을 고르시오.

①   ②   ③   ④   ⑤

17 대화를 듣고, Blue Water Resort에 관한 내용과 일치하지 <u>않는</u> 것을 고르시오.

① 필리핀에 있다.
② 편안하게 지낼 수 있는 휴양지이다.
③ 각종 수상 스포츠를 즐길 수 있다.
④ 대규모 수영장을 하나 갖추고 있다.
⑤ 현재 할인 행사 중이다.

18 다음을 듣고, Tom이 Cindy에게 할 말로 가장 적절한 것을 고르시오.

① I don't like this. Could you show me another one?
② Are you going to Anne's birthday party tomorrow?
③ How about having a surprise birthday party for Anne?
④ Let's go shopping together to buy presents for Anne.
⑤ I'm awfully sorry that I can't come to your birthday party.

[19-20] 대화를 듣고, 여자의 마지막 말에 이어질 남자의 응답으로 가장 적절한 것을 고르시오.

19
① Sure, take another.
② Are you going to go there now?
③ How much do you charge for delivery?
④ I want to send this package to Sydney.
⑤ Okay. I'll see that it's delivered there by 3.

20
① Oh, really? Congratulations!
② Let me help you to write a resume.
③ Don't worry. I'm sure you'll do well.
④ You can submit job applications online.
⑤ Why don't you participate in an internship program?

다음은 **Listening Test 03**의 주요 지문입니다. 녹음을 다시 듣고, 질문에 대한 답을 완성하세요.

Q3

1 Why doesn't the man look good?

↳ The reason is that he _____ and he is worried about how

_____.

Q5

2 What vehicles does the man buy parking permits for?

↳ He buys parking permits for _____.

Q7

3 What is the problem with the man's key?

↳ It fits _____ fine, but he can't easily _____

_____.

Q8

4 Why is the man late?

↳ The reason is that he _____.

Q10

5 Where is the no parking zone sign?

↳ It is _____.

Q11

6 What is Gyungchip?

↳ It is the day when _____

_____.

Q19

7 Why does the woman want the man to leave her package at the front desk?

↳ The reason is that _____.

Q20

8 Why is the woman so nervous?

↳ She has _____ at _____

in the morning.

● 자신의 상황에 맞게 내용을 완성하고 말해 보세요.

A Imagine you're going to write a memo to change an appointment. Complete the memo and show it to your classmates.

Changing an Appointment

(1) The receiver
(2) Your original plan
(3) Your reason to change it
(4) Your changed plan

Dear (1)_____

Hello. This is _____. I am writing this because I'd like to change our appointment. Our original plan was (2)_____

_____. However, I have to (3)_____

_____. So, if it is okay with you, I'd like to (4)_____

_____. I'm sorry for changing the appointment.

B Do you agree or disagree that students should wear school uniforms? Write your opinion giving two reasons and a supporting example for each.

School Uniforms

Reasons for agreeing/disagreeing	Supporting examples
(1)	(2)
(3)	(4)

I (agree/disagree) that students should wear school uniforms for two main reasons. First, (1)_____

_____. For example, (2)_____

_____. Second, (3)_____

_____. For example, (4)_____

_____. For these reasons, I am (for/against) school uniforms.

01

W I want to buy a pair of _____ _____.

M All right. How do you like these _____ ones with a _____-shaped _____?

W They're _____ _____. How about this emerald pair with a round-shaped frame?

M It is very _____ and the color suits you well.

W What about this _____-shaped frame with _____ colored _____?

M Oh, they are really nice. They have _____ _____ these days.

W OK, I'll take this pair.

02

W Were you able to get a look at the _____ _____?

M Yes. I remember exactly what he _____ _____.

W Can you describe the man in as much _____ as _____?

M Yes. He is _____ _____ and has got _____ _____ curly hair.

W Please tell us more about _____ _____.

M He has quite a big nose and a thick lower lip. Also, he has both a _____ and a _____.

W Is he fat or slim?

M Hmm. He is rather muscular.

03

W You don't look good today. What's going on?

M I _____ _____ _____. I'm just worried about how I'm going to _____ _____ _____.

W I'm sorry to hear that. Have you been looking for _____ _____?

M I've just started, but the _____ _____ is very _____ right now.

W That's tough. I have some friends who might be _____ to help you _____ _____ _____. I'll see what they can do.

M I really _____ _____ _____.

W No problem. In the meantime, don't worry so much. You'll _____ _____ this.

04

M Good morning. This is Mike Johnson, your _____ _____. Today is the first day of 'School Counseling Week.' Our focus for the week is 'Building _____ _____.'
This week, we will talk about how you can build _____ _____ and make it magical in the process. It starts with _____ a _____ for where you _____ _____ _____ and steadily _____ _____ that _____. If you need my help, you can _____ _____ and talk to me _____.

05

M Hi, I want to purchase a _____ _____ for next semester.

W Are you a full-time student or do you just _____ _____ _____ _____?

M I am a full-time student and all _____ _____ are during _____ _____.

W Will you be _____ a _____ or a _____?

M I have both of them but I will _____ _____ _____ to come to _____.

W OK, that will be _____ dollars. If you pay _____ dollars _____, you can get a _____ _____ for the _____.

M Really? It's cheaper than I expected. I'll buy _____ _____. Can I use a credit card?

W Sure.

06

W Good afternoon. May I have your _____ please?

M Here you go.

W Are you _____ _____ _____?

M Just one.

W Please place your _____ on the _____.

M I have a _____ in Toronto. Do I need to _____ _____ my luggage there?

W No, it'll go straight to your final destination. Here's your _____ _____. Your _____ _____ is 10 E.

M Thank you. Have a nice day.

07

M Good morning. Can I talk to you for a moment?

W Of course. Is there a _____ with your apartment?

M The _____ you gave me doesn't seem to _____ _____.

W OK, what's the problem? Doesn't the key _____ into the _____?

M It fits into the lock just fine, but I _____ _____ _____ it to the _____ or _____ _____.

W How long do you have to try before it'll open?

M About four or five minutes. It makes me quite angry!

W I see. Actually the man who was _____ _____ _____ _____ said the lock had a problem.

M Why didn't you _____ _____ _____ then?

W Sorry, I didn't have time. I will call a _____ right away.

08

M I'm sorry I'm late.

W It's okay. Why are you _____ anyway?

M I _____ _____ the bus stop _____ _____.

W I see. I was wondering whether you were _____ _____ _____ this place.

M Just my silly mistake. I had to _____ _____ at the next stop and run back.

W That's too bad. You must be _____ and _____.

M Bingo! Let's go in and order something to _____ _____ _____ _____ _____.

W Good. I'm _____ _____ _____.

09

① W A man is ordering hamburgers at a _____ _____ _____.

② W There are three people _____ _____ behind the man.

③ W The restaurant _____ is _____ a _____ and a _____.

④ W The restaurant employee has _____

⑤ W The man is going to _____ _____ _____.

10

M Excuse me, ma'am. Please show me your _____ _____.

W Why? What's the matter?

M You _____ a _____ _____.

W What? What rule?

M This is a no _____ _____, ma'am. You can't park here.

W I really _____ _____ why you are _____ me _____ _____ _____ parking here. Where is the sign?

M There's a sign _____ _____ _____ of the street. You should have seen it.

W Oh, _____ _____ _____. I'm so sorry. I didn't see it.

11

M Winter _____ almost _____ and spring _____ _____. Today is the day on which insects _____ _____ their holes _____ _____ _____. It is called "Gyungchip." However, we have bad news again, today. _____ _____ from China covers the sky and the sky looks gray. This _____ has continued _____ _____ _____ _____ _____. Since this fine dust may _____ many _____ _____, please wear a mask to cover your nose and mouth. Please try not to go out for a long time today and _____ _____ as long as you can.

12

W Excuse me, but may I _____ you _____?

M Sure. What is it?

W _____ _____ does Bus 333 come here?

M _____ _____ _____ _____.

W What time was the last bus?

M It was at 2:50.

W Thank you. I only have _____ _____ _____ to wait.

13

[Telephone rings.]

M Hello?

W Is that Jake? This is Julie.

M Hi. It's Jake. _____ _____?

W I'm calling to ask you to _____ _____ _____. Something urgent _____ _____.

M You sound sad. Did _____ _____ _____?

W My mom has been _____ _____ _____ since last week. The doctor said it might be pneumonia.

M I'm so _____ _____ _____ _____. When can we meet, then?

W I think I can _____ _____ the day _____ _____. My sister is going to _____ _____ _____ _____ and look after our mom on that day.

M That's fine with me. We can _____ _____ _____ and you can tell me how your mom's doing.

W Good. I _____ _____ _____ talking to you then.

14

M Do you remember the place where we met _____ _____ _____ _____?

W Umm, wasn't it _____ _____ _____ the library on the first day of school?

M No. Try to _____ it from your _____.

W Sorry. I really have a bad memory. Where was it?

M It was _____ _____ _____ _____ of the Grace _____ _____ last Christmas.

W Right. Right. Now I remember. I asked you where the _____ _____ _____ was.

M Yes. Then we met again in this classroom.

W Yeah. I was very _____ _____ _____ _____ again.

M So was I.

15

M Look at this _____!

W Oh, it's about _____ _____ _____. Are you interested in _____ _____?

M Interested? I'm _____ _____ his works, especially *The Water Lily*.

W Oh, I feel _____ _____ _____ _____. *The Water Lily* is _____ _____ _____ that I have ever seen.

M Then why don't you _____ _____ _____ _____ with me?

W Sure, I'd love to. I think we won't be able to get into it _____ a _____ because it's _____ _____.

M Okay. I'll _____ _____ _____ on the Internet.

16

① M Is it okay _____ _____ _____ _____ _____ here?

W I'm _____ I can't.

② M Is this your _____ _____ _____ _____ Jeju Island?

W Yes, I've _____ wanted to come here.

③ M Do you have any good _____ _____ _____?

W Well, I think you'll like *Tuesdays With Morrie*.

④ M Which team do you think will _____ _____ _____?

W I think _____ will win.

⑤ M You are _____ _____.

W I'm sorry, but _____ _____ was _____.

17

W Good afternoon, sir. How may I help you?

M Hello. I'm looking for the _____ _____ _____ for my family.

W Do you have any place _____ _____?

M I'm thinking of _____ in _____ _____.

W How about Blue Water Resort in Cebu? It is _____ _____ and _____ _____ with a variety of _____ and _____ _____.

M Good. I have always wanted to go to such a resort.

W You may also lounge on _____ _____ _____ and at one of the three _____ _____.

M Great. And what kinds of _____ _____ can I enjoy?

W You can enjoy wakeboarding, kayaking, snorkeling, and _____. Oh, they are offering _____ _____ _____ now. Don't miss out.

morning. I'm really _____.
M Don't worry. I'm sure you'll do well.

18

W Anne's _____ is _____. Tom is going to her _____ _____. But he hasn't decided _____ _____ _____ for her. He has to _____ _____ _____ _____ later today to _____ _____ _____. On his way to school, he meets Cindy. She says she also hasn't decided _____ _____ _____ for Anne. Tom wants to _____ _____ _____ _____ with Cindy and then they can _____ _____ _____ pick out _____ _____ for Anne. In this situation what would Tom most likely say to Cindy?

19

[Telephone rings.]

W Hello.
M Hello. This is ABC _____ _____. Is this Ms. Sue Robins?
W Yes, this is _____. Do you have _____ for me?
M Yes. Will you be in your office _____ _____ p.m.?
W Oh, sorry. I'll be _____ _____ _____ at that time. Can you _____ _____ at 1:30 p.m.?
M Let me see. Sorry, I _____ _____ _____.
W Then can you leave the package _____ _____ _____ _____?
M Okay. I'll see that it's delivered there by 3.

20

M You look _____. What's wrong with you?
W Well, I have _____ _____ _____ today.
M Oh, do you? What kind of _____ is it?
W I have _____ _____ _____ for a job. I applied for _____ _____ in _____ _____ _____ last month.
M Oh, great! When is it?
W _____ _____ _____ in the

Listening Test

01 대화를 듣고, 여자가 묘사하는 사람을 고르시오.

02 대화를 듣고, 두 사람이 구입할 물건이 <u>아닌</u> 것을 고르시오.

03 대화를 듣고, 두 사람의 관계로 가장 적절한 것을 고르시오.

① 식당 직원 — 손님　　　　② 상점 직원 — 손님
③ 직장 동료 — 동료　　　　④ 남편 — 아내
⑤ 선생님 — 학생

04 대화를 듣고, 남자가 지불할 금액을 고르시오.

① $33　　② $60　　③ $66　　④ $70　　⑤ $72.6

05 대화를 듣고, 여자의 심정으로 가장 적절한 것을 고르시오.

① proud　　　　② jealous　　　　③ grateful
④ guilty　　　　⑤ hopeless

06 다음을 듣고, Green Club Day Camp에 관해 언급되지 <u>않은</u> 것을 고르시오.

① 등록 대상　　　　　② 시작 시기　　　　　③ 프로그램
④ 가입 방법　　　　　⑤ 연락처

07 대화를 듣고, 두 사람이 할 일로 가장 적절한 것을 고르시오.

① 테니스경기 시청하기　　　　② 테니스 하기
③ 야구경기 시청하기　　　　　④ 농구 하기
⑤ TV 수리하러 가기

08 대화를 듣고, 여자가 졸린 이유를 고르시오.

① 새벽까지 TV를 봐서　　　　　② 숙제 하느라 늦게 자서
③ 불면증으로 밤을 새워서　　　　④ 일과표를 만드느라 피곤해서
⑤ 과학 수업이 지루해서

09 대화를 듣고, 남자가 가려고 하는 장소를 고르시오.

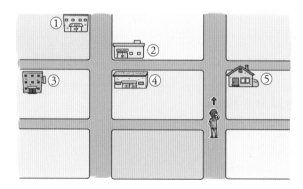

10 대화를 듣고, 남자가 이번 주말에 할 일이 <u>아닌</u> 것을 고르시오.

① 박물관 가기　　　　② 수학수업 하기　　　　③ 교회 가기
④ 방 청소 하기　　　　⑤ 숙제 하기

11 다음을 듣고, CYJ Speech Contest에 관한 내용과 일치하지 <u>않는</u> 것을 고르시오.

① 입상자에게는 메달과 상품이 준비되어 있다.
② 참가자 전원에게 상품권이 주어진다.
③ 추첨을 통해 방청객 5명에게 상품을 준다.
④ 유창성과 정확성이 주요 평가 기준이다.
⑤ 참가자에게 5분의 시간제한이 있다.

12 대화를 듣고, 두 사람이 만나기로 한 시각을 고르시오.

① 5:00   ② 5:30   ③ 6:00   ④ 6:30   ⑤ 7:00

13 대화를 듣고, 두 사람이 대화하는 장소로 가장 적절한 것을 고르시오.

① 우체국   ② 은행   ③ 공항   ④ 여행사   ⑤ 약국

14 대화를 듣고, 남자가 오늘 오후에 만날 사람을 고르시오.

① 체육관 회원들   ② 조정 동호회원들
③ 과제 팀원들   ④ 의사
⑤ 기하학 선생님

15 다음을 듣고, Royal Ice Rink에 관한 안내문의 내용과 일치하지 <u>않는</u> 것을 고르시오.

Royal Ice Rink

• **Hour**
    Weekdays: 14:00~18:00
    Weekend & Holidays: 12:00~18:00
    Summer & Winter Vacation: To be announced
    Closed on Lunar New Year's Day
• **Fee**
    Entrance: Adults $20, Students $10, Children 5~7 $5
    Skate Rental: Speed $25/for 2 hours
                   Figure $30/for 2 hours
• **Parking:** Free

---

①   ②   ③   ④   ⑤

16 대화를 듣고, 남자의 마지막 말에 담긴 의도로 가장 적절한 것을 고르시오.

① 수락　　　② 항의　　　③ 감사　　　④ 거절　　　⑤ 요청

17 다음을 듣고, 두 사람의 대화가 <u>어색한</u> 것을 고르시오.

①　　　　　②　　　　　③　　　　　④　　　　　⑤

18 대화를 듣고, 남자가 전하는 학교 소식과 일치하는 것을 고르시오.

① 태풍으로 인해 학교가 휴교할 것이다.
② 반일 보충수업이 예정되어 있다.
③ 보충수업은 일요일에 있을 것이다.
④ 보충수업일에 학생들은 교복을 입어야 한다.
⑤ 보충수업일에는 스쿨버스가 운행되지 않는다.

19 다음을 듣고, Judy가 남자에게 할 말로 가장 적절한 것을 고르시오.

① What is my uniform number?
② Where can I get the application form?
③ Does the club have rackets I can use?
④ Should I practice posing in front of a mirror?
⑤ How much do I have to pay for the membership?

20 대화를 듣고, 여자의 마지막 말에 이어질 남자의 응답으로 가장 적절한 것을 고르시오.

① That's what friends are for.
② Right. I'm with you on that.
③ I don't think I'm interested in science.
④ It is included as part of International Science Night.
⑤ The first thing we should do at the camp is to pitch a tent.

● 다음은 **Listening Test 04**의 주요 지문입니다. 녹음을 다시 듣고, 질문에 대한 답을 완성하세요.

Q2

1 Why do they need eggs and flour?

└→ The reason is that they have to _____ .

Q3

2 Why does the woman say "No" when the man wants to turn on the air-conditioner?

└→ The reason is that she's worried about _____ .

Q5

3 How did the man do well on the physics test this time?

└→ He _____ a student who is good at science in _____

_____ and _____ from him.

Q11

4 Which qualities of speech are the panel of judges going to judge?

└→ They are going to judge not only _____ but also

_____ .

Q13

5 Why does the man want to send his parcel by airmail?

└→ The reason is that he wants it _____ .

Q14

6 Why does the man look fit and trim?

└→ The reason is that he _____ in the fitness center at least

_____ a week.

Q19

7 Why does Judy ask the man whether the club has rackets for the members?

└→ The reason is that she _____ .

Q20

8 What is the man looking forward to doing in the science camp?

└→ He is looking forward to _____ .

● 자신의 상황에 맞게 내용을 완성하고 말해 보세요.

A Do you have any club that you are currently a member of? Introduce your club to your classmates.

My Club

Name/type of the club	(1)	
Activities in the club	(2)	
	(3)	
Special event it holds	(4)	
Requirement(s)	(5)	

I would like to introduce my club, (1)_____

_____. Two major activities in our club are these.

First, (2)_____.

Second, (3)_____.

My club also holds a special event, (4)_____.

To become a member, (5)_____.

B Compare and describe what you see in the pie chart, after filling in the table below.

How Ann Spends Her Free Time

- Using her cell phone
- Hanging out with friends
- Watching TV

20%
50%
30%

Describing a Pie Chart

(1) Title

(2) Activity Ann does most

(3) Comparing activities

(4) Activity Ann does least

(5) Your suggestion

This pie chart shows (1)_____. The biggest

portion of her free time is spent (2)_____. She spends

(3)_____

_____. (4)_____ is the activity

that Ann does least. Since she uses her cell phone too much, I recommend that

(5)_____.

01

W Have you seen Amanda's daughter?

M No, I haven't. I _____ _____ _____ Amanda has a daughter.

W Oh, yes she does! Her daughter, Jessica, is two years old. She is so _____ and _____.

M Tell me _____ _____ _____ _____.

W She has _____ _____ and beautiful _____ _____. She is also _____ some _____ _____.

M Is she big or small?

W She's not big but _____ _____ _____.

M Sounds like she is really adorable.

02

M Mom, when are you going _____ _____?

W This afternoon, maybe. Let's make a list. What do you _____?

M I need pretzels and mango juice.

W We also need _____ and _____. What fruits do you want me to buy?

M I want apples, _____, and _____.

W Alright, but I'll buy the plums _____. They are _____ _____ on Wednesday.

M Okay. Oh, mom! We also have to buy some _____ and _____ to make a cake for _____ _____.

W Yes, that's right. I almost forgot.

03

M It's _____ _____ and _____. Shall we turn on the air-conditioner?

W No, we shouldn't.

M No? Why do you say no?

W With the _____ _____ _____ _____, we'd better use these hand-held _____.

M That won't keep me cool. I _____ _____ it when I'm hot. Look! I'm _____ _____.

W How about turning on the electric fan then? It will keep you cool, and we can _____ _____.

M Okay. Okay. I will.

W Thanks for your understanding. It's better for our _____ _____ _____, too.

04

M Excuse me. I'm looking for a _____ in a _____ _____.

W Let's see, here's a nice _____ one. What do you think?

M I think I'd rather have it _____ _____.

W Okay, here it is. Would you like to _____ _____ _____?

M Yes, I would. I'll go to the _____ _____. [pause] It fits well. _____ _____ _____ _____?

W It is on sale. Just _____ dollars, including 10% tax.

M Then, I'll take _____ in a _____ size for my brother and _____ in a _____ size for me.

05

W Peter, you _____ _____ on this physics test. I almost failed it.

M Yes, I _____ _____ this time.

W Don't you _____ _____ physics tests?

M Things were _____ this time. I _____ next to a _____ _____.

W You mean you _____ _____ _____ at his test?

M No. I mean for three months I've sat _____ _____ him in _____ _____ and learned from him.

W Oh, wow. Is he kind and helpful?

M Absolutely. _____ _____ _____ not _____ _____ him, I would have _____ _____.

06

M Do you need a vacation _____ _____ _____? We are happy to share some _____ about the Green Club Day Camp. Our new day camp that starts in early June will be _____, _____ and _____. This year the kids will enjoy _____, _____,

_____, and doing _____ _____ _____. You will get some free time and have _____ _____ _____. If you need any information about _____, please contact Jane at 231-7823.

07

W What time is the baseball game on? I thought it _____ _____ _____.

M We _____ _____ the wrong time. Well, baseball's not my favorite sport anyway. I _____ _____ _____.

W Oh, really? I thought your favorite sport was basketball! I'm a _____ _____ _____ _____, too.

M How about playing a game sometime?

W Sure thing! _____ _____ _____ go to the _____ _____ _____?

M _____ _____? Let's go!

08

M Taeyeon, what's up? You _____ _____ _____.

W Yeah. Actually, I am very sleepy now. I stayed up late last night doing my _____ _____.

M Why did it take so long?

W Well, in fact I started to do it after watching Gag Concert.

M Now I see. You _____ _____ _____ your homework first before watching TV.

W I know. But the time just went so fast. I think I'd better _____ _____ _____ and try to follow a _____ _____ every day.

M That's the point. If you try to do that, you _____ _____ _____ at school.

W Thanks for your advice.

09

M Excuse me. Do you know _____ _____ _____ _____ Pizza Nara from here?

W Sure. _____ _____ for one block and turn left _____ _____ _____.

M And then?

W _____ _____ one block and _____ _____ at the corner.

M Okay. And?

W _____ _____ for one more block. At the end of the block, you'll see Pizza Nara _____ _____ _____. You _____ _____ _____.

M Thank you very much for helping me.

W _____ _____.

10

W David, what are you writing in the _____?

M I am writing down my _____ _____.

W Plans? What are you going to do?

M Well, I am going to _____ _____ _____ on Saturday morning, and then go to a math class _____ that.

W Oh, you'll be busy. _____ _____ _____ _____?

M On Sunday morning, I will _____ _____ _____. After lunch, I will _____ my room. _____, I've already done my _____.

W Then you _____ _____.

M That's right. It will be a _____ _____.

11

W Boys and Girls! Welcome to the CYJ _____ _____. We will _____ _____ and _____ to the top three speakers. Also, we'll give all the _____ a 5,000 won _____ _____ just _____ _____ _____ _____ the contest. Moreover, there will be a draw and two _____ _____ will receive an MP3 player. So please keep your tickets which have the numbers for the draw. The _____ of _____ not only judges the _____ but also the _____ _____ _____ _____. Each participant should observe the _____ _____ of five minutes. Are you ready? Don't be nervous. Let's start with number one.

12

[Telephone rings.]

M Hello.

W Hello, Tim. This is Kate. Are we _____ _____ _____ dinner?

M Of course, Kate. I am _____ _____

which restaurant is good for us. Would you like
Chinese food?

W _____ _____! What time shall we
meet?

M How about _____? Is it okay with you?

W Isn't that too early for dinner? How about
_____ _____ _____ that?

M Fine. I will stop by the library to _____ books
then. It _____ _____ _____
_____.

W Good. See you then.

13

W Good morning. _____ _____
_____ _____ _____ ?

M Good morning. I want to _____ _____
_____ _____ New Zealand.

W Okay. Do you want to send it _____
_____ or _____ _____ ?

M I think I'll send it by airmail. I want it to get there
_____ _____ _____ _____.
How much does it cost?

W It _____ _____ the _____.
Please put the parcel _____ _____
_____. Let's check.

M Okay. How much is it?

W It _____ 3 kilograms. That will be 25
dollars. Are you going to _____ _____
_____ or _____ _____ ?

M In cash. Here you are.

W Thank you.

14

W Don't you find these rowing machines _____
work?

M I certainly do, but they're supposed to be.

W _____ _____ do you come here for a
_____ ?

M Three times a week at least.

W No wonder you look so _____ and
_____.

M Thank you for saying that. _____ _____
_____ and you can be the same.

W By the way, did you finish the _____
_____ ?

M Not yet. I am going to _____ the _____
_____ this afternoon _____

_____ what to do.

15

① M It opens at 12:00 _____ _____
_____.

② M It does not open on _____ _____
_____ _____.

③ M The schedule for summer and winter vacations
_____ _____ _____ yet.

④ M Six-year-old _____ pay _____
dollars to enter the rink.

⑤ M _____ _____ can be rented at
_____ dollars _____ _____
_____.

16

W Tom, can you _____ _____
_____ ?

M Sure. What is it?

W Will you please help me _____ _____
_____ ?

M Okay. _____ _____ _____
_____ ?

W Will you please put paper, _____ and
_____ into the right _____ _____ ?

M [Pause] I'm _____. What else can I do for
you?

W Can you _____ _____ the _____
_____ ? Take it outside and put it in the food
waste _____ _____.

M No problem.

17

① M What's _____ _____ for the project?
W I'm thinking of _____ _____ of the
_____ _____.

② M Congratulations on _____ _____.
W Thank you so much.

③ M What would you do _____ _____
_____ _____ _____
_____ _____ ?
W I would take it _____ _____
_____ _____.

④ M My wallet was _____. What should I do?
W I called the police last night.

⑤ M You often _____ _____ _____
for you.

W _____ _____ _____ .

18

[Telephone rings.]

W Hello, _____ _____ . Who's calling, please?

M Hi, Megan. It's Sean. _____ _____ _____ _____ in the hospital?

W I'm dying to go home and to school. I'll _____ _____ in a few days.

M Congratulations! I have got some school news for you. We have a full day of _____ _____ _____ _____ . Will you go to them?

W Of course, I'll definitely go.

M It's for _____ _____ _____ last _____ , due to _____ Eagle. So _____ will follow _____ _____ _____ .

W Yes, I thought that was the reason. Can we _____ _____ _____ on that day?

M No. We will have to be in our _____ as usual. The school buses will run temporarily _____ the usual _____ , too.

19

M Judy wants to join _____ _____ _____ but she doesn't know _____ _____ _____ it. She calls _____ _____ _____ and asks _____ _____ _____ to join the club. The man on the phone says she can _____ at _____ _____ _____ . Now Judy has another question. As she doesn't have her own _____ _____ , she wants to know _____ the club has _____ for _____ _____ _____ _____ .

In this situation, what would Judy most likely say to the man?

20

M Mary, I'm going to take part in _____ _____ _____ in Silicon Valley _____ _____ .

W _____ _____ _____ in Silicon Valley? Sounds interesting.

M I feel that I have rekindled _____ _____ _____ in _____ .

W Good for you. I'm sure that you'll be _____ _____ _____ .

M I can't wait to meet many students _____ _____ _____ who will be there.

W Wow, it will be a great chance for you _____ _____ _____ _____ . Don't you think so?

M Right. I'm with you on that.

01 대화를 듣고, 여자가 탈 놀이기구를 고르시오.

①   ②   ③   ④   ⑤

02 다음을 듣고, 그림의 상황에 어울리는 대화를 고르시오.

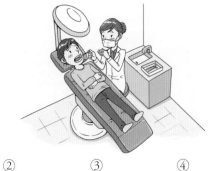

①   ②   ③   ④   ⑤

03 대화를 듣고, 여자의 심정으로 가장 적절한 것을 고르시오.

① upset   ② relieved   ③ depressed

④ impatient   ⑤ regretful

04 대화를 듣고, 두 사람의 관계로 가장 적절한 것을 고르시오.

① 판매원 ─ 고객   ② 교사 ─ 학생   ③ 경찰 ─ 운전자

④ 상사 ─ 직원   ⑤ 의사 ─ 환자

05 대화를 듣고, 남자가 전화를 건 목적을 고르시오.

① 약속 변경 통지   ② 참고 도서 문의   ③ 회의 참석 요청

④ 과제 내용 문의   ⑤ 학습 상담 요청

06 대화를 듣고, 두 사람이 현재 겪고 있는 문제를 고르시오.

① 시계가 없음   ② 버스를 놓침   ③ 버스를 잘못 탐
④ 차가 고장 남   ⑤ 문이 잠김

07 대화를 듣고, 남자가 여자에게 부탁한 일로 가장 적절한 것을 고르시오.

① 휴대전화 빌려주기   ② 책 돌려주기
③ 영화 표 예매하기   ④ 소금 건네주기
⑤ 오늘밤에 전화해주기

08 대화를 듣고, 여자가 주말에 축구경기를 보지 못한 이유를 고르시오.

① 가던 길에 전철이 고장 나서
② 동행인이 사고를 당해서
③ 집에서 쉬느라고
④ 몸이 불편해 병원에 가느라고
⑤ 교통혼잡으로 시간을 놓쳐서

09 대화를 듣고, 남자가 잘못 알고 있는 지역을 고르시오.

10 다음을 듣고, 무엇에 관한 설명인지 고르시오.

① 콜레스테롤의 순기능   ② 콜레스테롤의 역기능
③ 주요 성인병   ④ 혈액순환의 중요성
⑤ 과음의 위험성

11 다음을 듣고, 비행기가 도착하는 시각을 고르시오.

① 5:40 a.m.   ② 7:50 a.m.   ③ 8:00 p.m.
④ 9:50 p.m.   ⑤ 10:00 p.m.

12 대화를 듣고, 두 사람이 대화하는 장소로 가장 적절한 것을 고르시오.

① flower shop   ② ski resort   ③ gift shop
④ bakery   ⑤ classroom

13 대화를 듣고, 대화 내용과 일치하지 <u>않는</u> 것을 고르시오.

You're Invited to a
HOUSEWARMING PARTY!

Come help us celebrate our new home.

① Date: Sunday, July 25th
② Time: 5 p.m.
③ Buffet-Snacks-Drinks
④ 17 Rodeo Ave. Seoul
⑤ Reply to Jungmi, 010-0707-0007.

14 대화를 듣고, 두 사람이 사려고 하는 것을 고르시오.

① 방충망   ② 창문   ③ 커튼
④ 선글라스   ⑤ 벽지

15 대화를 듣고, 남자가 먼저 할 일로 가장 적절한 것을 고르시오.

① 책 주문하기   ② 건축 잡지 읽기
③ 지역문화센터 가기   ④ 극장에 가기
⑤ 여자에게 전화하기

16 다음을 듣고, 두 사람의 대화가 <u>어색한</u> 것을 고르시오.

① ② ③ ④ ⑤

17 대화를 듣고, Sunspot Farm 행사에 관한 내용과 일치하지 <u>않는</u> 것을 고르시오.

① 딸기 따기 행사이다.
② 참가자들은 단체로 참여할 것이다.
③ 참가비는 사전에 지불해야 한다.
④ 추가 비용을 내면 직접 딴 딸기를 가져갈 수 있다.
⑤ 행사 주최측에서 제공하는 교통편은 따로 없다.

18 다음을 듣고, Tom이 Ann에게 할 말로 가장 적절한 것을 고르시오.

① Is there too much homework?
② That's nice. We miss you a lot.
③ I hope you will make new friends soon.
④ Unfortunately, I don't like my new school either.
⑤ Well, the teachers are really nice. They always help me.

[19-20] 대화를 듣고, 남자의 마지막 말에 이어질 여자의 응답으로 가장 적절한 것을 고르시오.

19
① The news spread like wildfire.
② Out of the frying pan into the fire!
③ Summer is the perfect season for wildfires.
④ I use paper to start fires in my stove.
⑤ We should not have campfires in the dry season.

20
① Half the truth is always a whole lie.
② Don't be mad at me. It was not me.
③ If you tell the truth, they will forgive you.
④ It was careless of you to say so to your brother.
⑤ He's really funny. He tells a joke like it's the truth.

● 다음은 **Listening Test 05**의 주요 지문입니다. 녹음을 다시 듣고, 질문에 대한 답을 완성하세요.

Q1

1 Why does the girl's dad not want her to ride the green frog?

⤷ The reason is that there are too _____ waiting to _____

_____.

Q5

2 When is the man going to return Dr. Han's books?

⤷ He is going to _____.

Q7

3 What are the man and the woman doing now?

⤷ They are _____.

Q8

4 What happened to the woman's boyfriend?

⤷ He broke _____, so _____.

Q10

5 What does "good cholesterol" do in our bodies?

⤷ It helps prevent _____ and keep blood _____.

Q11

6 What do the passengers now have to do for their safety?

⤷ They have to _____ and _____.

Q15

7 What will the woman and the man do at 3 o'clock?

⤷ They will meet at _____ and play _____.

Q19

8 How do the police suspect the fire started?

⤷ They suspect _____.

자신의 상황에 맞게 내용을 완성하고 말해 보세요.

A Think about an incident that made you very embarrassed. Fill in the table below and tell your classmates about it.

My Embarrassing Moment

(1) When/where did it happen?

(2) What happened?

(3) How did it happen?

(4) What was embarrassing?

(5) How did you overcome it?

Let me tell you about an incident that made me so embarrassed. It happened

(1)_____. What happened was (2)_____

_____.

It happened because (3)_____

_____. I was embarrassed because (4)_____

_____. However, I could

overcome the situation as (5)_____

_____. Anyway, I hope it won't happen again to me.

B Do research on Valentine's Day. Then fill in the table below and talk to your classmates about it.

Valentine's Day

(1) When is it?

(2) What do people usually do?

(3) What do you do on the day?

(4) What do you think of the day?

I'm going to talk about Valentine's Day. It is on (1)_____. People

usually (2)_____

_____. On this day, I usually (3)_____

_____.

I think (4)_____.

01

W Dad, I want to ride that one.

M _____ _____ do you want to ride?

W I like that _____ frog wearing a _____ _____ _____.

M Look at that _____! How about the red-bellied frog with black spots on its back?

W Dad, it looks like a _____.

M Okay. Then I think the _____ yellow frog looks _____ _____ to ride.

W But Dad, I _____ _____ to ride the frog with the bow tie.

M I see. Let's _____ _____ _____ for it then.

02

① M I'd like some _____ for my _____.

W You need to get a _____.

② M When did you _____ _____ _____ last time?

W I did it this morning.

③ M My gums _____ so much that I _____ _____ anything.

W You'd _____ go see a _____.

④ M Why do I _____ _____ in my teeth?

W I'm afraid you have some _____.

⑤ M My leg's _____, and it's getting worse.

W It could be _____. Let's take some X-rays.

03

W Hi, Max! Wait till I tell you _____ _____ last night.

M What happened to you?

W While I was watching TV, I heard two guys _____ _____ _____ _____!
I ran to the phone and _____ _____ _____.

M Oh, no! What happened _____?

W The police _____ _____, chased and arrested them.

M Great. Is there _____ _____ to your car?

W You know what? _____ _____ it was mine but it was _____ _____.

04

M Would you like to _____ _____ _____ _____?

W Well, _____ _____ is it?

M It's only six years old.

W And what's the _____?

M Let me check. It's just 85,000 miles.

W That's _____ _____ _____. How much is it anyway?

M It's a _____ _____ at $10,500. But the price is only for today.

W Hmmm… What about the _____ _____? What kinds of items are _____?

05

[Telephone rings.]

W Hello.

M Hello. Can I talk to Dr. Han?

W I'm sorry, but he's _____ _____ _____ right now. Can I _____ _____ _____?

M Yes, please. I should _____ his books today, but _____ _____ _____ _____.

W So what do you want me to do for you?

M _____ _____ _____ tell him that I will give them back to him next _____?

W Sure. Please give me your name.

M This is Joe Smith _____ _____ _____ 505 class. Thank you.

06

M Here is the bus. Oh, no! It _____ _____ _____ us. I wonder what time the _____ _____ is!

W It says here the next bus comes at 9:30. We have to wait for _____ _____.

M Oh my, that's quite long. Hmm… Excuse me, but I have _____ _____ here several times before. Let me introduce myself. My name is Bart.

W I'm Angela. Nice to meet you. I have seen you, too. _____ do you _____?

M Not far from here. On Fernwood Drive. It's 10 minutes' drive from here. And you?

W My house is on Lake Road, a little _____
_____ _____.

M There is _____ _____ here behind us.
Would you like some tea _____ _____
_____?

W Sure, why not!

07

W May I _____ your cell phone to call my
mother after we finish lunch?

M Yes, of course. And do not forget to ask your
mother _____ _____ _____
_____ to the movies with me afterwards.

W Okay. Could you _____ _____
_____ _____, please?

M Sure, here it is.

W Thank you. Oh, did you _____ _____
_____ my *Harry Potter* book?

M I am sorry. I _____ _____ about it.
_____ _____ _____ to remind
me again tonight?

W Certainly.

08

M How was your _____? Did you _____
_____ at the soccer game?

W No. _____ _____ _____.

M Why?

W _____ _____ _____ to see the
game, my boyfriend had _____ _____.

M Really? What happened?

W My boyfriend _____ his _____
_____ when he _____ _____
at the subway station. We had to _____
_____ _____ _____ _____.

M I'm sorry to hear that. How is he?

W He is _____ _____ _____ and
_____ _____ _____ in his house.
It was an _____ weekend.

09

W Yoon, can I ask you about the _____ of
_____ _____?

M Sure. I'm quite _____ _____ their
locations. I learned about all the states in
_____ _____.

W Good. Can you tell me their locations _____

_____ _____ each other? For instance,
is Colorado _____ _____ _____
of Kansas?

M Well, Colorado is _____ _____ Kansas
and Kansas is _____ _____ Oklahoma.

W _____ _____ Utah and California?

M Utah is _____ _____ California, and
Utah is also _____ Nevada and Colorado.

W _____ _____. What about Arizona?

M It is _____ _____ New Mexico. I lived
there _____ _____ _____ when I
was young.

W Really? I _____ _____ _____
_____. Thank you anyway.

10

W Alcohol's _____ _____ the heart
are well documented. Studies have shown that
_____ _____ can raise levels of
"good cholesterol," which helps _____
harmful blood clots and keep blood _____
_____ through our bodies. _____,
there's _____ _____ that too much
alcohol can lead to _____ _____.
Excess alcohol can _____ _____
_____ _____ lots of diseases such as
liver disease, a stroke, and diabetes.

11

M _____ and _____. This is your
_____ _____. We are now going to
_____ _____ _____, so we will
_____ _____ you drinks and snacks for
a while. _____ _____ _____,
please _____ _____ and _____
_____ _____ _____. In two hours
and 10 minutes, we'll be _____ _____
Incheon International Airport. The local time is
now 7:50 in the evening. I hope you are _____
_____ _____. Thank you.

12

W Can I help you?

M Yes, I'm _____ _____ _____
_____.

W Are they _____ _____ _____
tomorrow?

M Yes, they are for my girlfriend. She loves pink. I will give them to her as a Valentine's gift.

W _____ _____! I'll check _____ we have any _____ _____ or not.

M Thank you.

W I'm sorry. We _____ _____ _____ _____ earlier today. But we will _____ _____ _____ at 7 a.m. tomorrow.

M OK. I will make sure I get here _____ _____.

13

M Did you _____ _____ _____ _____ from Jungmi?

W No. What kind of invitation card is it?

M She is going to _____ _____ _____ _____. She said she'd invite you.

W _____ _____. When is it?

M It will be on _____ _____, which is this _____.

W Will it be in the _____ or in the _____? If it is around noon, I can't make it. I have a _____ _____.

M It will start at _____ p.m. I think you _____ _____ _____. There will be a _____ along with snacks and drinks.

W How nice! Please tell me the _____ and give me _____ _____ _____. I don't think I have her number.

M The address is 70 Rodeo Avenue and the number is 010-0707-0007.

14

M Did you _____ which one you are going to buy?

W Not yet. I'm still _____ _____ the _____.

M Still? Why are you taking _____ _____? Don't you have a _____ _____ _____?

W I did. But when I look at all these pictures, it is so _____.

M I don't understand you. The only important thing is that it _____ _____ _____ _____ and people _____ _____ our house.

W Yes. But I have to choose the _____ and the

_____. It can make our house _____ _____ _____.

M I see. But _____ _____. Don't spend too much time on it. _____ you can choose will be _____.

W Alright.

15

[Telephone rings.]

M Hello.

W Hello, Jason. It's me, Judy. What are you doing?

M Oh, Judy. I'm _____ _____ on the Internet.

W What books are they?

M One is a _____ _____ _____ _____, and the other is a book about _____.

W Good. Jason, Jennie and I will _____ _____ _____ _____ and _____ _____ _____ at the community center. Will you join us?

M Hmm… I'm not sure if I can _____ _____ _____ _____. But I can join you _____ _____ _____ _____.

W Great. Let's meet at 3 _____ _____ _____ the center. Please _____ _____ when you arrive.

16

① M I'm writing _____ _____ for _____ _____ _____.

W That's great! I _____ _____ _____ _____ it.

② M What makes you think the movie will be _____ _____ _____?

W It has _____ _____ _____.

③ M Be sure _____ _____ _____ _____ when you _____ _____ _____.

W Sorry for the _____.

④ M I think _____ is the most important thing _____ _____.

W That's _____ _____ _____.

⑤ M Why do you look _____ _____?

W I have _____ _____. I shouldn't

have slept _____ _____ _____
_____.

17

M Jane, you like strawberries, don't you? I've decided to go to _____ _____ _____ _____ at Sunspot Farm. Would you like to go with me?

W Huh, when is it?

M Participants will be meeting at the _____ _____ of the farm _____ _____, at _____ _____ in the morning so this will be done in _____ _____.

W Is it free?

M No. There is a 5 dollar entry fee which includes all the _____ _____ _____ _____. You must _____ and pay _____ _____ _____ of the event.

W How can we go there? Is there any _____ _____ _____?

M No, but I will _____ you _____ _____ if you need one.

W OK, I'm in.

M Excellent choice. I'll register you and me. The fee _____ _____ _____.

18

W _____ _____ can be a very _____ _____ for a student. Tom's best friend, Ann, transferred _____ _____ _____ after her freshman year because her dad got _____ _____ _____. Tom calls Ann and asks _____ _____ _____ her _____ _____. She says she is _____ _____ _____ her new school because she doesn't have _____ _____. Tom is _____ because Ann was _____ _____ in her old school. In this situation, what would Tom most likely say to Ann?

19

W Karl, look at this _____ _____.

M What is it? What happened?

W _____ _____ broke out _____ Bicentennial _____. A lot of trees are _____.

M Is that _____ _____ we went to _____ _____?

W Yeah. The news says the police suspect _____ _____ wasn't _____ _____ _____.

M In this _____ _____, _____ easily catch fire.

W We should not have campfires in the dry season.

20

W You look _____. What's wrong?

M Well... I _____ _____ _____ of my brother's _____ _____.

W Didn't you say your parents bought it for _____ _____ _____ last month?

M Yes, I did. What would you do if you were _____ _____ _____?

W If I were you, I would tell him and your parents _____ _____ and say _____ _____ _____.

M I'm _____. They might be really _____ at me, especially _____ _____.

W If you tell the truth, they will forgive you.

01 대화를 듣고, 남자가 여자에게 줄 우표를 고르시오.

①   ②   ③   ④   ⑤

02 대화를 듣고, 두 사람이 구입할 동물로 가장 적절한 것을 고르시오.

①   ②   ③   ④   ⑤

03 대화를 듣고, 두 사람의 관계로 가장 적절한 것을 고르시오.

① 식당 종업원 ― 손님   ② 경찰관 ― 시민
③ 의사 ― 환자   ④ 선수 ― 코치
⑤ 아버지 ― 딸

04 대화를 듣고, 여자의 심정으로 가장 적절한 것을 고르시오.

① annoyed   ② embarrassed   ③ pleased
④ thankful   ⑤ sorrowful

05 대화를 듣고, 여자가 지불할 총 금액을 고르시오.

① $103   ② $105   ③ $107   ④ $108   ⑤ $125

06 대화를 듣고, 남자가 사야 할 물건을 고르시오.

① paper　　　　　② ink　　　　　③ cell phone
④ printer　　　　 ⑤ computer

07 다음을 듣고, 원그래프의 내용과 일치하지 <u>않는</u> 것을 고르시오.

Popular Sports in Cindy's Class

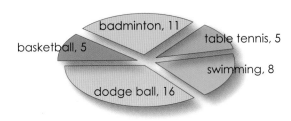

①　　　　②　　　　③　　　　④　　　　⑤

08 대화를 듣고, 여자가 남자를 위해 할 일로 가장 적절한 것을 고르시오.

① 다림질 하기　　　　② 양복 구입 하기
③ 설거지 하기　　　　④ 캠핑 같이 가기
⑤ 식사준비 하기

09 대화를 듣고, 남자가 당황한 이유를 고르시오.

① 음식이 잘못 나와서　　　② 주차를 할 수 없어서
③ 현금이 부족해서　　　　 ④ 신용카드를 분실해서
⑤ 길을 잃어버려서

10 대화를 듣고, 두 사람이 만나기로 한 시각을 고르시오.

① 2:00　　② 2:17　　③ 2:30　　④ 3:30　　⑤ 4:00

11 대화를 듣고, 여자에 대한 설명으로 일치하지 <u>않는</u> 것을 고르시오.

① 구직 면접 중이다.　　　　　　② 다수의 외국어에 능통하다.

③ 해외여행을 한 번 했다.　　　　④ 여행사 취업경험이 없다.

⑤ 언제든지 일을 시작할 수 있다.

12 대화를 듣고, 대화 내용과 일치하는 것을 고르시오.

KTX Reservation

① Time / Date:		10:25 a.m. / May 5
② Ticket Type:		Round trip
③ Depart / Arrive:		Seoul to Dongdaegu
④ Rate:		55,000 won
⑤ Car / Seat Number:		20 / 8D

13 대화를 듣고, 두 사람이 대화하는 장소로 가장 적절한 것을 고르시오.

① repair shop　　　　　　② police station

③ department store　　　④ bookstore

⑤ bank

14 다음을 듣고, 오늘 기온이 가장 높았던 지역을 고르시오.

① 서울　　② 인천　　③ 부산　　④ 울산　　⑤ 제주도

15 다음을 듣고, 무엇에 관한 안내인지 고르시오.

① 신규 강좌 개설　　　　② 선호과목 조사

③ 수강등록 방법　　　　④ 학교 규칙

⑤ 지도교수 상담

16 대화를 듣고, 두 사람이 먼저 해야 할 일로 가장 적절한 것을 고르시오.

① 병원에 병문안 가기　　　② 전철역에 친구 마중 가기
③ 선생님께 전화하기　　　④ 병원에서 발목 치료하기
⑤ 친구 집 들르기

17 다음을 듣고, 두 사람의 대화가 <u>어색한</u> 것을 고르시오.

① 　　　 ② 　　　 ③ 　　　 ④ 　　　 ⑤

18 대화를 듣고, 상황을 가장 잘 표현한 속담을 고르시오.

① 티끌 모아 태산.
② 고생 끝에 낙이 온다.
③ 쥐구멍에도 볕 들 날 있다.
④ 잘되면 내 탓 못되면 조상 탓.
⑤ 하늘은 스스로 돕는 자를 돕는다.

19 다음을 듣고, Sarah가 동아리 회장에게 할 말로 가장 적절한 것을 고르시오.

① What's today's special?
② What else should I bring?
③ Is everything set for the climb?
④ Do you enjoy mountain climbing?
⑤ How much time do you spend climbing?

20 대화를 듣고, 여자의 마지막 말에 이어질 남자의 응답으로 가장 적절한 것을 고르시오.

① What time was the party over?
② We want to invite you to our party.
③ Did you enjoy yourself at the party?
④ Why don't we get started by writing up a to-do list?
⑤ How about inviting our moms and dads to the party?

● 다음은 **Listening Test 06**의 주요 지문입니다. 녹음을 다시 듣고, 질문에 대한 답을 완성하세요.

Q1

1 Why can't the woman buy the animation character stamps that the man already bought?

  ↳ The reason is that the stamps are _____.

Q3

2 What is the man's bad habit when he plays tennis?

  ↳ He _____ with his eyes after he _____

  _____.

Q6

3 Why is the woman going to send the man a text message?

  ↳ The reason is that _____ has bad reception, so he _____

  _____ well.

Q11

4 How many languages can the woman speak fluently?

  ↳ She can speak _____ fluently.

Q12

5 Where are the woman and the man?

  ↳ They are at _____.

Q13

6 What does the woman want to do in the bank?

  ↳ She wants to _____.

Q16

7 Why is Hannah in the hospital?

  ↳ She _____ when _____

  _____ at the subway station.

Q20

8 Why do the girl and the boy want to have a party?

  ↳ They want to do _____ for _____

  _____.

● 자신의 상황에 맞게 내용을 완성하고 말해 보세요.

 A Describe what you see in the graph after filling in the table below.

Pets the Students in Mike's Class Raise

Describing a Graph

(1) Title

(2) The most popular pet

(3) Comparing pets

(4) The least popular pet

(5) Your suggestion
about raising a pet

This chart shows (1)_____.

The most popular pet is (2)_____. The students raise (3)_____

_____. (4)_____

are the least popular pet among Mike's classmates. It is a good idea to

(5)_____.

B Have you ever attended or hosted an impressive party? Fill in the table below and tell your classmates about it.

An Impressive Party

Who hosted it, when & where?	(1)
What was the purpose of the party?	(2)
	(3)
Why was the party impressive?	(4)
	(5)

I would like to tell you about an impressive party I had. It was hosted by

(1)_____. The purpose

of the party was (2)_____

_____. The party had many things that I think were impressive.

First, (3)_____.

Second, (4)_____.

Third, (5)_____.

It was a party that I'll never forget.

01

M Look at this. I _____ these _____ _____ _____ released by the United States Postal Service.

W Oh, they look awesome! _____ can I buy them?

M _____ _____. They are already _____ _____. But if you really want, I can give you _____ _____ _____.

W Really? Every one looks so cool. Which one is your _____?

M I love _____ stamps from the movie *Toy Story* and these _____ _____.

W Hmm…can I get this one with a _____ _____ and a _____?

M What about this one with a _____ _____ and a good-looking _____?

W That's also _____. Okay, I'll _____ that one.

02

W I love shopping at the mall! It's _____ so the weather is always nice.

M Exactly. _____ _____, it's raining outside, but we don't need any umbrellas in the mall.

W Oh, look at the _____ _____ _____ and there's a _____ one, too! Aren't they _____?

M Yes, they are. But I _____ _____ to cats. Why don't we buy that _____ _____?

W Honey, do you remember that I _____ to listen to its barking sound?

M I'm sorry, I just forgot. Look at that _____ haired silky guinea pig. It looks really _____.

W Absolutely, yes. Let's _____ _____ to our house.

03

M Even though I can run fast, I still _____ the _____ quite often while playing tennis.

W Try _____ _____ _____ the ball with your eyes after you _____ it.

M I know I have that _____ _____. I follow the ball all the way when it flies through the air.

W You need to _____ _____. Hit the ball and then _____ your eyes away from _____ _____ over to _____ _____.

M How can I shift my eyes _____?

W Practice makes _____.

M Okay. I'll practice a lot. Oh, our ordering number is now _____. I'll go get the _____.

04

W I'm happy you're coming for _____ tonight. Which do you like better, _____ or _____?

M Well, I don't eat _____ _____.

W Actually I don't eat much red meat, _____. What about some _____, then? Oysters? Squid?

M I _____ really _____ too much for seafood, either, Julia.

W That's okay. How about stewed chicken, then?

M Actually, Julia, I'm a _____. I _____ _____ any meat at all.

W I'm sorry. I _____ _____ _____ you what you _____ _____ before. I'll make the salad really delicious.

05

M May I help you, ma'am?

W Yes. My husband is a real _____ _____. I think he needs to play a sport. What can I buy him?

M What kind of sports does he like?

W _____ _____. He watches all kinds of sports on TV.

M Maybe this _____ _____ is good for him. It costs only _____ dollars.

W Oh, my! It's _____ _____. What about this one with a red handle?

M That is also a good item. It is _____ dollars. If you purchase this, you can get these _____ _____ for _____ dollars.

W I'll take it and I'll take _____ _____, _____.

06

[Telephone rings.]

W Hello.

M Hi, Stephanie. I'm Luke. How are things at the _____?

W Oh, Luke! Thank you for calling. I was about to call you. Can you please pick up _____ for the _____ _____ on your way back to the office?

M Pardon me? _____ _____ _____ _____, please?

W Pick up _____ _____, please.

M Did you say to pick up _____ for the _____? Sorry, the phone is _____ _____.

W Can you hear me now? Listen, I'll _____ you _____ I _____. Thanks, Luke. Talk to you later.

M OK, Stephanie. Sorry, my phone _____ _____ _____ _____ here.

07

① W Dodge ball is _____ _____ _____ any other sport.

② W Table tennis and basketball are the least popular sports in Cindy's class.

③ W Badminton is _____ _____ _____ _____ sport in Cindy's class.

④ W Swimming is _____ _____ _____ basketball and table tennis.

⑤ W No sport is _____ _____ _____ badminton in Cindy's class.

08

W _____ _____! Did you have a great time?

M It was _____. It was the best camping trip I've ever gone on. I _____ a lot of _____.

W Good. Anyway, what are you going to _____ _____ _____ _____ _____ this _____?

M The pants and shirt which you bought for me on my birthday.

W Oh, no! I forgot to _____ them.

M _____ _____ _____ do that for me? I'm not _____ _____ _____.

W Well, okay. Then can you _____ _____ _____? I will _____ _____ the iron first.

M Sure. Thank you.

09

W How was the dinner, sir?

M It was _____. If I _____ _____ _____, I'd like to come here again.

W _____ _____ _____ saying so. How would you like to pay _____?

M I'll _____ _____ _____. Let me _____ _____ _____. [pause] Oh no!

W _____ _____?

M I don't think I have enough cash in my wallet.

W Don't you have a _____ _____?

M _____ _____ _____. I left it in my car. Can I _____ _____ _____ _____ and come back _____ _____?

W No problem.

10

M If _____ _____ _____, how about watching the new movie called *The Attorney* with me?

W I'd love to. _____ _____ the movie start?

M There are _____ _____ in the Central Theater. We have to _____ which one we want to see.

W Are there showings in the afternoon, evening, and at night?

M Yes. When do you _____?

W The afternoon would be best for me.

M There are _____ _____, one at 2:30 and the other at 4:00.

W _____ _____ one is _____ for me. And let's meet 30 minutes before the show time _____ _____ _____ the _____ _____.

M Okay. See you then.

11

M Good afternoon. _____ _____
_____ _____ _____?

W _____ _____. I'm very nervous.

M Please relax. I'll ask you a few questions. First, so
you want to be a _____ _____?

W Yes, that's right. That's _____ _____
_____. I can even _____ four
_____ _____.

M That sounds _____. Then, _____
_____ _____ _____ in the travel
business?

W No, but I've traveled to several _____
_____. I think it will be a great help.

M Great. When can you start working?

W _____ _____ _____ you hire me.

12

W Welcome to Korail's _____ _____. How
may I help you?

M I'd like to make a reservation to go to Dongdaegu
from Seoul by KTX.

W _____ _____ _____ like to leave?

M This _____ _____. I mean, May 15.
And I'd like the 10:25 train in the morning.

W Do you need a _____ or a _____
_____?

M A one-way ticket, please.

W That's 50 thousand won. Would you like
_____ _____ _____
or _____ _____?

M _____ _____. Here you go.

W Thank you. OK, your _____ and _____
_____ is 12 and 8D. Have a nice day.

13

M Hello, ma'am. How may I help you?

W Hello. I need to _____ _____
_____, but I'm afraid the ATM outside
_____ _____ _____. What
should I do?

M Don't worry. You can go to a teller at the
_____ over there.

W I don't have my _____ with me.

M That's okay _____ _____ _____
you have a cash card for that account and some ID.

W That's good.

M Please _____ _____ _____,
_____ _____ this form, and
_____ _____ your _____.

W Thank you very much.

M _____ _____.

14

M Good evening. Did you enjoy the _____
_____ _____ _____ today? We had a high of
_____ _____ _____ Celsius in Seoul while
Incheon was _____ _____ _____
at 26.5. Busan and Ulsan _____ 23
_____ 25 respectively. Jeju Island _____
a high of 26. Tomorrow, the temperature will be
_____ _____ _____ _____ _____
_____ 27 in Seoul, so you can _____
_____ _____. This is Sunok Hwang
from KBC. Thank you.

15

W Good morning, students. We are pleased to
_____ that, due to _____ _____,
we have _____ two new courses to the
summer term! They are Elementary Algebra I and
Advanced Composition. Seats will _____
_____ _____, so log into our homepage
and _____ _____! Please contact an
_____ _____ if you would like to see
how these courses _____ _____ in
your _____ _____. They are here to
_____ _____ _____! They can be
reached at 123-6767.

16

M Do you know _____ Hannah _____
_____ today?

W She is _____ _____ _____. I'm
going to see her now.

M Is she _____ _____?

W She sprained her ankle, but she should be
_____ _____ _____.

M That's _____ _____. Do you know
_____ _____ _____ _____?

W When _____ _____ _____
suddenly at the subway station, she _____
_____ _____ and _____

_____.

M It could have been _____. Can I join you?

W Sure. She will be _____ _____ to see you. Let's _____ _____ her house first to _____ _____ _____ _____ for her.

17

① M I wish _____ _____ _____ _____.

W _____ _____ _____.

② M I went to the _____ _____ at dawn.

W You're always _____ _____ _____.

③ M I _____ _____ to jump in the water.

W _____ _____ you warm up before going in.

④ M I can't cook spaghetti.

W _____ _____ _____ _____.

⑤ M Are you _____ a trip to Disneyland?

W Yeah, I'm _____ _____ _____ it.

18

M Hi, Ashley. How were your tests?

W I think they're _____ _____. I got all _____ _____ on the tests this time. How about you?

M I got _____ _____ _____ on the _____ test.

W Wow, congratulations! It seems that _____ _____ from your brother _____ _____ _____ _____.

M It helps, but I don't completely agree. I studied really hard by myself, too.

W Wasn't your _____ _____ a B last time? Anyway, how was _____?

M I just got a C on that. My brother didn't _____ _____ carefully _____ _____ _____ difficult questions.

W Come on, you can't _____ it _____ _____ _____.

19

W Sarah is _____ _____ _____ a _____ _____. Next week, her club is going to climb Mt. Hood and _____ _____ _____ on the _____. Although it's summer now, _____ is covering _____ _____. So the head of the club says they should bring _____ _____, _____, and _____. It is the first time for Sarah to climb a mountain _____ _____ _____ _____ _____. She is wondering _____ there are any more things _____ _____ _____ _____. In this situation, what would Sarah most likely say to the head of the club?

20

W Bobby, I forgot what day mom and dad's _____ _____ is. I've drawn _____ _____. Do you know?

M Oh my god. It is _____ _____ _____ _____. I just _____ _____.

W Let's do _____ _____ for them.

M Do you have _____ _____ mind?

W How about _____ _____ _____?

M That's a good idea. But there are only _____ _____ _____ to prepare for the party. What should we do first?

W We need _____ _____ like _____, _____, and _____. We also need _____ _____ and _____. Oh, don't forget _____ _____. What else?

M Why don't we get started by writing up a to-do list?

01 대화를 듣고, 두 사람이 구매할 신발로 가장 적절한 것을 고르시오.

① ② ③ ④ ⑤

02 대화를 듣고, 여자가 찾고 있는 물건이 있는 장소를 고르시오.

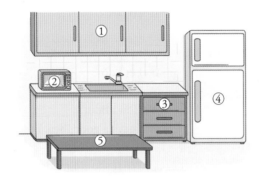

03 대화를 듣고, 남자의 심정으로 가장 적절한 것을 고르시오.

① impressed   ② nervous   ③ proud
④ jealous   ⑤ annoyed

04 대화를 듣고, 남자의 직업으로 가장 적절한 것을 고르시오.

① police officer   ② teacher   ③ reporter
④ salesclerk   ⑤ tour guide

05 대화를 듣고, 여자가 지불할 금액을 고르시오.

① $115   ② $150   ③ $250   ④ $315   ⑤ $350

06 다음을 듣고, 무엇에 관한 내용인지 고르시오.

① 구직의 어려움　　　　　　② 직장인의 스트레스
③ 원만한 직장생활　　　　　　④ 회사의 부당한 해고
⑤ 업무효율성 증진 방법

07 대화를 듣고, 여자가 남자에게 요청한 일로 가장 적절한 것을 고르시오.

① 요리 도와주기　　　　　　② 상 차리기
③ 후식 맛보기　　　　　　　④ 시험공부 하기
⑤ 숙제 하기

08 대화를 듣고, 두 사람이 만나기로 한 요일을 고르시오.

① Monday　　　　　② Tuesday　　　　　③ Wednesday
④ Thursday　　　　　⑤ Friday

09 다음을 듣고, 그림의 상황에 어울리는 대화를 고르시오.

① 　　　　② 　　　　③ 　　　　④ 　　　　⑤

10 대화를 듣고, 여자의 마지막 말에 담긴 의도로 가장 적절한 것을 고르시오.

① 칭찬　　　② 기대　　　③ 동의　　　④ 질투　　　⑤ 우려

11 대화를 듣고, 남자가 현재 하고 있는 일로 가장 적절한 것을 고르시오.

① 테니스 경기 관람   ② 테니스 경기 시청
③ 축구 경기 관람   ④ 축구 경기 시청
⑤ 콘서트 관람

12 다음을 듣고, 어느 나라에 관한 설명인지 고르시오.

① England   ② the Philippines   ③ France
④ Spain   ⑤ Swiss

13 대화를 듣고, 영어 글짓기 대회의 날짜로 가장 적절한 것을 고르시오.

MAY						
SUN	MON	TUE	WED	THU	FRI	SAT
					1	2
3	4	5	6	7	8	9
10	11	12	13	14	15	16
17	18	19	20	21	22	23
24 / 31	25	26	27	28	29	30

① May 8   ② May 14   ③ May 15   ④ May 21   ⑤ May 22

14 대화를 듣고, 여자가 전화를 건 목적으로 가장 적절한 것을 고르시오.

① 야근 수당을 청구하려고
② 원고 마감기한을 알려주려고
③ 딸을 유치원에 데려다 달라고 부탁하려고
④ 유치원에서 딸을 데려와 달라고 부탁하려고
⑤ 유치원까지의 소요 시간을 물어보려고

15 대화를 듣고, 두 사람이 대화하는 장소로 가장 적절한 것을 고르시오.

① art gallery   ② concert hall   ③ park
④ museum   ⑤ theater

16 다음을 듣고, 두 사람의 대화가 <u>어색한</u> 것을 고르시오.

① ② ③ ④ ⑤

17 대화를 듣고, 체육관에 관한 내용으로 일치하지 <u>않는</u> 것을 고르시오.

① 개점 1주년 행사를 진행 중이다.
② 행사는 5월 30일까지 계속된다.
③ 50% 할인되는 프로그램도 있다.
④ 신규 회원을 소개하면 할인 받을 수 있다.
⑤ 모든 회원들이 7일 무료 쿠폰을 이용할 수 있다.

18 다음을 듣고, Brad가 Carol에게 할 말로 가장 적절한 것을 고르시오.

① Have a nice trip.
② How was your trip to England?
③ When are you leaving for the trip?
④ I'd like to have some company on the trip.
⑤ Look to your right when you cross the street.

[19-20] 대화를 듣고, 여자의 마지막 말에 이어질 남자의 응답으로 가장 적절한 것을 고르시오.

19 ① Yes, with some honey in it.
② How long have you had this sore throat?
③ Do you have medicine for a sore throat?
④ You shouldn't forget to take the medicine 3 times a day.
⑤ Yes. It's hard to swallow food because of my sore throat.

20 ① It was really a nice restaurant. Try it out.
② The service was terrible when I went there.
③ That restaurant is among the best in this area.
④ Let's check out another restaurant down the street.
⑤ How come there are so many people in the restaurant?

● 다음은 **Listening Test 07**의 주요 지문입니다. 녹음을 다시 듣고, 질문에 대한 답을 완성하세요.

Q3

1 What is the woman supposed to do in her new job?

↳ She will arrange _____.

Q4

2 What did the girl get on her birthday from her sister?

↳ She got _____.

Q5

3 How much did the man pay for the three packs of doggy treats when he bought them?

↳ They were _____ each, so he paid _____ in total.

Q6

4 What are the three keywords for good on-the-job behavior?

↳ They are _____.

Q8

5 What do the members do in the DD Debate Club?

↳ They read _____ and have _____ _____ about news events.

Q10

6 What makes Jacob think he has achieved something?

↳ He has reached _____, _____.

Q13

7 What is the poster about?

↳ It is about an _____.

Q17

8 How will the woman get her friends to come to the gym?

↳ She will give them _____.

자신의 상황에 맞게 내용을 완성하고 말해 보세요.

A What motivates you to study hard? Fill in the table below and tell your classmates about it.

My Motivation to Study

What motivates me	Why they motivate me
(1)	(2)
(3)	(4)

I'm going to talk about what motivates me to study. First, I am motivated by

(1)_____. Since (2)_____

_____.

The second thing that motivates me to study is (3)_____

_____. Because (4)_____

_____.

These two things always motivate me to study hard.

B Think about a club you'd like to join at school. Fill in the table below and tell your classmates about it.

I Would Like to Join a Club...

(1) Name of the club
(2) Reason(s) you'd like to join
(3) Activities they do
(4) Time/place for regular meetings

I'm going to talk about a club which I would like to join. The club I would like to

join is (1)_____. I would like to join the club because

(2) _____

_____. Each club member (3)_____

_____

_____. The club meets (4)_____

_____. I can't wait to join the club and do all the fun activities.

01

M Now, we're done with shopping, right?

W Not yet. We have to buy Riona's _____ _____. Her preschool teacher asked me to send a _____ _____ of them.

M I see. There are lots of designs here. I like the ones with _____.

W She has the same pattern on a pair of her shoes. I want to buy her something _____ and _____.

M How about these _____ _____ ones with _____ _____?

W They look _____. What about these moccasins?

M Oh, I love their color. _____ on the front and _____ _____ on the back with a _____ _____!

W Yes, Riona will love them. Let's take them.

02

W Max, do you know _____ the _____ is? I need it to clean the dishes.

M Did you look on the _____ _____?

W It _____ _____. It was not in the _____ next to the _____, either.

M How about in the microwave oven? You sometimes _____ the dishcloth in _____ to sterilize it.

W No, it's not there.

M Oh, wait, I remember! Yesterday I used it when I _____ the _____. It may still be in the _____.

W Oh, yes. Here it is.

03

W Hey, good news. I _____ _____.

M Congratulations! What is _____ _____ now?

W I'm now a sales department _____. From now on, I will be _____ _____ of arranging _____ _____ in the sales department.

M Good for you. You got promoted _____ _____. On the other hand, I've _____ at the _____ _____ for three years.

04 (continued top right)

W I think it's because I have _____ _____. I had to work till very _____ _____ _____ so many times.

M Hey, I've been working hard, too. But _____ _____ _____ hasn't been _____ like yours. I _____ I _____ _____ as fast as you.

04

M What can I do for you?

W I'd like to _____ _____ _____ on these jeans.

M May I ask why you want to get a _____ for them?

W My sister bought them for my birthday, but I think they _____ _____ me.

M If that's the only reason, _____ _____ _____ _____ them for something else?

W I'm sorry, but I just want a refund.

M _____. Do you _____ _____ _____?

W Here it is.

M Please _____ _____ _____.

05

[Telephone rings.]

M Hello?

W Hello. I saw your _____ on the Internet. You're selling the Chihuahua puppy for _____ dollars, right?

M Yes, I paid _____ dollars when I _____ it in the _____ _____.

W Is it trained to _____ _____?

M Yes, it is. I'm also selling its portable doghouse for _____ dollars. Are you _____ _____ _____, too?

W Oh, well. That's good but…

M If you buy both of them, I'll give you three packs of doggy treats _____ _____. They were _____ dollars each when I bought them.

W Sounds good. I'll buy _____ _____ _____. Can I pick them up tomorrow?

06

M Why are people _____ from their jobs? In many cases, it's _____ because they are _____ _____ _____ _____. Instead, people are often fired because of a _____ _____. This is why it is important to _____ _____ _____ fellow workers. Getting along with other people is a _____ of _____ _____ _____. Here are three keywords for _____ on-the-job behavior: promptness, courtesy, and eagerness.

07

W How was school? How did you _____ _____ _____ _____?

M It was OK, and I _____ _____ on the test, Mom.

W I am _____ to hear that.

M By the way, what do we have _____ _____ tonight?

W I will make _____ _____ and mashed _____. For dessert, I've already made _____ _____ and _____.

M It has been _____ _____ _____ since you made roast beef. Do you need any help, mom?

W No, go do _____ _____ and leave the cooking to me.

M Thanks, mom. Call me whenever _____ _____ _____. I do not want to be late for this tasty dinner.

08

M Minju, I'm _____ _____ your _____ _____. Can you tell me a little bit about it?

W Why not? There are 13 members _____ me. Our club's name is "DD Debate."

M _____ _____ _____ _____ _____?

W We read English _____ and have weekly _____ _____ _____ about news events. The debates are every _____ right after school.

M Sounds interesting. Are you meeting _____

_____ then?

W No. This time we have _____ it _____ _____ _____.

M Okay. Can I go with you then?

W _____. Let's meet on that day and go to the _____ _____ _____.

09

① M Now, I _____ why this movie is a _____ _____.

W _____ _____ _____. It is so _____.

② M Why don't we go to the movies?

W I'd love to but I have to _____ _____ _____ my younger sisters.

③ M We'd like _____ _____ for the 2:30 show, please.

W _____ _____ _____. Enjoy the movie!

④ M I have a _____ _____.

W Let me look at your _____.

⑤ M Did you have a good weekend?

W Yes. I _____ to the _____ with my family.

10

W Hey, Jacob. Are you still _____ _____ _____?

M Judy, guess what! I got to _____ _____ _____ on this game.

W Really? _____ _____ is the highest?

M It goes up to _____ _____. I feel like I've really _____ _____ _____.

W Good for you! But you know what? You've been playing the game _____ _____ _____.

M Oh my god! Time flies so fast. I feel like _____ _____ _____ has _____.

W You spent too much time _____ _____ _____ that level. It's already 10 p.m.

11

[Telephone rings.]

M Hello.

W Hey, Jaesuk. _____ _____ _____ _____ now?

M Oh, hi, Misun. I'm watching a _____

_____ on TV. It's almost over.

W I _____ _____ much about _____,
   but is that the big game _____ _____
   _____ _____ I have heard so much
   about?

M No, that's a _____ _____. It's later
   tonight on channel 11. Are you going to watch it?

W Oh. I'm not much interested in sports anyway.
   By the way, do you _____ _____
   _____ tomorrow?

M _____, yes. Why?

W I'd like to go to a _____ _____ with
   you. Can you?

M Sure. I'll go with you.

12

M It is _____ _____ _____ in
   Western Europe. It is a _____ _____
   with significant _____, _____,
   _____, and _____ _____
   in Europe and around the world. It is the
   third _____ _____ in Europe and
   _____ in the world. The country's name
   comes from the Latin Francia, which means
   _____ _____ the _____. It has
   the Eiffel Tower, the Notre-Dame Cathedral, and
   the Palace of Versailles.

13

M Look at the _____!

W _____ _____ _____ _____?

M There will be an _____ _____
   _____ in May.

W Really? _____ it will be a very big one. Are
   you interested in it?

M Yeah, that _____ very _____, but I'm
   not sure yet.

W Why? Are you busy this month?

M Yes. I have to _____ a science report by the
   _____ _____ in May. But the contest
   will be right before that day.

W Oh, _____ _____ _____. I don't
   think you can _____ it then.

14

[Telephone rings.]

W Honey, are you _____ _____

_____?

M Yes. I am. Why? Are you _____ _____?

W No, it's _____ _____. I'm going to
   finish late today. I think I'll have to _____
   _____ _____ because tomorrow is the
   _____ _____ _____ _____.

M I see. What can I do for you?

W I need to _____ Hanul _____ at 5:30
   but I can't. She will be ready to be picked up at the
   kindergarten then.

M _____ _____ about it. I can pick her
   up. However, I might be late by 10 to 15 minutes
   because it's _____ _____.

W I'll call the teacher and _____ our
   _____. Thank you very much.

M No problem. Good luck with the manuscript.

15

M _____ _____ _____ _____
   do you like?

W Oh, I like all kinds of music _____
   _____ _____ it is not hard rock.

M Wow! Look at _____ _____
   _____ _____ who have already shown
   up for the _____.

W _____ do you want to _____? In the
   _____ or in the _____?

M In the shade, please. I have been in the sun too
   much lately.

W Okay, let's _____ _____ _____.
   How long ago did the band _____
   _____ at _____ _____?

M I think it started this tradition five years ago.

16

① M I heard that your sister _____ _____
      _____ _____. Is that true?

   W Yes, she did. I'm so _____ _____
      her.

② M _____ _____ _____ the news
      this morning?

   W _____ _____?

③ M What are you going to buy?

   W I'm going to buy _____ _____ and
      _____.

④ M _____ _____ and cross the street in
      front of the post office.

W _____ _____ _____
_____ again?

⑤ M I _____ _____ _____ in the
morning, so I was late for school.

W You _____ _____ _____.

17

M Good evening, what can I do for you?

W Hi, I'd like to _____ my registration.

M Thanks for your _____. Well, have you heard
about our _____ _____ _____?

W Yes, I have. But it's _____ _____ for me.

M In celebration of our _____ _____,
we are offering a _____% _____ for
members who buy the three-month personal
training program.

W Oh, are you? When does this _____ end?

M It is going on _____ _____ _____.
Also, you can get _____% _____ a
_____ _____ if a friend takes out a gym
membership _____ _____ _____.

W Oh, that's a good deal. Then do you have any
_____ _____ that I can give out?

M Seven-day trial vouchers are right here at
_____ _____ for our _____
_____. Help yourself.

18

W Winter vacation is _____ _____
_____. Last summer vacation, Brad took
a trip to England with his family _____
_____ _____. He enjoyed traveling
there _____, but he also had a _____
_____. He almost got _____
_____ _____ _____ while he
was crossing the street because he didn't look
_____ _____ _____. He didn't
remember that they drive _____ _____
_____ _____. Today Brad's best friend,
Carol, says she is going to take a trip to _____
_____ this vacation. She asks Brad for some
tips for the trip. In this situation, what would Brad
most likely say to Carol?

19

W Oh, my _____ is _____ _____.

M Do you have _____ _____?

W Yes. It is a bad cold and I'm taking some
_____. But there must be something else I
can do for _____ _____ _____.

M Well, if I were you, I would drink _____
_____ _____.

W What kind of _____?

M _____ _____ _____ it's
_____, it doesn't really matter. I prefer
_____ _____.

W It is quite _____, isn't it? Do you drink it with
_____ in it?

M Yes, with some honey in it.

20

W Oh, it's almost lunch time. I'm _____
_____ _____. What do you want to
have today?

M I'm _____ _____ _____ a bear. I
could _____ _____.

W Where shall we go? What about _____
_____?

M That would be _____ with me.

W The new Italian restaurant _____ _____
_____ got _____ _____ on the
Internet.

M No. Let's _____ _____ there.

W Why not?

M The service was terrible when I went there.

08 Listening Test

01 대화를 듣고, 두 사람이 묘사하는 사진을 고르시오.

①   ②   ③   ④   ⑤

02 대화를 듣고, 남자가 구입할 물건으로 가장 적절한 것을 고르시오.

①   ②   ③   ④  ⑤

03 대화를 듣고, 여자의 마지막 말에 담긴 의도로 가장 적절한 것을 고르시오.

① 감사   ② 경의   ③ 요청   ④ 비난   ⑤ 거절

04 대화를 듣고, 여자의 심정으로 가장 적절한 것을 고르시오.

① jealous   ② sorrowful   ③ irritated
④ nervous   ⑤ excited

05 대화를 듣고, 여자의 약속시간까지 남은 시간을 고르시오.

① 15분   ② 30분   ③ 45분   ④ 1시간   ⑤ 1시간 15분

06 대화를 듣고, 남자가 여자를 위해 할 일로 가장 적절한 것을 고르시오.

① 내일 아침에 전화하기   ② 음식 준비하기
③ 내일 여자 대신 운전하기   ④ 오늘밤 문자 보내기
⑤ 차에 기름 넣어주기

07 대화를 듣고, 여자가 딸의 선물로 사줄 물건을 고르시오.

① hairpin   ② CD   ③ notebooks
④ pencils   ⑤ pencil case

08 다음을 듣고, 도표의 내용과 일치하지 <u>않는</u> 것을 고르시오.

**Preferred Types of Volunteer Work
Among the Students in Tom's Class**

Mentoring children in orphanages 27%
Translating letters for charity organizations 9%
Cleaning streets 43%
Storytelling to the elderly at nursing homes 21%

0% 10% 20% 30% 40% 50%

①   ②   ③   ④   ⑤

09 대화를 듣고, 남자가 도서관에 가는 이유를 고르시오.

① 퀴즈대회 준비를 하려고   ② 책을 반납하려고
③ 보고서를 작성하려고   ④ 시험 공부를 하려고
⑤ 아르바이트를 하려고

10 대화를 듣고, 오늘 요일로 알맞은 것을 고르시오.

① Monday   ② Tuesday   ③ Wednesday
④ Thursday   ⑤ Friday

11 다음을 듣고, 무엇에 관한 광고인지 고르시오.

① fresh fruit ② organic food ③ milk
④ diet food ⑤ fruit juice

12 대화를 듣고, 대화 내용과 일치하는 것을 고르시오.

Susie's Field Trip Activities		
	Boring	Interesting
① Planting seeds	✓	
② Baking a cake	✓	
③ Horseback riding		✓
④ Cooking rice		✓
⑤ Swimming		✓

13 대화를 듣고, 두 사람이 대화하는 장소로 가장 적절한 것을 고르시오.

① 가구점 ② 파티장 ③ 극장 ④ 박물관 ⑤ 식당

14 대화를 듣고, 여자가 조언한 내용으로 가장 적절한 것을 고르시오.

① 컴퓨터 수리하기 ② 참고도서 구입하기
③ 컴퓨터 사용법 배우기 ④ 선생님과 상의하기
⑤ 친구에게 도움 요청하기

15 다음을 듣고, 교내 안내방송 내용과 일치하는 것을 고르시오.

① 기상 악화로 일부 방과 후 수업이 취소된다.
② 오늘 하교용 스쿨버스는 운행하지 않는다.
③ 수업이 끝나면 정규 시내버스로 하교해야 한다.
④ 내일 정상적으로 수업한다.
⑤ 등교관련 사항은 학교 웹사이트에만 공지한다.

16 대화를 듣고, 여자가 할 일로 가장 적절한 것을 고르시오.

① 줄 서기   ② 출국서류 작성하기

③ 수하물 부치기   ④ 비닐봉투에 화장품 담기

⑤ 생수병 버리기

17 다음을 듣고, 두 사람의 대화가 <u>어색한</u> 것을 고르시오.

①   ②   ③   ④   ⑤

18 대화를 듣고, 상황을 가장 잘 표현한 속담을 고르시오.

① It's a piece of cake.

② Make hay while the sun shines.

③ No smoke without fire.

④ A friend in need is a friend indeed.

⑤ Speak of devil and he will appear.

19 다음을 듣고, Christine이 친구에게 할 말로 가장 적절한 것을 고르시오.

① What does your pet dog look like?

② Be careful when you unleash your dog.

③ How many times a day should I feed the dog?

④ The dog is, so to speak, a member of my family.

⑤ Could you take care of my pet dog while I'm overseas?

20 대화를 듣고, 남자의 마지막 말에 이어질 여자의 응답으로 가장 적절한 것을 고르시오.

① It's really delicious.

② So am I. I can't wait.

③ Are you ready to order?

④ I'm waiting for my order.

⑤ What do you think we should order?

84

다음은 **Listening Test 08**의 주요 지문입니다. 녹음을 다시 듣고, 질문에 대한 답을 완성하세요.

Q3
1 How does the man say he sleeps in the library?

↳ He _____, and
goes to sleep.

Q4
2 Why is the woman taking the red-eye flight?

↳ The reason is that it is _____ as it costs _____.

Q5
3 What does the man ask the woman to do?

↳ He asks her to _____ and ask them _____
_____.

Q7
4 What is the woman doing?

↳ She is looking for _____.

Q10
5 Why do they think their homeroom teacher will be busy on Thursday?

↳ The reason is that she will have to _____.

Q13
6 Why does the woman want the non-smoking area?

↳ The reason is that she wants to _____
_____.

Q18
7 Why did the man feel betrayed by Gary?

↳ The reason is that Gary _____
until a few days ago.

Q19
8 Why did Christine's parents bring home an abandoned dog?

↳ They wanted the dog to _____.

● 자신의 상황에 맞게 내용을 완성하고 말해 보세요.

 A   Think about your school festival and tell your classmates about it.

My School Festival

(1) Events we have
(2) The most popular event
(3) Reason(s) it is popular
(4) An event I would add
(5) Reason(s) I would add it

I'm going to talk about the festival at my school. At the festival, we usually have

(1)_____. Students like

(2)_____ most. In my opinion, it is the most popular because

(3)_____

_____. If I could add an event to our school festival,

I would add (4)_____. That is because (5)_____

_____.

B   Suppose you have a foreign friend. What Korean food would you like to introduce to him/her? Fill in the table below and talk about it.

My Favorite Korean Dish

(1) What the food is
(2) Ingredients
(3) Tastes
(4) Reason(s) I like it
(5) My favorite way to eat it

I'm going to tell you about my favorite Korean dish. It is (1)_____

_____. To make it, you need (2)_____

_____.

It tastes (3)_____. I like it very much because

(4)_____.

My favorite way to eat it is (5)_____

_____. Try to make this delicious food and enjoy it.

08 Dictation Test

01

M I was told you are a photo specialist.

W No, I'm not. I'm just _____ _____ _____ _____.

M Do you have time to show me some of _____ _____?

W Sure. Just give me a minute. [pause] This is one of my photo albums.

M Let's see. Wow! I love this picture of a _____ with a _____. The _____ _____ in pink with _____ _____ looks like a real flower.

W Yes, and the _____ _____ makes the other colors look _____ _____.

M _____ gilding on the _____ and the _____ of the cup also makes it look elegant. Where did you take this photo?

W _____ _____ the teacup and saucer, I took the picture of them _____ _____.

02

W May I help you?

M Yes, please. These days I often _____ what I _____ _____ _____. So I think I need to buy Post-it Notes. Do you have any?

W Of course we do. There are lots of _____ and _____. What about these _____ _____ ones?

M They are cute, but I need some _____ ones.

W How about these _____ _____ ones?

M Do you have the _____ _____ ones?

W There you go. There are also _____ square Post-it Notes.

M It looks easier to write things down when it has _____. I'll take those Post-it Notes _____ _____, _____.

03

M I often _____ _____ _____ during the day.

W You do? _____ do you do it?

M Well, any place. Sometimes I _____ _____.

W Right here? How do you do that?

M I find a _____ _____ and just put _____ _____ on some _____ from the _____ and go to sleep.

W Are you serious? While others read books or study, you go to sleep? Do you _____ _____ _____ _____ for class?

M Oh, yes. I have an _____ _____.

W An alarm clock? _____ where people have to _____ _____?

04

W I bought a _____ _____ _____. I'm _____ _____ _____ seeing the city.

M Good for you! Traveling is _____ _____ _____. When are you _____?

W Next week. I'm taking the _____-_____ because of the _____ _____.

M How much is the _____?

W I paid $300 for a round-trip ticket.

M No way! _____ _____ _____ _____. How did you find it?

W There is a website which lets you bid on any ticket they are selling. I'll show you the site later.

M Thanks. Anyway, I'm _____ _____! I hope you have a great time there.

05

W What time is it? We're going to be _____!

M It's a _____ _____ _____. We're on time. Don't panic.

W But we have to be at the restaurant _____ _____ _____. We'll _____ _____ _____ there with all this evening traffic.

M Sure, we will. What time is Bill supposed to arrive for his surprise party?

W He is supposed to arrive at _____. But I _____ Janie I would be there _____ _____ _____. We will have many things to set up.

M We will get there by then. By the way, can you _____ the restaurant and ask them where we can _____ _____ _____?

W All right.

06

M Do you want me to _____ _____
_____ when we _____ _____
_____ _____ tomorrow?

W No, I'll drive. Trust me! I promise not to
_____ _____ _____ again!

M All right. But we also ran _____ _____
_____ last time. Don't forget to put gas in the
car _____ _____ _____ !

W OK! Oh, I'll prepare some sandwiches and fruit.
Could you bring your _____ _____ and
_____ ?

M Yes. And if you want, I'll _____ _____
in the morning and remind you _____
_____ _____ .

W Don't worry! I'll fill up the car tonight. But can you
_____ _____ _____ _____ ,
_____ ? You know I don't like getting up early.

M No problem. I'll call you then.

07

W Excuse me. I'm looking for a _____
_____ for my _____-year-old daughter.
Could you help me?

M Sure. _____ _____ a hairpin?

W I think she already has many of them. And she just
cut her hair short last week.

M If she likes to _____ _____ _____ ,
how about a CD or other _____ _____
with her favorite pop star's pictures on it?

W That's good. She's _____ _____
_____ _____ the K-pop group,
INFINITE. Can you show me something with the
group's picture on it?

M Here you are. We have _____ , clear files and
_____ _____ .

W I'll get the _____ _____ . She already
has many nice _____ and _____
_____ .

08

① W The chart displays the _____ of different
types of _____ _____ among the
students in _____ _____ .

② W According to the chart, _____ _____

is the most preferred type of volunteer work.

③ W Mentoring children _____ _____ is
less preferred than _____ to the elderly at
nursing homes.

④ W _____ _____ for _____
_____ is the least preferred type of
volunteer work.

⑤ W _____ _____ , ranking first,
accounted for _____% of the students.

09

W Hey, Robert. _____ _____ _____
_____ ?

M I'm going to the library.

W Why? The _____ _____ are
_____ . They were last week. Do you have any
books to return?

M No. I have to be ready for the _____
_____ . I need to study.

W What? What are you _____ _____ ?

M I'll be competing in the Golden Bell Quiz Show
_____ _____ _____ . So I'm
going to _____ _____ _____
_____ for that.

W Now I understand. Good luck.

M Thank you. Please come and _____
_____ _____ .

10

W What do you _____ _____ having
a _____ _____ for our _____
_____ ?

M Sounds like a _____ idea. Do you know when
her last day is?

W As I know, this Friday is her last day _____
_____ _____ .

M _____ ? Then when can we have the party?

W _____ _____ this _____ ?

M That would be good. I guess she will be busy
_____ _____ and _____
_____ to everyone _____ _____ .

W You're right. We will be busy _____
_____ _____ .

M Yeah. We only have two days to prepare.

11

M Do you want to make your _____ and _____ _____? Do you think you need more _____? _____ _____ _____ _____ our product? We have _____ _____ such as non-fat, low-fat, and regular. Besides plain, we have it in _____, _____, and _____. Each of those contains some _____ _____ _____. If you drink it every day, it will make your body _____ _____ _____. Please go to the market now and buy this Happy _____ _____.

12

W I really had a wonderful time on the _____ _____.

M Good for you. What did you do there?

W Well, I had a chance to _____ _____, bake a _____, ride a _____, swim in the river, and _____ _____.

M Wow! _____ _____ _____?

W Well, planting seeds was interesting. But _____ a cake was the _____ _____ I did there.

M What about the other activities?

W Horseback riding was _____, too, but cooking rice wasn't. Actually it was _____ _____ because I _____ _____ _____.

M Haha. How about swimming? Did you enjoy it?

W Not at all. It's really scary for me.

13

M Good morning. _____ _____ _____ are there _____ _____ _____?

W Four, two _____ and two _____.

M Then, _____ _____ _____ the non-smoking area?

W Sure. I want to have breakfast in a _____ _____.

M Please _____ _____ _____ _____. Let me check to see if there's a _____ _____ for you.

W Thanks. Can I have a _____ _____ for

my baby?

M Sure. We will bring it to you when you _____ _____.

W Thank you.

14

M _____ _____!

W Why? _____ _____ _____?

M My _____ just _____ while I was _____ _____ my English project.

W I'm sure you _____ _____ _____, didn't you?

M _____, no. I usually save it when _____ _____ _____ the work.

W Uh-oh. Then you _____ _____ _____ _____ _____.

M I know. It's terrible, but I have to finish this project _____ _____. What should I do?

W You'd _____ _____ to the teacher and _____ what just happened. She will _____ your _____.

M Okay, I will.

15

W Attention, students! _____ _____ the _____ and _____ _____, all after-school activities are _____ _____. There will be _____ _____ for after-school activities. All students _____ _____ _____ at the end of the school day on the _____ _____ _____. These, however, may be _____ because of the traffic conditions. The school plans to be open _____, Friday, with classes as normal. _____ _____ will be communicated by _____ and they will be put on the _____ _____.

16

M _____ _____ is filled with _____ today.

W Yeah. _____ _____ are so long.

M Are you carrying any _____ _____?

W No. I don't have any of them.

M Did you put your _____ in _____ _____? If you are carrying them now, _____ must be _____ml or _____, and stored in _____ _____ _____

_____.

W Don't worry about that.

M Then, don't forget to throw away your _____

_____ before you go through _____.

W Oh, I almost forgot.

17

① M How long will it take _____ _____ _____

_____ _____ _____?

　W Let me see.

② M Can I _____ _____ _____

_____ with the bookshelf?

　W Sure. That's very kind of you.

③ M Did you buy anything _____ _____

_____?

　W Not yet, but I'm thinking about buying some

clothes.

④ M _____ _____ _____

_____, horror or sci-fi movies?

　W Yes, I prefer them.

⑤ M I really want to have that pair of _____

_____.

　W I guess they'll _____ _____

_____ _____.

18

W Did you know that Gary has had a girlfriend

_____ _____ _____?

M Believe it or not, I heard it _____ _____

days ago.

W How come he didn't _____ this to you? You're

his best friend.

M That's why I _____ _____ for a couple

of days.

W Did he _____ her to you?

M Not yet, but we are going to _____

_____ _____ _____.

W Oh, he's coming. [pause] Hello, Gary. What's up?

19

W Christine has _____ _____ _____.

Her name is Snoopy. She was _____

_____ _____. Christine's parents

brought home _____ _____ to be

_____ _____ _____. Christine

was happy because she always wanted _____

_____ _____ _____. Christine

_____, _____, and _____ the dog.

This weekend, Christine's family is supposed to

_____ _____ _____ _____

Hong Kong. Christine has to find _____

_____ _____ who can _____

_____ _____ Snoopy. In this situation,

what would Christine most likely say to her friend?

20

M Does _____ _____ _____

_____ appeal to you?

W How about _____? It is _____

_____ the _____ _____ here.

M _____ _____. I like meat-filled tacos

with hot sauce.

W Me too. What do you want to _____?

M A _____ _____ for me. What about

you?

W I'll have _____. For dessert, let's try

_____ _____ cinnamon powder.

M Okay. I hope _____ _____ comes soon.

I'm really hungry.

W So am I. I can't wait.

01 대화를 듣고, 남자가 구입할 물건을 고르시오.

①  ②  ③   ④  ⑤

02 대화를 듣고, 두 사람이 결정한 신문 디자인을 고르시오.

①   ②  ③  ④  ⑤

03 대화를 듣고, 남자의 심정으로 가장 적절한 것을 고르시오.

① hopeful   ② determined   ③ proud
④ delighted   ⑤ nervous

04 대화를 듣고, 여자의 직업으로 가장 적절한 것을 고르시오.

① physician   ② veterinarian   ③ farmer
④ zoo keeper   ⑤ cook

05 대화를 듣고, 여자가 지불할 금액을 고르시오.

① $5.4   ② $6   ③ $10   ④ $30   ⑤ $50

06 대화를 듣고, 남자의 마지막 말에 담긴 의도로 가장 적절한 것을 고르시오.

① 동의 　　② 항의 　　③ 거절 　　④ 사과 　　⑤ 감사

07 대화를 듣고, 남자의 현재 신분으로 가장 적절한 것을 고르시오.

① 중학교 2학년생 　　② 신임 선생님 　　③ 대학 신입생
④ 2년차 회사원 　　⑤ 고교 신입생

08 대화를 듣고, 여자가 먼저 할 일로 가장 적절한 것을 고르시오.

① 영화표 구매하기 　　② 시간 확인하기
③ 식당 예약하기 　　④ 간식 사기
⑤ 메뉴 고르기

09 다음을 듣고, 그림의 상황에 어울리는 대화를 고르시오.

① 　　② 　　③ 　　④ 　　⑤

10 다음을 듣고, 무엇에 관한 내용인지 고르시오.

① 자원봉사 　　② 우정 　　③ 건강관리
④ 현대인의 삶 　　⑤ 직업훈련

11 대화를 듣고, 현재의 시각을 고르시오.

① 7:50   ② 8:10   ③ 8:30   ④ 8:45   ⑤ 8:50

12 다음을 듣고, Big Mart에 관한 내용과 일치하지 <u>않는</u> 것을 고르시오.

① 매장 내 방송으로 판매물품을 홍보 중이다.
② 모든 채소와 과일에 대해 가격할인행사 중이다.
③ 버섯을 한 팩 사면 한 팩을 덤으로 더 준다.
④ 현지 직송으로 농산물을 판매한다.
⑤ 과일과 채소 매장은 1층에 있다.

13 대화를 듣고, 두 사람이 주말에 함께 할 일로 가장 적절한 것을 고르시오.

① 줄넘기 하기   ② 체육관 가기   ③ 산책 가기
④ 마트 가기   ⑤ 달리기 하기

14 대화를 듣고, 두 사람이 대화하는 장소로 가장 적절한 것을 고르시오.

① 만화방   ② 극장   ③ DVD 대여점
④ 전화국   ⑤ 서점

15 대화를 듣고, 대화 내용과 일치하지 <u>않는</u> 것을 고르시오.

House for Rent

① **Bedrooms:** 3
② **Furniture:**   Fully furnished
③ **Location:**   Subway station in five minutes' walk
④ **Rent:** $550 per month / deposit $3,000
⑤ **Utilities:**   Everything included except the electric bill

---

16 다음을 듣고, 두 사람의 대화가 <u>어색한</u> 것을 고르시오.

①   ②   ③   ④   ⑤

17 대화를 듣고, 현장학습에 관한 내용과 일치하지 <u>않는</u> 것을 고르시오.

① 놀이공원으로 간다.

② 단체로 버스를 타고 간다.

③ 놀이기구 작동 장치에 대해 배운다.

④ 점심은 싸온 도시락으로 야외에서 먹는다.

⑤ 오후에는 자유시간이 주어진다.

18 다음을 듣고, Jim이 Cathy에게 할 말로 가장 적절한 것을 고르시오.

① What is the newest clothing trend?

② Sorry, we don't have the item in stock.

③ You should stop buying clothes online.

④ Where did you get all those nice clothes and shoes?

⑤ Don't be behind in fashion and enjoy shopping online.

[19-20] 대화를 듣고, 남자의 마지막 말에 이어질 여자의 응답으로 가장 적절한 것을 고르시오.

19 ① Do you have something to sell?

② I'd like to help you at the bazaar.

③ I guess you're right. Thank you for your advice.

④ Thank you for inviting me to this exciting bazaar.

⑤ Please join us. We hope to see you again at this event.

20 ① I will arrange that for you.

② It'll be added to your hotel bill.

③ I'll pick you up at your hotel at 6:00 p.m.

④ Its opening hours are from 5 a.m. to 1 a.m.

⑤ The Internet is available in the lobby 24 hours a day.

• 다음은 **Listening Test 09**의 주요 지문입니다. 녹음을 다시 듣고, 질문에 대한 답을 완성하세요.

Q5

1   What does the woman want to buy?

↳ She wants to buy _____ that can _____ _____.

Q6

2   What does the man think of the shirt that the woman would like to buy?

↳ He likes it because he _____.

Q7

3   What is the woman explaining to the man?

↳ She is explaining _____.

Q10

4   According to the man, what are the benefits of volunteering?

↳ ① To help you make _____

② To help you reach out to _____

③ To help you learn _____ and advance _____

④ To protect _____

Q12

5   What is the special price for mushrooms today?

↳ You can get _____ for the price of one pack.

Q13

6   What has Judy been doing to lose weight?

↳ She has_____ for a month or so.

Q14

7   What will happen if the woman doesn't return the DVDs by Saturday?

↳ She has to _____.

Q19

8   What was the woman supposed to do?

↳ She was supposed to _____ the day after tomorrow.

● 자신의 상황에 맞게 내용을 완성하고 말해 보세요.

A What do you think the three most important reasons that students should volunteer are? Fill in the table and tell your classmates about them.

Why Should Students Volunteer?

(1) First reason
(2) Second reason
(3) Third reason

I'd like to tell you about why volunteering is important for young students like us.

First, it is important because (1)_____

_____. Second, (2)_____

_____.

Finally, it is a valuable chance (3)_____

_____. So, let's not hesitate to

volunteer in our community.

B When was your most memorable school field trip? Fill in the table and tell your classmates about it.

My Most Memorable School Field Trip

Where	(1)
When	(2)
	(3)
What I did	(4)
	(5)
What was impressive	(6)

My most memorable school field trip was a trip to (1)_____.

I went there (2)_____. I did many things there. First,

(3)_____. Second,

(4)_____. Finally,

(5)_____. The reason

this field trip is the most memorable for me is that (6)_____

_____.

09 Dictation Test

01

W Hey, Thomas. What are you doing?

M I'm trying to buy a _____ _____ _____ on this website as a _____ _____ for Junsu.

W Wow, this site has a good selection.

M Yes, but it's really _____ _____ _____ one. Can you help me?

W Sure. What about this _____ _____ _____ wine bottle holder? It looks very _____ and _____.

M Wine in a shoe. Well, not a good idea. I love this zombie one. Looks like the zombie is _____ _____.

W That's _____ _____. Then, how about this _____ _____ one? Junsu is _____ _____ extraterrestrial life.

M I like _____ _____. I'll order it. Thanks for your help!

02

M Now, we have to _____ the contents of our _____ _____.

W Okay, why don't we put the _____ at the _____ _____ _____ _____ and the _____ _____ at the _____ of the paper?

M I think it looks a little _____. So let's put the issue date _____ _____ _____ _____.

W That's good. Then, how can we _____ the _____ _____?

M What about dividing the newspaper into _____ _____?

W Well, not bad. We can put the _____ _____ in the _____ column and the other in the _____.

M Yes. It will look _____.

03

W Minsu, why are you _____ _____?

M Mom, I'm _____ _____ sleeping.

W How come? The midterm exams _____ _____. You need to get _____ _____.

M I know, but the more I think about what I've studied, the more I _____ _____.

W You've studied _____ _____ this month. So what's the matter?

M Even though I studied hard for the last exams, I made lots of mistakes and got _____ _____.

W Let bygones be bygones. You have to _____ _____ each answer before submitting the answer sheet this time, OK?

M Yes, Mom. Now I'll _____ _____ _____ some _____. Good night, Mom.

04

W What can I help you with?

M It's about _____ _____. He is _____ yellow liquid continually.

W Sounds like _____ _____.

M He ate some _____. They fell and broke on the floor. I couldn't pick them up fast enough.

W _____ did he have the eggs?

M This morning, around 10 o'clock.

W Eggs can _____ _____ _____. But I think he will be okay. _____ _____ _____ as fast as possible.

M Yes, I'll do that right now.

05

W These sea animal squirts are _____ _____ to _____ and _____.

M Yes, they are _____ _____ _____ with little children.

W Good. My little boy seems to be _____ while _____. I'm looking for some bath toys that can _____ and _____ _____. How much are these?

M The regular price for a set of _____ squirts is _____ dollars, but now it's _____ _____. It's _____% _____.

W Oh, really? I'll take _____ _____. Can I use this _____% off coupon?

M I'm sorry, but you _____ _____ _____ on sale items.

W Okay. Here is my credit card.

06

M Hi, Minhee. Long time no see.

W Hi, Jim. What a _____! I haven't seen you since we graduated from university. What are you doing here?

M I just got a _____ _____ in this city, so I'm _____ _____ _____ _____. How about you?

W I'm looking for a _____ for my brother's birthday present. _____ do you _____ _____ this shirt?

M Well, you know how much I love _____. See? I've got _____ _____ shirt!

W You always did have _____ _____. I'll take this. _____ _____ this stuff, how about eating dinner together?

M Why not?

07

W Welcome to Brent _____ _____ _____. I'm Laura, a _____ _____ _____.

M Hello. Thank you for _____ _____. I'm Ben.

W How do you _____ _____ _____ a high school student?

M I'm very _____ and everything is so _____.

W Don't worry. You will be fine soon. Just _____ _____ _____ _____ and _____ the basic _____ _____.

M School rules? What are they? _____ _____ _____ tell me them?

W Okay. They are the following: speak in English only, always _____ your name tag, and _____ _____ _____ _____ your classes.

M I will _____ _____ _____ _____ _____ and try to follow them. Thank you.

W If you have any questions later on, just _____ _____ _____.

08

M The next one we can see is at 4:30.

W _____ _____ _____ _____ _____ now?

M It's _____ _____ _____ _____.

W We only have to wait for 45 minutes. That's fine with me.

M Okay. I will _____ _____ _____ _____ to buy tickets. Why don't you _____ _____ _____ some snacks and drinks?

W Alright. I will _____ _____ _____ because we will _____ _____ after the movie.

M I'm _____ _____ _____ now, but something light will be okay, I guess.

W I'll be _____ _____.

09

① M I want to _____ _____ my _____ _____.

W You _____ a new car?

② M Do you know why I _____ _____ _____?

W I don't know. All of a sudden I heard your siren.

③ M _____ _____ to your car?

W I _____ _____ _____ _____ in the parking lot.

④ M How long do we have to _____ _____ _____ _____?

W It will come here in 5 minutes.

⑤ M Loot at that! The car just ran a _____ _____ and _____ _____ _____!

W Is anyone hurt?

10

M With busy lives, it can be _____ to find time _____ _____ _____. However, the _____ of volunteering are enormous not only to _____ but also _____ _____ and _____ _____. It can help you _____ _____, reach out to the community, learn new skills, and even _____ _____ _____. Volunteering can also help protect _____ _____ and _____ _____. Today, let's learn more about the many _____ _____ _____ and find tips on getting started as a volunteer.

11

M Oh, no! _____ _____ _____
_____?

W _____ _____. What's wrong with you?

M It's eight thirty already. _____ _____
_____ eight fifty. I will be late for school.

W No, you won't. This clock has stopped. Anyway, it
looks like it's 40 minutes faster than the real time.

M Forty minutes faster? Good. There's _____
_____ _____ have breakfast.

W But hurry. _____ _____ to pack up all
the things you have to bring.

M I will. Could you please _____ _____
_____ for me, mom? I _____
_____ _____ in 15 minutes after
washing up.

W Okay.

12

W Hello, _____! _____ _____
for _____ at Big Mart. You can buy
_____ _____ and _____ like
apples, oranges, and cucumbers. We _____
_____ _____ _____ _____
on mushrooms today. If you buy one _____
of mushrooms, you can get the second pack
_____. As we said in our advertisement,
our fruit and vegetables are _____ directly
from _____ _____. So, _____
_____ to our fruit and vegetable section
on the first floor and _____ _____
_____ _____ them.

13

M Hi, Judy. You look really healthy and thin. What is
your _____?

W Actually, I've been _____ _____ every
day for a month or so.

M Really? What kind of _____ do you do?

W I _____ _____ for about _____
_____ _____ in the morning. It was
hard at first, but I feel better now.

M That's really a good _____. How much
_____ have you lost?

W I've lost _____ kilograms.

M Wow, I'll go buy _____ _____

_____, too. Do you have _____
_____ _____ at the YJ Mart? They're
having _____ _____ on this weekend.

W Oh, I want to buy _____ _____
_____. Let's go together.

14

M Hello. How may I help you?

W Can you _____ _____ an action
_____ an animation movie?

M Sure. _____ _____ _____ _Iron
Man_ or _Frozen_?

W No, I haven't seen either of them. I've missed all
my _____ to see them.

M They are _____. You should watch them.

W Then, I'd like to _____ those two movies.
_____ _____ _____ _____?

M Two thousand won each. What's your _____
_____?

W 736-9842. When is the _____ date?

M _____ _____ or there will be a
_____ _____.

15

W Best Eastern _____ _____. How may I
help you?

M Yes. Is the house you _____ _____
_____?

W Do you mean the one with three bedrooms
_____ _____?

M Yes, _____ _____ _____. Could
you please tell me more about it?

W My pleasure. It's _____ _____
_____ from a subway station, _____
_____ _____.

M How much is the _____?

W It's 515 dollars a month and has a _____
_____ _____ _____.

M What's _____ in the rent?

W All _____ are included _____
_____ the electric bill.

16

① M Can you tell me why you _____
_____ _____?

W Because they are _____ _____.

② M Do you need _____ _____

_____ the park?

W Yes. I know _____ _____ _____ there myself.

③ M Why don't you get Tom _____ _____ _____ _____?

W That's a good idea.

④ M Please _____ _____ _____ and sign here.

W I wonder _____ _____ _____. There is _____ _____ and _____.

⑤ M Did you enjoy _____ _____?

W Not much. I prefer _____ _____.

17

W I'm going to buy _____ _____ _____ _____ for this Friday.

M Okay. Then, are you going to _____ _____ on that day?

W Don't you remember? Our _____ _____ to the _____ _____ is this Friday. Aren't you coming?

M Oh, I completely forgot about that. Could you let me know _____ and _____ _____ _____ _____?

W Yes. We're going to meet at the _____ _____ of the school at _____ a.m. to _____ _____ the bus.

M As I remember, our teacher has not mentioned a _____ _____ yet.

W Yes, that's right. But I think in the morning we're going to learn about the _____ _____ for _____ _____.

M Oh, that's interesting.

W Right. The afternoon is _____ time. After we have _____ at the cafeteria, we have _____ _____ until _____ _____.

18

M Jim's friend, Cathy, spends too much time _____ _____ _____ because she enjoys _____ _____. She especially likes _____ _____ the latest, most popular _____ _____. Buying things in _____ _____ is usually _____ than buying them in _____ _____. But the problem is she spends almost all her allowance _____ _____ clothes. After she spends all of her allowance _____ _____, she sometimes _____ _____ from her friends. In this situation, what would Jim likely say to Cathy?

19

W Hi, Jack. I need _____ _____.

M Sure. What is it?

W I promised _____ _____ _____ with my friends at _____ _____ _____ the day after tomorrow.

M That will be fun! Then, what's the problem?

W This morning, my mom said I have to attend my grandfather's _____ _____ _____ on the same day.

M You mean _____ _____ _____ _____ your friends that you can't go?

W Exactly.

M I think you should tell them _____ _____ _____ _____. Your friends will understand you _____%.

W I guess you're right. Thank you for your advice.

20

W Good afternoon. Welcome to the Grand Hotel. How may I help you?

M I have _____ _____ for today. It's _____ _____ _____ _____ John Smith. Here's my ID.

W Thank you. We've reserved _____ _____ _____ _____ for you for _____ _____. Is that correct?

M Yes, it is.

W Excellent. Could you just _____ along the bottom, please?

M Whoa! _____ _____ a night! Hmm. OK, so what room am I in?

W You are in _____ _____. Here is your key. If you have any questions or requests, please dial '_____' from your room.

M Oh, when is _____ _____ _____ available?

W Its opening hours are from 5 a.m to 1 a.m.

01 대화를 듣고, 남자가 구입할 휴대전화 케이스를 고르시오.

① ② ③ ④ ⑤

02 대화를 듣고, 에스컬레이터의 위치로 알맞은 것을 고르시오.

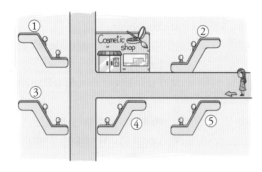

03 대화를 듣고, 두 사람의 관계로 가장 적절한 것을 고르시오.

① movie director — actress
② husband — wife
③ critic — reporter
④ clerk — customer
⑤ teacher — parent

04 대화를 듣고, 남자의 심정으로 가장 적절한 것을 고르시오.

① displeased
② interested
③ excited
④ disappointed
⑤ relieved

05 대화를 듣고, 두 사람이 만날 시각을 고르시오.

① 6:30
② 6:45
③ 7:00
④ 7:45
⑤ 8:00

06 다음을 듣고, 무엇에 관한 강의인지 가장 적절한 것을 고르시오.

① 그림 기법   ② 예술의 대중성
③ 미술 사조   ④ 시민운동의 역사
⑤ 미술 감상법

07 대화를 듣고, 여자의 마지막 말에 담긴 의도로 가장 적절한 것을 고르시오.

① 동의   ② 질투   ③ 감사   ④ 용인   ⑤ 사과

08 대화를 듣고, 대화 내용과 일치하지 <u>않는</u> 것을 고르시오.

Techno Mart
HOT DEALS

E-reader	$149
3D Smart LED HDTV	$679
①Laptop	$395

②Limited time offer: Prices valid only on Black Friday, November 28.
③Buy a 3D TV and get 4 pairs of 3D glasses.
④Buy two E-readers and get one for 50% off.
⑤Free delivery on all items.

09 대화를 듣고, 여자가 남자에게 부탁한 일로 가장 적절한 것을 고르시오.

① 책 빌려주기   ② 보고서 작성 도와주기
③ 책 반납해주기   ④ 도서관 이용시간 알려주기
⑤ 도서관 같이 가기

10 대화를 듣고, 여자가 약속 장소에 일찍 나온 이유를 고르시오.

① 시간이 남아서   ② 시계가 없어서
③ 시계가 틀려서   ④ 기다리는 걸 좋아해서
⑤ 미리 준비할 게 있어서

11 대화를 듣고, 학교 주최 파티에 대해 언급되지 <u>않은</u> 것을 고르시오.

① 시간　　　　　　　② 프로그램　　　　　　③ 메뉴
④ 참가자　　　　　　⑤ 장소

12 다음을 듣고, 표의 내용과 일치하는 것을 고르시오.

Film	Time	Theater Number
Miracle in Cell No.7	10:00 AM, 04:00 PM	1
Iron Man 3	11:30 AM, 05:00 PM	2
Les Miserables	03:00 PM, 06:00 PM	3
Frozen	04:30 PM, 07:30 PM	4
Lion King	11:30 AM, 05:00 PM	5

①　　　　　②　　　　　③　　　　　④　　　　　⑤

13 대화를 듣고, 두 사람이 대화하는 장소로 가장 적절한 것을 고르시오.

① flower shop　　　　② restaurant　　　　③ coffee shop
④ grocery store　　　⑤ kitchen

14 다음을 듣고, 무엇에 관한 내용인지 고르시오.

① 투표일 안내　　　　② 시정 홍보　　　　③ 개표 방송
④ 당선 인사　　　　　⑤ 선거 유세

15 대화를 듣고, 여자가 전화를 건 목적을 고르시오.

① 샌드위치를 갖다 주려고
② 영어 과제를 도와주려고
③ 선물을 전해 주려고
④ 함께 시험공부 하려고
⑤ 교과서를 갖다 주려고

16 대화를 듣고, 남자가 여자를 위해서 할 일로 가장 적절한 것을 고르시오.

① 함께 등산 하기   ② 초상화 그려주기
③ N서울타워에 같이 가기   ④ 함께 휴가 가기
⑤ 수영 가르쳐주기

17 다음을 듣고, 두 사람의 대화가 <u>어색한</u> 것을 고르시오.

①   ②   ③   ④   ⑤

18 대화를 듣고, 도서관 이용에 관한 내용과 일치하지 <u>않는</u> 것을 고르시오.

① 도서 대출시 학생증이 필요하다.
② 1회에 한해 대출기간을 연장할 수 있다.
③ 최대 대출기간은 2주일이다.
④ 대출 연장시 도서관을 방문해야 한다.
⑤ 신입생은 5권 이상 대출할 수 없다.

19 다음을 듣고, Judy가 전화 받은 사람에게 할 말로 가장 적절한 것을 고르시오.

① I'll reserve a table for us at the restaurant.
② Under what name do you want to reserve it?
③ We already have a reservation for our dinner party.
④ I'd like to reserve a table for ten next Saturday.
⑤ I'm calling to confirm the table that I reserved a few days ago.

20 대화를 듣고, 여자의 마지막 말에 이어질 남자의 응답으로 가장 적절한 것을 고르시오.

① How often do you exercise?
② Why don't you get exercise?
③ Yes, I try to exercise as often as I can.
④ No, you shouldn't exercise too much.
⑤ There are many people who don't like to exercise.

● 다음은 **Listening Test 10**의 주요 지문입니다. 녹음을 다시 듣고, 질문에 대한 답을 완성하세요.

Q2

1 Where does the woman want to go?

↳ She wants to go to _____.

Q4

2 Why does the man have dark circles under his eyes?

↳ The reason is that he sat up all night doing _____ for _____ _____.

Q5

3 What will the woman do for the man tonight?

↳ She will _____ before _____ starts.

Q7

4 How come they decide to do all the household chores?

↳ They want to _____.

Q11

5 For whom is the party?

↳ It is for _____.

Q13

6 What does the boy want to have for dinner?

↳ He wants _____.

Q14

7 What kind of election is it?

↳ It is a _____.

Q19

8 What is Judy planning to have and where will she have it?

↳ She is planning to have _____ at a _____.

● 자신의 상황에 맞게 내용을 완성하고 말해 보세요.

A Imagine you are one of the candidates for student council president. Make a poster and complete the speech transcript by filling in the blanks.

Vote
for

Your Name: _____!
Logo/Picture:

Slogan: _____

Hello, my name is _____, and I'm running for student council president. As president of the student council, I would fight for _____,

_____,

and _____

_____. I would always be open to your ideas on how the school can be improved and be more fun.

Vote for me!

B Have you ever done something special for your mom, dad, or any of your family members? Fill in the table and tell your classmates about it.

I Did...

For whom & When?	(1)
What did you do?	(2)
Why did you do it?	(3)
What did you feel?	(4)
	(5)

I would like to tell you about the special things that I did for my (1)_____

_____. I (2)_____

_____. I did it because (3)_____

_____.

After doing them, I felt two things. First, (4)_____

_____. Second, (5)_____

_____. Anyway, it always seems awesome

to help someone else.

01

M Mom, I want to buy Jane a _____ _____ _____ for her birthday present. Can you help me?

W Of course. There are _____ _____ _____ and _____ for any cell phone here.

M Yes. Do you think she will like this case with _____ _____?

W It doesn't look _____. What about this one with _____ _____ or that one with _____ _____?

M I _____ the patterns on both of them.

W Come on, Mike! It's _____ _____ _____ but for Jane.

M That's right. Okay then I'll buy that one with _____ _____.

02

W Excuse me, sir. Do you know how to get to the _____ _____ _____ _____?

M Yes. Take the escalator up to the _____ floor, then go through the furnishings department and it's _____ _____ the toy department.

W Thank you. Escalator to the _____ floor, _____ _____ _____ the furnishings department and then the toy department.

M Yes, that's right.

W And _____ _____ _____ _____?

M Can you see the _____ _____ over there? Go around the shop and the escalator is _____ _____ it.

W Okay, I see. Thank you so much.

03

M _____ _____ _____ _____ _____ the movie?

W Well, _____ _____ _____ _____ _____ _____, I was a little _____.

M Disappointed? Why? It got _____ _____, didn't it?

W It wasn't _____ _____ _____ _____ I

thought it would be.

M Really? All my friends told me it was _____ _____ _____ _____ they had ever seen.

W I really _____ it to be a lot _____ _____. By the way, what time do we have to _____ _____ tonight's family get-together?

M We _____ _____ at seven with the kids.

04

W Hey, Jim. What's wrong with _____ _____? Did you get in a _____ with your roommate?

M No. I just _____ _____ _____ _____ doing research for my term paper, so they look _____.

W Look at those _____ _____ under your eyes. You look like a _____ with them.

M Stop _____ _____ _____ _____. It's not a laughing matter.

W You look really _____ like a panda, though.

M Just _____ _____! Please leave me alone.

W Sorry. I _____ _____ to upset you.

05

[Telephone rings.]

W Hello?

M Is Jane there? This is Max speaking.

W Hi, Max! It's me. How are you?

M I'm fine. I was _____ _____ you'd like to go to a _____ _____ with me.

W Sure, I'd love to. What's _____?

M I was thinking about *Love in Paris*. _____ _____ _____ _____?

W Sounds great!

M Okay. The movie starts at _____ _____ so I'll pick you up at _____ o'clock.

W Well, how about meeting _____ _____ _____ _____ _____ _____ before the movie to get dinner? I'll treat you to dinner tonight.

M _____. See you then. Bye!

06

W Hello, everyone. Last class, I told you about the _____ _____ movement in the _____ _____. Today, we're going to be taking a look at the art movement called _____. This art movement _____ with a group of _____ _____ _____ in the 1800s. Their _____ _____ _____ brought them to _____, in spite of the _____ opposition from the conventional art community in France.

07

W Paul, let's give mom _____ _____ _____ and do some _____ _____ for her.
M That's a good idea. What do you want me to do?
W Would you _____ _____ _____?
M Sure. What should I do after that?
W Well, you can _____ _____ _____ in the _____ _____.
M Okay. But what are you going to do?
W I'm going to _____ _____ _____, and after that I have to _____ _____ _____.
M Do you think we can _____ _____? Yours seem _____.
W All right, all right.

08

M Have a look at this Techno Mart _____ _____. The laptop costs _____ _____ $400.
W Awesome. Until when can we _____ the listed items _____ _____ _____ prices?
M It says prices are valid until Black Friday, _____ _____. There's only _____ _____ _____. I'm planning to buy a _____ _____.
W Umm. The 3D TV costs $679 and that price includes _____ _____ _____ _____ _____.
M Are you interested in an E-reader? We can buy a second E-reader _____ _____ _____ if we buy one.

W I'm in. Let's buy them together and get the second one 50% off. Oh, there is _____ _____ _____ on all the items. Cool.

09

W Sangyoon, do you know when the _____ _____ _____ _____?
M It opens at 8:30 _____ _____ _____ and closes at 7 _____ _____ _____.
W What about on _____?
M I'm not sure. _____ _____ _____ on weekends.
W I see. If it is okay with you, please _____ _____ _____ _____.
M _____ _____. But then why do you want to know?
W That is because I need more _____ _____ for my report. Next Monday is the _____ _____.
M I see. I will _____ _____ _____ in 10 minutes.

10

M _____ _____ _____ _____ here, Haena?
W I'm waiting for Daeun. We _____ _____ _____ to meet here at seven o'clock.
M Then why are you here so early? You have to wait _____ _____ _____ _____.
W What? _____ _____ my watch, it's five to seven. Is that wrong?
M Yes. It's exactly twenty five after six.
W I see. Then my _____ must be _____. Thank you for letting me know.
M _____ _____. What are you going to do until seven?
W Well. I'll just sit here and wait for her.

11

M Look at the _____ _____ _____ _____.
W _____ _____ _____? I can't see it well. I have poor eyesight and too many people are _____ _____ _____ me.
M It says there will be _____ _____ _____ all students who were _____

_____ _____. It _____

_____ _____ _____ Room 101 at 3:00 p.m.

W Really? What else?

M They will _____ a large cake, pizza, fried chicken and _____ _____ _____ _____ drinks.

W I'm going. I was _____ _____ _____! Can I _____ _____ _____ who wasn't born in April?

M Yes, you can bring a friend but _____ _____.

W Any other _____?

M All the _____ and the _____ _____ of the school will be at the party too. And the party is _____.

12

① W *Miracle in Cell No.7* is _____ _____ in the morning.

② W *Iron Man 3* is _____ _____ Theater 3.

③ W *Les Miserables* is on both _____ _____ _____ and _____ _____ _____.

④ W *Frozen* is on _____ _____ a day in Theater 4.

⑤ W *Lion King* and *Iron Man 3* are on _____ _____ _____ _____.

13

M Mom, I'm _____. I want _____ _____ _____ _____.

W Let's buy the _____ for it.

M What are they?

W I don't think we have _____ _____, _____, and _____.

M Okay. They are in the vegetable _____. What else do we need to buy?

W If we add _____ _____, it will taste better.

M _____ _____ _____ _____ already. Thank you, mom.

W You're welcome. I'll get some oranges _____ _____.

14

M _____ and _____, I am here to swear _____ _____ _____ you that I will keep my _____ _____. _____ you _____ _____ where you are living now? Don't you want a _____ and _____ city? Here is the answer. _____ _____ me on _____ _____ _____ _____. Please remember my name, Gyomoon Kang. The future of our city _____ _____ _____ _____. One thing I can _____ you is that I won't _____ _____. I won't make you _____ _____ _____ _____. Please _____ for Number 1. Thank you.

15

[Telephone rings.]

M Hello?

W Hello. Is this Namgyu? This is Minji.

M Hi, Minji. What's up?

W You _____ your _____ _____ in my house.

M _____ _____ _____ _____. I was wondering where I had left it. I thought it was in my _____ _____.

W You _____ _____ English homework tonight, don't you?

M I do. I have to _____ _____ _____, the conversation part and the main text.

W Do you want me to take it to your house?

M _____. I will make a sandwich for you.

16

M Wow. What a beautiful view!

W Look at that! We can see the N Seoul Tower.

M The view here is _____! I'm happy that we _____ _____ here on a _____ _____.

W Yes. But I _____ a little _____.

M I think you need to get into _____ _____, so we'd better climb mountains _____ _____.

W Hey, what about this? Why don't you teach me _____ _____ _____?

M That's a great idea.

17

① M I won _____ _____ in a _____ contest.

W You must be _____.

② M What do you think of _____ _____?

W Good. Especially, _____ _____ _____ were very delicious.

③ M Excuse me, can I _____ here?

W Sorry, this section is only _____ _____ _____.

④ M Can I help you?

W Yes, please. I want to buy _____ _____ _____ Busan.

⑤ M Excuse me. Is _____ _____ _____?

W Yes. My friend will _____ _____ _____.

18

W Excuse me. Could you tell me how I can _____ _____ _____ _____? I am _____ _____.

M It's very simple. Just give me your _____ _____ _____ and the books you want.

W OK. _____ _____ can I _____ the books?

M You can actually keep them _____ _____ _____. But if you _____ _____ _____, you can keep them for another week. It is allowed once.

W Then, can I make _____ _____ _____?

M Sure. Just log into your _____ _____ on the _____ library website. Any other questions?

W Oh, _____ _____ books can I _____ at a time?

M _____ is the maximum for a _____.

W Thank you. You were very helpful.

19

W Judy is planning to have her _____ _____ _____ _____ at _____ p.m. _____ _____. She decides to reserve _____ _____ _____ first. Even though _____

_____ _____ _____ in her class was 40, _____ _____ _____ will be _____ _____. So she decides to make a reservation _____ _____ _____.

She searches for a good restaurant and calls it to make a reservation. In this situation, what would Judy likely say to the person on the phone?

20

W Is it my _____ or have you lost a lot of _____?

M Well, I'm on _____ _____ _____.

W What's that?

M I try to _____ _____ a low-carbohydrate and high-protein _____ these days and I try to eat lots of _____ and _____, too.

W I see. I'll try _____ _____ _____ from now on.

M Go for it. And don't forget to _____ for _____ _____ _____ in the morning. You can _____ _____ like me.

W Well, you like to exercise, don't you?

M Yes, I try to exercise as often as I can.

Listening Test

01 대화를 듣고, 남자가 구입할 수영복을 고르시오.

①  ②  ③  ④  ⑤

02 대화를 듣고, 남자가 그린 그림을 고르시오.

①  ②   ③   ④   ⑤

03 대화를 듣고, 여자의 심정으로 가장 적절한 것을 고르시오.

① frustrated ② pleased ③ sorrowful
④ ashamed ⑤ miserable

04 다음을 듣고, 여자가 전화를 건 목적으로 가장 적절한 것을 고르시오.

① 약속시간을 변경하려고 ② 생일파티에 초대하려고
③ 파티 불참을 통보하려고 ④ 함께 남동생 병문안 가려고
⑤ 깜짝파티 준비를 하려고

05 대화를 듣고, 남자가 지불할 금액을 고르시오.

① $450 ② $500 ③ $595 ④ $630 ⑤ $700

06 다음을 듣고, 남자가 방송을 하는 목적을 고르시오.

① 화재대피 훈련 안내
② 비상시스템 점검 안내
③ 재난대비 안전교육
④ 비상사태 발생 안내
⑤ 건물 청소 안내

07 대화를 듣고, 남자가 여자를 위해 할 일로 가장 적절한 것을 고르시오.

① 같이 선물 사기
② 꽃다발 골라주기
③ 점심 사주기
④ 돈 빌려주기
⑤ 차 태워 주기

08 대화를 듣고, 남자의 마지막 말에 담긴 의도로 가장 적절한 것을 고르시오.

① 제안　　　② 감사　　　③ 수락　　　④ 충고　　　⑤ 거절

09 다음을 듣고, 그림의 상황에 어울리는 대화를 고르시오.

①　　　　②　　　　③　　　　④　　　　⑤

10 대화를 듣고, 두 사람이 대화하는 장소로 가장 적절한 것을 고르시오.

① classroom
② dormitory
③ office
④ bookstore
⑤ library

11 대화를 듣고, 동균이의 현재 키를 고르시오.

① 149cm   ② 155cm   ③ 164cm   ④ 166cm   ⑤ 170cm

12 다음을 듣고, Bing Bing Toy Store에 관해 언급되지 <u>않은</u> 것을 고르시오.

① 세일 기간   ② 부대시설
③ 세일 규모   ④ 사은 행사
⑤ 매장 위치

13 대화를 듣고, Lisa의 직업 계획과 일치하지 <u>않는</u> 것을 고르시오.

Lisa's Career Plan	
① Original dream	a teacher
② Current major	education
③ Motivation for the current major	parents' recommendation
④ New major in mind	social welfare
⑤ Motivation for the new major	to help people

14 대화를 듣고, 남자가 일요일에 방문했던 장소를 고르시오.

① amusement park   ② fast food restaurant
③ train station   ④ museum
⑤ theater

15 대화를 듣고, 여자가 먼저 할 일로 가장 적절한 것을 고르시오.

① 식당 예약   ② 후식 주문
③ 사진 찍기   ④ 짐 싸기
⑤ 주변 관광

16 다음을 듣고, 두 사람의 대화가 <u>어색한</u> 것을 고르시오.

①   ②   ③   ④   ⑤

17 대화를 듣고, 야외에서의 번개 대처법으로 맞지 <u>않는</u> 것을 고르시오.

① 들판에 있다면 도랑을 찾아 피신한다.
② 평지에선 발을 바짝 붙이고 몸을 웅크린다.
③ 웅크린 자세에선 머리를 낮춘다.
④ 평지에선 납작한 자세로 눕지 않는다.
⑤ 차량은 감전의 위험이 있으므로 피한다.

18 다음을 듣고, 민호가 은행직원에게 할 말로 가장 적절한 것을 고르시오.

① I'd like to open an account.
② I'd like to cash this traveler's check, please.
③ I want to exchange Korean won into euros.
④ I want to close my bank account today, please.
⑤ Today's exchange rate is 1,400 won to the euro.

[19-20] 대화를 듣고, 남자의 마지막 말에 이어질 여자의 응답으로 가장 적절한 것을 고르시오.

19 ① I take pride in the work I did.
② I want to be a fashion model.
③ That model looks pretty cool.
④ I'm sure you're helping them a lot.
⑤ You seem to be worried about them.

20 ① Don't worry. I'll keep my word.
② Actually, I can't stand those movies.
③ I'm really into reading fantasy novels.
④ Wow! I'll keep my fingers crossed for you.
⑤ That's okay. I just want to play for fun.

● 다음은 **Listening Test 11**의 주요 지문입니다. 녹음을 다시 듣고, 질문에 대한 답을 완성하세요.

Q3
1 Why does the woman want to get a couple of days off?

↳ The reason is that she wants to _____ to attend _____

_____.

Q5
2 Why does the man decide to order 700 pens?

↳ The reason is that he can get _____ and _____

_____.

Q7
3 What did the woman buy and why did she buy it?

↳ She bought _____ because today is _____

_____.

Q8
4 What are all the members of Donghee's family going to do tomorrow?

↳ They are going to _____ in celebration

of _____.

Q11
5 Why does Donggyoon say "Hooray!"?

↳ The reason is that he _____ since last year.

Q12
6 When is the sale on at Bing Bing Toy Store?

↳ It will be on _____.

Q17
7 What happens when a car is struck by lightning?

↳ The electricity _____ and

_____.

Q19
8 According to the conversation, what day of the week do you guess today is?

↳ I guess it is _____ because yesterday was _____.

자신의 상황에 맞게 내용을 완성하고 말해 보세요.

A What are you going to do tomorrow? Talk to your classmates about it.

My Schedule for Tomorrow

In the morning	(1)
	(2)
In the afternoon	(3)
	(4)
In the evening	(5)
	(6)

I'm going to talk about what I am going to do tomorrow. In the morning, I will

(1)_____. Then I will

(2)_____. In the afternoon, I will

(3)_____. After that, I will

(4)_____. Finally, in the

evening, I will (5)_____.

And then, I will (6)_____.

B Do you have any foreign tourist attraction you'd like to recommend your friends visit? Fill in the table and tell your classmates about it.

My Favorite Foreign Tourist Attraction

Name & Location of the place	(1)
Nearby attractions	(2)
Reasons to recommend it	(3)
	(4)

I'd like to tell you about my favorite foreign tourist attraction that I have been to.

It is (1)_____ and is located _____. Famous

tourist attractions you can visit nearby are (2)_____

_____. I'd like to recommend this place because

(3)_____. Second,

(4)_____.

I really want to visit this place again sometime.

01

W What are you doing?

M I'm looking for a _____ for our son, John, on this website. How about these swim _____ with _____?

W They look cute, but he needs a swim _____, too.

M Those shorts match this _____ swim shirt _____ _____.

W Hmmmm… I think we'd better buy him a _____ - _____ shirt. Let's look at another _____ _____.

M Okay. This set includes a long-sleeved shirt and _____ _____ _____. I like it.

W So do I. Especially, I love the printed message on the shirt, _____ _____. That can make him cuter.

M Great! Let's go with that set.

02

M Yoomi! _____ _____ for _____ to the _____.

W I'm glad to be invited. Which one is yours, Namsoo? There are still-lifes, _____, and _____.

M _____ is a portrait of my dad.

W I see. Is it a _____-_____ portrait?

M No, it's not. It's a _____-_____ portrait.

W OK. I think I have to find it. The man in this painting has a generous and kind look. Your dad is like that.

M Oh, _____ _____ _____ _____ _____. My dad will be happy to hear that.

W Is he the one _____ _____?

M Well, he usually wears glasses but I painted him _____ _____.

03

W It's a _____ the boss is in _____ _____ _____ _____.

M I agree. I wish she were in a better mood.

W Actually, I was hoping I could _____ her for a couple of _____ _____.

M It looks like that's _____ _____ _____ _____.

W I have to go to Busan. My niece is getting married there. I want to attend _____ _____ _____.

M The boss is _____ _____ _____ _____ _____ right now.

W I know. What shall I do?

04

[Telephone rings.]

M Hello, this is Brian. I'm sorry _____ _____ _____ right now. Please _____ _____ _____ _____. I'll call you back.

[Beep]

W Hey Brian. This is Becky. I'm calling to _____ _____ _____ that I can't go to Tim's _____ _____ _____ tonight. My mom told me to _____ _____ _____ my younger brother because she will _____ _____ home _____ work tonight. I'm very sorry for _____ _____ _____ _____ go. Anyway, I'll call you again. Have fun. Bye.

05

W Can I help you?

M Yes, please. I want to _____ _____ _____ to give away as a promotional gift for the _____ of _____ _____.

W How many do you want to order?

M I'm thinking of _____ pens. I want ones that cost _____ dollar _____.

W Okay. These are the options that you can choose from.

M I love this pen. Do you have any _____ _____ if I buy a _____ _____? And is there a fee for _____ the _____?

W Logo printing is 5 cents per pen. And we can give you a _____% discount if you order 500 pens or _____.

M That's good.

W And if you order _____ pens or more, there

is a _____% discount and _____ logo printing.

M Oh, that's really cheap. I'll order _____ pens.

06

M This is an _____ from your Fire Safety Administrator. I'm sorry to _____ _____ _____ _____ by _____ _____ the building's intercom like this. However, this test is _____ to your well-being in case of an _____. We urge you to be _____ during this test so we can ensure _____ _____ in the future. Since this is only a test of the system, _____ _____ _____ _____, there will be _____ _____ to leave the building at this time. Thank you again for your patience.

07

W Hey, Peter! Where are you going?

M I'm going home. Oh, that is a very lovely _____ of _____. Who is it _____?

W It is for my sister, Jessica. Today is her _____ _____.

M It must have cost you a _____.

W I paid $60 for it but it is _____ it. Today is a very important day for my sister and I want to _____ _____ _____ for her.

M That is very nice of you. If you want, I _____ _____ _____ to her school.

W Can you? I _____ your kindness.

08

W Donghee, do you _____ _____ _____ _____ tomorrow?

M Yes. Tomorrow is my _____ _____ _____. All the members of my family will _____ together and _____ _____ with her.

W I see. What time will you come back?

M Around 5 p.m., _____ _____.

W What will you do when you come home?

M I have many things to do tomorrow _____ _____ _____.

W I see. I was wondering if we can _____ _____ _____.

M I'm sorry. I have to _____ _____.

_____ trimmed and _____ _____ _____ a report in the evening.

09

① **M** Hi, do you have any wall-mounted _____ _____?

W I'm sorry but we _____ _____ that kind of pot.

② **M** _____ _____ are these roses?

W They are $10 for a dozen.

③ **M** What are you _____ _____ _____ _____?

W I'm _____ _____ for a flower arrangement.

④ **M** What is your _____ _____?

W I do love tulips since they look elegant.

⑤ **M** _____ can I _____ this flower basket?

W Oh! It's beautiful. You can put it here _____ _____ _____ _____.

10

M Hey, Dorothy. Did you buy the _____ _____?

W Of course. I bought it with all my other textbooks last week. You _____ _____ it yet?

M _____, I didn't. I bought all the textbooks except it. How much is it?

W I bought a _____ _____ for $10.

M Wow! That's a _____ _____. Where did you get it?

W At the _____ _____ near the dormitory.

M Oh, I didn't know there is a _____ _____ near the _____. Here comes the _____ _____. Let's talk more about it _____ _____.

11

M Hooray! I _____ _____ this!

W What's up, Donggyoon?

M Please _____ _____ _____. I have grown a lot _____ last year.

W _____! How much have you grown?

M _____ centimeters. I guess I'm two centimeters taller than Jisung.

W _____ _____ _____ _____?

M He said he is _____ cm.

W Nice to hear that. I hope you will grow more until you _____ _____ _____ _____.

12

W This Saturday and Sunday, Bing Bing Toy Store is _____ _____ _____ _____. For two days, many children's toys are _____% _____. Each morning, we will serve free hot chocolate to the children and coffee to all adults. Also, we will give balloons to all _____ _____. Lastly, there will be a "Buy 2, get 1 for free" sale. If you buy two toy sets, you will get a third one for free. So _____ _____ the Bing Bing Toy Store on 3rd Street and _____ _____ _____ _____ the _____ _____ _____.

13

M Lisa, what do you want to be _____ _____ _____?

W When I was _____, I wanted to be a teacher.

M A teacher? Then why are you majoring in science?

W My parents _____ I choose it, but I think it _____ _____ _____ _____. So I _____ _____ change my major.

M _____ to the education _____?

W No. I'm thinking of entering the _____ _____ _____. I'd like to help people who need a hand.

M _____ _____ _____. That was what I wanted to do when I was young. But now I think _____ _____ _____ _____ _____ will be more fun.

W I see. You'll be a great _____.

14

W How was your Sunday? Did you _____ _____?

M Yes, very much.

W _____ _____ _____ _____?

M I _____ several _____. I also ate a bulbogi burger and churros.

W Rides?

M Yes. I rode a _____ _____, the Viking, and a _____ with my friends. I also enjoyed a _____ _____ and the _____ _____.

W Sounds great. _____ _____ did you do?

M I saw a _____ and _____ at night. I had a _____ _____.

15

W When are you leaving _____?

M I'm leaving _____ _____ _____ _____.

W Is there _____ _____ _____ _____ before you leave Sydney?

M I'd like to visit Australia Square. I heard that the view from _____ _____ _____ on top of the building is _____ _____.

W It really is. You can see _____ _____ _____ and the Harbor Bridge there. You shouldn't miss it.

M Yeah. I also heard that the building has been described as _____ _____ _____ building _____ _____.

W Why don't we _____ _____ _____ after this lunch? I'll _____ _____ for us.

M That sounds _____!

16

① **M** I'd like _____ _____ for _____ _____ _____ _____.

W I'm sorry. The tickets are _____ _____ _____.

② **M** I _____ the tennis match. It _____ _____ _____.

W I know how you feel. But don't _____ _____ _____ _____.

③ **M** It's nice weather, _____ _____?

W Yeah, it's perfect weather _____ _____ _____.

④ **M** Where's Cindy? Didn't you _____ _____?

W She invited us _____ _____ _____.

⑤ **M** Can't you stay _____ _____ _____?

W That's very _____ _____ _____, but I really can't.

17

W Can you guess how many people _____ by getting _____ _____ _____ in the U.S. every year?

M Well…maybe around 10 people?

W No, more than _____ die as a result of lightning strikes.

M What a surprise! Is there any way we can _____ ourselves _____ _____ _____ _____ ?

W If you get caught in _____ _____ _____ during _____ _____ _____ , find _____ _____ to lie in if possible.

M What if I can't find a ditch?

W Put your feet close together and _____ _____ with your _____ _____ and _____ _____ _____ .

M Any other ways to protect ourselves?

W Find _____ _____ and _____ _____ it. Even though it is _____ , the _____ will travel around the _____ of the vehicle and then go into _____ .

18

M Minho is traveling in England. He thinks he has to _____ _____ _____ _____ in Paris while he is traveling _____ _____ . So he takes the Eurostar _____ _____ _____ _____ . When he arrives _____ _____ _____ in Paris, he finds out he _____ _____ _____ _____ . He doesn't have _____ _____ now. Fortunately, he has some _____ _____ in his backpack. To buy a metro ticket to the Eiffel Tower, he needs to _____ _____ _____ . He goes to a bank. In this situation, what would Minho likely say to the teller at the bank?

19

W Hey, David! I saw you _____ _____ with your friends yesterday. Where did you go?

M My friends and I visited _____ _____ _____ _____ _____ .

W What did you do there?

M We played basketball with the children and then taught them _____ and _____ .

W You're like _____ _____ _____ to them.

M _____ _____ . We visit the kids _____ _____ and try hard to be _____ _____ _____ for them.

W I'm sure you're helping them a lot.

20

M I can't believe _____ _____ _____ _____ already.

W _____ _____ ! Time really flies. I regret spending last year _____ having _____ _____ _____ .

M You _____ _____ _____ _____ .

W By the way, do you have _____ _____ _____ for this year?

M Actually, I want to try something new. I've decided _____ _____ _____ _____ .

W Wow! That sounds exciting!

M Yeah, _____ _____ _____ ! I'll try out for _____ _____ _____ next week.

W Wow! I'll keep my fingers crossed for you.

01 대화를 듣고, 두 사람이 선택한 카드를 고르시오.

① ②  ③ ④  ⑤

02 대화를 듣고, 남자가 구입할 물건을 고르시오.

① ② ③ ④  ⑤

03 대화를 듣고, 여자가 남자를 찾아간 이유를 고르시오.

① 여행 상담   ② 휴가 요청   ③ 호텔 예약
④ 이민 상담   ⑤ 취업 의뢰

04 대화를 듣고, 남자의 성격으로 가장 적절한 것을 고르시오.

① thoughtful   ② generous   ③ inconsiderate
④ absent-minded   ⑤ responsible

05 대화를 듣고, 남자의 직업으로 가장 적절한 것을 고르시오.

① grocer   ② cook   ③ teacher   ④ farmer   ⑤ doctor

06 대화를 듣고, 남자가 지불할 금액을 고르시오.

① $250   ② $273   ③ $280   ④ $315   ⑤ $338

07 대화를 듣고, 남자가 무엇을 준비 중인지 가장 적절한 것을 고르시오.

① 파티 참가   ② 취업 면접
③ 패션 발표회   ④ 과제 제출
⑤ 옷 가게 개업

08 대화를 듣고, 여자가 할 일로 가장 적절한 것을 고르시오.

① 집 청소하기   ② 옷 사러 가기
③ 옷 정리하기   ④ 사촌 집 가기
⑤ 키 재어보기

09 대화를 듣고, 대화 내용과 일치하지 <u>않는</u> 것을 고르시오.

Vacancy Announcement
HOTEL KOREA

① **Position:** Chef
② **Requirement:** Chef's certificate
③ **Experience:** 2 years
④ **Documents:** - Curriculum Vitae (with names and contact details
　　　　　　　of 3 references)
　　　　　　　- Letter of application
⑤ **Send to:** Ivan Donovan, Manager,
　　　　　　at manager@hotelkorea.com

10 대화를 듣고, 두 사람이 만나기로 한 시각을 고르시오.

① 2:15   ② 2:45   ③ 2:58   ④ 3:15   ⑤ 3:30

11 다음을 듣고, 어떤 운동에 관한 설명인지 고르시오.

① badminton ② tennis ③ volleyball
④ table tennis ⑤ basketball

12 대화를 듣고, 오늘이 무슨 요일인지 고르시오.

Changdeokgung		
Day	Open	Close
Mon, Tue, Thu	9:30 a.m.	6:30 p.m.
Wed	Closed	
Fri	9:30 a.m.	5:00 p.m.
Sat	10:00 a.m.	4:00 p.m.
Sun	10:00 a.m.	2:00 p.m.

① 월요일 ② 수요일 ③ 금요일 ④ 토요일 ⑤ 일요일

13 대화를 듣고, 두 사람이 대화하는 장소로 가장 적절한 것을 고르시오.

① 병원 ② 패스트푸드점 ③ 일식점
④ 가구점 ⑤ 도서관

14 다음을 듣고, Clean Car Wash에 관해 언급되지 <u>않은</u> 것을 고르시오.

① 세차 장비 ② 서비스 차종 ③ 세차 가격
④ 위치 ⑤ 연락처

15 대화를 듣고, 여자가 파일을 열지 못하는 이유를 고르시오.

① 파일 용량이 커서
② 인터넷 연결이 불안정해서
③ 파일이 바이러스에 감염되어서
④ 파일의 압축을 풀지 못해서
⑤ 필요한 프로그램이 없어서

16 대화를 듣고, 두 사람이 먼저 할 일로 가장 적절한 것을 고르시오.

① 전화하기　　　　　　　　② 자리 양보하기

③ 시간 확인하기　　　　　　④ 지하철 하차하기

⑤ 버스표 예매하기

17 다음을 듣고, 두 사람의 대화가 <u>어색한</u> 것을 고르시오.

①　　　　　　②　　　　　　③　　　　　　④　　　　　　⑤

18 대화를 듣고, ABC Printing Services에 관한 내용과 일치하지 <u>않는</u> 것을 고르시오.

① 온라인으로도 인쇄 주문을 받는다.

② 고객은 인쇄 전 최종 디자인을 반드시 확인해야 한다.

③ 고객 변심에 의한 수정은 비용이 청구될 수 있다.

④ 사소한 본문 수정은 무료로 해준다.

⑤ 제작자의 실수는 무료로 수정해준다.

19 다음을 듣고, Sue가 John의 동생에게 할 말로 가장 적절한 것을 고르시오.

① I'll call first thing in the morning.

② Can you tell him to call me at 357-9864?

③ May I call you at a more convenient time?

④ Would you please call me when you're ready?

⑤ Will you tell him that I'll call him tomorrow afternoon?

20 대화를 듣고, 여자의 마지막 말에 이어질 남자의 응답으로 가장 적절한 것을 고르시오.

① That's right. I wouldn't buy it for a gift.

② Stop worrying. Nothing can be done now.

③ It's nothing really. I just wanted to say thank you.

④ I'm really grateful for the gift. Where did you get it?

⑤ It is the best gift I've ever received. Thank you so much.

● 다음은 Listening Test 12의 주요 지문입니다. 녹음을 다시 듣고, 질문에 대한 답을 완성하세요.

Q2

1 Why doesn't the man choose the multi-bin organizer that the woman recommends?

  ↳ The reason is that he thinks the big bins are _____ to hold his son's _____.

Q3

2 When does the woman's vacation start and end?

  ↳ It starts on _____ and ends on _____.

Q4

3 Why can't the woman come to work?

  ↳ The reason is that she _____ and _____ _____.

Q5

4 Why does the man spin the dough?

  ↳ He spins the dough _____.

Q10

5 Where are the man and the woman going to meet?

  ↳ They are going to meet _____.

Q15

6 What was the man's major?

  ↳ It was _____.

Q16

7 Why are they annoyed by the girl on the train?

  ↳ The reason is that she is _____ in a public place.

Q20

8 What did the woman do for the man last week?

  ↳ She _____.

● 자신의 상황에 맞게 내용을 완성하고 말해 보세요.

A Think about two places you'd recommend foreigners visit in your city and the reasons you recommend them. Then tell your classmates about those places.

My Favorite Places in My City

Places	Reasons I choose them
(1)	(2)
(3)	(4)

I live in _____ and there are lots of beautiful places in the city

I'd recommend foreigners visit. Now I'll tell you about two of them. Firstly, I

recommend (1)_____ because (2)_____

_____. Secondly,

I recommend (3)_____ because (4)_____

_____. I'm

sure foreigners will have a great time in the two places I recommend.

B Have you ever had help from someone you didn't know? Fill in the table and tell your classmates about it.

Help from Somebody Unknown

(1) When and where?
(2) What was the problem?
(3) Who helped you and how?
(4) Your feelings

I would like to talk about a time I got help from someone I didn't know. It

happened (1)_____. The problem

I had was this. (2)_____

_____. Then (3)_____

_____. I felt (4)_____

_____. Still I can't forget the person

who was willing to help me even though we didn't know each other.

12 Dictation Test

01

M Darling, we only have _____ _____ left before our wedding ceremony.

W Yes. I think it's time to send out the _____ _____ _____. Why don't we choose the _____ of the card from the ones on this website?

M Good. Do you have a card style _____ _____?

W Not really. What about this tri-fold card?

M It's good but as you know I do love simple things. I like this bi-fold one. It's simple as the card is only _____ _____ _____.

W Okay, then which is better _____ _____ _____? A _____ pattern or a _____?

M How about using one of the _____ _____ _____?

W Great idea! Now, let's think about the wording on the card.

02

W May I help you?

M Yes. I'd like to buy something to help _____ my son's _____.

W How about this _____ _____ _____? If he has a lot of large toys, you can also choose the _____ _____ here.

M Hmm. I want something to hold the toys according to their _____.

W Okay. What about this multi-bin organizer? There are _____ _____ bins, _____ _____ bins, and _____ _____ bins.

M Well, the big bins are _____ _____ _____ to hold his big toys.

W I think this toy box with _____ _____ is perfect for you then. You can put _____ toys in this _____ _____ and small ones in the removable _____ at the _____.

M Looks good. I'll take this one.

03

M Good morning! How can I help you?

W I have some time off from work next month and I was thinking of _____ _____ _____.

M That sounds great. _____ _____ is your vacation?

W Just _____ _____. My last day of work is July 21st and I'll go back on August 1st.

M Okay. This is a _____ about Denmark. _____ _____ _____ _____ it. Denmark has many beautiful spots to visit.

W Yeah, I really _____ _____ _____ _____ Tivoli Gardens in Copenhagen, the National Museum, and Legoland.

M I understand. Where do you want to stay while you're _____ _____?

W Copenhagen, of course.

M Great. The city has many nice hotels. OK, now I'll _____ _____ _____ _____ a great time in Denmark.

04

[Telephone rings.]

M Hello?

W Hello, is this Tim?

M Yes. Who is this?

W This is Amy. I'm afraid I _____ _____ to the office today as I _____ _____ the stairs and I hurt my ankle. The doctor told me _____ _____ _____ _____ all day.

M You should have been _____ _____! Listen, I can't do all this work _____.

W I feel really sorry, Tim. I will try to be in _____.

M Well, you _____ _____. There is a pile of things to do and I _____ _____ _____ _____.

W Don't worry! I will take care of it when I come in.

05

W Do you make _____?

M Yes, I do. That's my job.

126

W When do you work?

M I work _____ _____ in the morning _____ _____ in the evening.

W What is your job like?

M It's hard work but also fun. I _____ with the _____. I _____ _____ _____ to make it _____ _____ _____. Then, I put _____, _____, _____, _____, and more on top.

W Do you like your job?

M Yes, I really love what I am doing and I _____ _____ _____ my job.

06

W Sir, _____ _____ _____ the catalog for our in-flight shop? Would you like to _____ any _____ _____ _____?

M Yes, can I pay by credit card?

W Of course, all major credit cards are _____ but you can't spend _____ _____ _____ dollars.

M Okay, I'd like this _____ for my wife. It costs _____ dollars.

W Is there anything else you'd like, sir?

M Yes, I'd also like this _____ _____ _____ which is _____ dollars.

W Will that be all, sir?

M I've changed my mind. _____ _____ the _____, I want to get this _____ _____ which is _____ dollars. Here is my credit card.

07

M Can you give me a _____, Kate?

W Sure. What can I do for you?

M I don't know _____ _____ _____ to my _____ _____ tomorrow. Can you give me _____ _____ _____?

W You'd better wear a _____ _____ and not _____ clothing.

M Okay. What about the _____ of the suit? Which color will make me look _____ _____ and _____?

W I think a _____ _____ one would be great. By the way, did you _____ _____ _____ I asked you to in the morning?

M Yes, I did. As soon as I came to the campus, I _____ _____ the _____.

W Thanks. Now, what about your tie and shoes?

08

W Jinho, can you _____ _____ _____ for me? _____, _____ _____ _____, I can't open it _____ _____.

M Sure. What's the box you're _____? Do you want me to help you?

W It's okay. It's not _____. My cousin gave me her _____ _____. And I have to _____ them _____ my _____ and _____ them.

M Oh, really? Why did she give them to you anyway?

W They _____ _____ _____ anymore because she _____ _____ _____ since last year.

M I wish I had a cousin like that. I think _____ _____ _____ on to someone else who can use them is a _____ _____.

W Well, it is not always good, _____. My parents _____ _____ buy me clothes. I _____ would like to wear new _____.

M Hmm, I guess I would too.

09

W Hi, Tom. Are you still looking for _____ _____?

M Yes. Is there a good _____ you know of?

W Hotel Korea is looking for a _____.

M What are the _____?

W A _____ _____ is required, with a minimum of _____ _____ _____.

M What _____ should I submit?

W You need to submit a _____ _____ and a _____ _____ _____.

M I see. Anything else?

W You should include the _____ and _____ _____ of _____ _____ in your _____ _____.

M How should I send in the documents?

W Your documents should be sent in _____ _____.

10

M Shall we _____ _____ after school?

W _____ _____ _____ . But I have to _____ _____ _____ . I will meet Jessica and give her notebook back to her.

M _____ _____ will you meet her?

W At 2:45. But it _____ _____ _____ .

M When should I meet you then?

W _____ _____ 30 minutes after that?

M Good. Let's meet _____ _____ _____ the school gate.

W Okay. _____ _____ _____ .

11

W This is a game _____ _____ two or four players _____ _____ _____ .
It has been an _____ _____ _____ 1992. There is a high net _____ _____ _____ the court.
The players try to _____ _____ by hitting a _____ across the net using a racket.
The player or team winning the previous point always _____ . A _____ _____ _____ once the _____ _____ _____ _____ . A player or team must score 21 points first _____ _____ _____ _____ . The match ends when one team wins two games.

12

M Where are you going?

W I'm going to Changdeokgung to get some information to write a report for history class.

M Is it about the _____ of Changdeokgung?

W No, it's about how I felt after _____ _____ that _____ _____ _____ .

M Sounds interesting. Aren't they closed today?

W I don't think so. _____ _____ the _____ , they will _____ _____ _____ today.

M I see. I actually went there _____ _____ _____ _____ , and they closed _____ _____ _____ _____ on that day.

W Thanks for the _____ .

13

W How about _____ _____ _____ _____ for a while?

M I'd love to. _____ _____ _____ go out for lunch?

W Where do you want to go?

M How about a _____ _____ _____ near the _____ _____ ?

W I want to go to the _____ _____ _____ the street _____ here.

M Okay. Let's _____ _____ our _____ first and then keep looking for _____ _____ for our _____ .

W Alright. Let's _____ _____ _____ on the table so that no one will _____ _____ _____ .

M I'll do it.

14

M Do you want to make _____ _____ _____ _____ _____ ? Bring your car, taxi or van into Clean Car Wash today! We will _____ and _____ your _____ for an extremely reasonable price. It's _____ dollars for a car or taxi and _____ dollars for a van. Your car will _____ _____ _____ _____ ! Drive your car into our workshop located on Walnut Street. If you want to make an _____ , please call us at 474-1100. Thank you.

15

W _____ you _____ _____ computers?

M Yes. I _____ _____ computer engineering. Why?

W My friend in the U.S. _____ me _____ _____ with an _____ _____ , but I can't open it.

M Let me see. Oh, it's a PDF file.

W Oh, really? What should I do then?

M You _____ _____ _____ Acrobat Reader to open this file, first.

W Where and how can I download it?

M I will show you _____ _____ _____ _____ .

16

W I like using the _____ because it is easy to _____ _____ _____ some _____ while I'm on the train.

M Good. By the way, don't you think _____ _____ over there is _____ _____ _____ _____ too _____? This is a public place.

W Yeah, I agree with you.

M I think she's _____ _____ to talk so loudly _____ _____ _____ _____.

W It's really _____! Let's keep _____ _____ all the time.

M Anyway, how _____ _____ _____ _____ do we have to go?

W Oh, we have to _____ _____ the _____ at this station.

17

① M I'd like to send _____ _____ _____ _____.

   W Would you like to send it _____ _____ or _____ _____?

② M That was a hard test, _____ _____?

   W It was _____! I don't think I did very well.

③ M Can you tell me how to get to _____ _____ _____?

   W Sorry, but I don't know either. You'd better ask someone else.

④ M Look at _____ _____. You must not walk _____ _____ _____.

   W Sorry, I didn't see _____ _____.

⑤ M How do I _____ _____ _____ _____?

   W I'm _____ _____ a striped shirt.

18

[Telephone rings.]

W Thank you for calling ABC _____ _____. How may I help you?

M Hi, I've just uploaded my _____ _____ of a _____ _____ on your website under the name of Jeff. I need _____ _____ printed.

W OK, we'll check it out.

M _____ will they _____ _____? I can't wait to see how they look.

W They'll be done by this Friday. If you want to see the _____ _____ before it is sent to _____ _____, you can get it _____ _____ _____ for _____ dollars.

M Oh, that'll be great. Well, can I _____ any _____ after I see the design?

W Of course. Any mistake of ours, we'll fix for free. Otherwise, we'll charge you _____ dollars and _____ cents _____ _____.

M All right.

W Oh, please also remember that we'll do _____ _____ _____ free of _____.

19

M While _____ _____ _____, Sue finds that there's a Pompeii _____ at _____ _____ _____ by _____ _____. The exhibition is said to be very popular and it is expected to _____ _____ _____ on the weekend. So she thinks if she would like to go to the exhibition _____ _____ _____, she'd better _____ the tickets _____ _____. Since Sue knows John is interested in Pompeii, she calls John to see _____ he _____ _____ _____ her. However, his brother says _____ _____ _____. Sue wants John _____ _____ _____ back. In this situation, what would Sue likely say to John's brother?

20

M Surprise!

W Tom! _____ _____ _____!

M I just wanted to _____ _____ and thank you for _____ _____ to _____ _____ _____ _____.

W No. It was _____ _____ to do it. But, what's this?

M It's just _____ _____ _____.

W Wow, it's lovely, but you _____ _____ _____ bring _____ _____.

M It's nothing really. I just wanted to say thank you.

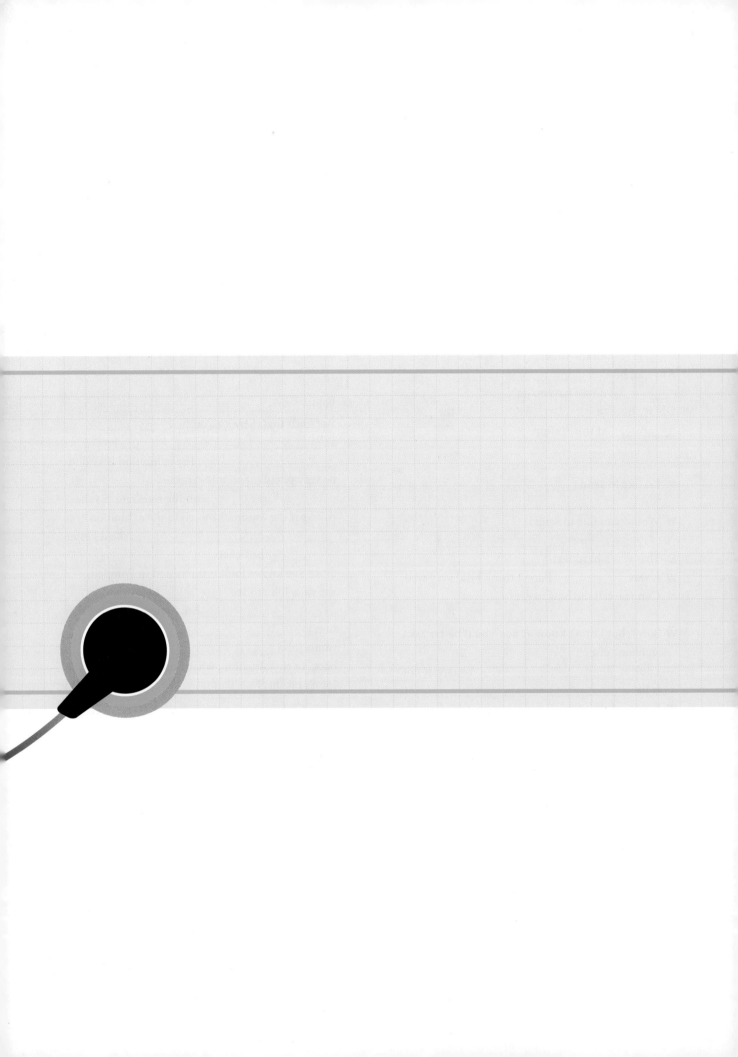

Actual Test
01~02회

01 Actual Test

01 대화를 듣고, 여자가 구입할 물건을 고르시오.

① 　② 　③ 　④ 　⑤

02 대화를 듣고, 여자가 만들기로 한 의장 디자인으로 가장 적절한 것을 고르시오.

① 　② 　③ 　④ 　⑤

03 대화를 듣고, 두 사람의 관계로 가장 적절한 것을 고르시오.

① 아들 — 엄마　　　　　　② 선생님 — 학생
③ 직장 상사 — 직원　　　　④ 점원 — 손님
⑤ 의사 — 환자

04 대화를 듣고, 여자의 성격으로 가장 적절한 것을 고르시오.

① sensible　　　② loose　　　③ considerate
④ passive　　　⑤ diligent

05 대화를 듣고, 남자가 꽃 구입에 사용한 총금액을 고르시오.

① $24　　② $36　　③ $96　　④ $144　　⑤ $216

6 다음을 듣고, 기내 방송이 끝난 후에 일어날 일을 고르시오.

① 비행기 이륙   ② 안전 교육

③ 기내식 배급   ④ 목적지 도착

⑤ 비상 착륙

7 대화를 듣고, 여자가 남자에게 부탁한 일로 가장 적절한 것을 고르시오.

① 장난감 분해하기   ② 장난감 치워주기

③ 비닐봉지 가져오기   ④ 동생과 놀아주기

⑤ 장난감 조립하기

8 대화를 듣고, 두 사람이 대화하는 장소로 가장 적절한 것을 고르시오.

① airplane   ② theater   ③ train

④ street   ⑤ bookstore

09 다음을 듣고, 그림의 상황에 어울리는 대화를 고르시오.

①   ②   ③   ④   ⑤

10 대화를 듣고, 여자가 먼저 할 일로 가장 적절한 것을 고르시오.

① 학교 가기   ② 체온 재기

③ 선생님께 전화하기   ④ 해열제 찾기

⑤ 병원 예약하기

11 대화를 듣고, Timothy의 생일파티가 열리는 날짜를 고르시오.

① March 10   ② March 13   ③ April 10

④ April 13   ⑤ May 10

12 다음을 듣고, 무엇에 관한 설명인지 고르시오.

① 씨름   ② 권투   ③ 유도   ④ 고싸움   ⑤ 태권도

13 대화를 듣고, 대화 내용과 일치하는 것을 고르시오.

	Departing	Ticket type	Day	Status
①	Seoul	One-way	Friday	Economy class
②	Seoul	One-way	Saturday	Business class
③	Seoul	Round-trip	Saturday	Business class
④	Busan	One-way	Sunday	Economy class
⑤	Busan	Round-trip	Saturday	Business class

14 대화를 듣고, 여자가 공항에 온 이유로 가장 적절한 것을 고르시오.

① 여행 가기 위해   ② 가족을 송별하려고

③ 친구를 만나려고   ④ 출장 가기 위해

⑤ 가족을 마중하려고

15 대화를 듣고, 남자가 할머니께 사 드릴 선물을 고르시오.

① 스카프   ② 신발   ③ 건강식품

④ 가요 CD   ⑤ 디너쇼 티켓

16 다음을 듣고, 두 사람의 대화가 <u>어색한</u> 것을 고르시오.

①   ②   ③   ④   ⑤

17 대화를 듣고, 동아리에 관한 내용과 일치하지 <u>않는</u> 것을 고르시오.

① 15세 이상의 남녀로 구성된 합창단이다.
② 회원은 악보를 읽을 수 있어야 한다.
③ 솔로 파트는 오디션을 받아야 한다.
④ 전문 성악가로부터 지도를 받는다.
⑤ 1년에 두 차례 콘서트를 연다.

18 다음을 듣고, Josh가 Nancy에게 할 말로 가장 적절한 것을 고르시오.

① Can I help you?
② I'm just looking around.
③ I don't want these pants.
④ Sorry, I'm busy at the moment.
⑤ Could you show me another one?

[19-20] 대화를 듣고, 여자의 마지막 말에 이어질 남자의 응답으로 가장 적절한 것을 고르시오.

19
① We can reschedule it for next week.
② I need a wake-up call in the morning.
③ Why don't you reschedule it for earlier?
④ No, that's fine. I will remember the date and time.
⑤ Right. I'll make a reminder here in my electronic organizer.

20
① We did it two weeks ago.
② It wasn't the original plan.
③ I plan on doing this for 2 years.
④ Thank you for helping me a lot.
⑤ It is supposed to be next month.

01

W   Hello. I'm looking for a _____ _____ for my three-year-old son.

M   Hello, ma'am! How about this _____ -_____ one? It is the _____ toy computer _____ _____. You can practice spelling and adding numbers with it.

W   Oh, but he already has too many toys with _____ _____ _____.

M   I see. Then how about this _____-_____ one with a _____? He can record his voice with this microphone.

W   Not bad. Can I see that _____-_____ one?

M   Yes, this is also a popular item for kids. It has a _____ and _____ playing function.

W   Hmm... I like the functions on _____ _____ _____ you recommended to me. And while I'm _____ _____ _____ of that _____, he is not.

02

M   What are you working on?

W   I'm trying to _____ a _____ for my club.

M   What's the _____ of the club?

W   We _____ _____ _____ _____ _____ such as elderly people living alone.

M   Then why don't you use a _____ as your logo?

W   That's good. And I want to _____ _____ _____ _____ each other in the heart.

M   Okay. And why don't you put some words _____ the heart? Do you have any words in mind?

W   Yes, I'm thinking of '_____ _____,' and _____ and _____ are meant to be _____.

M   That looks good. I'm sure it'll be a nice logo.

W   I hope so. _____ _____ for _____ _____.

03

M   You _____ _____ _____. Are you alright?

W   No. All this housework _____ _____ _____.

M   You'd better _____ _____ _____. Go and lie on the bed.

W   But I still have lots of things to do.

M   _____ _____. I'll _____ _____ _____ everything. _____ me.

W   Are you sure? Are you really going to do the _____ of the _____?

M   _____ _____ _____, Mom. I'll do my best to help you as you're not feeling well.

W   Oh, my little angel. I am _____ _____. Thank you.

04

M   You don't look good. How was your _____?

W   It was _____ _____ _____. I think I'd better stop _____ _____ _____ _____ and try something different.

M   Huh? With this current _____ _____, you _____ _____ to get a job! What else can you do?

W   What about _____ a coffee shop? It looks easy to do.

M   But have you prepared yourself _____?

W   I can start it by _____ _____ _____ from the _____. Once I open the coffee shop, I think I can _____ it.

M   You must _____ it carefully.

W   Oh, there won't be any problems. It's _____ _____ _____ a coffee shop.

05

W   Hi, Daniel. What are those flowers?

M   I'm going to plant flowers to _____ a _____ _____.

W   How many _____ of flowers did you buy?

M   I bought _____ kinds of them: daisies, tulips, roses, and orchids. And I've got _____ of each kind.

W   It seems that you spent lots of money. How much

are they?

M _____ dollars for each flower. They're giving _____ _____ _____ and selling all the different plants _____ _____ _____ _____.

W What a bargain! Do you need my help? I'm also _____ _____ _____.

M Really? Thank you. Then can you _____ some holes in the _____ here?

06

M Ladies and gentlemen, this is your captain speaking. I'm afraid we are _____ _____ _____ _____, so we'll have to make an _____ _____. Please make sure your _____ and _____ _____ are in their full _____ position. Make sure your seat belt is _____ and _____ _____ all electronic devices, as well. There is no cause for alarm as we can land _____ _____. I apologize for the inconvenience.

07

W Jake, can you give me a hand?

M Sure.

W I need to _____ this toy robot for my little brother. While I was putting it away, I accidentally _____ _____ and it broke into many pieces.

M How _____ you are! Does he know that?

W Yes. And I told him that I would assemble it _____ even though I _____ _____ how to do it.

M I'm sorry, I'm _____ _____ _____ _____ things _____. My brother is good at it, instead. Can I _____ the pieces to my house?

W Of course. Thank you! One moment, please. I'll _____ _____ a _____ _____ to put them in.

08

W Would you like a _____ to read, sir?

M Yes, please. I'll take that one.

W Here you go, sir. By the way, you look a little _____. Are you okay?

M Not so good. I'm always _____ before _____.

W Don't worry too much, sir. This is the _____ form of _____.

M I know that. I'm sure I'll be _____ after we _____ _____.

W You know we have some _____ _____ for you. You can find the _____ _____ in the pocket in front of you.

M Oh, good. A nice film will _____ _____ _____.

09

① M May I help you?
　W I'd like to _____ _____ _____ _____ San Francisco.
② M How much is the _____ _____?
　W It's $3 _____ _____, $1 _____ _____ from _____ to _____ years old and _____ for _____ _____ seven.
③ M Where can I find _____ _____?
　W They're _____ _____ seven.
④ M What's the _____ _____ _____ _____?
　W I'm here _____ _____.
⑤ M _____ _____ should I take this?
　W Three times a day _____ _____ _____ _____.

10

W Tom, hurry up! _____ _____, you will _____ _____ _____ school.

M But Mom, I think I _____ _____ _____.

W Really? I will _____ _____ _____. [pause] Let's check your _____ _____.

M What's my temperature?

W Yours is _____ _____.

M Should I go to school?

W It's probably not a good idea. I'll call your _____ and then find a _____ _____. I don't think the clinic _____ _____ _____.

M Alright. I will _____ _____ _____ _____.

11

M Hi, Sarah! _____ _____ _____
_____ now?

W I'm _____ _____ _____ for a
birthday party.

M Isn't your birthday _____ _____?

W Right. This is for Timothy. I want to _____
_____ _____ _____ for him.

M That will be _____. When is his birthday?

W It's _____ _____, _____
_____. But the party will be _____
_____ _____, on Saturday.

M Okay. Is there anything I can help you with?

W Please _____ these cards _____ the red
_____ _____ _____ _____.

12

W This is a _____ _____ _____.
Two people _____ _____ _____
_____ inside a circle. They have _____
_____ _____ cloth, either red or blue,
around their _____ and _____. During
the match, if one _____ forces the other
contestant to _____ _____ _____
with any part of his body, then he will be the
_____. We call the winner Chunha-Jangsa or
Baekdu-Jangsa _____ _____. What is
this?

13

[Telephone rings.]

W Happy _____. How can I help you?

M I'd like to _____ _____ _____ for
this Saturday _____ Tokyo.

W _____ _____ are you going to fly from,
_____ or Busan?

M From Seoul.

W Would you like to reserve a _____ or a
_____ _____?

M A round-trip ticket, please.

W Would you like _____ _____ or
_____?

M I _____ business class.

14

M Is this Jessica? _____ _____

_____! I didn't _____ _____ see
you here. What are you doing?

W Hi, Denny. I'm _____ _____ my
dad. He's _____ _____ _____
Washington today. How about you?

M I'm waiting for my dad, too. He left on _____
_____ _____ _____ England last
week and he is _____ today too.

W I see. Did his plane _____?

M No, not yet. I have to wait for him for _____
_____ _____ _____ more I guess.
How about your dad?

W _____ _____ the _____
_____, his plane landed a few minutes ago. I
can see him soon.

M _____ _____ _____.

15

M Kate, what will be _____ _____
_____ for my grandma? Her birthday is this
Friday.

W What about _____ _____?

M That was _____ _____ _____,
but my mom _____ _____ for her last
week.

W Oh, that's too bad. How about _____
_____ or _____ _____?

M They are _____ _____, aren't they? Is
there anything better?

W Let me think… Oh, what do you think of a famous
singer's _____ _____ _____
ticket?

M Wow! That would be great. She can _____
_____ _____ while _____
_____.

W Right. Hurry to _____ _____
_____.

16

① **M** Did you hear that Bill made it _____
_____ _____?

W Yes, I did. It's _____, isn't it?

② **M** Do you prefer _____ _____ to
_____ _____ _____?

W Yes, I do. _____ _____ is more
_____.

③ **M** Oz Air Travel. How may I help you?

W I'd like to book _____ to _____ for
_____ _____.

④ M _____ _____ _____
_____ me what's wrong with this alarm?

W I don't remember _____ _____
_____ it.

⑤ M You're late _____ _____ _____!

W I'm really sorry. _____ _____
_____ was terrible.

17

W Hi, I'm into _____ _____ so I'm
interested in this club. Could you tell me about it?

M Welcome. We are _____ _____
_____ for men and women _____
_____ _____ old. We enjoy singing
songs from _____ to _____,
_____ _____, and _____
_____.

W Great. To become a member, do I have to audition?

M You don't have to _____ to join us nor do
you need to _____ _____ _____
_____ music. We will only _____
someone if they want _____ _____
_____.

W Are there any special things about this club?

M We _____ _____ _____ a
professional mezzo-soprano, Mary Johnson. Under
her _____ _____ you can improve your
_____.

W Sounds really interesting. Do you give concerts,
too?

M Yes. We put on _____ _____
_____ _____.

18

W Josh _____ _____ _____ a denim
_____. He enters a shop and chooses the
shirt he would like to buy. But he realizes that he
_____ _____ _____ _____
_____. He doesn't have _____
_____ _____ _____ the shirt
at the moment. So, he decides to _____
_____ _____ and just _____
_____ _____. A clerk, named Nancy,
comes to him and asks _____ _____
_____ _____ _____. In this

situation, what would Josh most likely say to
Nancy?

19

[Telephone rings.]

W BF Dental Clinic. How may I help you?

M Hi there. I want to _____ _____
_____ with Dr. Smith _____
_____ _____ _____. I have a
_____ _____.

W I see. Please hold for a moment while I check
_____ _____ _____ _____
_____. [pause] Can you come in _____
at _____ p.m.?

M No, I can't. I have _____ _____
_____ _____. Do you have anything
_____ _____ _____?

W No, we don't have any openings in the morning.
How about _____ at _____ a.m.?

M I have to _____ _____ _____
_____ at the airport at 10 so I won't be able to
make it to your office by _____. Can I come
in at _____ _____ _____?

W Sure, _____ _____ in the morning
sounds good. Would you like _____
_____ _____ tomorrow?

M No, that's fine. I will remember the date and time.

20

W Hi, Ben. How was your weekend?

M Hey, Jenny. I was _____ _____. How
about you?

W _____ _____ for me. What did you do?

M My club had _____ _____ _____
to help the _____ at the community center.

W That sounds great! Did you _____
_____ _____ _____ _____?

M Because of _____ _____ _____,
not many people showed up. We raised _____
dollars, but we wanted to raise _____ dollars
more.

W Sorry to hear that. When do you plan to have
_____ _____ _____? I'd like to
help.

M It is supposed to be next month.

01 대화를 듣고, Jake가 누구인지 고르시오.

02 대화를 듣고, 두 사람이 구매할 물건으로 가장 적절한 것을 고르시오.

①  ② ③ ④  ⑤

03 대화를 듣고, 남자의 심정으로 가장 적절한 것을 고르시오.

① anxious   ② relieved   ③ indifferent
④ irritated   ⑤ hateful

04 대화를 듣고, 여자의 직업으로 가장 적절한 것을 고르시오.

① 의사   ② 간호사   ③ 입국 심사원
④ 경찰   ⑤ 교사

05 대화를 듣고, 두 사람이 만나기로 한 시각을 고르시오.

① 2:13   ② 2:30   ③ 3:30   ④ 4:13   ⑤ 4:30

06 대화를 듣고, 여자가 남자를 위해서 할 일로 가장 적절한 것을 고르시오.

① 손님 안내하기   ② 요리 도와주기
③ 청소 도와주기   ④ 상 차리기
⑤ 설거지 하기

07 대화를 듣고, 대화 내용과 일치하지 <u>않는</u> 것을 고르시오.

County Cup Final Match	
① Date	July 28
② Place	Donald Stadium
③ Teams	Mars vs. Venus
④ Score	3:2
⑤ MVP	Jake Johnson

08 대화를 듣고, 여자의 내일 일정이 <u>아닌</u> 것을 고르시오.

① 집 청소   ② 수학 수업   ③ 점심 약속
④ 바이올린 연습   ⑤ 저녁 약속

09 대화를 듣고, 남자가 환불 받을 수 <u>없는</u> 이유를 고르시오.

① 시간이 지나서   ② 이미 사용해서
③ 영수증이 없어서   ④ 상표를 제거해서
⑤ 환불규정이 바뀌어서

10 대화를 듣고, 남자의 출국 날짜로 알맞은 것을 고르시오.

① 4월 1일   ② 4월 8일   ③ 4월 15일
④ 4월 16일   ⑤ 4월 22일

11 다음을 듣고, 무엇에 관한 설명인지 고르시오.

① 도마　　② 가위　　③ 국자　　④ 칼　　⑤ 집게

12 다음을 듣고, 여자가 말을 하는 목적을 고르시오.

① 전학생 소개　　② 새 직원 소개　　③ 팀원 격려

④ 작별 인사　　⑤ 자기 소개

13 대화를 듣고, 두 사람이 대화하는 장소로 가장 적절한 것을 고르시오.

① 서점　　② 공항　　③ 버스　　④ 지하철　　⑤ 백화점

14 대화를 듣고, 자원을 절약하는 방법으로 언급되지 <u>않은</u> 것을 고르시오.

① 대중교통 이용하기　　② 카풀 하기

③ 전기 플러그 뽑기　　④ 걸어 다니기

⑤ 종이컵 사용 않기

15 다음을 듣고, 도표의 내용과 <u>다른</u> 것을 고르시오.

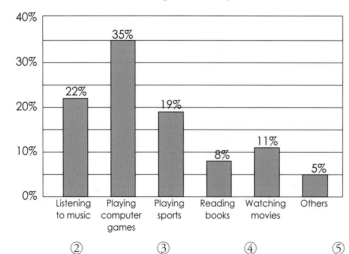

How Students in George's Class Spend Their Free Time

①　　②　　③　　④　　⑤

16 대화를 듣고, 두 사람이 보고 있는 광고로 가장 적절한 것을 고르시오.

① 애견샵 ② 애견호텔 ③ 애견사료

④ 식당 ⑤ 요리학원

17 다음을 듣고, 두 사람의 대화가 <u>어색한</u> 것을 고르시오.

① ② ③ ④ ⑤

18 대화를 듣고, 상황을 가장 잘 표현한 속담을 고르시오.

① Easy come, easy go.

② Look before you leap.

③ Don't judge a book by its cover.

④ An eye for an eye, a tooth for a tooth.

⑤ Don't put all your eggs in one basket.

19 다음을 듣고, Jessica가 남자에게 할 말로 가장 적절한 것을 고르시오.

① Is anyone sitting here?

② I'd like a table for four.

③ Where can I put this chair?

④ Would you like to put away this chair?

⑤ Is there an extra table around somewhere?

20 대화를 듣고, 여자의 마지막 말에 이어질 남자의 응답으로 가장 적절한 것을 고르시오.

① I hope so.

② I won't change my mind.

③ Thanks for your advice. I appreciate it.

④ I hope you'll enjoy your stay here. Please help yourself.

⑤ Please talk to her about it, so we can solve the problem.

01

M Hey, Angela. I have a _____ _____ _____.

W What is it this time?

M I'm setting you up on _____ _____ _____ with my classmate, Jake. I think you two would make a really _____ _____.

W Thanks, but I don't even know _____ _____ _____ _____.

M I know you put a _____ _____ on _____. He will _____ your expectation. Look at this photo. He is right _____ _____ _____.

W Where are you? Oh, here you are, with _____, _____ _____. Which guy is he?

M The guy with very short hair and a _____ _____. He is almost _____ _____ _____ than me. You will like him.

W Oh, he's tall and handsome.

02

W We have only _____ _____ _____ before Christmas. Why don't we buy a _____ _____ for the _____ _____?

M That's a good idea. Look at this website. What about this pair of _____ _____ with green leaves?

W I don't know, but I think a more _____ _____ would be _____.

M How about this wreath that has _____ berries, _____ leaves, _____ leaves, and _____ and _____ ribbons?

W That's good. But it would be so _____ _____ if there were a _____.

M Here you go! This is exactly what you want. A _____ _____ with a _____.

W Yes, it looks amazing. Let's order this one.

03

M Why the _____ _____?

W Haven't you heard the news about Roy?

M No, I haven't. What happened to him?

W He got in a _____ _____ on the way to school. I was told a van _____ _____

_____ while he was crossing the street.

M Is he all right? Where is he now?

W He's in the _____ _____ and he has _____ _____ _____ _____ _____.

M Oh my God! How could such a thing happen to him? _____ _____ _____ _____.

04

W Is this your _____ _____ _____?

M Yes, it is.

W Please _____ _____ this form. Do you have any _____?

M No, I don't.

W Please tell me _____ _____ _____ is.

M Well, recently I have been feeling _____, and sometimes I have really _____ _____ and an _____ _____.

W When did you start having those symptoms?

M I started feeling tired about _____ _____ _____ and after that the headaches came.

W OK. Please wait till it's your turn.

05

M Hey, Susan. Let's go work out later today.

W Sure. _____ _____ _____ _____ _____ are we going to work on today?

M How about working on our _____ _____ _____?

W I _____ if we can work on our arms and stomach today. As I _____ _____ _____ _____ six or seven times today, _____ _____ are _____ _____.

M No problem. _____ _____ do you want to go?

W How about at _____ _____?

M That sounds _____ _____ _____. Can we meet an _____ _____?

W Okay. Then, let's meet in front of the gym.

06

M Welcome to my house! Come on in!

W This present is for you, Sean. Thank you for _____ _____ to _____ _____ _____. Are the others here yet?

M Oh, thank you. Nobody has come here yet. So just _____ _____ _____ _____.

W Thanks. This is a great apartment! Do you mind if I _____ _____?

M No, go ahead.

W Oh, everything here is neat. Especially I like this _____ _____ and _____. How awesome!

M Jina, I hate to ask this, but would you mind helping me _____ _____ _____? I haven't cooked all the dishes yet.

W _____ _____ _____. I'm happy to help you.

07

W When is the County Cup _____ _____?

M It's _____ _____. It was on July 28.

W Oh, really? Where was it played? At Donald _____?

M Yes. Mars _____ _____ Venus.

W _____ _____ _____ _____?

M Mars! They _____ _____ _____. The score was _____ _____ _____.

W Hmm. Who was the MVP?

M Jake Johnson.

08

M _____ _____ _____ _____ do tomorrow?

W Well, tomorrow will be a _____ _____ _____ from _____ till _____.

M What are you going to do?

W First, I have to help my mom _____ _____ _____ in the morning, and then I have a _____ _____ at 11.

M And then?

W I will meet Sumi at one to _____ _____ _____. Then I have to _____ _____ _____ in the afternoon.

M Well, do you think you'll have time _____

_____ _____ to _____ _____ with me?

W _____ _____ _____ _____. I have to _____ _____ a report. It's due _____ _____ _____ _____.

M Oh, no! That's too bad.

09

M Hello, may I _____ _____ _____ for this beanie?

W No problem. Can I _____ _____ _____?

M Thanks. Here it is.

W Oh, you bought this _____ _____ _____ _____.

M Yes. I bought this when it _____ _____ _____. Is there a problem?

W I'm sorry, but yes. We don't give refunds _____ _____ _____. And we only give refunds _____ _____ _____.

M But I've never worn it and didn't _____ _____ _____ _____.

W I'm sorry, that's our _____ _____. There's nothing I can do.

10

W Are you _____ _____ here in Korea?

M Yes, very much. It's a beautiful country.

W _____ _____ _____ _____ to Korea?

M I came here _____ _____ _____ day of _____.

W What is your _____ of Korea?

M The people are really _____ and I _____ to see the _____ _____ at this time of year.

W _____ _____ are you going to stay?

M My _____ _____ was to stay for two weeks, but yesterday I _____ _____ stay a week longer.

W I see. I hope you will _____ _____ _____ _____.

11

M You can _____ _____ this in the kitchen. Its body _____ usually _____ _____ _____ while the _____ is _____ _____ _____ _____ or _____. This is used for cutting _____, _____, _____, etc. This is a very _____ and _____ _____ but you have to be really careful. That is because the metal part is _____ and has a _____ _____. If you are _____, you might _____ _____ or _____.

12

W Good afternoon, everyone. I'm pleased to _____ Mr. Mike Brown. He majored in business administration and has fifteen years of _____ in increasingly _____ _____ within marketing at several companies. He's going to be the _____ _____ of _____ _____ _____. I believe that his experience and knowledge will help this company _____. So please give a _____ _____ to Mr. Mike Brown.

13

W Hey, Taemin. Are you _____ here _____ _____ _____? I thought you _____ _____ _____ _____ _____ Taiwan.

M Hi, Yuna. _____ _____. I'm leaving this _____. Are you _____ _____ _____ _____ _____ now?

W No, I'm going to the _____. I want to look at _____ _____ _____ about the _____.

M Do you always buy that kind of book?

W _____ _____ _____. If there is an interesting one, that's the one I'll get. But I buy other kinds of books, too. _____ _____ _____ _____?

M I'm going to the _____ _____ to buy _____ _____ _____ for my mom.

W Oh, I have to _____ _____ at the next stop. I have to _____ _____.

_____. Why don't you _____ _____ _____?

M Thanks. _____ _____ _____ _____!

14

W Mingyu, do you know any good ways to _____ _____ _____?

M Well, it is helpful to _____ _____, _____, or trains _____ _____ _____.

W _____, it is. _____ can also be _____ _____ _____ but not many people do it because they don't feel safe.

M They don't feel safe?

W Yes. Some people don't feel it's safe to drive with someone they don't know well.

M Oh, _____ _____ _____. I think _____ _____ _____ when we aren't using them is helpful.

W _____ _____! What do you _____ _____ using _____ _____?

M _____ _____ we can _____ a lot of _____ if we don't use them.

W You're right.

15

① W _____ _____ _____ free-time _____ among the students in George's class is _____ _____ _____.

② W _____ percent said that they enjoy listening to music when they are free.

③ W The number of students who _____ playing sports was _____ _____ _____ _____ the number who answered playing computer games.

④ W _____ students enjoy _____ _____ than _____ _____.

⑤ W _____ _____ other activities, _____ _____ number of students in George's class want _____ _____ _____ in their free time.

16

W Ben, here is something that will make you happy. Have a look at _____ _____.

M Let me see. Oh, I _____ _____ _____ _____ for a sign that says, "_____ _____ _____!"

W Congratulations! From now on, you have _____ _____ _____ _____ to with your _____.

M Thanks. Why don't we _____ _____ _____ there today? They have a _____ _____ even _____ _____ _____.

W What do they have for a _____ _____ _____?

M _____ _____. The lunch special today is tacos.

W Oh, that's _____. Let's go!

17

① M Excuse me, I think you're sitting _____ _____ _____.

   W Oh, really? Let me _____ _____ _____. I'm sorry.

② M Does this bus go to _____ _____?

   W No, you should take _____ _____ _____.

③ M _____ _____ _____ _____ buy some mouthwash for my teeth.

   W How about this _____ _____ _____?

④ M Didn't you talk with her about _____ _____ _____?

   W Well, I tried to, but she didn't want to _____ _____ _____.

⑤ M What time should I get to _____ _____?

   W _____ _____ before the play starts.

18

M Jane, do you know who Jeff is?

W Do you mean _____ _____ _____ in our school?

M Yeah, that's him. He _____ _____ lots of _____ and the teachers always seemed to be angry about his behavior.

W Why are you talking about him _____ _____ _____ _____ _____? You aren't _____ to him.

M Are you _____ _____ this?

W Okay. What is it?

M He _____ _____ into Harvard _____.

W Wow, _____ _____ _____!

19

W Jessica arrives at a _____ _____ _____ to meet her friends. Because it's _____, almost every table _____ _____ _____ people. Fortunately, she sees _____ _____ _____ for four people. But there are _____ _____ _____. She sees _____ _____ _____ by a man sitting alone at another table. Since he is _____ _____ on his laptop, Jessica thinks that he _____ _____. So she would like to _____ _____ if she can _____ _____ _____. In this situation, what would Jessica most likely say to the man sitting alone at the table?

20

M Thank you for visiting. Please _____ _____ _____.

W Thank you. May I ask _____ _____ _____ to see me?

M Kate has always been a good student _____ _____ _____ _____ her _____. But these days I think one of her friends is bullying her.

W Oh, I didn't know that. Her behavior _____ _____ _____ _____ _____.

M Well, she isn't talkative and happy at school anymore. She is afraid to talk these days.

W I wasn't _____ _____ _____ _____. Thank you for _____ _____ _____.

M Please talk to her about it, so we can solve the problem.

Vocabulary **R**eview

01	orchid	난초	11	root for	응원하다
	plain	평범한		striker	공격수
	bouquet	꽃다발		absolutely	절대적으로, 물론
02	personality	성격	12	aisle	통로
	sociable	사교적인		at a time	한 번에
	cope with	~에 대처하다	13	journey	여행
	criticism	비난, 비평		fare	요금
03	report	신고하다		one-way	편도의
	burglary	가택 침입, 강도질		round-trip	왕복의
	graffiti	낙서	14	catch up to	~을 따라잡다
04	cancel	취소하다		winning	승리를 결정하는, 결승의
	around	대략	15	refund	환불
	client	고객		inconvenience	불편
05	document	서류	16	European	유럽 사람
	immediately	즉시		seem to-V	~인 것 같다
	charge	요금		German	독일의
06	gym	체육관	17	paradise	천국, 낙원
	trial	시도		senior	어르신
	sign up	등록하다		rate	등급을 매기다
07	poetry	(집합적) 시	18	be accompanied by	~을 동반하다
	rhyme	운이 맞다		a pair of	~ 한 켤레, ~ 한 벌
08	have a fever	열이 나다		sneakers	운동화
	cough	기침		would like to-V	~하고 싶다
	get better	(병이) 호전되다	19	avenger	복수자
09	avenue	거리		previous	이전의
	naughty	장난꾸러기의, 말을 안 듣는		follow	따르다
	for free	무료로	20	project	과제
10	backache	허리 통증		due	기한이 된, 예정된
	give ~ a hand	~을 도와주다		do one's best	최선을 다하다
	shoelace	신발끈			

02 Vocabulary Review

01	describe	묘사하다
	bright	밝은
02	niece	질녀
	nephew	조카
	magnifying glass	돋보기
	astronomer	천문학자
03	obey	준수하다, 복종하다
	speed limit	제한 속도
	keep in mind	명심하다
04	in detail	자세하게
	annoying	짜증나게 하는
	receipt	영수증
05	field trip	견학
	make a note of	~을 적어두다
	return	돌아오다, 돌아가다
06	go -ing	~하러 가다
	feel like	~을 하고 싶다
	Why don't we ~?	~하는 게 어때?
07	after-school	방과 후의
	session	수업 시간
	go over	복습하다, 잘 살펴보다
08	get together	모이다
	prefer	선호하다
09	literature	문학
	sophomore	2학년
10	cafeteria	구내식당
	had better+동사원형	~하는 게 더 낫다
	My goodness.	맙소사.
11	list off	하나씩 호명하다
	blank	텅 빈

	strive	노력하다
	concentrate on	집중하다
	the+비교급, the+비교급	~하면 할수록 더 ~하다
12	Same with me.	나도 마찬가지야.
	eyesight	시력
13	volunteer	자원봉사 하다
	meaningful	의미 있는
14	spring break	봄방학
	overseas	해외의
	especially	특히
15	leave	떠나다
	class	등급
	economy	값싼; 경제
16	weigh	무게가 ~ 나가다
	furry	털로 덮인
	endangered	멸종 위기에 처한
17	bracelet	팔찌
	warm-up exercise	준비운동
18	disembark	(탈것에서) 내리다
	transit	통과, 이동
	customs	세관
	immigration	입국, 입국심사
19	instruction	지시, 안내
	pregnant	임신한
	indirect	간접의
	public place	공공장소
20	via	~을 경유하여
	suit one's taste	입맛에 맞다

01	rectangular	직사각형의
	frame	틀, 테
	trendy	유행하는
02	suspect	용의자
	thick	두꺼운
	beard	턱수염
	mustache	콧수염
03	in the meantime	그동안에
	get through	빠져나가다, 종료하다
04	counselor	상담사
	set a goal	목표를 세우다
	steadily	꾸준히
05	purchase	구매하다
	permit	허가, 허가증
	semester	학기
06	scale	저울
	destination	목적지
	boarding pass	탑승권
07	fit into	~에 잘 맞다
	lock	자물쇠
	locksmith	자물쇠 수리공
08	pass by	지나치다
	by mistake	실수로
	starve	굶주리다
09	employee	종업원
	pay in cash	현금으로 지불하다
	driver's license	운전면허증
10	break	위반하다
	traffic rule	교통 법규
	parking zone	주차 구역

11	fine	미세한
	dust	먼지
	phenomenon	현상
	cause	야기하다
12	How often~?	얼마나 자주~?
	every+복수형 시간	매 ~마다
13	postpone	연기하다
	pneumonia	폐렴
	look after	돌보다
14	for the first time	처음으로
	recall	생각해내다
	memory	기억, 기억력
15	exhibition	전시회
	be crazy about	~에 푹 빠지다
	reservation	예약
16	park	주차하다
	heavy	심한, 무거운
	convenient	편리한
17	relaxing	느긋하게 하는
	lounge	느긋하게 보내다
	private	사적인
	miss out	놓치다
18	stop by	들르다
	on one's way to	~로 가는 길에
	delivery	배달
19	on business	업무차, 사업차
	come by	들르다
	make it	도착하다, 해내다
20	apply for	~에 지원하다
	nervous	긴장한

01	adorable	사랑스러운
	front tooth	앞니
	plump	통통한
02	grocery	식료품류, 식품점
	spinach	시금치
03	cost	비용
	electricity	전기
	stand	참다, 견디다
	sweaty	땀에 젖은
04	try on	입어보다
	fitting room	탈의실
	on sale	할인 중인
05	physics	물리학
	genius	천재
06	enjoyable	즐거운
	arts and crafts	공예
	registration	등록
	contact	연락하다, 접촉하다
07	have the wrong time	시간을 잘못 알다
	prefer	더 좋아하다
	court	뜰, 코트, 법정
08	organize	조직하다, 체계화하다
	routine	판에 박힌 일, 일과
09	go straight	직진하다
10	fortunately	운이 좋게도
	rest	쉬다
	participant	참가자
11	gift voucher	상품권
	take part in	~에 참가하다
	fluency	유창성

	accuracy	정확성
12	still	여전히, 아직도
	be on for	~을 원하다
13	parcel	꾸러미, 소포
	surface mail	(해상 포함) 육상우편
	as soon as possible	가능한 한 빨리
	depend on	~에 달려 있다
14	workout	운동
	trim	말쑥한
	stick at	~을 꾸준히 하다
	geometry	기하학
15	throughout	~ 동안 내내
	lunar	음력의
	rent	빌리다
16	separate	분리하다
	dispose of	~을 버리다
17	revolution	혁명
	graduation	졸업
	steal	훔치다
18	discharge	짐을 내리다, 퇴원시키다
	make-up class	보충수업
	temporarily	일시적으로
	timetable	시간표
19	how to-V	~하는 방법
	racket	채, 라켓
20	rekindle	다시 불붙이다
	pitch	던지다, 설치하다

05 Vocabulary Review

01	bow tie	나비넥타이
	queue	열, 줄
	crowned	왕관을 쓴
02	prescription	처방
	gum	잇몸
	ache	아프다, 쑤시다
	cavity	구멍, 충치
	swell	붓게 하다
03	break into	침입하다
	chase	추격하다
	arrest	체포하다
	damage	손상, 피해
04	bargain	매매, 싸게 산 물건
	extend	연장하다
	warranty	보증
05	economics	경제학
06	far from	~에서 멀리
	behind	~ 뒤에
07	afterwards	그 후에
	completely	완전히
	remind	상기시키다
08	wear a cast	깁스를 하다
	take a rest	휴식을 취하다
09	location	위치
	geography	지리
	relationship	관계
10	moderate	적당한, 보통의
	excess	과도(한)
	stroke	뇌졸중
	diabetes	당뇨병

11	turbulence	소란, 난기류
	for a while	잠시 동안
	safety	안전
	fasten	매다, 죄다
12	in stock	재고가 있는
13	invitation card	초대장
	housewarming party	집들이
14	catalog	목록
	confuse	혼란스럽게 하다
	block	막다
15	architecture	건축
	aqua basketball	수중농구
	community center	지역문화센터
16	pale	창백한
	shouldn't have p.p.	~하지 말았어야 했다
17	barn	헛간, 광
	register	등록하다
	prior to	~ 이전에
18	scary	두려운
	popular	인기 있는
19	breaking news	뉴스속보
	bicentennial	200주년 기념의
20	be in one's shoes	~의 입장이 되다
	tell the truth	진실을 말하다

01	release	발행하다
	be sold out	매진되다
	indoors	실내의
02	bark	짖다
	gorgeous	아주 멋진, 화려한
	air	공중
03	shift	옮기다, 바꾸다
	opponent	상대, 대항자
	care for	좋아하다
04	stew	뭉근한 불로 끓이다
	vegetarian	채식주의자
05	couch potato	소파에 앉아 TV만 보는 사람
	be about to-V	막 ～하려 하다
06	cut out	멈추다, 저절로 정지하다
	reception	수신
07	dodge ball	피구
	the second most	두 번째로 ～한
	iron	다리미; 다림질을 하다
08	do the dishes	설거지하다
	warm up	예열하다
09	fantastic	환상적인
	wallet	지갑
10	attorney	변호사
	ticket booth	매표소
	foreign	외국의
11	fluently	유창하게
	hire	고용하다
12	coming	다가오는
	thousand	1천
	withdraw	인출하다, 철수하다

13	teller	금전출납원, 은행직원
	bankbook	은행통장
	fill out	(양식을) 작성하다
	turn	차례, 순서
	degree	도, 정도
14	respectively	각각
	reach	～에 이르다
	temperature	기온
	on the rise	올라서, 상승중인
	demand	요구
15	elementary	기초의
	algebra	대수학
16	sprain	삐다
	relief	안도
	on vacation	휴가 중인
17	fish market	어시장
	dawn	새벽
	look forward to	～을 고대하다
	tricky	까다로운
18	average	평균의
	tutor	지도하다
	effect	효과
	plant	심다, 박다
19	summit	정상
	although	비록 ～이지만
	wedding anniversary	결혼기념일
20	draw a blank	실패하다, 생각나지 않다
	decoration	장식

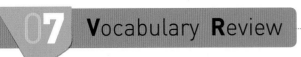

Vocabulary Review

01	be done with	~을 끝내다
	moccasin	뒤축 없는 신, 모카신
02	dishcloth	행주
	drawers	서랍장
	sterilize	살균하다
	cupboard	찬장
03	promote	승진시키다
	affair	일, 업무
	be in charge of	~을 담당하다
	on the other hand	반면에
04	fit	맞다, 어울리다
	exchange	교환하다
05	portable	휴대용의
	treat	간식, 한턱
06	fire	해고하다
	personal	사사로운, 개인적인
	conflict	충돌, 마찰
	promptness	신속
	courtesy	공손
	eagerness	열정
07	roast	구운
	mash	짓이기다
	tasty	맛있는
08	debate	토론
	including	~을 포함하여
09	touching	감동적인
	take care of	~을 돌보다
10	get to	~에 이르다
	achieve	달성하다
11	match	경기

	by the way	그런데
	significant	중대한
12	military	군사의
	palace	궁전
13	probably	아마도
	opposite	반대의
14	deadline	기한
	manuscript	원고
	kindergarten	유치원
15	as long as	~하는 한
	shade	그늘
	lately	최근에
	tradition	전통
16	be late for	~에 지각하다
	renew	갱신하다
17	in celebration of	~을 기념하여
	on one's recommendation	~의 추천으로
	potential	잠재적인
18	horrify	소름 끼치게 하다
	UK (United Kingdom)	영국
19	sore	아픈
	take medicine	약을 복용하다
	spicy	매운
20	death	죽음
	review	비평

08 Vocabulary Review

01	specialist	전문가
	be fond of	~을 좋아하다
	vivid	선명한
	rim	테, 가장자리
	elegant	우아한
02	formal	격식이 있는
	square	정사각형(의)
03	take a nap	낮잠 자다
	in time	늦지 않게
04	airfare	항공요금
	bid on	~에 입찰하다
05	quarter	1/4, 15분
	on time	제시간에
	panic	당황하다
	be supposed to-V	~할 예정이다
06	trust	신뢰하다
	run out of	~이 다 떨어지다
	depart	출발하다
07	school supplies	학용품
08	orphanage	고아원
	nursing home	양로원
	charity organization	자선단체
	account for	~을 차지하다
09	be over	끝나다
	be ready for	~에 준비가 되다
	compete	경쟁하다
	root for	~을 응원하다
10	farewell party	송별회
	pack up	짐을 꾸리다
	from now on	이제부터

	product	제품
11	plain	평이한, 보통의
	dairy product	유제품
12	seed	씨앗
	burn	태우다
13	party	일행
	adult	성인
	suggest	제안하다
	available	이용 가능한
14	crash	(컴퓨터) 갑자기 멈추다
	explain	설명하다
15	due to	~ 때문에
	delay	지연시키다
	because of	~ 때문에
16	flammable	가연성의
	liquid	액체
	go through	통과하다
	security	(공항) 보안 검색대
17	oversized	특대사이즈의
18	reveal	밝히다
	betray	배신하다
	abandon	버리다
	companion	반려, 친구
19	adopt	입양하다, 채택하다
	feed	먹이를 주다
	bathe	목욕시키다
20	appeal to	~의 마음에 들다

01	selection	(같은 종류의) 구색
	alien	외계인
	extraterrestrial	외계의, 지구 밖의
02	issue	발행
	distracting	산만한
	position	적당한 장소에 두다
03	have trouble -ing	~하는 데 어려움을 겪다
	midterm exam	중간고사
	bygone	지난 일, 과거사
	double check	다시 검토하다
04	vomit	토하다
	continually	계속해서
	food poisoning	식중독
05	squirt	물총
	squeeze	꽉 쥐다
	amuse	재미있게 하다
	entertain	즐겁게 하다
06	coincidence	우연의 일치
	graduate from	~을 졸업하다
07	basic	기초적인
	anytime	아무 때나
08	stand in line	줄을 서다
	kind of	다소, 좀
09	pull over	~에게 차를 대게 하다
	dent	움푹 팬 곳
	run a red light	정지신호에 달리다
10	benefit	이점, 장점
	enormous	막대한
	advance	향상시키다
	mental	정신의

11	calm down	진정하다
	set the table	식탁을 차리다
12	local	현지의
	producer	생산자
	take a look at	~을 보다
	thin	날씬한, 얇은
13	secret	비밀
	light	가벼운
	recommend	추천하다
14	either A or B	A나 B 둘 중 하나
	late fee	연체료
	real state	부동산
	furnish	(가구를) 비치하다
15	deposit	보증금
	utilities	(수도, 가스 등) 공익 설비, 공공요금
	electric bill	전기요금 고지서
16	cell phone	휴대전화
	amusement park	놀이공원
17	mention	언급하다
	mechanism	장치, 구조
	collect	수집하다
18	latest	최신의
	allowance	용돈
	charity bazaar	자선 바자회
19	attend	참석하다
	memorial service	추도식
	reserve	예약하다
20	bottom	밑바닥
	request	요청

	stud	장식 징, 장식 단추		staff	직원
01	attractive	매력적인	12	at the same time	동시에
	polka dot	물방울 무늬		section	구역
02	department	부, 과, (상품별) 매장	13	grind	갈다
	disappointed	실망한		water	침 흘리다
03	expect	기대하다		swear	맹세하다
	get-together	모임, 친목회		election	선거
	research	조사		pledge	서약
04	term paper	학기말 논문[숙제]	14	be satisfied with	~에 만족하다
	make fun of	~를 놀리다		mayoral	시장의
05	play	상영되다		vote for	~에 찬성 투표하다
	impressionism	인상주의		locker	사물함
	originate	유래하다	15	memorize	암기하다
06	prominence	탁월, 명성		breathtaking	깜짝 놀랄 만한
	opposition	반대	16	clear	화창한
	conventional	전통의, 재래의		shape	상태, 컨디션
	give[get] a day off	하루 휴가를 주다[받다]		side dish	반찬, 곁들임 요리
	vacuum	진공청소기로 청소하다	17	the handicapped	장애인들
07	fish tank	어항		check out	(절차를 밟고) 빌리다
	do the laundry	빨래하다		ID card	신분증
	switch	바꾸다	18	extension	연장
	advertisement	광고		account	계정, 계좌
08	reduce	줄이다	19	reunion	재회, 친목회
	valid	유효한		search	검색하다, 찾다
09	reference book	참고도서	20	imagination	상상, 망상
	make an appointment	약속하다		low-carbohydrate	저탄수화물의
10	according to	~에 따르면			
	exactly	정확하게			
	board	판자, 게시판			
11	be held	열리다			

01	swimsuit	수영복
	match	~에 어울리다
	long-sleeved	소매가 긴
	shorts	반바지
02	still-life	정물화
	portrait	초상화
	landscape	풍경, 풍경화
	full-length	전신의
03	It's a shame that	~해서 유감이다
	out of the question	불가능한
	ceremony	기념식
05	give away	나누어 주다
	promotional	판촉의
	policy	규정, 정책
06	administrator	관리자
	interrupt	방해하다
	essential	필수적인
	urge	촉구하다
	ensure	보장하다
	fire drill	화재대피 훈련
07	must have p.p	~였음에 틀림없다
	fortune	큰 돈, 운수
	worth	~의 가치가 있는
08	gather	모이다
09	mount	붙박다
	flower arrangement	꽃꽂이
10	biology	생물학
	used	중고의
	secondhand	중고의
	professor	교수

11	pinch	꼬집다
	ideal	이상적인
	height	키
12	customer	고객
	upcoming	다가오는
13	major in	~을 진공하다
	obviously	명백하게
	social welfare	사회 복지
14	fireworks	불꽃놀이
15	revolve	회전하다
	book	예약하다
16	perfect	완벽한
	invite	초대하다
17	lightning	번개
	ditch	도랑, 개천
	crouch	웅크리다
	surface	표면
18	backpack	배낭
19	neighborhood	이웃, 인근 지역
	computing	컴퓨터 사용
20	outstanding	두드러진, 뚜렷한
	achievement	성과
	keep one's fingers crossed for	~에 행운을 빌다

12 Vocabulary Review

01	tri-fold	삼중으로 접은
	bi-fold	이중으로 접은
	floral	꽃의, 꽃무늬의
	wording	말로 나타내기
02	organizer	정리함
	bin	용기, 통
	roomy	널찍한
03	work	일, 직장
	brochure	소책자
04	stairs	계단
	alone	혼자
05	dough	반죽 덩어리
	spin	돌리다
	be proud of	~을 자랑스러워 하다
06	in-flight	기내의
	duty free goods	면세품
	accept	받아들이다
	perfume	향수
07	formal suit	정장
	casual	격식을 차리지 않은
	intelligent	지적인
	head	향하다
08	by oneself	혼자서
	closet	옷장
	arrange	정리하다
	hand on	양도하다
	hardly	거의 ~ 아니다
	certificate	증명서, 인가증
	requirement	자격
09	curriculum vitae	이력서

11	application	지원, 지원서
	reference	신원보증인, 참고
	since	~ 이후로
	shuttlecock	(배드민턴) 셔틀콕
12	heritage	유산
	information	정보
13	take a break	짧은 휴식을 취하다
	Shall we~?	~하는 것 어때?
	fill up	채우다
14	brand new	아주 새로운
	polish	윤을 내다
	extremely	극단적으로
	reasonable	(가격이) 적정한
15	be good at	~을 잘하다
	engineering	공학
	attach	첨부하다
16	catch up on	~을 따라잡다, 만회하다
	public place	공공장소
17	striped	줄무늬의
18	draft	초안, 문안
	fix	고치다
	per	~당
	free of charge	무료로
19	in advance	미리
20	pleasure	기쁨
	lovely	멋진, 사랑스러운

번호	영어	한글
01	bestselling	가장 잘 팔리는
	function	기능
	be sick of	~에 질리다
02	capitalize	대문자로 쓰다
	suggestion	제안
03	rest	휴식, 나머지
	touched	감동한
04	current	현재의
	downturn	침체
	run	경영하다
	financially	제정적으로
	loan	대출
05	gardening	원예
	emergency landing	비상착륙
	upright	똑바로 선
06	securely	안전하게, 튼튼하게
	alarm	불안, 공포
	apologize	사과하다
	assemble	조립하다
	put away	치우다
07	break into pieces	산산조각 나다
	clumsy	솜씨 없는, 서투른
	plastic bag	비닐봉지
08	take off	이륙하다
	entertainment	오락, 오락물
09	monthly magazine	월간 잡지
	have a fever	열이 있다
10	thermometer	온도계
	fever reducer	해열제
11	envelope	봉투

번호	영어	한글
	one by one	하나씩 차례로
	traditional	전통의
12	kneel	무릎을 꿇다
	thigh	허벅지
	contestant	경쟁자, 참가자
13	economy class	일반석
	land	착륙하다
14	at least	최소한
	arrivals board	(공항) 도착안내판
15	comfortable	편안한
	common	평범한
	make it to	~에 이르다
16	final	결승전
	incredible	믿을 수 없는
	traffic jam	교통체증
	choir	합창단
	in unison	제창으로
17	audition	음성 테스트를 하다[받다]
	expert	전문가(의)
	improve	향상시키다
	put on	상연하다
18	at the moment	지금은
	clerk	점원
19	send off	배웅하다
	flea market	벼룩시장
20	raise money	돈을 모금하다

14 Vocabulary Review

01	value	가치
	appearance	외모
	meet	충족시키다
	expectation	기대
02	wreath	화환, 리스
	mittens	벙어리 장갑
03	long face	우울한 표정
	run into	～와 충돌하다
	coma	혼수상태
	What a pity.	안됐다.
04	headache	두통
	upset stomach	배탈
06	chop	잘게 썰다
07	final match	결승전
	stadium	경기장
	play against	～을 상대로 경기하다
08	till	～ 때까지
	practice	연습하다
	the day after tomorrow	내일 모레
09	remove	제거하다
	price tag	가격표
10	impression	인상
	blossom	꽃, 개화
11	be made of	～으로 만들어지다
	metal	금속
	grip	손잡이
	keen	날카로운
	edge	테두리, 날
	wound	상처를 입히다
	be pleased to-V	～하게 되어 기쁘다

12	administration	경영, 관리
	increasingly	더욱 더
	knowledge	지식
13	newly	새롭게
	get off	내리다
	natural resources	자연 자원
14	definitely	분명히, 확실히
	carpooling	자가용 탑승, 카풀
	unplug	플러그를 뽑다
	electronic device	전자기기
15	activity	활동
	except for	～을 제외하고
17	mouthwash	양치약
	goggle	보안경, 고글
	theater	극장
18	troublemaker	문제아, 말썽꾼
	behavior	행동
	all of a sudden	갑자기
19	be filled with	～로 가득 차다
	empty	텅 빈
20	when it comes to	～에 관해서라면
	bully	(약한 자를) 괴롭히다
	talkative	수다스러운
	be aware of	～을 알다

MEMO

MEMO

MEMO

MEMO

MEMO

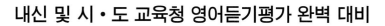

내신 및 시·도 교육청 영어듣기평가 완벽 대비

Listening

올리고

중학영어듣기 모의고사

Level 3

정답 및 해석

01 ②	02 ④	03 ⑤	04 ①	05 ⑤
06 ③	07 ①	08 ③	09 ③	10 ②
11 ⑤	12 ①	13 ⑤	14 ②	15 ④
16 ①	17 ②	18 ④	19 ③	20 ②

01

M I'd like to get some <u>flowers</u> for my mother's birthday.

W Do you have <u>anything special in mind</u>?

M A <u>corsage</u> would be nice. Do you have an <u>orchid</u> corsage?

W I'm <u>afraid</u> we don't have any orchids today. How about this red carnation corsage?

M That's <u>too plain</u>. Do you have pink ones?

W Sorry, we don't have any. Then, what about a <u>bouquet</u> of spring flowers with a <u>pretty vase</u>?

M That sounds <u>wonderful</u>. I know my mother will like that.

··

남 엄마 생신에 드릴 꽃을 사고 싶어요.

여 특별히 생각하신 것이 있나요?

남 코르사주가 좋을 것 같아요. 난초 코르사주 있나요?

여 죄송하지만, 오늘 난초가 없네요. 이 빨간색 카네이션 코르사주는 어때요?

남 너무 평범한 것 같아요. 분홍색 있나요?

여 죄송하지만 없어요. 그럼, 봄꽃 한 다발을 예쁜 화병에 담아 드리는 것은 어때요?

남 좋아요. 엄마가 좋아하실 거예요.

••
have ~ in mind ~을 마음에 두다 **corsage** 꽃 장식, 코르사주 **orchid** 난초 **plain** 평범한 **bouquet** 꽃다발

02

W Hey, Ben. I can guess <u>how</u> you <u>fall asleep</u>. You lie on <u>your back</u> with both arms straight at your sides, right?

M <u>That's right</u>. How do you know it?

W I read an article about <u>sleeping positions</u>. It says <u>how you sleep</u> shows your personality.

M Wow, that's amazing. Then can you guess my brother's <u>personality</u>?

W Of course, tell me <u>how he sleeps</u>.

M He sleeps on his <u>stomach</u> with his <u>head</u> turned to the <u>side</u> and <u>arms curled</u> near the <u>pillow</u>.

W His position is called freefall. He may be <u>sociable</u> but cannot cope with <u>personal criticism</u>.

M Yes, he is exactly like that.

··

여 안녕, Ben. 나는 네가 어떻게 자는지 추측할 수 있어. 너는 바로 누워서 양 팔을 양 옆에 똑바로 두고 자, 그렇지?

남 맞아. 너 그걸 어떻게 알아?

여 잠자는 자세에 관한 기사를 읽었어. 그 기사에 따르면 잠자는 방식은 성격을 보여준대.

남 와, 놀라운데. 그럼 우리 형의 성격을 맞춰볼래?

여 물론이지, 그가 어떻게 자는지 말해봐.

남 형은 엎드려서 얼굴을 옆으로 하고 팔을 베개 가까이에 구부리고 자.

여 그의 자세는 자유낙하라 불리는 거야. 사교적일 순 있지만 개인적 비난에 대해서는 대처를 못 할 수 있어.

남 그래, 형은 정확히 그래.

••
article 기사 **personality** 성격 **curl** 곱슬곱슬하게 하다, 웅크리다 **stomach** 배 **sociable** 사교적인 **cope with** ~에 대처하다 **criticism** 비난, 비평

03

M What can I do for you?

W I'm calling to <u>report</u> that my house <u>has been burgled</u>.

M When did you <u>discover</u> the <u>burglary</u>?

W It was <u>five minutes ago</u> when I got home from work.

M Was anything <u>stolen</u>?

W Yes, all my jewelry was <u>gone</u>. And they <u>sprayed graffiti</u> all over the walls.

M Where do you live?

W I live at 19 Saemunan-ro.

M An <u>officer</u> will be there in about <u>half an hour</u>. Please don't touch anything.

··

남 무엇을 도와드릴까요?

여 우리 집에 강도가 들어서 신고 하려고 전화했어요.

남 강도가 들었다는 건 언제 발견하셨어요?

여 5분 전에 퇴근해서 집에 도착했을 때요.

남 도둑 맞은 것이 있습니까?

여 네, 보석들이 모두 없어졌어요. 그리고 벽에다 온통 스프레이로 낙서를 해뒀어요.

남 사시는 곳은요?

여 새문안로 19번지에 살아요.

남 경찰관이 30분쯤 후에 거기에 갈 겁니다. 아무것도 만지지 마세요.

① 기분 좋은　　　② 수치스러운　　　③ 슬픈
④ 만족하는　　　⑤ 겁에 질린

●●
report 신고하다　**burgle** 강도질하다　**burglary** 가택 침입, 강도질
graffiti 낙서

04

W Hello, Alex. I'm calling to let you know I'm going to be late. I'm very sorry.

M What's going on, Cathy? The meeting won't start for another hour.

W Well, I'm still at the railway station. My train was canceled at the last minute. I have to wait for the next one.

M At what time will you be here?

W The next train is coming in 25 minutes, so I'll be there at around eleven ten.

M Then just ten minutes late for the meeting. Should we wait for you?

W Please start without me. Don't make the clients wait.

M Okay. Get here as soon as possible.

- - - - - - - - - -

여 안녕하세요, Alex. 제가 늦게 도착하는 것을 알려드리려고 전화 드렸습니다. 정말 죄송합니다.

남 무슨 일이지요, Cathy? 회의는 한 시간 후에나 시작할 겁니다.

여 그게, 아직 기차역이에요. 제가 탈 기차가 출발 바로 전에 운행이 취소되었어요. 다음 기차를 기다려야 해요.

남 언제 여기에 도착하죠?

여 다음 기차가 25분 후에 올 거여요. 그러면 11시 10분경에 거기에 도착할 것 같습니다.

남 그럼 회의에 딱 10분 지각하는군요. 우리가 기다릴까요?

여 저 없이 그냥 시작하세요. 고객을 기다리게 하지 마세요.

남 알겠습니다. 최대한 빨리 여기에 오세요.

●●
cancel 최소하다　**around** 대략　**client** 고객　**as + 부사 + as possible**
가능한 한 ~하게

05

M Can you give me a wake-up call tomorrow?

W Certainly. What time would you like us to call you?

M I need the call at seven.

W No problem. We'll call you tomorrow morning at seven.

M One more thing! I need to copy a document immediately.

W We have a copier in our business center, located on the first floor.

M Great! Is there a charge?

W It's twenty cents a copy, sir.

- - - - - - - - - -

남 내일 모닝콜 해주시겠어요?

여 물론이죠. 언제 전화 드릴까요?

남 7시에 전화해주세요.

여 네. 내일 아침 7시에 전화 드리겠습니다.

남 한 가지 더요! 서류 하나를 당장 복사해야 해요.

여 1층에 위치한 사무 센터에 복사기가 있습니다.

남 좋아요. 요금을 내야 하나요?

여 복사 한 장당 20센트입니다.

●●
wake-up call 모닝콜, 아침에 깨우는 전화　**document** 서류
immediately 즉시　**locate** 위치시키다　**charge** 요금

06

W How may I help you?

M I'm looking around for a gym to use.

W Great. You came to the right place. Are you looking to get a membership?

M I think so. What kinds of memberships do you have?

W We have two membership packages: a three-month package and a twelve-month package.

M I'll be here for a year but I don't know if I want to be a member for that long.

W Our three-month package would be perfect, then.

It's just like a trial package.

M That sounds good. After signing up, could you show me around?

··

여 어떻게 도와드릴까요?

남 사용할 헬스장을 찾아 둘러보고 있는 중입니다.

여 좋아요. 제대로 찾아 오셨습니다. 회원권 가입을 하려고 하세요?

남 네, 맞아요. 어떤 종류의 회원권이 있나요?

여 두 가지 종류가 있는데, 3개월 상품과, 12개월 상품입니다.

남 일 년은 여기에 있을 테지만, 그렇게 오랫동안 회원이 되고 싶을지는 잘 모르겠습니다.

여 그럼 3개월 상품이 좋을 것 같습니다. 시험 삼아 한 번 해보는 상품 같은 거죠.

남 좋아요. 등록한 후에 헬스장을 구경시켜 주시겠습니까?

··
gym 체육관 **right** 적당한 **trial** 시도 **sign up** 등록하다

07

M When two things go together, you can call them a couple. In poetry, when two lines that rhyme go together, they are called a rhyming couplet. The sound that ends the first line is repeated in the second line. Rhyming couplets are fun to hear, and they are easy to remember. Read these poems. Which ones have rhyming couplets and what are the rhyming words?

··

남 두 가지 사물이 함께 있을 때, 당신은 그것들을 커플이라고 부를 수 있습니다. 시에서 운이 맞는 두 행이 함께 오면, 그 행들은 운이 맞는 2행 연구라고 불립니다. 첫 행의 마지막에 오는 소리는 두 번째 행에서 반복됩니다. 운이 맞는 2행 연구는 듣기에 재미있고, 기억하기에 쉽습니다. 이 시들을 읽어보세요. 어떤 시가 운이 맞는 2행 연구를 가지고 있고 운이 맞는 단어는 무엇인가요?

··
poetry (집합적) 시 **rhyme** 운이 맞다 **couplet** (시의) 대구, 2행 연구
poem (한 편의) 시

08

M Minji, are you okay? You look sick.

W I have a fever and a bad cough.

M I'm sorry to hear that. Did you take some medicine?

W Yeah, I already did this morning but it's not getting better.

M Why don't you go see a doctor, then?

W I need to study for a math test tomorrow.

M Your health is more important than the test.

W You're right.

··

남 민지야, 너 괜찮니? 아파 보여.

여 나 열이 나고 기침이 심해.

남 안됐구나. 약은 먹었니?

여 응, 오늘 아침에 먹었는데 괜찮아지지를 않네.

남 그러면 병원에 가는 게 어때?

여 내일 수학 시험이 있어서 공부를 해야 해.

남 네 건강이 시험보다 더 중요해.

여 네 말이 맞아.

··
have a fever 열이 나다 **cough** 기침 **take medicine** 약을 복용하다
get better (병이) 호전되다

09

① W Where is the nearest coffee shop?

  M It's on 5th Avenue.

② W My brother is very naughty.

  M So is my brother. Is your brother in the living room now?

③ W You always drink coffee.

  M Yeah, I like it very much.

④ W I have a job interview in the next room soon.

  M I'll keep my fingers crossed for you.

⑤ W How much was this sandwich?

  M I got it for free.

··

① 여 가장 가까운 커피숍이 어디인가요?

  남 5번가에 있습니다.

② 여 내 남동생은 장난이 아주 심해.

  남 내 남동생도 그래. 네 남동생 이젠 거실에 있니?

③ 여 항상 커피를 마시는군요.

  남 네, 커피를 아주 좋아합니다.

④ 여 나 옆 호실에서 곧 취업 면접 있어.

  남 행운을 빌게.

⑤ 여 이 샌드위치 얼마였니?

  남 공짜로 얻었어.

avenue 거리 **naughty** 장난꾸러기의, 말을 안 듣는 **job interview** 취업 면접 **keep one's fingers crossed for** ~에 행운을 빌다 **for free** 무료로

10

W Hi, James.

M Hi, Cathy. How's your backache?

W Actually, it still hurts a lot. It's difficult for me to bend forward or stand for long.

M I'm sorry to hear that. Is there anything I can do for you?

W Well, then can you give me a hand?

M Sure. What is it?

W I can't tie my shoelaces.

여 안녕, James.

남 안녕, Cathy. 허리 통증은 어때?

여 사실 아직 심하게 아파. 앞으로 구부리거나 오래 서있는 게 힘들어.

남 그 말 들으니 안됐네. 내가 뭐 도와줄 일 있니?

여 저, 그럼 나 좀 도와 줄래?

남 물론이야. 그게 뭐니?

여 내가 신발끈을 묶을 수가 없어.

backache 허리 통증 **bend** 구부리다 **forward** 앞으로 **give ~ a hand** ~을 도와주다 **shoelace** 신발끈

11

W Hey, Minjae, it's Monday again. What are you doing?

M Hi, Yujin. I'm buying tickets online for the soccer game between the Dragons and Hawks.

W The game between the Dragons and Hawks! Anyway, which team do you root for?

M I'm a big fan of the Dragons.

W Really? Me too. I especially like Jaeil Lee. I think he is the best striker.

M Do you want to go with me, then?

W Absolutely! When is the game?

M It's the day after tomorrow at noon.

W Perfect.

여 민재야, 또다시 월요일이네. 너 뭐 하니?

남 안녕, 유진아. 온라인으로 Dragons와 Hawks 간의 축구 경기 표를 구매 중이야.

여 Dragons와 Hawks 간의 경기라고! 어쨌든 넌 어느 팀 응원해?

남 나는 Dragons의 광 팬이야.

여 정말? 나도 그래. 나는 특히 이재일 선수가 좋아. 내 생각에는 그가 최고의 공격수인 것 같아.

남 그러면 나랑 같이 갈래?

여 물론이지! 경기가 언젠데?

남 내일 모레 정오야.

여 좋았어.

root for 응원하다 **striker** 공격수 **absolutely** 절대적으로, 물론 **the day after tomorrow** 내일 모레

12

M Excuse me, ma'am. Where can I find books about World War II?

W You can find them in aisle F. It's in the history section.

M Thank you. By the way, how many books can I check out at a time?

W Five. And you can keep them for two weeks.

M Good. That's long enough for me to write the report.

W If you have any problem finding a book, please tell me.

M Alright. Thank you very much.

W My pleasure.

남 실례합니다. 제2차 세계대전에 관한 책을 어디서 찾을 수 있나요?

여 통로 F에서 찾으실 수 있습니다. 역사 구역에 있습니다.

남 고맙습니다. 그런데 한 번에 몇 권이나 빌릴 수 있나요?

여 5권입니다. 그리고 2주 동안 빌리실 수 있습니다.

남 좋습니다. 보고서 작성하기엔 충분한 시간이네요.

여 책 찾는 데 어려움이 있으면 말씀해 주세요.

남 네. 감사합니다.

여 천만에요.

① 도서관   ② 서점   ③ 구내식당
④ 박물관   ⑤ 미술관

aisle 통로 **check out** (절차를 밟고) 빌리다, 나가다 **at a time** 한 번에

13

[Telephone rings.]

W Thank you for calling ABC Airlines. How may I help you?

M Hi. Do you have a flight to Guam tomorrow, April 14th? I have urgent business.

W Yes, it leaves at 10:10 in the morning. Fortunately, we have four seats left.

M Good. How long does the trip take exactly?

W It will take about 8 hours and 40 minutes. It will be a long journey.

M I see. How much is the fare?

W A one-way ticket is $1,800, and a round-trip ticket costs $2,200.

M Okay. I will book a round-trip ticket.

탑승권 정보			
목적지	① 괌	날짜	② 4월 14일
시간	③ 오전 10시 10분	소요 시간	④ 8시간 40분
표 구분	왕복	요금	⑤ $1,800

[전화벨이 울린다.]

여 ABC 항공에 전화 주셔서 감사합니다. 도와드릴까요?

남 안녕하세요. 내일, 4월 14일에 괌으로 가는 비행편이 있습니까? 급한 용무가 생겨서요.

여 네, 아침 10시 10분에 떠나는 게 있습니다. 다행히 네 석이 남아 있습니다.

남 좋습니다. 가는 데 시간이 정확히 얼마나 걸리죠?

여 약 8시간 40분 걸릴 거예요. 긴 여행이 될 것입니다.

남 그렇군요. 가격은 얼마인가요?

여 편도는 1,800 달러이고, 왕복은 2,200 달러입니다.

남 알겠습니다. 왕복으로 예약하겠습니다.

journey 여행 **fare** 요금 **one-way** 편도의 **round-trip** 왕복의
book (차표를) 사다, 예약하다

14

W The Sharks had a very good year this year. They won more games than any other team. And they won the championship. The final game was exciting. The Sharks were three runs behind in the ninth inning. The team had to play hard to catch up to their opponent. Luckily, they did that. David Wilson hit a home run. He ran to home base with a big smile. He was very excited to score the winning run.

여 Sharks 팀은 올해 매우 좋은 해를 보냈습니다. 그들은 다른 어떤 팀보다도 더 많은 경기를 이겼습니다. 그리고 우승도 했습니다. 마지막 경기는 흥미진진했습니다. Sharks 팀은 9회에 3점을 뒤지고 있었습니다. 팀은 상대 팀을 따라잡기 위해 열심히 해야 했습니다. 운 좋게도 그들은 해냈습니다. David Wilson이 홈런을 쳤습니다. 그는 함박미소를 지으며 홈으로 달렸습니다. 그는 결승점을 낸 것을 매우 기뻐했습니다.

① 탁구 ② 야구 ③ 배구 ④ 축구 ⑤ 농구

catch up to ~를 따라잡다 **winning** 승리를 결정하는, 결승의

15

M Hello! How may I help you?

W I'd like to get a refund for this jacket.

M What's wrong with it?

W The jacket is nice, but the zipper is broken.

M Don't you want to exchange it for another one?

W OK. But let me check the zipper first.

M No problem. Sorry for the inconvenience.

W That's okay. I should have checked it before I bought it.

남 안녕하세요? 무엇을 도와드릴까요?

여 이 재킷을 환불하고 싶습니다.

남 무슨 문제인가요?

여 재킷은 예쁜데 지퍼가 고장 났어요.

남 다른 것과 교환은 원하지 않으세요?

여 좋아요. 하지만 지퍼를 먼저 확인해볼게요.

남 물론이죠. 불편을 끼쳐드려 죄송합니다.

여 괜찮습니다. 사기 전에 제가 확인을 했어야 했는걸요.

refund 환불 **broken** 고장 난 **inconvenience** 불편

16

① M Would you mind reading my writing?

W Yes, of course. What is it about?

② M What are you reading?

W I'm reading a book called *The Giving Tree*.

③ M You look so happy.

W I just passed my driving test.

④ M Have you ever met any Europeans?

W Yes. I once met a German man.

⑤ M What seems to be the problem?

W I have a bad cough.

....

① 남 내 글을 읽어봐 주겠니?

여 물론 싫지. 무엇에 관한 것인데?

② 남 너 무슨 책을 읽고 있니?

여 〈아낌없이 주는 나무〉라는 책을 읽고 있어.

③ 남 너 행복해 보이는구나.

여 나 운전면허 시험에 막 합격했어.

④ 남 유럽 사람 만나본 적 있니?

여 응, 독일인을 한 번 만났어.

⑤ 남 어디가 불편하세요?

여 기침이 심해요.

●●
mind -ing ~하는 것을 꺼리다 **European** 유럽 사람 **seem to-V** ~인 것 같다 **German** 독일의 **cough** 기침

17

[Telephone rings.]

W Thank you for calling the Cinema Paradise Theater. How may I help you?

M Hi. What movies are now playing?

W A new 007 movie, *The Virus*, and *Romantic Holiday* are now playing at the theater.

M How much is a ticket?

W A ticket is 9 dollars and 50 cents for adults and 5 dollars for children up to age 12. A ticket for seniors is 3 dollars.

M Does the movie *Romantic Holiday* have an age limit?

W That's an R-rated movie, so you must be at least 18 years old or be accompanied by a parent. For more information, please visit our website at www.cinemaparadise.com.

M OK, thank you.

[전화벨이 울린다.]

여 시네마천국 극장에 전화 주셔서 감사합니다. 무엇을 도와드릴까요?

남 안녕하세요. 현재 상영되고 있는 영화들은 무엇인가요?

여 새 〈007〉 영화, 〈바이러스〉, 〈로맨틱 홀리데이〉가 현재 상영 중입니다.

남 표는 얼마인가요?

여 어른 9달러 50센트, 12세까지의 어린이는 5달러입니다. 경로우대표는 3달러입니다.

남 영화 〈로맨틱 홀리데이〉는 연령제한이 있나요?

여 그건 R등급의 영화입니다. 적어도 18세 이상이거나 부모 중 한 분이 동행해야 합니다. 더 자세한 정보를 원하시면 저희 웹사이트 www.cinemaparadise.com을 방문해주세요.

남 알겠습니다. 감사합니다.

●●
paradise 천국, 낙원 **up to** ~까지 **senior** 어른신 **limit** 제한 **rate** 등급을 매기다 **at least** 적어도 **be accompanied by** ~을 동반하다

18

W Tom wants to buy a pair of sneakers. He goes to a shop and finds the style of sneakers he would like to buy. He asks the clerk to bring him the sneakers in his size, but the clerk says that they don't have them in his size. The sizes they do have are either too big or too small for him. Tom doesn't want to buy another style of sneakers. In this situation, what would Tom most likely say to the clerk?

....

여 Tom은 운동화를 사기로 결심한다. 그는 상점으로 가서 그가 사고 싶은 스타일의 운동화를 발견한다. 그는 점원에게 그에게 맞는 사이즈의 운동화를 가져다 달라고 부탁하지만 점원은 그에게 맞는 사이즈가 없다고 한다. 있는 사이즈는 그에게 너무 크거나 너무 작다. Tom은 다른 스타일의 운동화를 사고 싶어하지 않는다. 이 상황에서 Tom은 점원에게 뭐라고 말하겠는가?

① 도와드릴까요?

② 죄송하지만 전 모릅니다.

③ 운동화를 사고 싶습니다.

④ 저를 위해 한 켤레 주문해주시겠습니까?

⑤ 전 이런 큰 셔츠는 원치 않습니다.

●●
a pair of ~ 한 켤레, ~ 한 벌 **sneakers** 운동화 **would like to-V** ~하고 싶다 **clerk** 점원 **either A or B** A나 B 둘 중 하나

19

W Would you like to see a movie this weekend?

M I'd like to. What would you like to see?

W How about *The Avengers 3*?

M *The Avengers 3*? I haven't watched the previous two yet. Do you think it'll be okay?

W Yes. Don't worry. I heard that the movie is easy to follow and interesting.

M What kind of movie is it?

W It's a fantasy adventure movie.

- -

여 이번 주말에 영화 보러 갈래?

남 좋아. 넌 뭘 보고 싶니?

여 〈어벤저스 3〉 어때?

남 〈어벤저스 3〉? 난 아직 두 전편들을 보지 못했어. 괜찮을까?

여 응. 걱정 마. 그 영화 따라가기 쉽고 재미도 있다고 들었어.

남 어떤 종류의 영화니?

여 공상모험 영화야.

① 표는 8달러 50센트야.
② 마지막 상영이 밤 11시 30분이야.
③ 공상모험 영화야.
④ 그 영화는 오후 4시 30분과 오후 7시에 있어.
⑤ 극장 앞에서 3시에 만나는 거 어때?

••
avenger 복수자 **previous** 이전의 **follow** 따르다 **fantasy** 공상(의)
adventure 모험

20

W Hi, Tom. How's everything going?

M Amy, I'll give up on my science project.

W Do you mean the project due tomorrow?

M Yes. It's too difficult for me and I only have a day left.

W Come on, just do your best and at least you won't fail.

M But I don't think I have enough time.

W Don't think like that. I'll help you.

- -

여 안녕, Tom. 모든 일이 잘 되고 있니?

남 Amy, 나 과학 과제 포기할까봐.

여 내일이 기한인 과제 말하는 거니?

남 응. 그건 내게 너무 어렵고 이젠 딱 하루밖에 안 남았어.

여 힘내, 시도라도 하면 적어도 낙제는 면할 거야.

남 그렇지만 시도해 보기엔 너무 늦은 것 같아.

여 그렇게 생각하지 마. 내가 널 도와줄게.

① 그 말 들으니 기뻐.
② 그렇게 생각하지 마. 내가 널 도와줄게.
③ 그냥 포기하고 우리 영화나 보러 가자.
④ 네가 일찍 끝나면 나를 좀 도와줄래?
⑤ 제 시간에 과제를 끝내려고 밤낮으로 작업하고 있구나.

••
project 과제 **due** 기한이 된, 예정된 **do one's best** 최선을 다하다

Further Study 정답   p. 14

1. She guesses it from his personality.

2. The train was canceled and she has to wait for the next one for 25 more minutes.

3. The reason is that he is not quite sure if he wants to be a member for a year.

4. She needs to study for a math test tomorrow.

5. He is busy buying tickets online for a soccer game.

6. It takes about 8 hours and 40 minutes.

7. The reason is that he hasn't watched the previous two yet.

8. The reason is that the project is too difficult for him and he only has a day left.

On Your Own 모범답안   p. 15

A

School Lunches	
Reasons for agreeing	Supporting examples
(1) without school lunches, some students skip their lunch for this or that reason	(2) some students' parents are too busy working hard to make a lunch box for them
(3) school lunches not only keep students physically healthy but also mentally healthy	(4) by having the same lunch at their regular seats, no student needs to feel bad about having no lunch, a poor lunch, or being alone

I believe that schools have to provide lunches for students for two main reasons. First, (1)without school lunches, some students skip their lunch for this or that reason. For example, (2)some students' parents are too busy working hard to make a lunch box for them. Second, (3)school lunches not only keep students physically healthy but also mentally healthy. For example, (4)by having the same lunch at their regular seats, no student needs to feel bad about having no lunch, a poor lunch, or being alone. In conclusion, I agree that schools should have lunch programs.

학교 급식	
찬성하는 이유	뒷받침 예
(1) 학교 급식이 없다면 어떤 학생들은 이런 저런 이유로 점심을 거름	(2) 어떤 학생들의 부모는 열심히 일하느라 너무 바빠서 점심 도시락을 싸줄 수가 없음
(3) 학교 급식은 학생들을 육체적으로 건강하게 해줄 뿐만 아니라 정신적으로도 건강하게 해줌	(4) 자신들의 정규 좌석에서 똑같은 점심을 먹음으로써 어떤 학생도 점심이 없거나, 초라하거나 혹은 혼자 있는 것에 대해 기분이 안 좋을 필요가 없음

저는 두 가지 중요 이유로 학교는 급식을 제공해야 한다고 생각합니다. 첫 번째로, 학교 급식이 없다면 어떤 학생들은 이런 저런 이유로 점심을 거르게 됩니다. 예를 들어, 어떤 학생들의 부모는 열심히 일하느라 너무 바빠서 점심 도시락을 싸줄 수가 없습니다. 두 번째로 학교 급식은 학생들을 육체적으로 건강하게 해줄 뿐만 아니라 정신적으로도 건강하게 해줍니다. 예를 들어, 자신들의 정규 좌석에서 똑같은 점심을 먹음으로써 어떤 학생도 점심이 없거나, 초라하거나 혹은 혼자 있는 것에 대해 기분이 안 좋을 필요가 없습니다. 결론적으로, 저는 학교가 급식 프로그램을 가져야 한다는 데 동의합니다.

B

To See Movies or to Read Novels?	
Reasons I prefer movies	Supporting examples
(1) it takes a far shorter time to see a movie than to read a novel	(2) when you read a book in the *Harry Potter* series, it takes at least a few days; when you see the same story in a movie, it takes only about three hours
(3) all the fantastic visuals and sounds make the story more realistic, vivid, and fun	(4) it's more fun to watch Harry playing Quidditch, flying in the air, than to read about it

I prefer seeing movies to reading novels for two main reasons. First, (1)it takes a far shorter time to see a movie than to read a novel. For example, (2)when you read a book in the *Harry Potter* series, it takes at least a few days. However, when you see the same story in a movie, it takes only about three hours. Second, (3)all the fantastic visuals and sounds make the story more realistic, vivid, and fun. For example, (4)it's more fun to watch Harry playing Quidditch, flying in the air, than to read about it. In conclusion, I think it is better to see movies than to read books.

영화를 볼 것인가, 소설을 읽을 것인가?	
영화를 더 좋아하는 이유	뒷받침 예
(1) 소설을 읽는 것보다 영화를 보는 것이 시간이 훨씬 덜 걸림	(2) 〈해리포터〉 시리즈 한 권을 읽을 때 적어도 며칠은 걸릴 것임; 같은 이야기를 영화로 볼 때는 약 3시간밖에 안 걸림
(3) 그 모든 환상적인 영상과 소리는 이야기를 더욱 더 현실적이고, 생생하고, 재미있게 해줌	(4) Harry가 공중에서 날면서 Quidditch를 하는 것을 보는 것은 책으로 읽을 때보다 더 재미가 있음

저는 두 가지 중요한 이유로 소설책을 읽는 것보다 영화를 보는 것을 더 좋아합니다. 첫 번째로 소설을 읽는 것보다 영화를 보는 것이 시간이 훨씬 덜 걸립니다. 예를 들어 〈해리포터〉 시리즈 한 권을 읽을 때 적어도 며칠은 걸릴 것입니다. 하지만 같은 이야기를 영화로 볼 때는 약 3시간밖에 안 걸립니다. 두 번째로 그 모든 환상적인 영상과 소리는 이야기를 더욱 더 현실적이고, 생생하고, 재미있게 해줍니다. 예를 들어 Harry가 공중에서 날면서 Quidditch를 하는 것을 보는 것은 책으로 읽을 때보다 더 재미가 있습니다. 결론적으로 저는 책을 읽는 것보다 영화를 보는 것이 더 좋다고 생각합니다.

01 ③	02 ④	03 ①	04 ③	05 ④
06 ①	07 ①	08 ⑤	09 ③	10 ⑤
11 ①	12 ②	13 ②	14 ④	15 ②
16 ⑤	17 ⑤	18 ②	19 ④	20 ④

01

W Excuse me, could you please help me? I can't find my bag.

M Oh, I'm sorry to hear that. Can you describe it to me?

W It is a bright pink bag with a pocket on the front.

M Does it have a name tag on it?

W Yes. Also it has a heart-shaped keychain attached to the handle.

M Okay, that helps a lot. Please wait while I check.

W Thank you. I hope you can find it soon.

여 실례지만, 도와주실 수 있으세요? 제 짐을 찾을 수가 없어요.
남 아, 유감입니다. 그 수하물 모양을 설명해주시겠습니까?
여 앞주머니가 있는 밝은 분홍색 가방이에요.
남 이름표가 있나요?
여 네. 손잡이에 하트 모양의 열쇠고리도 달려 있어요.
남 알겠습니다. 도움이 많이 되네요. 제가 알아보는 동안 기다려주세요.
여 감사합니다. 제 짐을 곧 찾으면 좋겠어요.

••
describe 묘사하다 bright 밝은 name tag 이름표 keychain 열쇠고리

02

M That's a nice photo. Did you take it?

W Yes. I took it last month and got it printed yesterday.

M Who are they in this picture?

W They are my seven-year-old niece and five-year-old nephew.

M They are so cute but they look really serious. Why is she pointing up at the full moon?

W She has a magnifying glass in her hand. She was explaining to her brother how far away the moon is from the earth.

M Wow, she will be an astronomer someday.

남 사진 멋지다. 네가 찍었어?
여 응. 지난달에 찍었고 어제 인화했어.
남 이 사진에 있는 사람들은 누구야?
여 내 7살 된 조카딸과 5살 된 조카야.
남 무척 귀여운데 아주 진지해 보여. 그녀는 왜 보름달을 가리키고 있어?
여 그녀는 손에 돋보기를 들고 있어. 달이 지구에서 얼마나 멀리 있는지를 동생에게 설명하고 있는 중이었어.
남 와, 그녀는 언젠가 천문학자가 되겠다.

••
niece 조카딸, 질녀 nephew 조카 magnifying glass 돋보기 point up 가리키다 full moon 보름달 astronomer 천문학자

03

W What do you usually do in your job?

M I give speeding tickets to people. I mean to drivers.

W What kind of drivers are they?

M They are the people who don't obey the speed limit.

W What is the most difficult part of your job?

M Well, it is when people don't follow the traffic rules.

W Is there anything that you'd like to tell them?

M Well, they should keep in mind that following the traffic rules is very important. Accidents happen when people don't follow them.

여 업무상 대개 무엇을 하세요?
남 저는 사람들, 그러니까 운전자들에게 속도위반 딱지를 끊습니다.
여 그들은 어떤 운전자들인가요?
남 제한 속도를 지키지 않는 사람들입니다.
여 당신의 직업에서 가장 어려운 부분은 무엇입니까?
남 글쎄요. 사람들이 교통신호를 지키지 않을 때입니다.
여 그들에게 해주실 말씀이 있으신가요?
남 음. 그들은 교통 법규를 지키는 것이 매우 중요하다는 것을 명심해야 합니다. 사고는 사람들이 그것들을 안 지킬 때 일어납니다.

••
speeding ticket 속도위반 딱지 obey 준수하다, 복종하다 speed limit 제한 속도 keep in mind 명심하다 follow 따르다

04

M Good afternoon, can I help you?

W I hope so. I bought these earphones here about two months ago, but the sound quality is awful.

M Can you tell me the problem with the sound in more detail?

W There is an annoying hissing sound in the background, so I want a refund.

M Do you have your receipt?

W No, I lost it.

M I'm sorry but it isn't our policy to give refunds without the receipt.

W I want to see the manager.

남 안녕하세요, 도와드릴까요?

여 네. 이 이어폰을 여기에서 약 두 달 전에 구매했는데 음질이 너무 나빠요.

남 음질 문제에 대해서 좀 더 구체적으로 말씀해주시겠습니까?

여 쉬익 하는 짜증스런 소리가 배경 소리로 계속 나와서 환불하고 싶어요.

남 영수증 있으십니까?

여 아니요. 잃어버렸어요.

남 죄송하지만 저희 정책상 영수증 없이는 환불을 해드릴 수 없습니다.

여 매니저를 만나고 싶어요.

① 부러워하는   ② 안도하는   ③ 짜증난
④ 슬픔에 젖은   ⑤ 비참한

•• **sound quality** 음질   **in detail** 자세하게   **annoying** 짜증나게 하는 **hiss** 쉿 소리를 내다   **receipt** 영수증   **policy** 정책

05

W What date will our field trip be on?

M It will be Tuesday, September 15th. It's next Tuesday. Make a note of that in your calendar.

W Yes, I will write that down.

M We will leave at 9 in the morning. Be at school half an hour early to get your bags on the bus.

W When are we going to come back?

M We will return six days later and arrive at our school at 7 p.m. Any more questions?

W No. I am really looking forward to the trip.

여 우리 견학 가는 날짜가 언제예요?

남 9월 15일, 화요일이란다. 다음 주 화요일이지. 달력에 적어둬.

여 네, 적어두겠습니다.

남 아침 9시에 출발할 거야. 버스에 짐을 싣기 위해서 30분 먼저 학교에 와야 한다.

여 언제 돌아오나요?

남 6일 후에 돌아올 것이고 학교에는 저녁 7시에 도착할 거란다. 더 궁금한 것 있니?

여 아니요. 여행이 정말 기대돼요.

•• **field trip** 견학   **make a note of** ~을 적어두다   **half an hour** 30분 **return** 돌아오다, 돌아가다

06

M Amy, you like inline skating, don't you?

W Yes, I do.

M Well, would you like to go inline skating today?

W Sorry, I don't feel like it today.

M Then, what would you like to do?

W Why don't we go shopping? Didn't you say you'd like to buy a spring coat?

M OK. Let's go out now.

남 Amy, 인라인스케이트 타는 거 좋아하지, 그렇지 않아?

여 응, 좋아하지.

남 그럼, 오늘 인라인스케이트 타러 갈까?

여 미안해. 난 오늘은 별로 타고 싶지 않아.

남 그럼, 뭘 하고 싶어?

여 우리 쇼핑 가는 거 어때? 봄 코트 사고 싶다고 말하지 않았어?

남 좋아. 지금 나가자.

•• **go -ing** ~하러 가다   **feel like** ~을 하고 싶다   **Why don't we ~?** ~하는 게 어때?

07

M What are you doing?

W I have been trying to solve this math problem for the last 20 minutes but I still have no idea how to solve it.

M Is the homework for tomorrow?

W No, it is due at the end of next week.

M Why don't you get some after-school tutoring?

W Why haven't I thought of it? I'll <u>sign up</u> for it tomorrow.

M Before going to the session, you <u>should go over</u> all the problems <u>again</u>. Then you can <u>prepare some questions</u> for the tutor.

W Thanks for your advice. I'll <u>do that now</u>.

....

남 뭐 해?

여 20분째 이 수학 문제를 풀려고 애쓰고 있지만 어떻게 풀어야 할지 여전히 모르겠어.

남 그 숙제 내일 내야 하는 거야?

여 아니, 다음 주 말이야.

남 방과 후 과외 수업을 받는 거 어때?

여 내가 왜 그 생각을 안 해봤지? 내일 등록해야겠어.

남 수업에 가기 전에, 그 문제들을 다 다시 봐야 해. 그렇게 하면 선생님께 여쭤 볼 문제를 준비할 수 있잖아.

여 충고 고마워. 지금 해야겠어.

••
after-school 방과 후의 **tutor** (가정교사로서) 지도하다; 가정교사
session 수업 시간 **go over** 복습하다. 잘 살펴보다

08

M Do you <u>have any plans</u> this Saturday?

W Why?

M If you're free, let's <u>get together</u> and <u>see the new</u> movie, *Frozen*.

W *Frozen*? I really want to see it. When is the movie showing?

M Do you prefer <u>in the morning</u>, <u>afternoon</u>, or <u>evening</u>?

W Well, let's go in the afternoon.

M Sure. There are <u>two showings</u> in the afternoon; <u>one</u> at 2:30 and <u>the other</u> at 4:50.

W Let's go to the <u>later</u> one.

M No problem. I'll <u>pick you up</u> at 4:20.

....

남 이번 토요일에 계획 있니?

여 왜?

남 만일 한가하면 우리 만나서 새 영화 〈겨울왕국〉을 보자.

여 〈겨울왕국〉? 나 그거 정말 보고 싶어. 영화 언제 상영해?

남 너는 오전, 오후, 저녁 중에 언제를 더 좋아해?

여 음. 오후에 보자.

남 알았어. 오후에는 2시 30분이랑 4시 50분 두 번 상영해.

여 나중 것으로 하자.

남 알았어. 4시 20분에 데리러 갈게.

••
get together 모이다 **prefer** 선호하다 **show** 상영하다. 상영되다

09

W Are you Seungyoon Lee, the new <u>student teacher</u>? I'm the <u>principal</u> of this school, Mary Jones. Nice to meet you.

M Hello. I'm <u>glad to meet you</u>, too.

W How do you feel?

M I'm <u>nervous</u> about whether I can teach well or not. But <u>on the other hand</u>, I'm very <u>excited to start</u> teaching.

W I know how you feel now because I had the same feeling when I was <u>in your shoes</u>. <u>Anyway</u>, what's your major?

M I used to major in <u>English literature</u> but now I'm majoring in <u>English education</u>. I changed it two years ago when I was a <u>sophomore</u>.

W I see. What's your <u>hobby</u>?

M I love <u>horseback riding</u>. I go to the horse-riding track <u>every other Saturday</u>.

....

직위	① 교생
현재 전공	② 영어 교육
현재 학년	③ 2학년
취미	④ 무엇인가 – 말 타기 ⑤ 얼마나 자주 하는가 – 약 한 달에 두 번

여 새 교생선생님이신 이승윤 선생님이세요? 저는 이 학교의 교장인 Mary Jones입니다. 만나서 반갑습니다.

남 안녕하세요. 만나 뵙게 되어 저도 기쁩니다.

여 기분이 어떠세요?

남 잘 가르칠 수 있을지 아닐지 걱정됩니다. 하지만 반면에 가르치는 걸 시작할 수 있어 무척 신이 납니다.

여 저도 그런 시절이 있었기 때문에 지금 선생님의 기분이 어떤지 압니다. 어쨌든, 전공이 무엇인가요?

남 영문학이었는데 현재는 영어교육을 전공하고 있습니다. 2년 전 2학년이었을 때 바꾸었습니다.

여 그렇군요. 취미는 무엇인가요?

남 승마를 무척 좋아합니다. 격주 토요일에 승마장에 갑니다.

student teacher 교생　**on the other hand** 반면에　**in one's shoes** ~의 입장에　**major in** ~을 전공하다　**literature** 문학　**education** 교육　**sophomore** 2학년　**every other** 하나 걸러

10

M　Olivia, do you have the activity book for our English class?

W　I'm sorry. I left it at home because I don't have an English class today.

M　Oh, no. I need to borrow that book before the class begins. What should I do?

W　Why don't you ask Tommy? He keeps all his books in his locker.

M　Really? Thanks for the information. Do you know where he is now?

W　I saw him in the cafeteria a few minutes ago. He was with Rica.

M　Good. I will ask Rica if I can't borrow Tommy's book.

W　You'd better hurry up. The bell will ring in three minutes.

M　My goodness. Bye. See you.

남　Olivia, 영어 시간에 쓰는 활동 책 있니?
여　미안. 오늘 영어 수업이 없어서 집에 놔두고 왔어.
남　이런. 수업 시작하기 전에 그 책을 빌려야 하는데, 어떻게 하지?
여　Tommy에게 물어봐. 걘 모든 책을 사물함에 두고 다녀.
남　정말? 정보 고마워. 걔 지금 어디에 있는지 아니?
여　몇 분 전에 구내식당에서 봤어. Rica랑 같이 있었어.
남　잘됐다. Tommy의 책을 못 빌리면 Rica에게 물어봐야지.
여　서둘러. 3분 후에 종이 칠 거야.
남　맙소사. 안녕. 또 봐.

① 책 사러 서점에 가기
② 책 빌리러 도서관 가기
③ 수업 하러 교실에 가기
④ 영어 선생님을 찾아가 질문하기
⑤ 식당에 가서 친구를 찾기

information 정보　**cafeteria** 구내식당　**had better + 동사원형** ~하는 게 더 낫다　**My goodness**. 맙소사.

11

M　Good evening, ladies and gentlemen. I'm very glad to receive this award for best actor this year. I can't begin to say how much I appreciate this honor. There are so many people I'd like to thank but I can't list off all of them. As soon as I got on the stage, my head went blank. I really appreciate their help. I will strive to concentrate on acting, so I will be worthy of getting this award. Thank you again for this award.

남　신사숙녀 여러분, 안녕하세요? 제가 이 올해의 남우주연상을 받게 되어 너무나 기쁩니다. 이 영예가 얼마나 감사한지 말로 할 수가 없습니다. 제가 감사하고 싶은 분들이 정말 많지만 일일이 다 호명할 수가 없네요. 무대에 올라오자마자 머릿속이 하얘졌습니다. 그분들의 도움에 진심으로 감사 드립니다. 연기에 매진해서 제가 이 상을 받을 자격이 되도록 하겠습니다. 다시 한 번 이 상을 주심에 감사 드립니다.

appreciate 감사하다　**list off** 하나씩 호명하다　**go + 형용사** ~한 상태가 되다　**blank** 텅 빈　**strive** 노력하다　**concentrate on** 집중하다　**be worthy of -ing** ~할 가치가 있다

12

M　Alison, what is most important to you when choosing a cellular phone?

W　To me, the design is most important.

M　What else?

W　Maybe the size of the screen. The bigger the better.

M　Same with me. Since I have bad eyesight, a small screen makes my eyes easily tired.

W　What about the color?

M　I actually don't care about it.

W　I see. Anyway, we can change the color by changing the phone case.

남　Alison, 휴대전화기를 고를 때 가장 중요한 것이 뭐니?
여　나는 디자인이 가장 중요해.
남　또?
여　아마도 화면 크기겠지. 클수록 더 좋아.
남　나랑 똑같네. 나는 시력이 나빠서 화면이 작으면 눈이 쉽게 피로해져.

여 색은?

남 나는 사실상 색은 중요하지 않아.

여 그렇구나. 어쨌든 색은 휴대전화 케이스를 바꾸면 되니까.

••
cellular phone 휴대전화 **the + 비교급, the + 비교급** ~하면 할수록 더 ~하다 **Same with me.** 나도 마찬가지야. **eyesight** 시력

13

W Where shall we go for our vacation this year, Luke?

M How about Busan? The weather is always good, and we can rest on the beach.

W I'd rather do something more meaningful this year, such as volunteering in a poor country.

M That's a good idea, but I want to have a relaxing time during my vacation.

W By the way, when did we order? It is taking too long.

M It's been just 10 minutes since we gave her the order.

W I'm so hungry that I could eat a horse.

여 올해 우리 어디로 휴가를 갈 거야, Luke?

남 부산 어때? 날씨가 항상 좋고 우린 해변에서 쉴 수 있어.

여 나는 올해에는 가난한 나라에서 자원봉사 하기와 같은 뭔가 더 의미 있는 일을 하고 싶어.

남 좋은 생각이긴 하지만, 나는 휴가 동안 편안한 시간을 보내고 싶어.

여 그런데 우리 언제 주문했지? 너무 오래 걸리는 것 같아.

남 주문하고 10분밖에 안 됐어.

여 너무 배고파서 말이라도 먹어 치울 수 있을 것 같아.

① 여행사   ② 음식점   ③ 수영장

④ 동물원   ⑤ 슈퍼마켓

••
rest 쉬다 **volunteer** 자원봉사 하다 **meaningful** 의미 있는 **relax** 긴장을 풀다, 편히 하다

14

M Sally, what are you going to do this spring break?

W I really want to go abroad. I've never been overseas because I'm too scared to fly.

M Are you serious?

W Yes. I can't get on a plane! Have you ever traveled abroad?

M Yeah, I traveled to Europe for 15 days last year with my family.

W Sounds great. Which country did you like most?

M I especially loved Italy. The Duomo in Milano was very beautiful.

W I wish I could go to Italy.

M Don't let fear control you. Every great journey begins with a single step.

남 Sally, 이번 봄방학에 무엇을 할 거니?

여 나는 정말로 해외로 가고 싶어. 비행기 타는 걸 너무 무서워해서 해외에 한 번도 가본 적이 없거든.

남 정말이야?

여 응. 비행기에 올라 탈 수가 없어. 너는 해외 여행 해봤니?

남 응. 나는 작년에 가족과 함께 15일 동안 유럽 여행을 했어.

여 멋지다. 어떤 나라가 가장 좋았니?

남 나는 특히 이탈리아가 좋았어. 밀라노의 두오모 성당이 정말 아름답더라고.

여 나도 이탈리아로 갈 수 있으면 좋겠다.

남 두려움에 지배당하지 마. 모든 멋진 여행은 한 걸음부터 시작하는 거야.

••
spring break 봄방학 **overseas** 해외의 **especially** 특히 **fear** 두려움

15

[Telephone rings.]

W ABC Airlines. How may I help you?

M I'd like to book a round-trip ticket from New York to Seoul.

W What day would you like to leave?

M I'd like to leave on December 28th.

W When will you be returning?

M I'd like to return two weeks later, on the 11th of January, 2015.

W Which class would you like?

M Economy class, please.

W That's 1,986 dollars, please.

비행편 정보	
① 표 유형	왕복
② 출발	뉴욕 / 2013년 12월 28일
③ 도착	서울 / 2015년 1월 11일
④ 등급	일반석
⑤ 요금	$1,986

[전화벨이 울린다.]

여 ABC 항공입니다. 어떻게 도와 드릴까요?

남 뉴욕에서 서울로 가는 왕복표 한 장 예약하고 싶습니다.

여 언제 출발하실 겁니까?

남 12월 28일에 떠나고 싶습니다.

여 언제 돌아오실 건가요?

남 2주 후인 2015년 1월 11일에 돌아올 겁니다.

여 어떤 좌석을 원하세요?

남 일반석으로 부탁 드립니다.

여 요금은 1,986달러입니다.

•• **leave** 떠나다 **class** 등급 **economy** 값싼; 경제

16

W Let me tell you about giant pandas, today. Giant pandas are large black-and-white animals that look like teddy bears. They grow to be about five feet tall and can weigh up to 200 pounds. The black furry circles around their eyes make them look cute and cuddly. However, they are so rare that only a small number still live in the world. People fear that one day in the future, there will be no more pandas. We must save these cute but endangered animals.

여 오늘은 여러분에게 자이언트 팬더에 대해 말하겠습니다. 자이언트 팬더는 곰 인형처럼 생긴, 큰 흑백색의 동물입니다. 약 5피트까지 자라고 몸무게가 200파운드까지 나갈 수 있습니다. 눈 주위의 검은 털 원으로 인해 귀엽고 꼭 껴안아주고 싶게 보입니다. 하지만 너무 희귀해서 세상에 소수만 아직 살고 있습니다. 사람들은 미래 어느 날 팬더들이 더 이상 없게 될까 걱정합니다. 우리는 이 귀엽지만 멸종위기에 처한 동물을 구해야 합니다.

•• **weigh** 무게가 ~ 나가다 **furry** 털로 덮인 **cuddly** 꼭 껴안고 싶은 **rare** 드문, 진귀한 **endangered** 멸종 위기에 처한

17

① M Do you know any Italian restaurants around here?

W A place called 'Naples' opened two weeks ago.

② M Where can I find children's clothes?

W They are on the fifth floor.

③ M Do you remember when you went out?

W I think it was around noon.

④ M I'd like to buy this bracelet for Mom.

W She will probably like it.

⑤ M Be sure to do warm-up exercises before you go in the water.

W I exercise twice a week.

① 남 너 이 근처에 있는 이탈리아 식당을 아니?

여 '나폴리'라는 곳이 2주 전에 문을 열었어.

② 남 아동복은 어디에 있나요?

여 5층에 있습니다.

③ 남 너는 네가 언제 외출했는지 기억하니?

여 내 생각에 정오쯤이었던 것 같아.

④ 남 엄마를 위해 이 팔찌를 사고 싶어.

여 엄마가 아마도 좋아하시겠네.

⑤ 남 물에 들어가기 전에 준비운동을 반드시 하도록 해.

여 나는 일주일에 두 번 운동해.

•• **remember** 기억하다 **go out** 외출하다 **bracelet** 팔찌 **warm-up exercise** 준비운동

18

M Excuse me, could you let me know what the captain said? I missed it listening to music with earphones.

W No problem. First of all, we are approaching Tokyo Narita Airport. Are you going to transfer to another plane in Tokyo?

M Yes.

W OK, when we arrive in Tokyo, passengers who are transferring like you should disembark first.

M Should I go through customs or immigration?

W No. No transit passengers should do that.

M Do you think I can catch my connecting flight, OZ837 bound for London?

W Oh, because of our delay, passengers who were to transfer to that flight should go to our main office to receive further instructions.

....

남 죄송하지만, 기장님이 뭐라고 말씀하셨는지 알려주실 수 있을까요? 이어폰을 끼고 음악을 듣고 있다가 놓쳤어요.
여 네, 먼저 저희는 도쿄 나리타 공항에 접근하고 있습니다. 도쿄에서 다른 비행기로 갈아타십니까?
남 네.
여 그럼, 도쿄에 도착하면 손님 같은 환승 승객들은 먼저 내리셔야 합니다.
남 제가 세관이나 입국심사를 거쳐야 하나요?
여 아니요. 환승 승객은 모두 그렇게 하시면 안 됩니다.
남 제가 런던행 OZ837 연결 비행편을 탈수 있을 것 같은가요?
여 아, 비행기 지연으로 인해서 그 비행편으로 환승 예정이었던 승객들은 저희 본사 사무실로 가셔서 추가 안내를 받으셔야 합니다.

passenger 승객 **disembark** (탈것에서) 내리다 **transfer** 환승하다
transit 통과, 이동 **bound for** ~행인 **customs** 세관 **immigration**
입국, 입국심사 **instruction** 지시, 안내

19

W Suji is waiting for her friends at a restaurant. There's a no smoking sign on the wall. However, she sees a man smoking next to a pregnant woman in the restaurant. That makes Suji upset. She knows smoking, direct or indirect, is bad for our health, especially to women and children. She also knows that these days, smoking is not allowed in public places. In this situation, what would Suji most likely say to the man?

....

여 수지는 한 식당에서 그녀의 친구들을 기다리고 있다. 벽에는 금연 사인이 있다. 하지만 그녀는 그 식당에서 임신부 옆에서 담배를 피고 있는 한 남자를 본다. 수지는 화가 난다. 흡연은 직접적이든 간접적이든 우리 건강에, 특히 여성들과 어린이들에게 나쁘다는 걸 그녀는 안다. 그녀는 또한 요즘은 공공장소에서 흡연이 허용되지 않는다는 것도 알고 있다. 이 상황에서 수지는 그 남자에게 뭐라고 말하겠는가?

① 그거 참 안됐네요.
② 당신은 얼마나 자주 담배를 피세요?
③ 언제 처음 담배를 피기 시작했나요?
④ 당신은 여기서 담배를 필 수 없습니다.

⑤ 당신은 이 건물 어디서든 담배를 필 수 있습니다.

next to ~ 옆에 **pregnant** 임신한 **indirect** 간접의 **public place**
공공장소 **allow** 허용하다

20

W Is this your first time to visit Korea?
M Yes, it is. But I went to London via Incheon last year.
W How long will you be here this time?
M For two days.
W Have you ever tried any Korean foods?
M Sure. I have tried kimchi, bibimbap and bulgogi.
W How did you like them?
M The foods were fantastic and suited my taste.

....

여 한국에 방문하신 것은 이번이 처음인가요?
남 네, 그렇습니다. 하지만 작년에 인천을 경유해 런던으로 간 적은 있습니다.
여 이번에 여기 얼마나 계실 거죠?
남 이틀 동안요.
여 한국음식 드셔 보셨나요?
남 물론이죠. 김치, 비빔밥, 불고기를 먹어봤습니다.
여 어땠나요?
남 음식들이 환상적이었고 제 입맛에도 맞았습니다.

① 음식이 맛있으면 좋겠습니다.
② 저는 짠 음식을 먹으면 안 됩니다.
③ 김치는 한국 전통음식이지요.
④ 음식들이 환상적이었고 제 입맛에도 맞았습니다.
⑤ 저는 매운 음식을 먹고 나면 늘 속이 쓰려요.

via ~을 경유하여 **suit one's taste** 입맛에 맞다

Further Study 정답   p. 24

1 The reason is that the girl is teaching the boy about how far away the moon is from the Earth.
2. They make an annoying hissing sound in the background, so the sound quality is awful.
3. They are going to see the new movie, *Frozen*.
4. He feels nervous but very excited to start teaching.

5. To her, the design is most important.

6. He wants to go to Busan because he thinks the weather is good and they can rest on the beach.

7. The man wants to stay in Seoul for two weeks.

8. She is upset because a man is smoking next to a pregnant woman in a restaurant.

On Your Own 모범답안

p. 25

A

Describing a Picture	
(1) What does the picture show?	a man helping a girl ride a bike on a park road
(2) What do you think is happening now?	a father is teaching his daughter how to ride a bike
(3) Explain how you think the situation occurred.	the girl wanted to learn how to ride a bike and asked her dad to teach her how to do it

This picture shows (1)a man helping a girl ride a bike on a park road. It seems that (2)a father is teaching his daughter how to ride a bike. I think that (3)the girl wanted to learn how to ride a bike and asked her dad to teach her how to do it.

그림 묘사하기	
(1) 그림은 무엇을 보여주나요?	공원 길에서 한 여자 어린이가 자전거 타는 것을 도와주는 한 남자
(2) 무슨 일이 일어나고 있는 것 같나요?	한 아빠가 딸에게 자전거 타는 법을 가르치고 있는 중임
(3) 어떻게 일어난 상황이라고 생각하는지 설명해보세요.	여자 어린이가 자전거 타는 법을 배우기를 원해서 아빠에게 그 방법을 가르쳐 달라고 요청했음

그림은 공원 길에서 한 여자 어린이가 자전거 타는 것을 도와주는 한 남자를 보여준다. 한 아빠가 딸에게 자전거 타는 법을 가르치고 있는 것처럼 보인다. 나는 여자 어린이가 자전거 타는 법을 배우기 원해서 아빠에게 그 방법을 가르쳐 달라고 요청했다고 생각한다.

B

Following the Latest Fashion Trend	
Reasons for disagreeing	Supporting examples
(1) following fashion trends is a waste of money	(2) some of the latest dresses can cost a couple months' worth of savings; besides, fashion styles are changing all the time
(3) can lose creativity by just following fashion trends	(4) if everyone followed the same fashion trend, everybody would dress alike; they wouldn't need to be creative

I disagree that everyone should dress according to the latest fashion trend for two reasons. First, (1)following fashion trends is a waste of money. For example, (2)some of the latest dresses can cost a couple months' worth of savings. Besides, fashion styles are changing all the time. Second, (3)you can lose your creativity by just following fashion trends. For example, (4)if everyone followed the same fashion trend, everybody would dress alike. Then, they wouldn't need to be creative. In conclusion, I don't believe that everyone should dress according to the latest fashion trend.

최신유행 따르기	
반대하는 이유	뒷받침 예
(1) 유행을 따르는 것은 돈을 낭비하는 것임	(2) 몇몇 최신 옷들은 몇 달 동안 모으는 액수만큼의 비용이 들 수 있음; 게다가 유행 스타일은 언제나 변화함
(3) 단지 유행을 따름으로써 창의성을 잃어버릴 수 있음	(4) 모든 사람이 같은 유행을 따른다면, 모두가 똑같이 옷을 입게 될 것임; 그들은 창의적일 필요가 없을 것임

저는 두 가지 이유로 모든 사람이 최신유행에 따라 옷을 입어야 한다는 것에 반대합니다. 첫 번째로, 유행을 따르는 것은 돈을 낭비하는 것입니다. 예를 들면, 몇몇 최신 옷들은 당신이 몇 달 동안 모으는 액수만큼의 비용이 들 수 있습니다. 게다가 유행 스타일은 언제나 변화하고 있습니다. 두 번째로, 단지 유행을 따름으로써, 당신은 창의성을 잃어버릴 수 있습니다. 예를 들어, 모든 사람들이 같은 유행을 따른다면, 모두가 똑같이 옷을 입게 될 것입니다. 그러면, 그들은 창의적일 필요가 없게 될 것입니다. 결론적으로, 저는 모든 사람이 최신유행에 맞춰 옷을 입어야 한다고 생각하지 않습니다.

01 ①	02 ③	03 ①	04 ②	05 ④
06 ④	07 ②	08 ②	09 ⑤	10 ①
11 ④	12 ⑤	13 ④	14 ⑤	15 ③
16 ①	17 ④	18 ④	19 ⑤	20 ③

01

w I want to buy a pair of fashionable sunglasses.
M All right. How do you like these black ones with a rectangular-shaped frame?
w They're too normal. How about this emerald pair with a round-shaped frame?
M It is very unique and the color suits you well.
w What about this heart-shaped frame with brown colored lenses?
M Oh, they are really nice. They have become trendy these days.
w OK, I'll take this pair.

여 멋진 선글라스를 사고 싶어요.
남 좋아요. 직사각형 테로 된 이 검은색 선글라스 어때요?
여 그건 너무 평범한 것 같아요. 이 둥근 테의 에메랄드 색 선글라스는 어때요?
남 아주 독특한 데다 색깔이 당신과 잘 어울리네요.
여 이 갈색 렌즈에 하트 모양 테는 어때요?
남 오, 정말 좋아요. 요즘 유행입니다.
여 좋아요, 이것으로 할게요.

fashionable 멋진, 유행하는 **rectangular** 직사각형의 **frame** 틀, 테
normal 평범한 **unique** 독특한 **suit** ~에 어울리다 **trendy** 유행하는

02

w Were you able to get a look at the suspect's face?
M Yes. I remember exactly what he looks like.
w Can you describe the man in as much detail as possible?
M Yes. He is medium height and has got shoulder length curly hair.
w Please tell us more about his face.

M He has quite a big nose and a thick lower lip. Also, he has both a beard and a mustache.
w Is he fat or slim?
M Hmm. He is rather muscular.

여 용의자의 얼굴을 볼 수 있으셨습니까?
남 네. 저는 그가 어떻게 생겼는지 정확하게 기억합니다.
여 그 남자를 가능한 한 자세히 묘사해 주시겠습니까?
남 네. 그는 중간 키에 어깨 길이의 곱슬머리였어요.
여 그의 얼굴에 대해서 더 말씀해주세요.
남 코가 상당히 크고 아랫입술이 두꺼웠어요. 또 턱수염과 콧수염 둘 다 있었어요.
여 뚱뚱한가요, 말랐나요?
남 음. 다소 근육질이었어요.

suspect 용의자 **medium** 중간의 **thick** 두꺼운 **lower lip** 아랫입술
beard 턱수염 **mustache** 콧수염

03

w You don't look good today. What's going on?
M I lost my job. I'm just worried about how I'm going to pay the bills.
w I'm sorry to hear that. Have you been looking for another job?
M I've just started, but the job market is very bad right now.
w That's tough. I have some friends who might be able to help you find a job. I'll see what they can do.
M I really appreciate your help.
w No problem. In the meantime, don't worry so much. You'll get through this.

여 오늘 안 좋아 보여요. 무슨 일이에요?
남 일자리를 잃었어요. 공과금들을 어떻게 지불할지 걱정입니다.
여 유감이에요. 다른 일자리를 구하고 있는 중이죠?
남 막 시작했지만, 지금 구직 시장이 매우 상황이 나빠요.
여 어렵네요. 제게 당신이 일자리를 찾을 수 있도록 도울 수도 있을 친구들이 있어요. 그들이 무엇을 해줄 수 있을지 알아볼게요.
남 당신의 도움에 정말 감사 드립니다.
여 천만에요. 그 동안, 너무 걱정하지 마세요. 당신은 이 상황을 꼭 극복해낼 거예요.

① 도움을 주는　②열정적인　③게으른
④ 유머가 있는　⑤겸손한

bill 계산서, 청구서　**job market** 구직시장　**tough** 어려운　**appreciate** 감사하다　**in the meantime** 그동안에　**get through** 빠져나가다, 종료하다

04

M Good morning. This is Mike Johnson, your <u>school</u> <u>counselor</u>. Today is the first day of 'School Counseling Week.' Our focus for the week is 'Building <u>Magical</u> <u>Futures</u>.' This week, we will talk about how you can build <u>your</u> <u>future</u> and make it magical in the process. It starts with <u>setting</u> a <u>goal</u> for where you <u>want to be</u> and steadily <u>working</u> <u>toward</u> that <u>goal</u>. If you need my help, you can <u>come</u> <u>by</u> and talk to me <u>anytime</u>.

남 안녕하세요. 여러분 학교의 상담교사인 Mike Johnson입니다. 오늘은 '학교 상담 주간'의 첫 날입니다. 이 주간의 주안점은 '신비스러운 미래 건설하기'입니다. 이번 주에 우리는, 여러분이 어떻게 미래를 건설하고 그 과정에서 그것을 멋지게 만들 수 있는지에 대해 이야기를 나눌 것입니다. 그것은 여러분이 도달하고 싶은 곳에 대한 목표를 설정하고 꾸준히 그 목표를 향해 노력하는 것으로 시작합니다. 도움이 필요하다면, 여러분은 언제든지 와서 저와 이야기를 나눌 수 있습니다.

counselor 상담사　**focus** 주안점, 초점　**magical** 마법의　**set a goal** 목표를 세우다　**steadily** 꾸준히　**come by** 들르다　**anytime** 언제든지

05

M Hi, I want to purchase a <u>parking</u> <u>permit</u> for next semester.

W Are you a full-time student or do you just <u>come in</u> <u>the evenings</u>?

M I am a full-time student and all <u>my</u> classes are during <u>the</u> <u>day</u>.

W Will you be <u>driving</u> a <u>motorcycle</u> or a <u>car</u>?

M I have both of them but I will <u>use the car</u> to come to <u>school</u>.

W OK, that will be <u>35</u> dollars. If you pay <u>15</u> dollars <u>more</u>, you can get a <u>second</u> <u>permit</u> for the

motorcycle.

M Really? It's cheaper than I expected. I'll buy <u>both</u> <u>permits</u>. Can I use a credit card?

W Sure.

남 안녕하세요. 다음 학기 주차허가증을 사고 싶어요.
여 정규학생인가요, 야간학생인가요?
남 정규학생인데 제 수업이 모두 주간에 있습니다.
여 오토바이와 자동차 중 어떤 것을 이용하실 건가요?
남 둘 다 있지만, 학교에 올 때에는 차를 사용하려고요.
여 네, 그럼 35불이에요. 15불 더 내시면 오토바이에 대한 또 다른 허가증을 받을 수 있습니다.
남 그래요? 예상했던 것보다 더 싸네요. 두 가지 허가증을 다 사겠습니다. 신용카드를 사용해도 되죠?
여 물론이죠.

purchase 구매하다　**permit** 허가, 허가증　**semester** 학기　**full-time** 정규의　**cheap** 값싼

06

W Good afternoon. May I have your <u>ticket</u> please?

M Here you go.

W Are you <u>checking</u> <u>any</u> <u>bags</u>?

M Just one.

W Please place your <u>bag</u> on the <u>scale</u>.

M I have a <u>stopover</u> in Toronto. Do I need to <u>pick up</u> my luggage there?

W No, it'll go straight to your final destination. Here's your <u>boarding</u> <u>pass</u>. Your <u>seat</u> <u>number</u> is 10 E.

M Thank you. Have a nice day.

여 안녕하세요. 탑승권 주시겠어요?
남 여기 있습니다.
여 보낼 짐 있으세요?
남 딱 하나 있습니다.
여 저울에 올려놔 주세요.
남 저는 토론토에서 비행기를 갈아탑니다. 제 짐을 거기에서 찾아야 합니까?
여 아뇨. 짐은 곧장 당신의 최종 목적지로 갈 겁니다. 여기 탑승권 있습니다. 좌석번호는 10E입니다.
남 감사합니다. 즐거운 하루 보내십시오.

① 경찰서　②체육관　③버스정류장
④ 공항　⑤지하철역

scale 저울   **stopover** 도중 하차   **luggage** 여행가방, 수하물
destination 목적지   **boarding pass** 탑승권

07

M Good morning. Can I talk to you for a moment?

W Of course. Is there a problem with your apartment?

M The key you gave me doesn't seem to work well.

W OK, what's the problem? Doesn't the key fit into the lock?

M It fits into the lock just fine, but I can't easily turn it to the right or the left.

W How long do you have to try before it'll open?

M About four or five minutes. It makes me quite angry!

W I see. Actually the man who was living there before you said the lock had a problem.

M Why didn't you get it fixed then?

W Sorry, I didn't have time. I will call a locksmith right away.

남 안녕하세요. 잠깐 이야기 나눌 수 있을까요?

여 물론이죠. 아파트에 무슨 문제라도 있나요?

남 당신이 준 열쇠가 잘 작동하지 않는 것 같아요.

여 어떤 문제인가요? 열쇠가 자물쇠에 잘 안 들어가요?

남 자물쇠에는 잘 들어가는데 오른쪽이나 왼쪽으로 잘 돌릴 수가 없어요.

여 열릴 때까지 얼마나 오랫동안 시도해야 하죠?

남 약 4, 5분 정도요. 정말 화가 납니다!

여 알겠습니다. 사실은 전에 살던 분이 자물쇠에 문제가 있다고 말을 했습니다.

남 그런데 왜 수리를 안 하셨죠?

여 죄송합니다. 시간이 없어서요. 바로 자물쇠 수리공에게 전화하겠습니다.

for a moment 잠시 동안   **work** 작동하다   **fit into** ~에 잘 맞다   **lock** 자물쇠   **locksmith** 자물쇠[열쇠] 수리공

08

M I'm sorry I'm late.

W It's okay. Why are you late anyway?

M I passed by the bus stop by mistake.

W I see. I was wondering whether you were having

M Just my silly mistake. I had to get off at the next stop and run back.

W That's too bad. You must be exhausted and starving.

M Bingo! Let's go in and order something to fill up our stomachs.

W Good. I'm starving to death.

남 늦어서 미안해.

여 괜찮아. 어쨌든 왜 늦었어?

남 실수로 정류장을 지나쳤어.

여 그렇구나. 여기 찾는 데 무슨 문제가 있나 걱정했어.

남 내가 바보 같이 착각한 거지. 다음 정류장에 내려서는 뛰어서 되돌아 왔어.

여 안됐구나. 지치고 배고프겠다.

남 맞아! 들어가서 배를 채울 음식을 주문하자.

여 좋아. 배고파 죽겠어.

pass by 지나치다   **by mistake** 실수로   **silly** 어리석은   **exhaust** 지치게 하다   **fill up** 가득 채우다   **starve** 굶주리다

09

① W A man is ordering hamburgers at a fast food restaurant.

② W There are three people lined up behind the man.

③ W The restaurant employee is wearing a uniform and a cap.

④ W The restaurant employee has black hair.

⑤ W The man is going to pay in cash.

① 여 한 남자가 패스트푸드 레스토랑에서 햄버거를 주문하고 있다.

② 여 그 남자 뒤에는 세 명의 사람들이 줄 서 있다.

③ 여 레스토랑의 종업원은 유니폼에 모자를 쓰고 있다.

④ 여 레스토랑의 종업원은 검은 머리를 하고 있다.

⑤ 여 그 남자는 현금으로 계산할 것이다.

line up 일렬로 세우다, 줄을 서다   **employee** 종업원   **pay in cash** 현금으로 지불하다

10

M Excuse me, ma'am. Please show me your driver's

license.

W　Why? What's the matter?

M　You broke a traffic rule.

W　What? What rule?

M　This is a no parking zone, ma'am. You can't park here.

W　I really don't understand why you are giving me a ticket for parking here. Where is the sign?

M　There's a sign at the corner of the street. You should have seen it.

W　Oh, there it is. I'm so sorry. I didn't see it.

....

남　실례합니다. 부인. 운전면허증을 보여주세요.

여　왜요? 무슨 문제죠?

남　교통 법규를 어기셨습니다.

여　뭐라고요? 무슨 법규를요?

남　이곳은 주차 불가 구역입니다. 부인. 여기서 주차할 수 없습니다.

여　여기 주차했다고 위반 딱지를 주는 것이 정말 이해가 안 되네요.
　　표지판이 어디 있어요?

남　길 모퉁이에 있습니다. 보셨어야 했습니다.

여　오, 저기에 있군요. 죄송합니다. 못 봤어요.

driver's license 운전면허증　**break** 위반하다　**traffic rule** 교통 법규
parking zone 주차 구역

11

M　Winter has almost gone and spring has come. Today is the day on which insects appear from their holes in the earth. It is called "Gyungchip." However, we have bad news again, today. Fine dust from China covers the sky and the sky looks gray. This phenomenon has continued for the last three days. Since this fine dust may cause many health problems, please wear a mask to cover your nose and mouth. Please try not to go out for a long time today and stay inside as long as you can.

....

남　겨울은 거의 다 갔고 봄이 왔습니다. 오늘은 땅속 구멍에서 곤충들이
　　나오는 날입니다. "경칩"이라고 불리지요. 그런데, 오늘 다시 나쁜
　　소식이 있습니다. 중국발 미세먼지가 하늘을 덮어서 하늘이 회색으로
　　보입니다. 이 현상은 지난 3일간 계속돼 왔습니다. 미세먼지는 많은
　　건강 문제를 일으킬 수 있으므로 코와 입을 가릴 마스크를 착용하세요.
　　오늘은 가능한 한 밖에 오랫동안 나가 있지 마시고 최대한 실내에
　　머무십시오.

fine 미세한　**dust** 먼지　**phenomenon** 현상　**cause** 야기하다

12

W　Excuse me, but may I ask you a question?

M　Sure. What is it?

W　How often does Bus 333 come here?

M　Every twenty minutes.

W　What time was the last bus?

M　It was at 2:50.

W　Thank you. I only have ten more minutes to wait.

....

여　실례지만 뭐 좀 여쭤봐도 될까요?

남　물론이죠. 뭡니까?

여　333번 버스는 이곳에 얼마나 자주 오나요?

남　20분마다 옵니다.

여　마지막 버스는 언제였나요?

남　2시 50분이었습니다.

여　감사합니다. 10분만 더 기다리면 되네요.

How often ~? 얼마나 자주~?　**every + 복수형 시간** 매 ~마다

13

[Telephone rings.]

M　Hello?

W　Is that Jake? This is Julie.

M　Hi. It's Jake. What's up?

W　I'm calling to ask you to postpone our appointment. Something urgent came up.

M　You sound sad. Did something bad happen?

W　My mom has been in the hospital since last week. The doctor said it might be pneumonia.

M　I'm so sorry to hear that. When can we meet, then?

W　I think I can make it the day after tomorrow. My sister is going to take a day off work and look after our mom on that day.

M　That's fine with me. We can have lunch then and you can tell me how your mom's doing.

W　Good. I look forward to talking to you then.

....

[전화벨이 울린다.]

남 여보세요?

여 Jake니? 나 Julie야.

남 안녕. 나 Jake야. 무슨 일이야?

여 약속 연기할 수 있는지 물어보려고 전화했어. 급한 일이 생겨서.

남 목소리가 안 좋아 보이네. 안 좋은 일이라도 생긴 거야?

여 엄마가 지난 주부터 병원에 입원해 계셔. 의사선생님이 폐렴일 수도 있대.

남 그 얘길 들으니 마음이 안됐다. 그러면 우리 언제 만날 수 있어?

여 내 생각에 내일모레 괜찮을 것 같아. 언니가 그날 하루 회사에서 휴가 내고 엄마를 돌볼 거거든.

남 나도 괜찮아. 그러면 점심 같이 먹고 엄마가 어떠신지 나한테 얘기해주면 되겠다.

여 알았어. 그날 만나서 얘기하자.

•
postpone 연기하다 **come up** 생기다 **pneumonia** 폐렴 **the day after tomorrow** 내일모레 **look after** 돌보다 **look forward to -ing** ~하는 것을 고대하다

14

M Do you remember the place where we met for the first time?

W Umm, wasn't it in front of the library on the first day of school?

M No. Try to recall it from your memory.

W Sorry. I really have a bad memory. Where was it?

M It was at the front entrance of the Grace Department Store last Christmas.

W Right. Right. Now I remember. I asked you where the ice cream shop was.

M Yes. Then we met again in this classroom.

W Yeah. I was very glad to meet you again.

M So was I.

남 우리가 맨 처음 만났던 장소 기억해?

여 음. 내가 첫 등교하던 날 도서관 앞에서였나?

남 아니. 기억을 떠올려봐.

여 미안해. 나는 정말로 기억력이 안 좋아. 어디였니?

남 지난 크리스마스 때 그레이스 백화점 정문이었어.

여 맞아. 맞아. 이제 기억 나. 내가 너한테 아이스크림 가게가 어디 있는지 물어봤었어.

남 응. 그리고 이 교실에서 다시 만났지.

여 응. 너를 다시 만나서 정말 반가웠어.

남 나도.

••
for the first time 처음으로 **in front of** ~ 앞에 **entrance** 입구, 입장 **recall** 생각해내다 **memory** 기억, 기억력

15

M Look at this poster!

W Oh, it's about the Monet exhibition. Are you interested in his paintings?

M Interested? I'm crazy about his works, especially *The Water Lily*.

W Oh, I feel the same as you. *The Water Lily* is the greatest painting that I have ever seen.

M Then why don't you go to the exhibition with me?

W Sure, I'd love to. I think we won't be able to get into it without a reservation because it's so popular.

M Okay. I'll make a reservation on the Internet.

남 이 포스터 좀 봐!

여 오, 모네 전시회에 관한 거네. 너 그의 그림에 관심 있니?

남 관심 있냐고? 나는 그의 작품들, 특히 〈수련〉을 미칠 듯이 좋아해.

여 오, 동감이야. 〈수련〉은 내가 본 최고의 그림이야.

남 그럼 나랑 그 전시회에 가지 않을래?

여 물론이지. 나도 가고 싶어. 이 전시회는 인기가 많아서 예매 안 하면 들어가기 힘들 것 같아.

남 알았어. 내가 인터넷으로 예매할게.

••
exhibition 전시회 **be interested in** ~에 관심이 있다 **be crazy about** ~에 푹 빠지다 **without** ~ 없이 **reservation** 예약

16

① M Is it okay if I park my car here?

  W I'm afraid I can't.

② M Is this your first time to visit Jeju Island?

  W Yes, I've always wanted to come here.

③ M Do you have any good books to recommend?

W Well, I think you'll like *Tuesdays With Morrie*.
④ M Which team do you think will win the game?
W I think Korea will win.
⑤ M You are late again.
W I'm sorry, but the traffic was heavy.

---

① 남 제 차를 여기에 주차해도 될까요?
여 죄송하지만 저는 할 수 없어요.
② 남 제주도 방문이 처음이니?
여 응, 난 늘 여기에 오고 싶었어.
③ 남 추천할 만한 좋은 책이 있니?
여 글쎄, 나는 네가 〈모리와 함께한 화요일〉을 좋아할 거라고 생각해.
④ 남 너는 어느 팀이 경기에서 이길 거라고 생각하니?
여 나는 한국이 이길 거라고 생각해.
⑤ 남 너 또 늦었구나.
여 미안해. 하지만 교통체증이 심했어.

park 주차하다 **recommend** 추천하다 **heavy** 심한, 무거운

17

W Good afternoon, sir. How may I help you?
M Hello. I'm looking for the perfect vacation spot for my family.
W Do you have any place in mind?
M I'm thinking of somewhere in the Philippines.
W How about Blue Water Resort in Cebu? It is a convenient and relaxing resort with a variety of leisure and sporting activities.
M Good. I have always wanted to go to such a resort.
W You may also lounge on the private beach and at one of the three swimming pools.
M Great. And what kinds of water sports can I enjoy?
W You can enjoy wakeboarding, kayaking, snorkeling, and fishing. Oh, they are offering a special rate now. Don't miss out.

여 안녕하세요. 손님. 어떻게 도와드릴까요?
남 안녕하세요. 가족을 위한 완벽한 휴가지를 찾고 있습니다.
여 마음에 두신 곳이 있습니까?
남 필리핀 어딘가를 생각하고 있습니다.
여 Cebu에 있는 Blue Water 리조트는 어떠세요? 다양한 레저와 스포츠 활동을 할 수 있는 편리하고 편안한 휴양지입니다.
남 좋습니다. 전 항상 그런 곳에 가보고 싶었습니다.

여 전용 해변가와 세 개의 수영장 중 하나에서 느긋하게 시간을 보낼 수도 있습니다.
남 멋지네요. 그런데 어떤 해양 스포츠를 즐길 수 있을까요?
여 웨이크보딩 타기, 카약 타기, 스노클링, 낚시 등을 하실 수 있습니다. 오, 지금 특별 할인가를 제공하고 있네요. 놓치지 마세요.

convenient 편리한 **relaxing** 느긋하게 하는 **lounge** 느긋하게 보내다
private 사적인 **rate** 요금 **miss out** 놓치다

18

W Anne's birthday is tomorrow. Tom is going to her birthday party. But he hasn't decided what to buy for her. He has to stop by a mall later today to buy a present. On his way to school, he meets Cindy. She says she also hasn't decided what to buy for Anne. Tom wants to go to the mall with Cindy and then they can help each other pick out something nice for Anne. In this situation what would Tom most likely say to Cindy?

여 Anne의 생일이 내일이다. Tom은 그녀의 생일파티에 갈 예정이다. 하지만 그는 그녀를 위해 무엇을 살지 아직 결정하지 못했다. 그는 오늘 나중에 선물 사러 가게에 들러야 한다. 학교에 가는 길에, 그는 Cindy를 만난다. 그녀는 자신도 아직 Anne을 위해 뭘 사야 할지 결정하지 못했다고 말한다. Tom은 Cindy와 함께 가게에 가고 싶어하는데 그러면 그들은 Anne을 위한 뭔가 좋은 것을 고르는 데 서로 도움이 될 수 있다. 이 상황에서 Tom은 Cindy에게 뭐라고 말할 것 같은가?

① 이건 마음에 안 드네요. 다른 거 보여주실래요?
② 너 내일 Anne의 생일파티에 갈 거니?
③ Anne을 위해 깜짝 생일파티 여는 거 어때?
④ 같이 쇼핑 가서 Anne에게 줄 선물을 사자.
⑤ 네 생일파티에 갈 수 없어서 정말 미안해.

stop by 들르다 **mall** 상점가 **later** 나중에, 뒤에 **present** 선물 **on one's way to** ~로 가는 길에

19

[Telephone rings.]
W Hello.
M Hello. This is ABC Delivery Service. Is this Ms. Sue Robins?

W Yes, this is <u>she</u>. Do you have <u>something</u> for me?

M Yes. Will you be in your office <u>around</u> 3 p.m.?

W Oh, sorry. I'll be <u>out</u> <u>on</u> <u>business</u> at that time. Can you <u>come</u> <u>by</u> at <u>1:30</u> p.m.?

M Let me see. Sorry, I <u>can't</u> <u>make</u> <u>it</u>.

W Then can you leave the package <u>at</u> <u>the</u> <u>front</u> <u>desk</u>?

M Okay. I'll see that it's delivered there by 3.

. . . .

[전화벨이 울린다.]

여 여보세요.

남 여보세요. ABC 택배서비스입니다. Sue Robins 씨이신가요?

여 네, 접니다. 제게 배달할 것이 있습니까?

남 네. 오후 3시쯤 사무실에 계실 건가요?

여 오, 죄송해요. 그 시간에는 업무차 외근 나갈 겁니다. 1시 30분에 들를 수 있겠습니까?

남 어디 볼까요. 죄송합니다. 안 되겠네요.

여 그럼 프런트데스크에 짐다발을 두고 가시겠습니까?

남 좋아요. 오후 3시까지 거기로 배달되도록 하겠습니다.

① 물론이죠. 다른 걸로 가져가세요.
② 지금 그곳에 갈 건가요?
③ 배달 비용은 얼마죠?
④ 이 꾸러미를 시드니로 보내고 싶어요.
⑤ 좋아요. 오후 3시까지 거기로 배달되도록 하겠습니다.

delivery 배달 **on business** 업무차, 사업차 **come by** 들르다 **make it** 도착하다, 해내다 **leave** 남기고 가다

20

M You look <u>worried</u>. What's wrong with you?

W Well, I have <u>a</u> <u>big</u> <u>interview</u> today.

M Oh, do you? What kind of <u>interview</u> is it?

W I have <u>a</u> <u>final</u> <u>interview</u> for a job. I applied for <u>a</u> <u>job</u> in <u>a</u> <u>large</u> <u>company</u> last month.

M Oh, great! When is it?

W <u>At</u> <u>eleven</u> <u>thirty</u> in the morning. I'm really <u>nervous</u>.

M Don't worry. I'm sure you'll do well.

. . . .

남 너 걱정 있어 보여. 무슨 문제 있니?

여 음, 오늘 중요한 인터뷰가 있어.

남 오, 그래? 어떤 종류의 인터뷰야?

여 최종 취업 면접이 있어. 지난달 어느 대기업 일자리에 지원했거든.

남 오, 멋진데! 언제니?

여 오전 11시 30분이야. 나 너무 긴장 돼.

남 걱정하지 마. 난 네가 잘 할 거라고 확신해.

① 오, 정말? 축하해!
② 내가 이력서 쓰는 거 도와줄게.
③ 걱정하지 마. 난 네가 잘 할 거라고 확신해.
④ 넌 입사 지원서를 온라인으로 제출해도 돼.
⑤ 수련 프로그램에 참가해보는 건 어때?

apply for ~에 지원하다 **nervous** 긴장한

Further Study 정답   p. 34

1. The reason is that he <u>lost his job</u> and he is worried about how <u>he is going to pay the bills</u>.

2. He buys parking permits for <u>both a car and a motorcycle</u>.

3. It fits <u>into the lock</u> fine, but he can't easily <u>turn it to the right or the left</u>.

4. The reason is that he <u>passed by the bus stop by mistake</u>.

5. It is <u>at the corner of the street</u>.

6. It is the day when <u>insects appear from their holes in the earth</u>.

7. The reason is that <u>she will be out on business around 3 p.m.</u>

8. She has <u>a final interview for a job</u> at <u>11:30</u> in the morning.

On Your Own 모범답안   p. 35

A

Changing an Appointment	
(1) The receiver	Hyerim
(2) Your original plan	meet at 2:00 p.m. on Saturday in front of the school gate to go shopping
(3) Your reason to change it	have to go to my nephew's 1st birthday party on the same day at noon
(4) Your changed plan	meet her around 5:00 p.m. in front of her apartment building

Dear (1)Hyerim,

Hello. This is Mina. I am writing this because I'd like to change our appointment. Our original plan was (2)to meet at 2:00 p.m. on Saturday in front of the school gate to go shopping. However, I have to (3)go to my nephew's 1st birthday party on the same day at noon. So, if it is okay with you, I'd like to (4)meet you around 5:00 p.m. in front of your apartment building instead. I'm sorry for changing the appointment.

약속 변경	
(1) 받는 사람	혜림
(2) 원래 계획	토요일 오후 2시에 학교 정문 앞에서 만나 쇼핑 가기로 함
(3) 변경 이유	같은 날 정오에 조카의 돌잔치에 가야 함
(4) 변경된 계획	오후 5시경 그녀의 아파트 건물 앞에서 만남

혜림이에게,
안녕. 나 미나야. 나는 우리 약속을 변경하고 싶어서 이 글을 써. 우리가 원래는 쇼핑하러 가려고 토요일 오후 2시에 우리 학교 정문 앞에서 만나기로 했었지. 그런데 그날 정오에 내 조카 돌잔치에 가야 해. 그래서 만일 네가 괜찮다면 대신 오후 5시경에 너네 아파트 건물 앞에서 만났으면 해. 약속을 변경하게 되어 미안해.

B

School Uniforms	
Reasons for agreeing	Supporting examples
(1) can help students to focus on their school work better	(2) students don't have to waste time picking out clothes every morning; have more time to study
(3) can help reduce bullying at school	(4) students can often get bullied for wearing certain clothes that are unique or different from others'

I agree that students should wear school uniforms for two main reasons. First, (1)wearing school uniforms can help them to focus on their school work better. For example, (2)students don't have to waste time picking out clothes every morning. Then, they have more time to study. Second, (3)uniforms can help reduce bullying at school. For example, (4)students can often get bullied for wearing certain clothes that are unique or different from others'. For these reasons, I am for school uniforms.

교복	
찬성하는 이유	뒷받침 예
(1) 학생들이 학교 공부에 더 집중하는 데 도움이 됨	(2) 학생들이 매일 아침 옷을 고르느라 시간을 낭비할 필요가 없음; 공부하는 데 더 많은 시간을 가질 수 있음
(3) 학교에서 집단 괴롭힘을 줄이는 데 도움이 됨	(4) 학생들이 독특하거나 다른 사람들과 다른 옷을 입는 것으로 인해 집단 괴롭힘을 당하는 경우가 종종 있음

나는 두 가지 중요한 이유로 학생들은 교복을 입어야 한다는 것에 동의합니다. 첫 번째로, 교복을 입는 것은 그들이 학교 공부에 더 집중하는 데 도움이 됩니다. 예를 들면 학생들이 매일 아침 옷을 고르느라 시간을 낭비할 필요가 없습니다. 그러면 그들은 공부하는 데 더 많은 시간을 가질 수 있습니다. 두 번째로, 교복은 학교에서 집단 괴롭힘을 줄이는 데 도움이 될 수 있습니다. 예를 들면, 학생들이 독특하거나 다른 사람들과 다른 옷을 입는 것으로 인해 집단 괴롭힘을 당하는 경우가 종종 있습니다. 이런 이유들로 인해, 저는 교복 착용에 찬성합니다.

04 Listening Test 정답   p. 40

01 ⑤	02 ⑤	03 ④	04 ③	05 ②
06 ④	07 ②	08 ②	09 ①	10 ⑤
11 ③	12 ③	13 ①	14 ③	15 ①
16 ①	17 ④	18 ④	19 ③	20 ②

01

W Have you seen Amanda's daughter?
M No, I haven't. I didn't even know Amanda has a daughter.

W Oh, yes she does! Her daughter, Jessica, is two years old. She is so <u>cute</u> and <u>adorable</u>.

M Tell me <u>what she looks like</u>.

W She has <u>blonde hair</u> and beautiful <u>blue eyes</u>. She is also <u>growing</u> some <u>front teeth</u>.

M Is she big or small?

W She's not big but <u>a little plump</u>.

M Sounds like she is really adorable.

여 Amanda의 딸을 본 적 있니?

남 아니. 나는 Amanda가 딸이 있는 줄도 몰랐어.

여 오, 그녀에게는 딸이 있어. 그녀의 딸, Jessica는 두 살이야. 그녀는 너무 귀엽고 사랑스러워.

남 아기가 어떻게 생겼는지 말해줘.

여 금발에 아름다운 푸른 눈을 가졌어. 또한 앞니 몇 개가 자라나고 있어.

남 아기가 큰 편이야, 작은 편이야?

여 크진 않지만, 약간 통통해.

남 정말 사랑스러울 것 같아.

adorable 사랑스러운 **blonde** 금발의 **front tooth** 앞니 **plump** 통통한

02

M Mom, when are you going <u>grocery shopping</u>?

W This afternoon, maybe. Let's make a list. What do you <u>need</u>?

M I need pretzels and mango juice.

W We also need <u>spinach</u> and <u>cabbage</u>. What fruits do you want me to buy?

M I want apples, <u>strawberries</u>, and <u>plums</u>.

W Alright, but I'll buy the plums <u>tomorrow</u>. They are <u>on sale</u> on Wednesday.

M Okay. Oh, mom! We also have to buy some <u>eggs</u> and <u>flour</u> to make a cake for <u>Dad's birthday</u>.

W Yes, that's right. I almost forgot.

남 엄마, 장 보러 언제 가실 거예요?

여 아마도 오늘 오후에 갈 것 같다. 목록을 만들어보자. 넌 뭐가 필요하니?

남 저는 프리첼과 망고 주스가 필요해요.

여 시금치와 양배추도 필요해. 과일은 어떤 걸 샀으면 하니?

남 저는 사과, 딸기, 그리고 자두를 먹고 싶어요.

여 좋아, 하지만 자두는 내일 사야겠어. 수요일에 할인판매를 하거든.

남 좋아요. 참, 엄마! 아빠 생일 케이크를 만들려면 달걀과 밀가루도 사야 해요.

여 그래, 맞아. 나는 거의 잊고 있었구나.

grocery 식료품류, 식품점 **spinach** 시금치 **plum** 자두 **flour** 밀가루

03

M It's <u>getting hotter</u> and <u>hotter</u>. Shall we turn on the air-conditioner?

W No, we shouldn't.

M No? Why do you say no?

W With the <u>rising cost of electricity</u>, we'd better use these hand-held <u>fans</u>.

M That won't keep me cool. I <u>can't stand</u> it when I'm hot. Look! I'm <u>all sweaty</u>.

W How about turning on the electric fan then? It will keep you cool, and we can <u>save energy</u>.

M Okay. Okay. I will.

W Thanks for your understanding. It's better for our <u>two little boys</u>, too.

남 점점 더 더워지네. 에어컨 켤까?

여 아니. 안 돼.

남 안 돼? 왜 안 된다고 해?

여 전기료가 인상되고 있어서 이 손에 잡는 부채를 사용하는 게 나아.

남 그걸로는 난 시원하지 않을 거야. 난 더위는 못 참아. 봐! 나 땀에 다 젖었잖아.

여 그러면 선풍기를 켜는 건 어때? 시원하기도 하고, 전기료도 절약할 수 있어.

남 알았어. 알았어. 그렇게 할게.

여 이해해줘서 고마워. 선풍기가 우리 어린 두 아들에게도 더 나아.

비교급＋비교급 점점 더 ~한 **cost** 비용 **electricity** 전기 **stand** 참다, 견디다 **sweaty** 땀에 젖은 **save** 절약하다, 저축하다

04

M Excuse me. I'm looking for a <u>shirt</u> in a <u>medium size</u>.

W Let's see, here's a nice <u>blue</u> one. What do you think?

M I think I'd rather have it <u>in white</u>.

W Okay, here it is. Would you like to <u>try it on</u>?

M Yes, I would. I'll go to the <u>fitting room</u>. [pause] It fits well. <u>How much is it</u>?

W It is on sale. Just <u>33</u> dollars, including 10% tax.

M Then, I'll take <u>one</u> in a <u>large</u> size for my brother and <u>one</u> in a <u>medium</u> size for me.

남 실례합니다. 중간 치수의 셔츠를 사려고 합니다.
여 네, 여기에 괜찮은 파란색 셔츠가 있어요. 어떠세요?
남 하얀색이 더 좋을 것 같아요.
여 네, 여기 있습니다. 한번 입어보시겠어요?
남 네, 좋아요. 탈의실에 가야겠어요. 저한테 잘 맞네요. 얼마입니까?
여 할인 중이에요. 10% 세금 포함해서 33달러입니다.
남 그럼, 형에게 줄 큰 사이즈 하나와, 제가 입을 중간 사이즈 하나 주세요.

••
try on 입어보다 **fitting room** 탈의실 **fit** 꼭 맞다 **on sale** 할인 중인
tax 세금

05

W Peter, you <u>did well</u> on this physics test. I almost failed it.

M Yes, I <u>passed it</u> this time.

W Don't you <u>usually fail</u> physics tests?

M Things were <u>different</u> this time. I <u>sat</u> next to a <u>science genius</u>.

W You mean you <u>took a peek</u> at his test?

M No. I mean for three months I've sat <u>next to</u> him in <u>physics class</u> and learned from him.

W Oh, wow. Is he kind and helpful?

M Absolutely. <u>If it had</u> not <u>been for</u> him, I would have <u>failed again</u>.

여 Peter, 너 물리시험 잘 봤구나. 난 거의 낙제인데.
남 응, 이번에는 통과했지.
여 너 물리시험에서 대개 낙제하지 않았어?
남 이번에는 달랐어. 내가 과학 천재 옆에 앉았거든.
여 그의 시험지를 엿봤다는 거니?
남 아니. 세 달 동안 물리 시간에 걔 옆에 앉아서 배웠다는 거지.
여 아, 우와. 그가 친절하고 잘 도와주니?
남 완전히. 만약 걔가 아니었더라면 난 다시 낙제했을 거야.

① 자랑스러워하는   ② 부러워하는   ③ 감사하는
④ 죄책감이 드는   ⑤ 절망적인

••
physics 물리학 **genius** 천재 **If it had not been for** (가정법

과거완료) 만약 ~이 없었다면

06

M Do you need a vacation <u>from your children</u>? We are happy to share some <u>information</u> about the Green Club Day Camp. Our new day camp that starts in early June will be <u>fun</u>, <u>exciting</u> and <u>enjoyable</u>. This year the kids will enjoy <u>hiking</u>, <u>swimming</u>, <u>singing</u>, and doing <u>arts and crafts</u>. You will get some free time and have <u>peace of mind</u>. If you need any information about <u>registration</u>, please contact Jane at 231-7823.

남 자녀로부터의 휴가가 필요하십니까? Green Club 주간캠프에 대한 몇 가지 정보를 드리게 되어서 기쁩니다. 6월 초에 시작되는 저희의 새로운 주간캠프는 재미있고, 신나며 즐거울 것입니다. 올해에는 아이들이 하이킹, 수영, 노래 부르기, 그리고 공예를 즐길 것입니다. 여러분들은 자유 시간을 얻고 마음의 평안을 갖게 될 겁니다. 등록에 관한 정보가 필요하시다면, 231-7823번 Jane에게 연락해주세요.

••
enjoyable 즐거운 **arts and crafts** 공예 **registration** 등록
contact 연락하다, 접촉하다

07

W What time is the baseball game on? I thought it <u>started at noon</u>.

M We <u>must have</u> the wrong time. Well, baseball's not my favorite sport anyway. I <u>much prefer tennis</u>.

W Oh, really? I thought your favorite sport was basketball! I'm a <u>big fan of tennis</u>, too.

M How about playing a game sometime?

W Sure thing! <u>Why don't we</u> go to the <u>grass court now</u>?

M <u>Why not</u>? Let's go!

여 그 야구경기 언제 방송해? 나는 정오에 시작한다고 생각했거든.
남 우리가 시간을 잘못 안 것 같아. 어쨌든 야구는 내가 좋아하는 스포츠도 아니야. 나는 테니스를 훨씬 좋아해.
여 정말? 나는 네가 농구를 좋아하는 줄 알았어. 나도 테니스를 엄청 좋아해.
남 언제 게임 한 번 하는 거 어때?
여 물론이지! 지금 잔디 코트로 갈까?

남 그러자. 가자!

have the wrong time 시간을 잘못 알다   **prefer** 더 좋아하다   **court** 뜰,
코트, 법정

08

M Taeyeon, what's up? You look so tired.

W Yeah. Actually, I am very sleepy now. I stayed up late last night doing my science homework.

M Why did it take so long?

W Well, in fact I started to do it after watching Gag Concert.

M Now I see. You should have done your homework first before watching TV.

W I know. But the time just went so fast. I think I'd better organize my schedule and try to follow a regular routine every day.

M That's the point. If you try to do that, you won't be sleepy at school.

W Thanks for your advice.

남 태연아, 무슨 일이야? 무척 피곤해 보여.

여 응. 사실은 지금 너무 졸려. 과학 숙제 하느라고 어젯밤 늦게까지 깨어있었거든.

남 왜 그렇게 시간이 많이 걸렸던 거야?

여 음, 사실은 개그콘서트 다 보고 시작했거든.

남 이제 알겠네. TV를 보기 전에 숙제를 먼저 했어야지.

여 알아. 그런데 이번에 시간이 너무 빨리 지나갔어. 일정을 체계적으로 잘 정리해서 매일 규칙적인 일과를 따르도록 노력해야 할 것 같아.

남 바로 그거야. 네가 그렇게 한다면 학교에서 졸릴 이유도 없을 거야.

여 충고 고마워.

stay up 자지 않고 깨어있다   **organize** 조직하다, 체계화하다   **should
have p.p.** ~했어야 했다   **regular** 규칙적인, 일상의   **routine** 판에 박힌
일, 일과

09

M Excuse me. Do you know how to get to Pizza Nara from here?

W Sure. Go straight for one block and turn left at the corner.

M And then?

W Keep going one block and turn right at the corner.

M Okay. And?

W Go straight for one more block. At the end of the block, you'll see Pizza Nara on your left. You can't miss it.

M Thank you very much for helping me.

W My pleasure.

남 실례합니다. 여기서 Pizza Nara까지 어떻게 가는지 아시나요?

여 물론입니다. 한 블록을 곧장 가신 후 길 모퉁이에서 왼쪽으로 두세요.

남 그리고요?

여 계속해서 한 블록 가서 길 모퉁이에서 오른쪽으로 도세요.

남 네. 그리고요?

여 한 블록 더 곧장 가세요. 블록 끝에서 당신의 왼쪽에 Pizza Nara가 있을 겁니다. 쉽게 찾을 거예요.

남 도와주셔서 정말 감사합니다.

여 천만에요.

go straight 직진하다   **turn left[right]** 왼쪽[오른쪽]으로 돌다   **You
can't miss it**. 쉽게 찾을 겁니다.

10

W David, what are you writing in the planner?

M I am writing down my weekend plans.

W Plans? What are you going to do?

M Well, I am going to go to the museum on Saturday morning, and then go to a math class right after that.

W Oh, you'll be busy. What about on Sunday?

M On Sunday morning, I will go to church. After lunch, I will clean my room. Fortunately, I've already done my homework.

W Then you can rest.

M That's right. It will be a good weekend.

여 David, 일정장부에 무엇을 적고 있는 거니?

남 주말 계획을 적고 있어.

여 계획? 뭐 할 건데?

남 음. 토요일 오전에 박물관에 가고, 그런 다음에 곧바로 수학수업에 갈 거야.

여 오, 바쁘겠네. 일요일은 어때?

남 일요일 아침에는 교회에 갈 거야. 점심 먹은 후엔 방 청소를 할 거고. 다행히 숙제는 다 했어.

여 그러면 쉴 수 있겠다.

남 맞아. 괜찮은 주말이 될 거야.

•• **fortunately** 운이 좋게도 **rest** 쉬다

11

w Boys and Girls! Welcome to the CYJ Speech Contest. We will award medals and prizes to the top three speakers. Also, we'll give all the participants a 5,000 won gift voucher just for taking part in the contest. Moreover, there will be a draw and two audience members will receive an MP3 player. So please keep your tickets which have the numbers for the draw. The panel of judges not only judges the fluency but also the accuracy of the pronunciation. Each participant should observe the time limit of five minutes. Are you ready? Don't be nervous. Let's start with number one.

여 소년 소녀 여러분! CYJ 말하기 경연대회에 오신 것을 환영합니다. 제일 잘한 3명의 연사에게는 메달과 상품을 수여할 것입니다. 또한, 모든 참가자들에게는 대회에 참가한 것만으로도 5,000원 상품권이 주어집니다. 더 나아가, 추첨이 있을 것인데 두 명의 방청객이 mp3 플레이어를 받게 될 것입니다. 그러니 추첨을 위한 번호가 있는 표를 잘 가지고 계십시오. 심사위원들은 유창성뿐만 아니라 발음의 정확성도 채점할 것입니다. 모든 참가자들은 제한 시간 5분을 준수해야 합니다. 준비되셨나요? 떨지 마세요. 1번부터 시작하겠습니다.

•• **participant** 참가자 **gift voucher** 상품권 **take part in** ~에 참가하다 **draw** 추첨 **panel** 심사원단, 토론집단 **not only A but also B** A뿐만 아니라 B도 **fluency** 유창성 **accuracy** 정확성

12

[Telephone rings.]

M Hello.

w Hello, Tim. This is Kate. Are we still on for dinner?

M Of course, Kate. I am thinking about which restaurant is good for us. Would you like Chinese food?

w Sounds great! What time shall we meet?

M How about five? Is it okay with you?

w Isn't that too early for dinner? How about an hour after that?

M Fine. I will stop by the library to return books then. It closes at five thirty.

w Good. See you then.

[전화벨이 울린다.]

남 여보세요.

여 안녕, Tim. 나 Kate야. 우리 저녁 식사 유효한 거야?

남 물론이지, Kate. 우리한테 어떤 식당이 좋을까 생각하고 있어. 중국음식 괜찮겠어?

여 좋아! 몇 시에 만날까?

남 5시 어때? 괜찮아?

여 저녁으로는 좀 이르지 않아? 그 시간의 한 시간 후 어때?

남 좋아. 그러면 책 반납하러 도서관에 들러야겠다. 5시 30분에 문 닫거든.

여 그래. 이따 보자.

•• **still** 여전히, 아직도 **be on for** ~을 원하다 **stop by** 들르다 **return** 반환하다

13

w Good morning. How may I help you?

M Good morning. I want to send this parcel to New Zealand.

w Okay. Do you want to send it by airmail or surface mail?

M I think I'll send it by airmail. I want it to get there as soon as possible. How much does it cost?

w It depends on the weight. Please put the parcel on the scale. Let's check.

M Okay. How much is it?

w It weighs 3 kilograms. That will be 25 dollars. Are you going to pay in cash or by card?

M In cash. Here you are.

w Thank you.

여 안녕하세요. 무엇을 도와드릴까요?

남 안녕하세요. 이 소포를 뉴질랜드로 보내고 싶습니다.

여 네. 항공우편으로 보내시겠습니까, 육상우편으로 보내시겠습니까?

남 항공우편으로 해주세요. 가능한 한 빨리 도착하길 원해서요. 얼마죠?

여 무게에 따라 다릅니다. 소포를 저울 위에 올려주세요. 확인해 볼게요.

남 네. 얼마입니까?

여 3킬로그램이네요. 그러면 25달러입니다. 현금으로 하시겠어요, 카드로 하시겠어요?

남 현금요. 여기 있습니다.

여 감사합니다.

··
parcel 꾸러미, 소포 **airmail** 항공우편 **surface mail** (해상 포함)
육상우편 **as soon as possible** 가능한 한 빨리 **depend on** ~에 달려
있다

14

W Don't you find these rowing machines <u>hard</u> work?

M I certainly do, but they're supposed to be.

W <u>How</u> <u>often</u> do you come here for a <u>workout</u>?

M Three times a week at least.

W No wonder you look so <u>fit</u> and <u>trim</u>.

M Thank you for saying that. <u>Stick</u> <u>at</u> <u>it</u> and you can be the same.

W By the way, did you finish the <u>geometry</u> <u>project</u>?

M Not yet. I am going to <u>meet</u> the <u>project</u> <u>members</u> this afternoon <u>to discuss</u> what to do.

여 이 로잉머신들 너무 힘들지 않아?

남 나도 힘들지만 이것들은 원래 힘든 거야.

여 너는 운동하러 여기에 얼마나 자주 오니?

남 적어도 일주일에 세 번은 와.

여 그래서 그렇게 건강하고 말쑥하게 보이는구나.

남 그렇게 말해줘서 고마워. 꾸준히 하면 너도 그렇게 될 거야.

여 그런데, 기하학 과제 했니?

남 아니, 아직. 오늘 오후에 과제 팀원들 만나서 무엇을 할지 의논하기로 했어.

··
row 노 젓다 **workout** 운동 **at least** 최소한 **fit** 건강한 **trim** 말쑥한
stick at ~을 꾸준히 하다 **geometry** 기하학

15

① M It opens at 12:00 <u>throughout</u> <u>the</u> <u>year</u>.

② M It does not open on <u>Lunar</u> <u>New</u> Year's Day.

③ M The schedule for summer and winter vacations <u>hasn't</u> <u>been</u> <u>decided</u> yet.

④ M Six-year-old <u>children</u> pay <u>5</u> dollars to enter the rink.

⑤ M <u>Figure</u> <u>skates</u> can be rented at <u>30</u> dollars <u>for</u> <u>2</u>

hours.

```
Royal 아이스 링크

• 시간
  주중 : 14:00~18:00
  주말 & 공휴일 : 12:00~18:00
  여름방학 & 겨울방학 : 추후 공지 예정
  설날 휴관
• 요금
  입장 : 성인 20달러, 학생 10달러, 5~7세 어린이 5달러
  스케이트 대여 : 스피드 2시간 25달러
              피겨 2시간 30달러
• 주차 : 무료
```

① 남 1년 내내 낮 12시에 개장한다.

② 남 설날에는 문을 열지 않는다.

③ 남 여름방학과 겨울방학 일정은 아직 결정되지 않았다.

④ 남 6세 어린이는 5달러에 입장 가능하다.

⑤ 남 피겨스케이트는 2시간에 30달러로 빌릴 수 있다.

··
throughout ~ 동안 내내 **lunar** 음력의 **schedule** 일정 **decide**
결정하다, 결심하다 **enter** 입장하다 **rent** 빌리다

16

W Tom, can you <u>do</u> <u>me</u> <u>a</u> <u>favor</u>?

M Sure. What is it?

W Will you please help me <u>separate</u> <u>the</u> <u>garbage</u>?

M Okay. <u>What</u> <u>should</u> <u>I</u> <u>do</u>?

W Will you please put paper, <u>cans</u> and <u>plastics</u> into the right <u>recycling</u> <u>bins</u>?

M [Pause] I'm <u>done</u>. What else can I do for you?

W Can you <u>dispose</u> <u>of</u> the <u>food</u> <u>waste</u>? Take it outside and put it in the food waste <u>garbage</u> <u>can</u>.

M No problem.

여 Tom, 내 부탁 좀 들어줄래?

남 그럼. 뭐야?

여 내가 쓰레기 분리하는 거 좀 도와줄래?

남 좋아. 난 뭘 해야 돼?

여 이 종이와 캔, 플라스틱들을 올바른 재활용함에 넣어줄래?

남 다 했어. 다른 거 또 뭐 하지?

여 음식 쓰레기를 버려줄래? 밖으로 가져가서 음식 쓰레기통에 넣어줘.

남 알았어.

17

① M What's your topic for the project?

　W I'm thinking of the history of the French Revolution.

② M Congratulations on your graduation.

　W Thank you so much.

③ M What would you do if you found money on the street?

　W I would take it to the police station.

④ M My wallet was stolen. What should I do?

　W I called the police last night.

⑤ M You often make me wait for you.

　W Sorry about that.

- -

① 남 너 프로젝트 주제가 뭐니?

　여 프랑스 혁명의 역사에 관해 생각하고 있어.

② 남 졸업 축하해.

　여 정말 고마워.

③ 남 만약에 길에서 돈을 발견한다면, 너는 어떻게 할 거니?

　여 나는 경찰서에 가져다 줄 거야.

④ 남 지갑을 도둑맞았어. 어떻게 해야 하지?

　여 내가 어젯밤에 경찰에 전화했어.

⑤ 남 넌 자주 내가 너를 기다리게 만들어.

　여 그 점 미안해.

18

[Telephone rings.]

W Hello, Megan speaking. Who's calling, please?

M Hi, Megan. It's Sean. How are you doing in the hospital?

W I'm dying to go home and to school. I'll be discharged in a few days.

M Congratulations! I have got some school news for you. We have a full day of make-up classes this Saturday. Will you go to them?

W Of course, I'll definitely go.

M It's for the cancelled classes last Wednesday, due to Typhoon Eagle. So classes will follow the Wednesday schedule.

W Yes, I thought that was the reason. Can we wear casual clothes on that day?

M No. We will have to be in our uniform as usual. The school buses will run temporarily on the usual timetable, too.

- -

[전화벨이 울린다.]

여 여보세요, Megan입니다. 전화하신 분은 누구죠?

남 안녕, Megan. 나야 Sean. 병원에서 잘 지내고 있니?

여 집이랑 학교에 가고 싶어 죽겠어. 며칠 내로 퇴원할 거야.

남 축하해! 네게 들려줄 학교 소식이 좀 있어. 이번 토요일에 전일 보충수업이 있어. 너 갈 거니?

여 물론이지. 나 꼭 갈 거야.

남 태풍 독수리로 인해 지난 수요일에 취소되었던 수업을 위한 거야. 그래서 수업은 수요일 일정을 따른대.

여 응, 그게 이유일 줄 알았어. 그날 사복을 입어도 되니?

남 안 돼. 평소대로 교복을 입어야 돼. 스쿨버스도 평상시 시간표에 따라 일시적으로 운행될 거래.

19

M Judy wants to join the tennis club but she doesn't know how to join it. She calls the club office and asks how to apply to join the club. The man on the phone says she can apply at the club website. Now Judy has another question. As she doesn't have her own tennis racket, she wants to know if the club has rackets for the members to use. In this situation, what would Judy most likely say to the man?

- -

남 Judy는 테니스 클럽에 가입하고 싶지만 가입방법을 모른다. 그녀는 클럽 사무실에 전화해서 클럽에 지원하는 방법을 묻는다. 전화상의 남자는 클럽 웹사이트에서 지원할 수 있다고 말한다. 이제 Judy는 다른 질문이 있다. 그녀는 테니스 라켓이 없기 때문에 회원들이 사용할 라켓을 클럽이 구비하고 있는지 알고 싶어 한다. 이 상황에서 Judy는 남자에게 뭐라고 말하겠는가?

① 제 등 번호가 어떻게 되나요?
② 어디에서 지원서를 받을 수 있을까요?
③ 제가 사용할 수 있는 라켓이 클럽에 있습니까?
④ 거울 앞에서 자세 잡는 연습을 해야 할까요?
⑤ 회비로 얼마를 지불해야 하나요?

●●
join 가입하다, 합류하다 **how to-V** ∼하는 방법 **racket** 채, 라켓

20

M Mary, I'm going to take part in a science camp in Silicon Valley this vacation.

W A science camp in Silicon Valley? Sounds interesting.

M I feel that I have rekindled an old interest in science.

W Good for you. I'm sure that you'll be a good scientist.

M I can't wait to meet many students from other countries who will be there.

W Wow, it will be a great chance for you to make foreign friends. Don't you think so?

M Right. I'm with you on that.

남 Mary, 나 이번 방학에 실리콘 밸리에서 열리는 과학캠프에 참가할 예정이야.
여 실리콘 밸리에서 열리는 과학캠프라고? 재미있겠는데.
남 과학에 대한 옛 관심이 다시 불붙는 기분이야.
여 잘됐다. 난 네가 훌륭한 과학자가 될 거라 믿어.
남 거기 참가할 다른 나라 출신의 많은 학생들을 빨리 만나고 싶어.
여 와, 해외 친구를 사귈 멋진 기회가 될 거야. 그렇게 생각하지 않니?
남 맞아. 동감이야.

① 친구 좋다는 게 뭐겠니.
② 맞아. 동감이야.
③ 난 과학에 흥미가 있는 것 같지 않아.
④ 그것은 국제 과학의 밤 행사의 일부로 포함되어 있다.
⑤ 캠프장에서 제일 먼저 할 일은 텐트를 치는 거야.

●●
rekindle 다시 불붙이다 **interest** 흥미, 관심 **international** 국제적인
pitch 던지다, 설치하다

1. The reason is that they have to make a cake for his dad's birthday.
2. The reason is that she's worried about the rising cost of electricity.
3. He sat next to a student who is good at science in physics class and learned from him.
4. They are going to judge not only the fluency but also the accuracy of the pronunciation.
5. The reason is that he wants it to get to New Zealand as soon as possible.
6. The reason is that he works out in the fitness center at least three times a week.
7. The reason is that she doesn't have her own racket.
8. He is looking forward to meeting many students from other countries.

A

My Club	
Name/type of the club	(1) SAIE, which stands for Sing Along In English; an American pop song singing club
Activities in the club	(2) listen to the various hit pop songs and try to sing them ourselves
	(3) study the lyrics of the pop songs to learn English
Special event it holds	(4) Pop Song Singing Contest, in December
Requirement(s)	(5) a passion for pop music

I would like to introduce my club, (1)SAIE, which stands for Sing Along In English. It is an American pop song singing club. Two major activities in our club are these. First, (2)we listen to the various hit pop songs and try to sing them ourselves. Second, (3)we study the lyrics of the pop songs to learn English. My club also holds a special event, (4)Pop Song Singing Contest, in December. To become a member, (5)just bring your passion for pop music.

나의 동아리	
동아리 이름/유형	(1) '영어 노래 부르기'의 약자인 SAIE; 미국 팝송 부르기 동아리
동아리 활동들	(2) 다양한 인기 팝송을 듣고 직접 불러보기 (3) 영어를 배우기 위해 팝송 가사를 공부
특별 행사	(4) 12월에 있는 팝송 부르기 경연대회
자격조건	(5) 팝송을 향한 열정

저의 동아리, SAIE를 소개하고 싶습니다. SAIE는 '영어 노래 부르기'의 약자인데 미국 팝송 부르기 동아리입니다. 두 가지 주요 동아리 활동은 이런 것입니다. 첫째, 다양한 인기 팝송을 듣고 직접 불러보기도 합니다. 둘째, 우리는 영어를 배우기 위해 팝송가사를 공부합니다. 제 동아리는 12월에 팝송 부르기 경연대회라는 특별한 행사도 주최합니다. 회원이 되고 싶다면 팝송을 향한 여러분들의 열정만 가지고 오세요.

B

Describing a Pie Chart	
(1) Title	how Ann spends her free time
(2) Activity Ann does most	using her cell phone
(3) Comparing activities	spends less time hanging out with friends than using her cell phone, but spends more time hanging out with friends than watching TV
(4) Activity Ann does least	watching TV
(5) Your suggestion	she should reduce cell phone use gradually

This pie chart shows (1)how Ann spends her free time. The biggest portion of her free time is spent (2)using her cell phone. She spends (3)less time hanging out with friends than using her cell phone, but spends more time hanging out with friends than watching TV. (4) Watching TV is the activity that Ann does least. Since she uses her cell phone too much, I recommend that (5)she should reduce her cell phone use gradually.

Ann이 여가시간을 보내는 방법
- 휴대전화 사용
- 친구와 어울리기
- TV 시청

20%
50%
30%

원그래프 설명하기	
(1) 제목	Ann이 어떻게 여가시간을 보내는가
(2) Ann이 가장 많이 하는 활동	휴대전화 사용하기
(3) 활동들 간 비교	친구와 어울리는 데에 휴대전화를 사용하는 것보다 더 적은 시간을 사용하지만, TV 시청하는 것보다는 친구들과 노는 데에 더 많은 시간을 보냄
(4) Ann이 가장 적게 하는 활동	TV 시청하기
(5) 당신의 제안	점차적으로 휴대전화 사용을 줄여야 함

이 원그래프는 Ann이 어떻게 그녀의 여가시간을 보내는지 보여줍니다. 그녀의 여가시간 중에서 가장 큰 부분은 휴대전화 사용하는 것에 쓰입니다. 그녀는 친구와 어울리는 데에 휴대전화를 사용하는 것보다 더 적은 시간을 사용하지만, TV 시청하는 것보다는 친구들과 노는 데에 더 많은 시간을 보냅니다. TV 시청하기는 그녀가 가장 적게 하는 활동입니다. 그녀는 휴대전화를 너무 많이 사용하므로 저는 그녀가 점차적으로 휴대전화 사용량을 줄일 것을 권합니다.

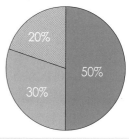

05 Listening Test 정답 p. 50

01 ④	02 ④	03 ②	04 ①	05 ①
06 ②	07 ⑤	08 ②	09 ⑤	10 ⑤
11 ⑤	12 ①	13 ④	14 ③	15 ①
16 ③	17 ④	18 ③	19 ⑤	20 ③

01

W Dad, I want to ride that one.
M Which frog do you want to ride?

W I like that green frog wearing a black bow tie.

M Look at that queue! How about the red-bellied frog with black spots on its back?

W Dad, it looks like a monster.

M Okay. Then I think the crowned yellow frog looks more fun to ride.

W But Dad, I only want to ride the frog with the bow tie.

M I see. Let's wait in line for it then.

. . . .

여 아빠, 저거 타고 싶어요.

남 어떤 개구리 타고 싶니?

여 검은색 나비넥타이를 매고 있는 녹색 개구리요.

남 저 긴 줄 좀 봐! 등에 검은 점 무늬가 있는 무당개구리는 어때?

여 아빠, 그건 괴물같이 생겼어요.

남 그래. 그럼 내 생각에는 왕관을 쓴 노란색 개구리가 타기에 더 재미날 것 같구나.

여 하지만 아빠, 저는 나비넥타이를 맨 그 개구리만 타고 싶어요.

남 알겠다. 그럼 줄 서자.

bow tie 나비넥타이 **queue** 열, 줄 **red-bellied frog** 무당개구리 **spot** 점 **crowned** 왕관을 쓴 **in line** 줄 서서, 정렬하여

02

① M I'd like some medicine for my stomach.
  W You need to get a prescription.

② M When did you brush your teeth last time?
  W I did it this morning.

③ M My gums ache so much that I can't eat anything.
  W You'd better go see a dentist.

④ M Why do I feel pain in my teeth?
  W I'm afraid you have some cavities.

⑤ M My leg's swollen, and it's getting worse.
  W It could be broken. Let's take some X-rays.

. . . .

① 남 위 약 좀 사고 싶어요.
  여 처방전을 받아와야 합니다.

② 남 언제 마지막으로 이를 닦으셨나요?
  여 오늘 아침요.

③ 남 잇몸이 너무 아파서 아무것도 먹을 수가 없어요.
  여 치과에 가보세요.

④ 남 왜 이렇게 이가 아픈 거죠?
  여 충치가 있는 것 같네요.

⑤ 남 다리가 부어있고 부기가 점점 더 심해져요.
  여 부러졌을 수 있습니다. 엑스레이를 찍어봅시다.

. .
medicine 약 **prescription** 처방 **gum** 잇몸 **ache** 아프다, 쑤시다 **cavity** 구멍, 충치 **swell** 붓게 하다

03

W Hi, Max! Wait till I tell you what happened last night.

M What happened to you?

W While I was watching TV, I heard two guys breaking into my car! I ran to the phone and called the police.

M Oh, no! What happened next?

W The police came immediately, chased and arrested them.

M Great. Is there any damage to your car?

W You know what? I thought it was mine but it was my neighbor's.

. . . .

여 안녕, Max. 지난밤에 무슨 일이 있었는지 너에게 말해줄 테니 기다려봐.

남 무슨 일이 있었는데?

여 내가 TV를 보고 있는데, 두 남자가 내 차에 침입하는 소리를 들었어. 나는 전화기로 달려가서 경찰을 불렀지.

남 이를 어째. 그리고 나서 어떻게 됐어?

여 경찰이 즉시 출동했고, 그 남자들을 추격해서 체포했어.

남 잘됐네. 차 손상된 거 있어?

여 그런데 말이야. 내 차라고 생각했는데 내 이웃사람 차였어.

① 속상한   ② 안도하는   ③ 우울한
④ 애타는   ⑤ 후회하는

. .
break into 침입하다 **immediately** 즉시 **chase** 추격하다 **arrest** 체포하다 **damage** 손상, 피해

04

M Would you like to test drive this car?

W Well, how old is it?

M It's only six years old.

W And what's the mileage?

M Let me check. It's just 85,000 miles.

W That's quite a lot. How much is it anyway?

M It's a real bargain at $10,500. But the price is only for today.

W Hmmm… What about the extended warranty? What kinds of items are covered?

남 이 차 시험운전하고 싶으세요?

여 글쎄요. 몇 년 된 차예요?

남 6년밖에 안 됐어요.

여 주행거리는 어떻게 되죠?

남 확인해보겠습니다. 8만 5천 마일밖에 안 되네요.

여 꽤 많이 탔네요. 어쨌든 얼마인가요?

남 가격이 정말 싼 10,500달러에 모십니다. 하지만 그 가격은 오늘만입니다.

여 음… 보증기간 연장은 어떻게 되나요? 어떤 항목들이 보장되나요?

●●
test drive 시험운전하다 **mileage** 마일 수, 주행 거리 **bargain** 매매, 싸게 산 물건 **extend** 연장하다 **warranty** 보증

05

[Telephone rings.]

W Hello.

M Hello. Can I talk to Dr. Han?

W I'm sorry, but he's in a meeting right now. Can I take a message?

M Yes, please. I should return his books today, but I'm afraid I can't.

W So what do you want me to do for you?

M Could you please tell him that I will give them back to him next Monday?

W Sure. Please give me your name.

M This is Joe Smith in his Economics 505 class. Thank you.

[전화벨이 울린다.]

여 여보세요.

남 여보세요. 한 박사님과 통화할 수 있을까요?

여 죄송하지만 지금 회의 중이십니다. 메시지를 남겨드릴까요?

남 네. 오늘까지 책을 돌려드려야 하는데 그럴 수가 없을 것 같아서요.

여 그럼 제가 어떻게 하면 될까요?

남 다음 주 월요일에 돌려드린다고 전해 주시겠습니까?

여 물론이지요. 이름을 알려주세요.

남 저는 경제학 505 수업을 듣는 Joe Smith입니다. 감사합니다.

●●
economics 경제학

06

M Here is the bus. Oh, no! It went right past us. I wonder what time the next bus is!

W It says here the next bus comes at 9:30. We have to wait for 20 minutes.

M Oh my, that's quite long. Hmm… Excuse me, but I have seen you here several times before. Let me introduce myself. My name is Bart.

W I'm Angela. Nice to meet you. I have seen you, too. Where do you live?

M Not far from here. On Fernwood Drive. It's 10 minutes' drive from here. And you?

W My house is on Lake Road, a little farther than yours.

M There is a cafe here behind us. Would you like some tea while we wait?

W Sure, why not!

남 버스가 여기 오네요. 오, 이런! 우리를 그냥 지나쳤네요. 다음 버스가 언제인지 궁금하군요.

여 다음 버스는 9시 30분에 온다고 되어 있네요. 20분 기다려야 해요.

남 이런, 오래 기다려야 되네요. 저… 실례합니다만 전에 여기서 당신을 여러 번 봤습니다. 제 소개를 할게요. 제 이름은 Bart입니다.

여 전 Angela예요. 만나서 반갑습니다. 저도 당신을 봤어요. 어디 사세요?

남 여기서 멀지 않습니다. Fernwood Drive요. 여기서 차로 10분 거리지요. 당신은요?

여 우리 집은 Lake Road에 있는데 당신의 집보다 조금 더 멉니다.

남 여기 우리 뒤에 카페가 있네요. 기다리는 동안 저랑 차 한 잔 하시겠습니까?

여 네, 좋아요.

●●
introduce 소개하다 **far from** ~에서 멀리 **behind** ~ 뒤에

07

W May I borrow your cell phone to call my mother after we finish lunch?

M Yes, of course. And do not forget to ask your mother whether you may go to the movies with me afterwards.

W   Okay. Could you pass me the salt, please?

M   Sure, here it is.

W   Thank you. Oh, did you remember to bring my *Harry Potter* book?

M   I am sorry. I completely forgot about it. Could you call to remind me again tonight?

W   Certainly.

··

여   점심식시 후에 우리 엄마한테 전화하게 네 휴대전화 좀 빌려줄래?

남   응. 그리고 너의 어머니께 나랑 이따 영화 보러 가도 되는지 여쭤보는 거 잊지 마.

여   알았어. 소금 좀 건네줄래?

남   그래, 여기 있어.

여   고마워. 아, 내 〈해리포터〉 책 가지고 오는 거 기억했니?

남   미안해, 완전히 까먹고 있었어. 오늘밤에 전화해서 다시 한 번 더 말해줄래?

여   물론이지.

··
afterwards 그 후에   **completely** 완전히   **remind** 상기시키다

08

M   How was your weekend? Did you enjoy yourself at the soccer game?

W   No. Not at all.

M   Why?

W   On the way to see the game, my boyfriend had an accident.

M   Really? What happened?

W   My boyfriend broke his right leg when he fell down at the subway station. We had to go to the hospital.

M   I'm sorry to hear that. How is he?

W   He is wearing a cast and taking a rest in his house. It was an awful weekend.

··

남   주말 어땠니? 축구 경기는 재미있었니?

여   아니. 전혀.

남   왜?

여   경기를 보러 가는 길에 남자친구가 사고가 났어.

남   정말? 무슨 일인데?

여   내 남자친구가 지하철역에서 넘어지면서 오른쪽 다리가 부러졌어. 그래서 병원에 가야 했어.

남   안됐구나. 남자 친구는 어때?

여   깁스를 하고 집에서 쉬고 있어. 끔찍한 주말이었어.

··
Not at all. 전혀 아니다.   **wear a cast** 깁스를 하다   **take a rest** 휴식을 취하다

09

W   Yoon, can I ask you about the locations of some states?

M   Sure. I'm quite familiar with their locations. I learned about all the states in geography class.

W   Good. Can you tell me their locations in relationship to each other? For instance, is Colorado west or east of Kansas?

M   Well, Colorado is west of Kansas and Kansas is north of Oklahoma.

W   How about Utah and California?

M   Utah is east of California, and Utah is also between Nevada and Colorado.

W   Last question. What about Arizona?

M   It is south of New Mexico. I lived there for five years when I was young.

W   Really? I didn't know about that. Thank you anyway.

··

여   윤아, 몇몇 주의 위치에 대해 물어봐도 될까?

남   물론이지. 주 위치에 대해 꽤 잘 알아. 지리 시간에 모든 주에 관해 배웠거든.

여   좋아. 주들 서로 간의 관계로 위치를 말해줄 수 있니? 예를 들어 Colorado는 Kansas의 서쪽이야, 동쪽이야?

남   그러니까, Colorado는 Kansas의 서쪽에 있고 Kansas는 Oklahoma의 북쪽에 있어.

여   Utah랑 California는?

남   Utah는 California의 동쪽에 있는데 Utah는 또한 Nevada와 Colorado 사이에 있어.

여   마지막 질문이야. Arizona는?

남   그것은 New Mexico의 남쪽에 있어. 어렸을 때 그곳에서 5년 동안 살았어.

여   정말? 몰랐어. 어쨌든 고마워.

··
location 위치   **state** 주, 국가   **geography** 지리   **relationship** 관계
west 서쪽   **east** 동쪽   **north** 북쪽   **south** 남쪽

10

W Alcohol's <u>effects</u> <u>on</u> the heart are well documented. Studies have shown that <u>moderate drinking</u> can raise levels of "good cholesterol," which helps <u>prevent</u> harmful blood clots and keep blood <u>flowing</u> <u>smoothly</u> through our bodies. <u>However</u>, there's <u>no</u> <u>denying</u> that too much alcohol can lead to <u>serious</u> <u>problems</u>. Excess alcohol can <u>increase</u> <u>your</u> <u>risk</u> <u>of</u> lots of diseases such as liver disease, a stroke, and diabetes.

여 알코올이 심장에 미치는 영향은 잘 기록되어 있다. 많은 연구들이 적당한 음주가 좋은 콜레스테롤 수치를 높인다는 점을 보여주는데, 이 콜레스테롤은 해로운 혈전을 방지하고 온 몸으로 혈액이 부드럽게 흐를 수 있도록 도와준다. 하지만 과음은 심각한 문제들을 일으킬 수 있다는 것은 부인할 수 없다. 과도한 알코올은 간 질병, 뇌졸중, 당뇨병 같은 여러 질병에 걸릴 위험을 증가시킬 수 있다.

●● **document** 기록하다 **moderate** 적당한, 보통의 **blood clot** 혈전 **There is no denying that** ~을 부인할 수 없다 **excess** 과도(한) **liver** 간 **stroke** 뇌졸중 **diabetes** 당뇨병

11

M <u>Ladies</u> and <u>gentlemen</u>. This is your <u>captain</u> <u>speaking</u>. We are now going to <u>pass</u> <u>through</u> <u>turbulence</u>, so we will <u>stop</u> <u>serving</u> you drinks and snacks for a while. <u>For</u> <u>your</u> <u>safety</u>, please <u>be</u> <u>seated</u> and <u>fasten</u> <u>your</u> <u>seat</u> <u>belts</u>. In two hours and 10 minutes, we'll be <u>arriving</u> <u>at</u> Incheon International Airport. The local time is now 7:50 in the evening. I hope you are <u>enjoying</u> <u>your</u> <u>flight</u>. Thank you.

남 신사 숙녀 여러분, 안녕하십니까. 저는 기장입니다. 지금 난기류를 통과할 예정이어서 음료와 간식 제공을 잠시 중단하겠습니다. 승객 여러분의 안전을 위해서 자리에 앉아주시고, 안전벨트를 매주십시오. 2시간 10분 후에 인천국제공항에 도착할 것입니다. 현지 시간은 현재 저녁 7시 50분입니다. 즐거운 여행 되십시오. 감사합니다.

●● **turbulence** 소란, 난기류 **for a while** 잠시 동안 **safety** 안전 **fasten** 매다, 죄다

12

W Can I help you?

M Yes, I'm <u>looking</u> <u>for</u> <u>pink roses</u>.

W Are they <u>for Valentine's Day</u> tomorrow?

M Yes, they are for my girlfriend. She loves pink. I will give them to her as a Valentine's gift.

W <u>How</u> <u>sweet</u>! I'll check <u>whether</u> we have any <u>in</u> <u>stock</u> or not.

M Thank you.

W I'm sorry. We <u>sold</u> <u>out</u> <u>of</u> <u>them</u> earlier today. But we will <u>get a</u> <u>delivery</u> at 7 a.m. tomorrow.

M OK. I will make sure I get here <u>early</u> <u>tomorrow</u>.

여 무엇을 도와드릴까요?
남 네, 저는 분홍색 장미를 찾고 있습니다.
여 내일 발렌타인데이를 위한 것인가요?
남 네, 제 여자친구를 위한 것입니다. 그녀는 분홍색을 좋아하거든요. 발렌타인데이 선물로 그녀에게 주려고요.
여 정말 다정다감하시네요! 재고가 있는지 없는지 확인하겠습니다.
남 감사합니다.
여 죄송합니다. 오늘 일찍 다 팔렸습니다. 하지만 내일 아침 7시에 배달을 받습니다.
남 좋습니다. 내일 일찍 여기 꼭 오겠습니다.

① 꽃 가게　　② 스키 리조트　　③ 선물 가게
④ 빵 가게　　⑤ 교실

●● **in stock** 재고가 있는 **sell out of** ~을 다 팔다 **delivery** 배달

13

M Did you <u>receive</u> <u>an</u> <u>invitation</u> <u>card</u> from Jungmi?

W No. What kind of invitation card is it?

M She is going to <u>have a</u> <u>housewarming</u> <u>party</u>. She said she'd invite you.

W <u>Sounds</u> <u>interesting</u>. When is it?

M It will be on <u>July 25th</u>, which is this <u>Sunday</u>.

W Will it be in the <u>afternoon</u> or in the <u>evening</u>? If it is around noon, I can't make it. I have a <u>previous</u> <u>appointment</u>.

M It will start at <u>5 p.m.</u> I think you <u>can</u> <u>make</u> <u>it</u>. There will be a <u>buffet</u> along with snacks and drinks.

W How nice! Please tell me the address and give me her phone number. I don't think I have her number.

M The address is 70 Rodeo Avenue and the number is 010-0707-0007.

집들이에 초대되셨습니다!

오셔서 우리 새 집을 축하해 주세요.

① 날짜 : 7월 25일 일요일
② 시간 : 오후 5시
③ 뷔페-간식-음료
④ 서울 로데오길 17번지
⑤ 010-0707-0007번으로 정미에게 회답해주세요.

남 정미에게서 초대장 받았어?
여 아니. 무슨 초대장?
남 집들이 할 거래. 너도 초대할 거라고 했어.
여 재미있겠다. 언제야?
남 7월 25일, 이번 일요일이야.
여 오후야, 저녁이야? 정오쯤이면 난 못 가. 선약이 있어.
남 오후 5시에 시작할 거야. 내 생각에는 네가 올 수 있을 것 같은데. 간식과 음료가 제공되는 뷔페가 있을 거야.
여 괜찮은데! 그녀의 주소랑 연락처를 좀 알려줘. 내가 전화번호를 갖고 있는 것 같지 않아.
남 주소는 로데오길 70번지이고, 전화번호는 010-0707-0007이야.

invitation card 초대장 **housewarming party** 집들이 **previous** 이전의

14

M Did you decide which one you are going to buy?

W Not yet. I'm still looking at the catalog.

M Still? Why are you taking so long? Don't you have a style in mind?

W I did. But when I look at all these pictures, it is so confusing.

M I don't understand you. The only important thing is that it blocks out the sun and people can't see inside our house.

W Yes. But I have to choose the material and the design. It can make our house look more beautiful.

M I see. But hurry up. Don't spend too much time on it. Anything you can choose will be beautiful.

W Alright.

남 무엇을 살 건지 결정했어?
여 아니 아직. 아직 목록을 보고 있어.
남 아직도? 왜 그렇게 오래 걸려? 생각해 둔 스타일 없어?
여 있었지. 그런데 이걸 보니 너무 혼란스러워.
남 이해가 안 가. 중요한 것은 오직 햇빛을 가려주고 사람들이 우리 집 안을 못 보는 거잖아.
여 맞아. 하지만 난 재질과 디자인을 골라야 해. 그것이 우리 집을 더 아름답게 만들어줄 수도 있어.
남 그렇구나. 그렇지만 서둘러. 그것에 너무 많은 시간을 소비하지 마. 당신이 고르는 건 다 멋질 거야.
여 알았어.

catalog 목록 **confuse** 혼란스럽게 하다 **block** 막다 **material** 재료

15

[Telephone rings.]

M Hello.

W Hello, Jason. It's me, Judy. What are you doing?

M Oh, Judy. I'm ordering books on the Internet.

W What books are they?

M One is a travel book on Spain, and the other is a book about architecture.

W Good. Jason, Jennie and I will go to a movie and play aqua basketball at the community center. Will you join us?

M Hmm… I'm not sure if I can go to a movie. But I can join you at the community center.

W Great. Let's meet at 3 in front of the center. Please call me when you arrive.

[전화벨이 울린다.]

남 여보세요.
여 안녕, Jason. 나야, Judy. 너 뭐 하고 있니?
남 응, Judy. 인터넷으로 책을 주문하고 있어.
여 어떤 책이야?
남 하나는 스페인 여행서고, 다른 하나는 건축에 관한 책이야.
여 그렇구나. Jason, Jennie와 나는 영화 보고 지역문화센터에서 수중농구를 할 거야. 너도 우리와 함께 할래?
남 음… 내가 영화 보러 갈 수 있을지 잘 모르겠어. 하지만 지역문화센터에서 너희랑 함께 할 순 있어.
여 좋아. 센터 앞에서 3시에 만나자. 도착하면 내게 전화해.

order 주문하다 **architecture** 건축 **aqua basketball** 수중농구

community center 지역문화센터

16

① M I'm writing an article for the school newspaper.

　W That's great! I can't wait to read it.

② M What makes you think the movie will be a big hit?

　W It has great special effects.

③ M Be sure to wear a helmet when you ride a bike.

　W Sorry for the inconvenience.

④ M I think trust is the most important thing between friends.

　W That's a good point.

⑤ M Why do you look so pale?

　W I have a cold. I shouldn't have slept with the window open.

⋯⋯⋯⋯⋯⋯⋯⋯⋯⋯⋯⋯⋯⋯⋯⋯⋯⋯⋯⋯⋯

① 남 나 학교 신문 기사를 쓰고 있어.

　여 그거 멋지다! 빨리 읽고 싶어.

② 남 너는 왜 그 영화가 대성공할 것이라고 생각하니?

　여 특수효과가 뛰어나거든.

③ 남 자전거를 탈 때는 반드시 헬멧을 쓰도록 해.

　여 불편을 끼쳐드려 죄송합니다.

④ 남 내 생각에 신뢰가 친구 사이에 가장 중요한 것 같아.

　여 그거 좋은 지적이야.

⑤ 남 너 왜 그렇게 창백해 보이니?

　여 감기에 걸렸어. 창문을 열어 둔 채로 자지 말았어야 했어.

••
big hit 대성공 **trust** 신뢰 **pale** 창백한 **shouldn't have p.p.** ~하지 말았어야 했다

17

M Jane, you like strawberries, don't you? I've decided to go to the strawberry picking event at Sunspot Farm. Would you like to go with me?

W Huh, when is it?

M Participants will be meeting at the red barn of the farm this Saturday, at nine thirty in the morning so this will be done in a group.

W Is it free?

M No. There is a 5 dollar entry fee which includes all the strawberries you can pick. You must register and pay prior to the date of the event.

W How can we go there? Is there any shuttle bus available?

M No, but I will give you a ride if you need one.

W OK, I'm in.

M Excellent choice. I'll register you and me. The fee is on me.

⋯⋯⋯⋯⋯⋯⋯⋯⋯⋯⋯⋯⋯⋯⋯⋯⋯⋯⋯⋯⋯

남 Jane, 너 딸기 좋아하지, 그렇지 않니? 나 Sunspot 농장에서 열리는 딸기 따기 행사에 가기로 결정했어. 나랑 함께 가지 않을래?

여 어, 언제니?

남 참가자들이 단체로 참여하도록 그 농장의 붉은 헛간에서 이번 토요일 오전 9시 30분에 만날 거야.

여 무료니?

남 아니. 딸 수 있는 모든 딸기를 포함한 5달러의 참가비가 있어. 행사날 이전에 등록하고 지불을 해야 해

여 거기엔 어떻게 가니? 셔틀버스 이용 가능해?

남 아니, 하지만 네가 필요하다면 내가 태워줄게.

여 좋아, 동참할게.

남 현명한 선택이야. 너랑 나 등록할게. 비용은 내가 낸다.

••
barn 헛간, 광 **entry fee** 참가비 **register** 등록하다 **prior to** ~ 이전에

18

W Changing schools can be a very scary time for a student. Tom's best friend, Ann, transferred to another school after her freshman year because her dad got a new job. Tom calls Ann and asks how she likes her new school. She says she is not happy with her new school because she doesn't have any friends. Tom is shocked because Ann was very popular in her old school. In this situation, what would Tom most likely say to Ann?

⋯⋯⋯⋯⋯⋯⋯⋯⋯⋯⋯⋯⋯⋯⋯⋯⋯⋯⋯⋯⋯

여 전학한다는 것은 학생에게 매우 두려운 시간일 수 있다. Tom의 단짝인, Ann은 아빠가 새로운 일자리를 얻으셔서 1학년을 마치고 다른 학교로 전학 갔다. Tom은 Ann에게 전화해서 새 학교가 마음에 드는지 물어본다. 그녀는 친구가 아무도 없어서 새 학교가 만족스럽지 않다고 말한다. Tom은 Ann이 그녀의 옛 학교에서 아주 인기 있었기 때문에 충격을 받는다. 이 상황에서 Tom은 Ann에게 뭐라고 말하겠는가?

① 숙제가 너무 많니?

② 그거 다행이다. 우리는 네가 많이 그리워.
③ 나는 네가 곧 새 친구들을 사귀기를 바래.
④ 불행하게도, 나도 새 학교가 싫어.
⑤ 글쎄, 선생님들은 정말 좋으셔. 항상 나를 도와주시거든.

scary 두려운 **transfer** 옮기다 **freshman** 1학년 **popular** 인기 있는

19

W Karl, look at this breaking news.
M What is it? What happened?
W A fire broke out at Bicentennial Park. A lot of trees are burning.
M Is that the park we went to last weekend?
W Yeah. The news says the police suspect a campfire wasn't put out completely.
M In this dry weather, trees easily catch fire.
W We should not have campfires in the dry season.

여 Karl, 이 뉴스속보 좀 봐.
남 왜? 무슨 일이야?
여 200주년기념공원에 불이 났대. 많은 나무들이 불타고 있어.
남 우리가 지난 주말에 갔던 그 공원 말이야?
여 응. 뉴스에서 경찰은 캠프파이어가 완전히 꺼지지 않은 것을 원인으로 의심하고 있대.
남 이런 건조한 날씨에는 나무에 불이 쉽게 붙지.
여 건조한 계절에는 우린 캠프파이어를 해서는 안 돼.

① 그 소식은 들불처럼 퍼졌다.
② 엎친 데 덮친 격이야!
③ 여름은 산불에 최적의 계절이다.
④ 나는 종이를 써서 난로에 불을 붙여.
⑤ 건조한 계절에는 우린 캠프파이어를 해서는 안 돼.

breaking news 뉴스속보 **bicentennial** 200주년 기념의 **suspect** ~이 아닌가 의심하다

20

W You look worried. What's wrong?
M Well... I broke the screen of my brother's tablet PC.
W Didn't you say your parents bought it for his birthday present last month?
M Yes, I did. What would you do if you were in my

shoes?
W If I were you, I would tell him and your parents what happened and say I was sorry.
M I'm scared. They might be really mad at me, especially my brother.
W If you tell the truth, they will forgive you.

여 너 걱정 있어 보여. 무슨 일이니?
남 응… 형의 태블릿 PC 화면을 깨뜨렸어.
여 지난달 그의 생일 선물로 너희 부모님께서 그것을 사주셨다고 네가 말하지 않았니?
남 응, 그랬지. 만약 네가 내 입장이라면 넌 어떻게 하겠니?
여 만약 내가 너라면, 난 그와 부모님께 무슨 일이 있었는지 말하고 미안하다고 말하겠어.
남 난 무서워. 그들은 내게 미칠 듯 화를 낼지도 몰라, 특히 형이.
여 네가 진실을 말하면, 그들은 널 용서할 거야.

① 반만 진실인 것은 언제나 완전한 거짓이다.
② 내게 화내지 마. 내가 그런 게 아니야.
③ 네가 진실을 말하면, 그들은 널 용서할 거야.
④ 형에게 그런 말을 하다니 네가 경솔했어.
⑤ 그는 정말 재미있어. 농담을 진담처럼 이야기해.

be in one's shoes ~의 입장이 되다 **scared** 겁먹은 **especially** 특히
tell the truth 진실을 말하다

Further Study 정답   p. 54

1. The reason is that there are too many people waiting to ride it.
2. He is going to return them next Monday.
3. They are eating lunch.
4. He broke his right leg, so had to go to the hospital.
5. It helps prevent blood clots and keep blood flowing smoothly.
6. They have to be seated and fasten their seatbelts.
7. They will meet at the community center and play aqua basketball.
8. They suspect a campfire wasn't put out completely.

A

My Embarrassing Moment	
(1) When/where did it happen?	in the living room of my home last month
(2) What happened?	stepped on my brother's tablet PC on the floor by accident and broke its screen
(3) How did it happen?	in a hurry not to be late for an appointment with my friend
(4) What was embarrassing?	it is very expensive and was my brother's graduation present from my parents
(5) How did you overcome it?	told the truth to him and said I was sorry

Let me tell you about an incident that made me so embarrassed. It happened (1)in the living room of my home last month. What happened was (2)I stepped on my brother's tablet PC on the floor by accident and broke its screen. It happened because (3)I was in a hurry not to be late for an appointment with my friend. I was embarrassed because (4)it is very expensive and was my brother's graduation present from my parents. However, I could overcome the situation as (5)I told the truth to him and said I was sorry. Anyway, I hope it won't happen again to me.

나의 난처한 순간	
(1) 언제/어디서 일어났습니까?	우리 집 거실에서 지난 달에
(2) 무슨 일이 있었습니까?	바닥에 있던 형의 태블릿 PC를 실수로 밟아서 화면을 깨뜨렸음
(3) 어떻게 일어났습니까?	친구와의 약속에 늦지 않기 위해 서둘렀음
(4) 무엇이 당황스러웠나요?	그것이 고가이고 부모님이 주신 형의 졸업 선물이었음
(5) 어떻게 극복했습니까?	형에게 사실을 말하고 사과했음

저를 너무나 난처하게 만들었던 한 사건에 대해 말씀 드리겠습니다. 그 일은 저희 집 거실에서 지난 달 발생했습니다. 사건은 제가 바닥에 있던 형의 태블릿 PC를 실수로 밟아서 화면을 깨뜨린 것입니다. 이 일이 일어난 이유는 제가 친구와의 약속에 늦지 않기 위해 서둘렀기 때문입니다. 그 태블릿 PC가 고가이고 부모님이 주신 형의 졸업 선물이었기 때문에 저는 난처했습니다. 하지만 저는 그에게 사실을 말하고 사과함으로써 그 상황을

B

극복할 수 있었습니다. 어쨌든 저는 다시는 그런 일이 제게 일어나지 않기를 바랍니다.

Valentine's Day	
(1) When is it?	February 14th
(2) What do people usually do?	give chocolates to whoever they love, confess their love to those persons
(3) What do you do on the day?	make chocolates by myself, give them to my close friends and family members
(4) What do you think of the day?	a great and lovely day to celebrate

I'm going to talk about Valentine's Day. It is on (1)February 14th. People usually (2)give chocolates to whoever they love and confess their love to those persons. On this day, I usually (3)make chocolates by myself and give them to my close friends and my family members. I think (4)it is a great and lovely day to celebrate.

발렌타인 데이	
(1) 언제입니까?	2월 14일
(2) 사람들은 대개 무엇을 합니까?	사랑하는 사람이라면 누구에게나 초콜릿 주기, 그 사람에게 사랑 고백하기
(3) 당신은 그날 무엇을 합니까?	직접 초콜릿을 만들어 친한 친구들과 가족들에게 줌
(4) 이날에 대해 어떻게 생각합니까?	멋지고 사랑 넘치는 기념일

저는 발렌타인데이에 대하여 이야기를 할 것입니다. 날짜는 2월 14일입니다. 사람들은 대개 그들이 사랑하는 사람이라면 누구에게나 초콜릿을 주고 사랑을 고백합니다. 저는 이날 대개 직접 초콜릿을 만들어 제 친한 친구들과 가족들에게 줍니다. 저는 이날이 멋지고 사랑 넘치는 기념일이라고 생각합니다.

01 ②	02 ⑤	03 ④	04 ②	05 ③
06 ①	07 ⑤	08 ①	09 ③	10 ①
11 ③	12 ③	13 ⑤	14 ④	15 ①
16 ⑤	17 ②	18 ④	19 ②	20 ④

01

M Look at this. I bought these animation character stamps released by the United States Postal Service.

W Oh, they look awesome! Where can I buy them?

M You can't. They are already sold out. But if you really want, I can give you one of these.

W Really? Every one looks so cool. Which one is your favorite?

M I love robot stamps from the movie *Toy Story* and these car stamps.

W Hmm…can I get this one with a cute dog and a grandpa?

M What about this one with a little mouse and a good-looking cook?

W That's also good. Okay, I'll take that one.

남 이것 좀 봐. 내가 미국 우정공사에서 발행한 이 만화영화 캐릭터 우표를 샀어.
여 오, 멋지다! 어디서 살 수 있는 거니?
남 못 사. 이미 다 판매되었어. 하지만 네가 정말 원한다면, 이것들 중에서 하나 줄게.
여 정말? 다 너무 멋져 보여. 네가 제일 좋아하는 건 어떤 거야?
남 〈토이 스토리〉에 나오는 로봇 우표와 이 자동차 우표를 좋아해.
여 그럼… 귀여운 개와 할아버지가 있는 이 우표 가져도 되니?
남 작은 생쥐와 잘 생긴 요리사가 있는 이 우표는 어때?
여 그것도 좋아, 응, 그걸로 할게.

release 발행하다 **awesome** 근사한 **be sold out** 매진되다 **cook** 요리사

02

W I love shopping at the mall! It's indoors so the weather is always nice.

M Exactly. Like today, it's raining outside, but we don't need any umbrellas in the mall.

W Oh, look at the little white kitten and there's a black one, too! Aren't they adorable?

M Yes, they are. But I prefer dogs to cats. Why don't we buy that brown poodle?

W Honey, do you remember that I hate to listen to its barking sound?

M I'm sorry, I just forgot. Look at that black haired silky guinea pig. It looks really gorgeous.

W Absolutely, yes. Let's take him to our house.

여 나는 몰에서 쇼핑하는 걸 좋아해. 실내에 있으니까 항상 좋은 날씨야.
남 맞아. 오늘처럼 밖에 비가 와도 몰 안에 있으면 우산이 필요 없지.
여 오, 작은 흰색 고양이를 봐. 그리고 검은색 고양이도 있어. 사랑스럽지 않아?
남 맞아. 하지만 나는 고양이보다 개가 더 좋아. 저 갈색 푸들 사는 거 어때?
여 자기야, 나 개 짖는 소리 싫어하는 거 기억하지?
남 미안해, 잊어버렸어. 저 검은 비단 털을 가진 기니피그 봐봐. 정말 너무 멋진데.
여 정말 그래. 우리 집에 데려가자.

indoors 실내의 **prefer A to B** B보다 A를 더 좋아하다 **bark** 짖다
gorgeous 아주 멋진, 화려한 **take A to B** A를 B로 데려가다

03

M Even though I can run fast, I still miss the ball quite often while playing tennis.

W Try not to follow the ball with your eyes after you hit it.

M I know I have that bad habit. I follow the ball all the way when it flies through the air.

W You need to trust yourself. Hit the ball and then shift your eyes away from the ball over to your opponent.

M How can I shift my eyes fast?

W Practice makes perfect.

M Okay. I'll practice a lot. Oh, our ordering number is now showing. I'll go get the dishes.

남 나는 테니스 할 때 빨리 달리지만, 여전히 공을 꽤 자주 놓쳐요.

여 공을 던진 후에 눈이 그 공을 따라가지 않도록 하세요.

남 저도 제가 그런 나쁜 습관이 있다는 걸 알아요. 저는 공이 공중으로 날아갈 때 계속해서 공을 따라가게 돼요.

여 스스로를 믿어야 해요. 공을 치고 나면 눈을 공에서 떼어 상대 선수 쪽으로 옮기세요.

남 어떻게 하면 눈을 빨리 움직일 수 있을까요?

여 연습하면 돼요.

남 네, 연습 많이 할게요. 오, 우리 주문 번호가 지금 보이네요. 제가 가서 음식들 가져올게요.

•• **air** 공중 **shift** 옮기다. 바꾸다 **opponent** 상대. 대항자 **practice** 연습; 연습하다

04

W I'm happy you're coming for dinner tonight. Which do you like better, beef or pork?

M Well, I don't eat red meat.

W Actually I don't eat much red meat, either. What about some seafood, then? Oysters? Squid?

M I don't really care too much for seafood, either, Julia.

W That's okay. How about stewed chicken, then?

M Actually, Julia, I'm a vegetarian. I don't eat any meat at all.

W I'm sorry. I should have asked you what you couldn't eat before. I'll make the salad really delicious.

여 오늘밤 저녁 식사 하러 온다니 기뻐. 소고기와 돼지고기 중에서 어떤 것을 더 좋아해?

남 음, 난 붉은 고기는 먹지 않아.

여 사실 나도 붉은 고기는 많이 먹지 않아. 그럼 해산물은 어때? 굴? 오징어?

남 난 해산물도 그렇게 좋아하진 않아, Julia.

여 괜찮아. 그럼 닭고기 스튜는 어때?

남 사실, Julia, 나 채식주의자야. 고기는 전혀 먹지 않아.

여 미안해. 뭘 못 먹는지 전에 물어봤어야 했는데. 샐러드 정말 맛있게 만들어 줄게.

① 화가 난　　　　② 당황한　　　　③ 기쁜
④ 감사하는　　　　⑤ 슬픈

•• **oyster** 굴 **squid** 오징어 **care for** 좋아하다 **stew** 뭉근한 불로 끓이다

vegetarian 채식주의자

05

M May I help you, ma'am?

W Yes. My husband is a real couch potato. I think he needs to play a sport. What can I buy him?

M What kind of sports does he like?

W All sports. He watches all kinds of sports on TV.

M Maybe this tennis racket is good for him. It costs only 125 dollars.

W Oh, my! It's too expensive. What about this one with a red handle?

M That is also a good item. It is 105 dollars. If you purchase this, you can get these three balls for two dollars.

W I'll take it and I'll take those balls, too.

남 도와드릴까요?

여 네. 제 남편이 정말 앉아서 TV만 보는 사람이에요. 운동하는 게 필요하다고 생각하는데 뭘 사줄 수 있을까요?

남 남편께서 어떤 종류의 스포츠를 좋아하시죠?

여 스포츠라면 뭐든요. TV로 모든 종류의 스포츠를 봐요.

남 아마도 이 테니스 라켓이 좋겠네요. 125달러밖에 안 합니다.

여 세상에! 너무 비싸요. 빨간색 손잡이가 있는 이 라켓은 어때요?

남 그것도 좋은 품목입니다. 가격은 105달러입니다. 만약 이걸 구매하신다면, 이 공 세 개를 2달러에 사실 수 있습니다.

여 그것도 사고 저 공들도 살게요.

•• **couch potato** 소파에 앉아 TV만 보는 사람 **cost** ~의 비용이 들다

06

[Telephone rings.]

W Hello.

M Hi, Stephanie. I'm Luke. How are things at the office?

W Oh, Luke! Thank you for calling. I was about to call you. Can you please pick up paper for the computer printer on your way back to the office?

M Pardon me? Can you repeat that, please?

W Pick up computer paper, please.

M Did you say to pick up ink for the printer? Sorry, the

phone is cutting out.

W Can you hear me now? Listen, I'll text you what I need. Thanks, Luke. Talk to you later.

M OK, Stephanie. Sorry, my phone has really bad reception here.

[전화벨이 울린다.]

여 여보세요.

남 안녕하세요. Stephanie. Luke입니다. 사무실은 어때요?

여 오, Luke! 전화해줘서 고마워요. 막 전화하려던 참이었어요. 사무실로 오는 길에 컴퓨터 프린터 용지를 좀 사다 줄래요?

남 뭐라고요? 다시 한 번 말해주시죠?

여 컴퓨터 용지를 좀 사달라고요.

남 프린터 잉크를 좀 사달라고 한 겁니까? 미안해요. 전화가 끊겨지네요.

여 지금 들리나요? 있잖아요. 제가 필요한 걸 문자로 알려줄게요. 고마워요, Luke. 나중에 얘기해요.

남 알았어요, Stephanie. 미안해요. 내 전화기 수신 상태가 여기서 정말 안 좋네요.

① 종이　　　② 잉크　　　③ 휴대전화
④ 프린터　　　⑤ 컴퓨터

be about to-V 막 ~하려 하다　**pick up** 집다, 사다　**cut out** 멈추다, 저절로 정지하다　**text** 문자를 보내다　**reception** 수신

07

① W Dodge ball is more popular than any other sport.

② W Table tennis and basketball are the least popular sports in Cindy's class.

③ W Badminton is the second most popular sport in Cindy's class.

④ W Swimming is more popular than basketball and table tennis.

⑤ W No sport is as popular as badminton in Cindy's class.

Cindy네 반의 인기 스포츠

① 여 피구는 다른 어떤 운동보다 더 인기 있다.

② 여 탁구와 농구는 Cindy네 반에서 가장 인기가 없는 운동이다.

③ 여 배드민턴은 Cindy네 반에서 두 번째로 인기 있는 운동이다.

④ 여 수영은 농구나 탁구보다 더 인기 있다.

⑤ 여 Cindy네 반에서 배드민턴만큼 인기 있는 스포츠는 없다.

dodge ball 피구　**table tennis** 탁구　**the second most** 두 번째로 ~한

08

W Welcome home! Did you have a great time?

M It was awesome. It was the best camping trip I've ever gone on. I took a lot of pictures.

W Good. Anyway, what are you going to wear to the party this evening?

M The pants and shirt which you bought for me on my birthday.

W Oh, no! I forgot to iron them.

M Could you please do that for me? I'm not good at ironing.

W Well, okay. Then can you do the dishes? I will warm up the iron first.

M Sure. Thank you.

여 집에 온 것을 환영해! 즐거운 시간 보냈니?

남 아주 좋았어요. 제가 다녀본 캠핑여행 중에 최고였어요. 사진도 많이 찍었어요.

여 잘됐네. 어쨌든, 오늘 저녁 파티에 뭘 입을 거니?

남 엄마가 제 생일에 사주신 바지와 셔츠를 입을 거예요.

여 오, 이런! 다림질 하는 것을 잊었네.

남 다림질 좀 해주시겠어요? 제가 다림질을 잘 못해서요.

여 그래. 그러면 설거지 좀 해줄래? 나는 다리미를 먼저 예열할게.

남 물론이죠. 고맙습니다.

iron 다리미; 다림질을 하다　**do the dishes** 설거지하다　**warm up** 예열하다

09

W How was the dinner, sir?

M It was fantastic. If I have a chance, I'd like to come here again.

W Thank you for saying so. How would you like to pay

anyway?

M I'll pay in cash. Let me get the wallet. [pause] Oh no!

W What's wrong?

M I don't think I have enough cash in my wallet.

W Don't you have a credit card?

M Not on me. I left it in my car. Can I go to my car and come back right away?

W No problem.

여 저녁 식사는 어떠셨습니까?

남 아주 훌륭했습니다. 기회가 오면 다시 오고 싶습니다.

여 그렇게 말씀해주셔서 감사합니다. 그런데 지불은 어떻게 하실 건가요?

남 현금으로 하겠습니다. 지갑 좀 꺼내고요. 오, 이런!

여 무슨 문제인가요?

남 제 지갑에 현금이 충분하게 있지 않네요.

여 신용카드 없으세요?

남 내가 갖고 있지 않아요. 차에 놓고 왔습니다. 차에 갔다가 바로 와도 될까요?

여 물론이죠.

•• **fantastic** 환상적인 **wallet** 지갑

10

M If you're free today, how about watching the new movie called *The Attorney* with me?

W I'd love to. When does the movie start?

M There are several showings in the Central Theater. We have to decide which one we want to see.

W Are there showings in the afternoon, evening, and at night?

M Yes. When do you prefer?

W The afternoon would be best for me.

M There are two showings, one at 2:30 and the other at 4:00.

W The earlier one is better for me. And let's meet 30 minutes before the show time in front of the ticket booth.

M Okay. See you then.

남 오늘 한가하다면, 나랑 같이 〈변호인〉이라는 새 영화 보는 거 어때?

여 좋아. 영화가 언제 시작해?

남 Central Theater에서 여러 번의 상영이 있어. 어떤 걸 볼지를 결정해야 해.

여 오후, 저녁, 밤에도 상영이 있니?

남 응. 언제가 좋아?

여 오후가 내겐 가장 좋아.

남 2시 30분과 4시, 두 번이 있어.

여 빠른 게 내겐 더 좋아. 그리고 매표소 앞에서 상영 시간 30분 전에 만나자.

남 그래. 그럼 이따 봐.

•• **attorney** 변호사 **ticket booth** 매표소

11

M Good afternoon. How do you feel now?

W Good afternoon. I'm very nervous.

M Please relax. I'll ask you a few questions. First, so you want to be a tour guide?

W Yes, that's right. That's my dream job. I can even speak four languages fluently.

M That sounds wonderful. Then, have you ever worked in the travel business?

W No, but I've traveled to several foreign countries. I think it will be a great help.

M Great. When can you start working?

W As soon as you hire me.

남 안녕하세요. 지금 기분이 어떠세요?

여 안녕하세요. 무척 떨립니다.

남 편하게 계셔도 됩니다. 몇 가지만 물어볼게요. 먼저, 관광 가이드가 되고 싶으시다고요?

여 네. 맞습니다. 제 꿈의 직업이에요. 전 4개국어를 유창하게 말할 수도 있습니다.

남 멋지네요. 그러면 여행사에서 일해본 적이 있으세요?

여 아니요. 그렇지만 여러 외국을 여행해 봤습니다. 이것이 많은 도움이 되리라 생각합니다.

남 좋습니다. 언제 일을 시작하실 수 있죠?

여 저를 채용하시는 즉시요.

•• **tour guide** 관광 가이드 **foreign** 외국의 **fluently** 유창하게 **hire** 고용하다

12

W Welcome to Korail's reservation center. How may I help you?

M I'd like to make a reservation to go to Dongdaegu from Seoul by KTX.

W When would you like to leave?

M This coming Saturday. I mean, May 15. And I'd like the 10:25 train in the morning.

W Do you need a one-way or a round-trip ticket?

M A one-way ticket, please.

W That's 50 thousand won. Would you like to pay in cash or by card?

M In cash. Here you go.

W Thank you. OK, your car and seat number is 12 and 8D. Have a nice day.

....

KTX 예약	
① 시간 / 날짜:	오전 10시 25분 / 5월 5일
② 표의 구분:	왕복
③ 출발 / 도착:	서울에서 동대구로
④ 운임:	55,000원
⑤ 차량 / 좌석 번호:	20 / 8D

여 Korail 예약센터에 오신 걸 환영합니다. 무엇을 도와드릴까요?

남 서울에서 동대구로 가는 KTX표를 예약하고 싶습니다.

여 언제 떠나실 건가요?

남 이번 주 토요일요. 그러니까 5월 15일입니다. 그리고 오전 10시 25분 기차로 해주세요.

여 편도표가 필요하세요, 왕복표가 필요하세요?

남 편도로 주세요.

여 네. 그럼 5만원입니다. 현금으로 지불하시겠습니까, 카드로 하시겠습니까?

남 현금요. 여기 있습니다.

여 감사합니다. 네, 차량번호와 좌석번호는 각각 12번과 8D입니다. 안녕히 가세요.

....

make a reservation 예약하다 **coming** 다가오는 **thousand** 1천

13

M Hello, ma'am. How may I help you?

W Hello. I need to withdraw some cash, but I'm afraid

the ATM outside is not working. What should I do?

M Don't worry. You can go to a teller at the counter over there.

W I don't have my bankbook with me.

M That's okay as long as you have a cash card for that account and some ID.

W That's good.

M Please get a number, fill out this form, and wait for your turn.

W Thank you very much.

M My pleasure.

....

남 안녕하세요. 무엇을 도와드릴까요?

여 안녕하세요. 현금을 인출하고 싶은데, 현금인출기가 작동을 안 하는 것 같아요. 어떻게 해야 하죠?

남 걱정하지 마세요. 저 쪽에 창구에 있는 직원에게 가세요.

여 통장이 없는데요.

남 그 계좌 현금 카드와 신분증이 될 만한 게 있으면 괜찮습니다.

여 다행이네요.

남 번호표를 뽑으시고 이 양식을 작성하셔서 순서를 기다리세요.

여 정말 감사합니다.

남 천만에요.

① 수리점　　　② 경찰서　　　③ 백화점
④ 서점　　　　⑤ 은행

withdraw 인출하다, 철수하다 **ATM(Automated Teller Machine)** 현금인출기 **teller** 금전출납원, 은행직원 **bankbook** 은행통장 **fill out** (양식을) 작성하다 **turn** 차례, 순서

14

M Good evening. Did you enjoy the beautiful spring day today? We had a high of 22 degrees Celsius in Seoul while Incheon was a little warmer at 26.5. Busan and Ulsan were 23 and 25 respectively. Jeju Island reached a high of 26. Tomorrow, the temperature will be on the rise up to 27 in Seoul, so you can wear light clothing. This is Sunok Hwang from KBC. Thank you.

....

남 안녕하십니까. 오늘 아름다운 봄 날을 즐기셨습니까? 서울은 최고 섭씨 22도까지 올라갔는데 인천은 26.5도로 조금 더 따뜻했습니다. 부산과 울산은 각각 23도와 25도였습니다. 제주도는 최고 26도까지

올라갔습니다. 내일은 서울의 기온이 계속 올라서 27도까지 오르겠으니 가벼운 옷차림을 하셔도 좋겠습니다. 이상 KBC 황순옥이었습니다. 감사합니다.

•• **degree** 도, 정도　**Celsius** 섭씨의　**respectively** 각각　**reach** ~에 이르다　**temperature** 기온　**on the rise** 올라서, 상승 중인

15

W　Good morning, students. We are pleased to announce that, due to student demand, we have added two new courses to the summer term! They are Elementary Algebra I and Advanced Composition. Seats will fill up fast, so log into our homepage and register today! Please contact an academic advisor if you would like to see how these courses would fit in your educational plan. They are here to help you succeed! They can be reached at 123-6767.

여　안녕하세요, 학생 여러분. 학생들의 요구로 여름학기에 새로운 두 강좌를 추가 개설함을 공지하게 되어 기쁩니다. 두 강좌는 기초 대수학 1과 고급 작문입니다. 좌석이 빨리 찰 예정이니 홈페이지에 접속해서 오늘 등록하세요! 그 강좌들이 여러분의 학업 계획과 어떻게 조화되는지 알고 싶다면, 학사지도교수에게 연락하세요. 그들은 여러분의 성공을 돕기 위해서 여기에 있습니다. 123-6767번으로 연락하시면 됩니다.

•• **announce** 알리다　**demand** 요구　**term** 학기　**elementary** 기초의 **algebra** 대수학　**advanced** 상급의, 발전된　**academic advisor** 학사지도교수　**educational** 교육의, 학업의

16

M　Do you know why Hannah is absent today?

W　She is in the hospital. I'm going to see her now.

M　Is she all right?

W　She sprained her ankle, but she should be all right soon.

M　That's a relief. Do you know how she got hurt?

W　When the escalator stopped suddenly at the subway station, she lost her balance and fell down.

M　It could have been worse. Can I join you?

W　Sure. She will be real glad to see you. Let's stop by

her house first to pick up some stuff for her.

남　너 Hannah가 오늘 왜 결석한지 아니?

여　병원에 입원 중이야. 지금 걔를 보러 갈 거야.

남　괜찮은 거니?

여　발목을 삐었지만, 금방 나을 거야.

남　그거 다행이다. 어쩌다가 다쳤는지 아니?

여　지하철역에서 에스컬레이터가 갑자기 멈췄을 때, 균형을 잃고 넘어졌어.

남　상황이 더 나쁠 수도 있었네. 너랑 함께 가도 될까?

여　물론이지. 널 보면 정말로 기뻐할 거야. 걔 물건 챙기러 걔네 집부터 먼저 들르자.

•• **absent** 결석한　**be in the hospital** 입원 중이다　**sprain** 삐다　**relief** 안도　**escalator** 에스컬레이터　**stuff** 물건, 소지품

17

① M　I wish I were on vacation.

　W　So do I.

② M　I went to the fish market at dawn.

　W　You're always complaining about others.

③ M　I can't wait to jump in the water.

　W　Make sure you warm up before going in.

④ M　I can't cook spaghetti.

　W　Let me help you.

⑤ M　Are you planning a trip to Disneyland?

　W　Yeah, I'm looking forward to it.

① 남　내가 지금 휴가 중이라면 좋을 텐데.

　여　나도 그래.

② 남　나 오늘 새벽에 어시장에 갔어.

　여　넌 언제나 남들에 대해 불평을 하는구나.

③ 남　물 속에 빨리 뛰어들고 싶어요.

　여　들어가기 전에 준비운동 하는 것을 잊지 마라.

④ 남　나는 스파게티를 만들 줄 몰라.

　여　내가 도와줄게.

⑤ 남　너는 디즈니랜드에 여행 갈 계획이니?

　여　응, 무척 기대돼.

•• **on vacation** 휴가 중인　**fish market** 어시장　**dawn** 새벽　**complain** 불평하다　**look forward to** ~을 고대하다

18

M Hi, Ashley. How were your tests?

W I think they're getting trickier. I got all average grades on the tests this time. How about you?

M I got a perfect score on the English test.

W Wow, congratulations! It seems that the tutoring from your brother is having an effect.

M It helps, but I don't completely agree. I studied really hard by myself, too.

W Wasn't your English grade a B last time? Anyway, how was math?

M I just got a C on that. My brother didn't teach me carefully how to handle difficult questions.

W Come on, you can't blame it on your brother.

남　안녕, Ashley. 시험은 어땠니?

여　점점 까다로워지고 있는 것 같아. 이번 시험에서 모두 딱 평균을 받았어. 너는?

남　나 영어 시험에서 만점 받았어.

여　와, 축하해! 네 형이 지도해준 게 효과를 발휘한 것 같네.

남　도움은 됐지만 완전히 동의는 안 해. 나 스스로도 진짜 열심히 공부했단 말이야.

여　너 지난번에 영어 성적이 B 아니었니? 어쨌든, 수학은 어땠어?

남　그냥 C 받았어. 형이 어려운 문제를 다루는 법을 꼼꼼하게 가르쳐 주지 않았어.

여　왜 그래. 형을 원망할 순 없지.

●●
tricky 까다로운　**average** 평균의　**perfect score** 만점　**tutor** 지도하다
effect 효과　**blame A on B** A의 책임을 B에게 돌리다

19

W Sarah is a member of a travel club. Next week, her club is going to climb Mt. Hood and plant a flag on the summit. Although it's summer now, snow is covering the mountaintop. So the head of the club says they should bring their coats, gloves, and scarves. It is the first time for Sarah to climb a mountain covered with snow in summer. She is wondering if there are any more things she needs to bring. In this situation, what would Sarah most likely say to the head of the club?

여　Sarah는 여행 동아리의 회원이다. 다음 주에 그녀의 동아리는 Hood 산에 올라 정상에 깃발을 꽂을 예정이다. 비록 지금 여름이지만, 그 산꼭대기에는 눈이 덮여있다. 그래서 동아리 회장은 코트, 장갑, 목도리를 가져와야 한다고 말한다. Sarah는 여름에 눈 덮인 산을 오르는 것이 처음이다. 그녀는 더 가지고 가야 할 것이 있는지 궁금하다. 이 상황에서 Sarah는 동아리 회장에게 뭐라고 말하겠는가?

① 오늘의 특별요리는 뭔가요?
② 그밖에 다른 무엇을 가지고 와야 하나요?
③ 등산 갈 준비가 다 되었나요?
④ 등산하는 걸 좋아하나요?
⑤ 등산하는 데 얼마나 시간을 투자하세요?

●●
plant 심다, 박다　**summit** 정상　**mountaintop** 산꼭대기　**although** 비록 ~이지만

20

W Bobby, I forgot what day mom and dad's wedding anniversary is. I've drawn a blank. Do you know?

M Oh my god. It is the day after tomorrow. I just completely forgot.

W Let's do something special for them.

M Do you have anything in mind?

W How about a surprise party?

M That's a good idea. But there are only two days left to prepare for the party. What should we do first?

W We need party decorations like balloons, banners, and candles. We also need a cake and flowers. Oh, don't forget the present. What else?

M Why don't we get started by writing up a to-do list?

여　Bobby, 엄마 아빠의 결혼기념일이 언제인지 잊어버렸어. 생각이 안 나. 오빤 알아?

남　오 이런. 내일 모레야. 까맣게 잊고 있었어.

여　엄마 아빠를 위해 뭔가 특별한 것을 하자.

남　특별히 생각해 둔 게 있니?

여　깜짝 파티 어때?

남　좋은 생각이다. 그런데 파티 준비를 할 수 있는 날이 딱 이틀밖에 남지 않았어. 뭘 먼저 해야 할까?

여　우린 풍선, 현수막, 양초 같은 파티 장식물들이 필요해. 또한 케이크랑 꽃도 필요하고. 오, 선물도 잊지 마. 또 뭐가 있지?

남　할 일 목록을 쓰는 것부터 시작해 보는 게 어때?

① 파티가 몇 시에 끝났니?
② 우리는 당신을 파티에 초대하고 싶어요.
③ 파티에서 재미있었니?
④ 할 일 목록을 쓰는 것부터 시작해 보는 게 어때?
⑤ 파티에 엄마 아빠들을 초대하면 어떨까?

●●
wedding anniversary 결혼기념일 **draw a blank** 실패하다, 생각나지 않다 **completely** 완전히 **decoration** 장식 **banner** 기, 현수막

Further Study 정답   p. 64

1. The reason is that the stamps are already sold out.
2. He follows the ball with his eyes after he hits it.
3. The reason is that his phone has bad reception, so he can't hear her well.
4. She can speak four languages fluently.
5. They are at Korail's reservation center.
6. She wants to withdraw some cash.
7. She sprained her ankle when the escalator stopped suddenly at the subway station.
8. They want to do something special for their parents' wedding anniversary.

On Your Own 모범답안   p. 65

A

Describing a Graph	
(1) Title	pets the students in Mike's class raise
(2) The most popular pet	dog
(3) Comparing pets	students raise more hamsters than iguanas, but raise fewer hamsters than cats
(4) The least popular pet	iguanas
(5) Your suggestion about raising a pet	by raising a pet, young people are likely to learn to be more responsible

This chart shows (1)the popularity of different pets that the students in Mike's class raise in their homes. The most popular pet is (2)a dog. The students raise

(3)more hamsters than iguanas, but raise fewer hamsters than cats. (4)Iguanas are the least popular pets among Mike's classmates. It is a good idea to (5)raise a pet because young people are likely to learn to be more responsible.

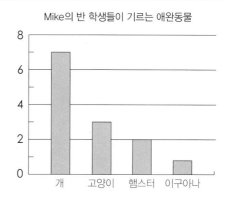

Mike의 반 학생들이 기르는 애완동물

그래프 설명하기	
(1) 제목	Mike의 반 학생들이 기르는 애완동물
(2) 가장 인기 있는 애완동물	개
(3) 애완동물 간 비교하기	학생들은 이구아나보다는 햄스터를 더 많이 기르지만 고양이보다는 햄스터를 덜 기름
(4) 가장 인기 없는 애완동물	이구아나
(5) 애완동물 기르기에 대한 당신의 제안사항	애완동물을 기름으로써 청소년들이 더 책임감을 갖도록 배우게 됨

이 그래프는 Mike의 반 학생들이 집에서 기르는 각기 다른 애완동물의 인기를 보여줍니다. 가장 인기 있는 애완동물은 개입니다. 학생들은 이구아나보다는 햄스터를 더 많이 기르지만 고양이보다는 햄스터를 덜 기릅니다. 이구아나는 Mike의 반 친구들에게 가장 인기 없는 애완동물입니다. 청소년들이 더 책임감을 갖도록 배울 것이므로 애완동물을 기르는 것은 좋은 생각입니다.

B

An Impressive Party	
Who hosted it, when & where?	(1) my brother and I hosted it at our home in February 2014
What was the purpose of the party?	(2) to congratulate my mom and dad on their 17th wedding anniversary
Why was the party impressive?	(3) the first party that my brother and I had ever hosted (4) decorated the party place ourselves with balloons, ribbons, candles, and banners (5) baked a cake ourselves to congratulate them

I would like to tell you about an impressive party I had. It was hosted by (1)my brother and me at our home in February 2014. The purpose of the party was (2)to congratulate my mom and dad on their 17th wedding anniversary. The party had many things that I think were impressive. First, (3)it was the first party that my brother and I had ever hosted. Second, (4)we decorated the party place ourselves with balloons, ribbons, candles, and banners. Third, (5)we baked a cake ourselves to congratulate them. It was a party that I'll never forget.

인상적인 파티	
누가 언제 어디서 열었나요?	(1) 오빠와 내가 2014년 2월 집에서 엶
파티의 목적은?	(2) 엄마 아빠의 17번째 결혼기념일을 축하하기 위해서
파티가 인상적이었던 이유는?	(3) 오빠와 내가 처음으로 연 파티
	(4) 우리가 직접 풍선, 리본, 양초, 현수막으로 파티 장소를 장식함
	(5) 엄마와 아빠께 축하 드리기 위해 케이크를 직접 만듦

제가 경험한 인상적인 파티를 소개하고 싶습니다. 이 파티는 오빠와 제가 2014년 2월 집에서 열었습니다. 파티의 목적은 엄마 아빠의 17번째 결혼기념일을 축하하기 위해서였습니다. 그 파티에는 제가 인상적이라고 생각하는 것이 여러 가지가 있었습니다. 첫째, 그것은 오빠와 제가 처음으로 연 파티였습니다. 둘째, 우리가 직접 풍선, 리본, 양초, 현수막으로 파티 장소를 장식했습니다. 셋째, 우리는 엄마와 아빠께 축하 드리기 위해 케이크를 직접 만들었습니다. 그것은 제가 결코 잊지 못할 파티였습니다.

01 ③	02 ①	03 ④	04 ④	05 ①
06 ③	07 ⑤	08 ⑤	09 ①	10 ⑤
11 ②	12 ④	13 ②	14 ④	15 ③
16 ①	17 ⑤	18 ③	19 ①	20 ②

01

M Now, we're done with shopping, right?

W Not yet. We have to buy Riona's classroom shoes. Her preschool teacher asked me to send a new pair of them.

M I see. There are lots of designs here. I like the ones with butterflies.

W She has the same pattern on a pair of her shoes. I want to buy her something unique and comfortable.

M How about these leopard print ones with wide shoelaces?

W They look uncomfortable. What about these moccasins?

M Oh, I love their color. Pink on the front and dark purple on the back with a brown trim!

W Yes, Riona will love them. Let's take them.

남 이제 우리 쇼핑 끝난 거지?

여 아직. Riona 실내화를 사야 해요. 유치원 선생님이 걔가 신을 새 실내화 한 켤레를 보내달라고 하셨어요.

남 알았어. 여기에 여러 디자인들이 있네. 난 나비 무늬가 있는 것이 마음에 들어.

여 같은 무늬의 신발 한 켤레가 있어요. 난 뭔가 독특하고 편안한 신발을 사주고 싶어요.

남 그럼 넓은 신발끈이 있는 이 표범 무늬 신발은 어때?

여 불편해 보여요. 이 모카신은 어때요?

남 오, 색깔이 마음에 드네. 앞부분은 분홍색이고 갈색 테두리 장식이 있는 뒷부분은 짙은 보라색!

여 응, Riona가 좋아할 거예요. 이것으로 사요.

••
be done with ~을 끝내다   **unique** 독특한   **shoelace** 신발끈
moccasin 뒤축 없는 신, 모카신   **trim** (장식이 되는) 테두리

02

W Max, do you know where the dishcloth is? I need it to clean the dishes.

M Did you look on the kitchen table?

W It wasn't there. It was not in the drawers next to the refrigerator, either.

M How about in the microwave oven? You sometimes put the dishcloth in there to sterilize it.

W No, it's not there.

M Oh, wait, I remember! Yesterday I used it when I arranged the cups. It may still be in the cupboard.

W Oh, yes. Here it is.

....

여 Max, 행주 어디에 있는지 아세요? 접시 닦는 데 필요해요.

남 식탁 위에 봤어요?

여 거기에 없었어요. 냉장고 옆에 있는 서랍장에도 없어요.

남 전자레인지 안은 어때요? 가끔 행주를 소독한다고 거기에 넣잖아요.

여 아뇨, 거기에도 없어요.

남 오, 잠깐만. 기억났어요. 어제 내가 컵 정리할 때 행주를 사용했어요. 아마 아직 찬장 안에 있을 거예요.

여 오, 네. 여기 있어요.

••
dishcloth 행주 **drawers** 서랍장 **refrigerator** 냉장고 **microwave oven** 전자레인지 **sterilize** 살균하다 **cupboard** 찬장

03

W Hey, good news. I got promoted.

M Congratulations! What is your title now?

W I'm now a sales department manager. From now on, I will be in charge of arranging all affairs in the sales department.

M Good for you. You got promoted quite quickly. On the other hand, I've stayed at the same position for three years.

W I think it's because I have worked hard. I had to work till very late at night so many times.

M Hey, I've been working hard, too. But my hard work hasn't been noticed like yours. I wish I could be promoted as fast as you.

....

여 이봐, 좋은 소식이야. 나 승진했어.

남 축하해! 이제 직함이 뭐야?

여 이제 영업부 부장이야. 이제부터 영업부에서 모든 일의 관리를 내가 맡게 될 거야.

남 잘됐다. 너는 아주 빨리 승진했어. 반면에 나는 3년 동안 같은 직급에 머물러 있지.

여 나는 내가 일을 열심히 했기 때문이라고 생각해. 너무나 여러 번 아주 밤늦게까지 일해야 했어.

남 이봐, 나도 열심히 일해왔어. 하지만 내가 한 일은 네가 한 일만큼 주목을 받지 못했어. 나도 너처럼 빨리 승진을 하면 좋을 텐데.

① 감명받은   ② 불안한   ③ 뽐내는
④ 부러워하는   ⑤ 화난

••
promote 승진시키다 **title** 직함 **department** 국, 부 **affair** 일, 업무 **be in charge of** ~을 담당하다 **on the other hand** 반면에

04

M What can I do for you?

W I'd like to get a refund on these jeans.

M May I ask why you want to get a refund for them?

W My sister bought them for my birthday, but I think they don't fit me.

M If that's the only reason, why don't you exchange them for something else?

W I'm sorry, but I just want a refund.

M Alright. Do you have the receipt?

W Here it is.

M Please wait a minute.

....

남 무엇을 도와드릴까요?

여 이 청바지를 환불하고 싶어요.

남 왜 환불을 원하시는지 여쭤봐도 될까요?

여 언니가 제 생일 선물로 사줬는데 제게 어울리는 것 같지 않아요.

남 그게 유일한 이유라면 다른 것으로 교환하시는 것은 어떠세요?

여 죄송합니다만 환불을 원합니다.

남 알겠습니다. 영수증 있으세요?

여 여기 있습니다.

남 잠시만 기다려 주세요.

① 경찰   ② 선생님   ③ 기자
④ 판매원   ⑤ 관광 가이드

••
refund 환불 **fit** 맞다, 어울리다 **exchange** 교환하다 **receipt** 영수증

05

[Telephone rings.]

M Hello?

W Hello. I saw your ad on the Internet. You're selling the Chihuahua puppy for 100 dollars, right?

M Yes, I paid 200 dollars when I bought it in the pet store.

W Is it trained to live indoors?

M Yes, it is. I'm also selling its portable doghouse for 15 dollars. Are you interested in it, too?

W Oh, well. That's good but…

M If you buy both of them, I'll give you three packs of doggy treats for free. They were 5 dollars each when I bought them.

W Sounds good. I'll buy both of them. Can I pick them up tomorrow?

··

[전화벨이 울린다.]

남 여보세요.

여 여보세요. 인터넷에 올리신 광고 봤어요. 100달러에 치와와 강아지 파시는 거 맞죠?

남 네. 애완동물 가게에서 살 때 200달러 지불했어요.

여 실내생활에 훈련되어 있나요?

남 네. 휴대용 개집도 15달러에 팔아요. 이것도 관심 있습니까?

여 오, 글쎄요. 좋긴 한데…

남 둘 다 사시면, 강아지 간식 세 봉지를 공짜로 드릴게요. 제가 한 봉지당 5달러에 샀던 거예요.

여 좋아요. 둘 다 살게요. 내일 데리러 가도 되나요?

•• **ad** 광고 **puppy** 강아지 **indoors** 실내에서 **portable** 휴대용의 **treat** 간식, 한턱

06

M Why are people fired from their jobs? In many cases, it's not because they are doing a bad job. Instead, people are often fired because of a personal conflict. This is why it is important to get along with fellow workers. Getting along with other people is a matter of good work habits. Here are three keywords for good on-the-job behavior: promptness, courtesy, and eagerness.

남 왜 사람들은 그들의 직장에서 해고당할까요? 많은 경우, 그들이 일을 못해서가 아닙니다. 대신에, 사사로운 마찰 때문에 종종 사람들이 해고당합니다. 이것이 동료들과 잘 지내야 하는 것이 중요한 이유입니다. 다른 사람들과 잘 지낸다는 것은 좋은 업무 습관의 문제입니다. 이제 바른 직장 내 행동에 대한 세 가지 핵심어를 말씀 드리려고 하는데 그것은 바로 신속, 공손 그리고 열정입니다.

•• **fire** 해고하다 **personal** 사사로운, 개인적인 **conflict** 충돌, 마찰 **get along with** ~와 사이 좋게 지내다 **promptness** 신속 **courtesy** 공손 **eagerness** 열정

07

W How was school? How did you do on the test?

M It was OK, and I did great on the test, Mom.

W I am glad to hear that.

M By the way, what do we have for dinner tonight?

W I will make roast beef and mashed potatoes. For dessert, I've already made carrot cake and muffins.

M It has been a long time since you made roast beef. Do you need any help, mom?

W No, go do your homework and leave the cooking to me.

M Thanks, mom. Call me whenever dinner is ready. I do not want to be late for this tasty dinner.

··

여 학교에서 잘 지냈니? 시험은 어떻게 봤니?

남 괜찮았어요, 그리고 시험은 잘 봤어요, 엄마.

여 그 이야기를 들으니 기쁘구나.

남 그런데 오늘밤 저녁으로 뭐 먹어요?

여 쇠고기 구이와 으깬 감자를 만들 거야. 후식으로 당근 케이크와 머핀도 이미 만들어놨어.

남 오랜만에 쇠고기 구이를 만드시네요. 도와드릴까요, 엄마?

여 아니, 가서 숙제 하고 요리는 나에게 맡기렴.

남 고마워요, 엄마. 저녁이 준비되면 언제든지 저를 부르세요. 이런 맛있는 저녁에 늦기 싫어요.

•• **roast** 구운 **mash** 짓이기다 **tasty** 맛있는

08

M Minju, I'm interested in your debate club. Can you tell me a little bit about it?

W Why not? There are 13 members including me. Our

club's name is "DD Debate."

M What do you usually do?

W We read English newspapers and have weekly debates in English about news events. The debates are every Wednesday right after school.

M Sounds interesting. Are you meeting this Wednesday then?

W No. This time we have postponed it for two days.

M Okay. Can I go with you then?

W Definitely. Let's meet on that day and go to the club meeting together.

남 민주야, 난 너의 토론 클럽에 관심이 있어. 그 클럽에 대해 이야기 좀 해줄래?

여 좋아. 나 포함해서 13명의 회원이 있어. 우리 클럽 이름은 "DD 토론"이야.

남 보통 뭐 해?

여 우리는 영어 신문을 읽고 영어로 시사 사건에 대한 토론을 매주 해. 토론은 매주 수요일 수업 끝난 직후에 있어.

남 재미있겠다. 그러면 이번 수요일에도 만나니?

여 아니. 이번에는 이틀 미뤘어.

남 좋아. 그때 나도 같이 가도 돼?

여 당연하지. 그날 만나서 클럽 모임에 같이 가자.

① 월요일　　　② 화요일　　　③ 수요일
④ 목요일　　　⑤ 금요일

••
be interested in ~에 흥미가 있다　**debate** 토론　**including** ~을 포함하여　**postpone** 연기하다　**definitely** 그렇고 말고

09

① M Now, I understand why this movie is a big hit.

　W So do I. It is so touching.

② M Why don't we go to the movies?

　W I'd love to but I have to take care of my younger sisters.

③ M We'd like two tickets for the 2:30 show, please.

　W Here you go. Enjoy the movie!

④ M I have a bad cough.

　W Let me look at your throat.

⑤ M Did you have a good weekend?

　W Yes. I went to the cinema with my family.

---

① 남 이제 이 영화가 왜 크게 히트를 치고 있는지 알겠어.

　여 나도 그래. 너무나 감동적이야.

② 남 영화 보러 가는 거 어때?

　여 가고 싶지만, 내 여동생들을 돌봐야 해.

③ 남 2시 30분 영화 두 장 주세요.

　여 여기 있습니다. 영화 즐겁게 관람하세요!

④ 남 기침이 심해요.

　여 목 좀 보여주세요.

⑤ 남 주말 잘 보냈니?

　여 응. 가족들과 함께 극장에 갔어.

••
touching 감동적인　**take care of** ~을 돌보다　**throat** 목

10

W Hey, Jacob. Are you still playing that game?

M Judy, guess what! I got to the highest level on this game.

W Really? What level is the highest?

M It goes up to level 12. I feel like I've really achieved something.

W Good for you! But you know what? You've been playing the game for two hours.

M Oh my god! Time flies so fast. I feel like only 20 minutes has passed.

W You spent too much time to get to that level. It's already 10 p.m.

여 이봐, Jacob. 너 아직 그 게임 하고 있는 거니?

남 Judy, 맞춰봐! 나 이 게임에서 최고 단계에 올랐어.

여 정말? 몇 단계가 최고인데?

남 12단계까지 있어. 내가 정말 뭔가를 해낸 것처럼 느껴져.

여 잘했네! 그런데 너 그거 아니? 너 2시간 동안 그 게임 하고 있다는 거.

남 오 이런! 시간 진짜 빨리 간다. 20분밖에 안 지난 것 같은데.

여 그 단계에 가려고 넌 너무 많은 시간을 보냈어. 벌써 10시야.

••
get to ~에 이르다　**achieve** 달성하다

11

[Telephone rings.]

M Hello.

W Hey, Jaesuk. What are you doing now?

M Oh, hi, Misun. I'm watching a <u>tennis</u> <u>match</u> on TV. It's almost over.

W I <u>don't</u> <u>know</u> much about <u>tennis</u>, but is that the big game <u>between</u> <u>Spain</u> <u>and</u> <u>Korea</u> I have heard so much about?

M No, that's a <u>soccer</u> <u>game</u>. It's later tonight on channel 11. Are you going to watch it?

W Oh. I'm not much interested in sports anyway. By the way, do you <u>have</u> <u>free</u> <u>time</u> tomorrow?

M <u>Probably</u>, yes. Why?

W I'd like to go to a <u>music</u> <u>concert</u> with you. Can you?

M Sure. I'll go with you.

- -

[전화벨이 울린다.]
남 여보세요.
여 안녕, 재석아. 너 지금 뭐 해?
남 아, 안녕 미선아. 텔레비전으로 테니스 경기를 보고 있어. 거의 끝나가.
여 난 테니스에 대해선 잘 모르는데 그게 내가 그렇게도 많이 들었던 한국과 스페인 간의 대경기야?
남 아니, 그건 축구 경기야. 그건 이따 밤에 11번 채널에서 해. 그거 볼 거야?
여 아. 난 스포츠에 별 관심이 없어. 그런데, 너 내일 시간 있니?
남 아마도 그럴 걸. 왜?
여 너랑 같이 음악 콘서트에 가고 싶어. 갈 수 있어?
남 물론이지. 같이 갈게.

••
match 경기 **by the way** 그런데

12

M It is <u>the</u> <u>largest</u> <u>country</u> in Western Europe. It is a <u>great</u> <u>power</u> with significant <u>cultural</u>, <u>economic</u>, <u>military</u>, and <u>political</u> <u>influence</u> in Europe and around the world. It is the third <u>wealthiest</u> <u>nation</u> in Europe and <u>ninth</u> in the world. The country's name comes from the Latin Francia, which means <u>country</u> <u>of</u> the <u>Franks</u>. It has the Eiffel Tower, the Notre-Dame Cathedral, and the Palace of Versailles.

- -

남 이 나라는 서유럽에서 가장 큰 나라입니다. 이 나라는 유럽과 전 세계에서 문화, 경제, 군사, 그리고 정치적으로 큰 영향력을 가진 강국입니다. 유럽에서는 세 번째로 부자 나라이며 세계에서는 아홉 번째입니다. 나라의 이름은 프랑크족의 나라라는 의미의 라틴어 Francia에서 유래되었습니다. 이 나라에는 에펠 탑, 노트르담 성당,

그리고 베르사이유 궁전이 있습니다.

① 영국　　　　② 필리핀　　　　③ 프랑스
④ 스페인　　　　⑤ 스위스

••
significant 중대한 **cultural** 문화의 **economic** 경제의 **military** 군사의 **influence** 영향(력) **come from** ~에서 유래하다 **palace** 궁전

13

M Look at the <u>poster</u>!

W <u>What</u> <u>is</u> <u>it</u> <u>about</u>?

M There will be an <u>English</u> <u>writing</u> <u>contest</u> in May.

W Really? <u>Probably</u> it will be a very big one. Are you interested in it?

M Yeah, that <u>sounds</u> very <u>interesting</u>, but I'm not sure yet.

W Why? Are you busy this month?

M Yes. I have to <u>submit</u> a science report by the <u>third</u> <u>Friday</u> in May. But the contest will be right before that day.

W Oh, <u>that's</u> <u>too</u> <u>bad</u>. I don't think you can <u>enter</u> it then.

- -

남 포스터를 봐봐!
여 무엇에 관한 건데?
남 5월에 영어 글짓기 대회가 있대.
여 정말? 아마도 큰 대회가 될 것 같아. 관심 있니?
남 응, 흥미롭게 들리긴 하는데 아직 잘 모르겠어.
여 왜? 이번 달에 바쁘니?
남 응. 5월 셋째 주 금요일까지 과학 보고서를 제출해야 해. 그런데 그 대회가 제출일 바로 전날이야.
여 안됐구나. 그럼 네가 대회에 참가할 수 없을 것 같네.

① 5월 8일　　　② 5월 14일　　　③ 5월 15일
④ 5월 21일　　　⑤ 5월 22일

••
probably 아마도 **submit** 제출하다

14

[Telephone rings.]

W Honey, are you <u>still</u> <u>at</u> <u>work</u>?

M Yes. I am. Why? Are you <u>already</u> <u>finished</u>?

W No, it's the opposite. I'm going to finish late today. I think I'll have to work very late because tomorrow is the deadline for the manuscript.

M I see. What can I do for you?

W I need to pick Hanul up at 5:30 but I can't. She will be ready to be picked up at the kindergarten then.

M Don't worry about it. I can pick her up. However, I might be late by 10 to 15 minutes because it's rush hour.

W I'll call the teacher and explain our situation. Thank you very much.

M No problem. Good luck with the manuscript.

[전화벨이 울린다.]

여 여보, 아직 사무실이에요?

남 응. 왜? 벌써 끝났어요?

여 아니, 그 반대예요. 오늘 늦게 끝날 거예요. 내일이 원고 마감일이라 아주 늦게까지 일해야 할 것 같아요.

남 그렇구나. 내가 무엇을 하면 될까요?

여 한울이를 5시 30분에 데리러 가야 하지만 내가 할 수가 없어요. 그때 한울이는 유치원에서 우리가 데려가도록 준비가 되어 있을 거예요.

남 걱정 말아요. 내가 데려올 수 있어요. 그런데 지금이 혼잡 시간대라 10분에서 15분 정도까지 늦을 수도 있을 것 같아요.

여 내가 선생님께 전화 드려서 우리 상황을 설명할게요. 정말 고마워요.

남 고맙긴. 원고 쓰는 것에 행운을 빌어요.

●●
opposite 반대의 **deadline** 기한 **manuscript** 원고 **kindergarten** 유치원 **rush hour** 혼잡한 시간 **explain** 설명하다

15

M What kind of music do you like?

W Oh, I like all kinds of music as long as it is not hard rock.

M Wow! Look at the number of people who have already shown up for the concert.

W Where do you want to sit? In the shade or in the sun?

M In the shade, please. I have been in the sun too much lately.

W Okay, let's sit down here. How long ago did the band start playing at this park?

M I think it started this tradition five years ago.

남 넌 어떤 종류의 음악을 좋아하니?

여 오, 나는 하드록만 아니면 모든 종류의 음악을 다 좋아해.

남 왜! 콘서트를 보려고 벌써 온 사람들의 수를 봐.

여 어디에 앉고 싶니? 그늘 아니면 햇볕?

남 그늘에 앉자. 최근에 햇볕에 너무 많이 있었어.

여 그래, 여기 앉자. 그 밴드는 얼마나 오래 전에 이 공원에서 연주를 하기 시작했던 거야?

남 이 전통은 5년 전에 시작된 것 같아.

① 미술관   ② 콘서트 홀   ③ 공원
④ 박물관   ⑤ 극장

●●
as long as ~하는 한 **show up** 나타나다 **shade** 그늘 **lately** 최근에 **tradition** 전통

16

① **M** I heard that your sister had a car accident. Is that true?

  W Yes, she did. I'm so proud of her.

② **M** Have you heard the news this morning?

  W What news?

③ **M** What are you going to buy?

  W I'm going to buy some books and CDs.

④ **M** Turn left and cross the street in front of the post office.

  W Would you say that again?

⑤ **M** I missed the bus in the morning, so I was late for school.

  W You must be upset.

---

①남 네 여동생이 교통사고를 당했다고 들었어. 정말이니?

  여 응, 그래. 나는 그녀가 무척 자랑스러워.

②남 오늘 아침에 뉴스 들었니?

  여 무슨 뉴스?

③남 너 뭐 살 예정이니?

  여 책 몇 권이랑 CD 몇 장 살 예정이야.

④남 우체국 앞에서 왼쪽으로 돌아 길을 건너세요.

  여 다시 말씀해 주시겠어요?

⑤남 오늘 아침에 버스를 놓쳐서 학교에 늦었어.

  여 너 짜증 났겠구나.

●●
be proud of ~을 자랑스러워 하다 **be late for** ~에 지각하다

17

M Good evening, what can I do for you?

W Hi, I'd like to <u>renew</u> my registration.

M Thanks for your <u>renewal</u>. Well, have you heard about our <u>personal training program</u>?

W Yes, I have. But it's <u>too expensive</u> for me.

M In celebration of our <u>first anniversary</u>, we are offering a <u>50</u>% <u>discount</u> for members who buy the three-month personal training program.

W Oh, are you? When does this <u>offer</u> end?

M It is going on <u>till May 30th</u>. Also, you can get <u>30% off</u> a <u>gym renewal</u> if a friend takes out a gym membership <u>on your recommendation</u>.

W Oh, that's a good deal. Then do you have any <u>trial vouchers</u> that I can give out?

M Seven-day trial vouchers are right here at <u>the counter</u> for our <u>potential members</u>. Help yourself.

남 안녕하세요, 무엇을 도와드릴까요?

여 안녕하세요. 등록을 갱신하려고요.

남 재등록 감사합니다. 혹시, 저희의 개인지도 프로그램에 관해 들어보신 적 있으세요?

여 네, 들어봤어요. 그런데 제겐 너무 비싸요.

남 1주년 기념으로, 3개월 개인지도 프로그램을 구매하시는 회원님께는 50%를 할인해 드리고 있습니다.

여 오, 그런가요? 이 행사는 언제 끝나나요?

남 이 행사는 5월 30일까지 계속됩니다. 또한 친구가 회원님의 추천으로 체육관 회원이 되시면 회원님이 체육관 회원권을 갱신하실 때 쓸 30% 할인을 받으실 수 있습니다.

여 오, 좋은 조건이네요. 그러면 제가 나누어 줄 수 있는 무료 체험권 같은 거 있나요?

남 잠재 회원들을 위한 7일 체험권이 바로 여기 카운터에 있습니다. 마음껏 이용하세요.

renew 갱신하다 **registration** 등록 **in celebration of** ~을 기념하여 **take out** 획득하다 **on one's recommendation** ~의 추천으로 **voucher** 할인권, 사은권 **potential** 잠재적인

18

W Winter vacation is <u>around the corner</u>. Last summer vacation, Brad took a trip to England with his family <u>for two weeks</u>. He enjoyed traveling there greatly, but he also had a <u>horrifying moment</u>. He almost got <u>hit by a car</u> while he was crossing the street because he didn't look <u>to his right</u>. He didn't remember that they drive <u>on the left side</u>. Today Brad's best friend, Carol, says she is going to take a trip to <u>the UK</u> this vacation. She asks Brad for some tips for the trip. In this situation, what would Brad most likely say to Carol?

어 겨울방학이 코앞에 와있다. 지난 여름방학에 Brad는 2주간 가족과 함께 잉글랜드 여행을 했다. 그는 거기서 여행을 무척 즐겼지만 한 가지 소름 끼쳤던 순간도 있었다. 그는 오른쪽을 보지 않아서 길을 건널 때 거의 차에 치일 뻔했던 것이다. 그는 거기 사람들이 왼쪽에서 운전한다는 것을 기억하지 못했다. 오늘 Brad의 단짝인 Carol이 이번 방학에 영국으로 여행갈 예정이라고 말한다. 그녀는 Brad에게 여행에 대한 조언을 구한다. 이 상황에서 Brad는 Carol에게 뭐라고 말하겠는가?

① 여행 잘 해.
② 잉글랜드 여행은 어땠니?
③ 여행 언제 떠나니?
④ 나는 여행에 함께 가는 사람이 좀 있으면 좋겠어.
⑤ 길 건널 땐 오른쪽을 봐.

horrify 소름 끼치게 하다 **UK** (United Kingdom) 영국 **tip** 정보, 비결

19

W Oh, my <u>throat</u> is <u>killing me</u>.

M Do you have <u>a cold</u>?

W Yes. It is a bad cold and I'm taking some <u>medicine</u>. But there must be something else I can do for <u>my sore throat</u>.

M Well, if I were you, I would drink <u>some hot tea</u>.

W What kind of <u>tea</u>?

M <u>As long as</u> it's <u>hot</u>, it doesn't really matter. I prefer <u>ginger</u> tea.

W It is quite <u>spicy</u>, isn't it? Do you drink it with <u>something in it</u>?

M <u>Yes, with some honey in it.</u>

여 오, 목이 너무 아파.

남 너 감기 걸린 거야?

여 응. 심한 감기여서 약을 먹고 있어. 하지만 인후통을 위해 약 이외에

내가 할 수 있는 일이 분명 있을 거야.

남　음, 내가 너라면, 뜨거운 차를 좀 마시겠어.

여　무슨 차?

남　뜨거운 거면 뭐든 괜찮아. 나는 생강차를 선호해.

여　그거 꽤 매운데, 그렇지 않니? 거기다 뭘 넣어서 마시니?

남　응, 꿀을 넣어서.

① 응, 꿀을 넣어서.
② 목 아픈 증상이 얼마나 오래 됐나요?
③ 목 아픈 데 먹는 약 있나요?
④ 하루 세 번씩 약 먹는 것을 잊어선 안됩니다.
⑤ 네. 목이 아파서 음식을 넘기기가 힘들어요.

throat 목구멍　**sore** 아픈　**take medicine** 약을 복용하다　**ginger** 생강
spicy 매운

20

W　Oh, it's almost lunch time. I'm starving to death.
　　What do you want to have today?

M　I'm as hungry as a bear. I could eat anything.

W　Where shall we go? What about Italian food?

M　That would be fine with me.

W　The new Italian restaurant across the street got
　　good reviews on the Internet.

M　No. Let's not go there.

W　Why not?

M　The service was terrible when I went there.

여　오, 점심시간 거의 다 됐어. 배고파 죽겠어. 너 오늘 뭐 먹고 싶니?

남　나 너무나 배가 고파. 아무거나 다 먹을 수 있어.

여　어디로 갈까? 이탈리아음식 어때?

남　난 좋아.

여　길 건너편에 새로 생긴 이탈리아음식점이 인터넷에서 좋은 평가를
　　받던데.

남　안 돼. 거긴 가지 말자.

여　왜 안 돼?

남　내가 갔을 때 서비스가 형편없었어.

① 거긴 정말 좋은 식당이었어. 가서 먹어봐.
② 내가 갔을 때 서비스가 형편없었어.
③ 그 식당은 이 일대에서는 최고에 속해.
④ 이 길에 있는 다른 식당을 확인해보자.
⑤ 이 식당엔 왜 사람이 이렇게 많죠?

death 죽음　**review** 비평

p. 74

Further Study 정답

1. She will arrange all affairs in the sales department.
2. She got a pair of jeans.
3. They were 5 dollars each, so he paid 15 dollars in total.
4. They are promptness, courtesy, and eagerness.
5. They read English newspapers and have weekly debates in English about news events.
6. He has reached level 12, the highest level on the game.
7. It is about an English writing contest.
8. She will give them a seven-day trial vouchers.

p. 75

On Your Own 모범답안

A

My Motivation to Study	
What motivates me	Why they motivate me
(1) a desire not to let down my parents	(2) they always root for me and I love them very much; I want to make them happy
(3) a desire to become a pilot	(4) love flying and traveling in foreign countries; really want to realize my dream

I'm going to talk about what motivates me to study.
First, I am motivated by (1)a desire not to let down
my parents. Since (2)they always root for me and I
love them very much, I want to make them happy.
The second thing that motivates me to study is (3)my
desire to become a pilot. Because (4)I love flying and
traveling in foreign countries, I really want to realize
my dream. These two things always motivate me to
study hard.

내가 공부하도록 동기를 부여하는 것	
내게 동기를 주는 것	그것이 동기가 되는 이유
(1) 부모님을 실망 시켜드리지 않겠다는 바램	(2) 부모님이 항상 나를 응원해주시고 난 그분들을 너무나 사랑하므로 그분들을 행복하게 해드리고 싶음
(3) 조종사가 되고 싶은 바램	(4) 비행과 외국 여행을 좋아하므로 내 꿈을 정말로 이루고 싶음

저는 제가 공부하도록 동기를 부여해주는 것에 대해서 이야기하려고 합니다. 첫 번째로, 제 부모님을 실망시켜 드리지 않겠다는 바램에 의해서 동기부여를 받습니다. 부모님이 항상 저를 응원해주시고 전 그분들을 너무나 사랑하기 때문에 저는 그 분들을 행복하게 해드리고 싶습니다. 저를 공부하게 하는 두 번째 것은 비행기조종사가 되고 싶은 바램입니다. 저는 비행과 외국 여행을 좋아하기 때문에 저는 정말로 제 꿈을 이루고 싶습니다. 이런 두 가지 바램이 항상 제가 열심히 공부하도록 동기를 부여해줍니다.

B

I Would Like to Join a Club...	
(1) Name of the club	the Guitar Club
(2) Reason(s) you'd like to join	love playing the guitar very much, it releases all of my stress
(3) Activities they do	each member brings a new song they'd like to play on the guitar with all the club members, learns and then plays all the new songs on the guitar
(4) Time/place for regular meetings	in the music room every Tuesday right after school

I'm going to talk about a club which I would like to join. The club I would like to join is (1)the Guitar Club. I would like to join the club because (2)I love playing the guitar very much and it releases all of my stress. Each club member (3)brings a new song they'd like to play on the guitar with all the club members. Everyone learns and then plays all the new songs on the guitar. The club meets (4)in the music room every Tuesday right after school. I can't wait to join the club and do all the fun activities.

저는 … 동아리에 가입하고 싶습니다	
(1) 동아리 이름	기타 동아리
(2) 가입을 원하는 이유	기타 연주를 아주 좋아함, 그것이 내 모든 스트레스를 해소함
(3) 그들이 하는 활동	다른 모든 회원과 함께 기타로 연주하고 싶은 새 노래를 각자 가져옴, 그 모든 새 노래를 배운 후 기타로 연주함
(4) 정기 모임을 위한 시간과 장소	매주 화요일 방과 후 곧바로 음악실에서

저는 제가 가입하고 싶은 동아리에 대해 이야기할 것입니다. 제가 가입하고 싶은 동아리는 기타 동아리입니다. 저는 기타 연주를 무척 좋아하며 그것이 저의 모든 스트레스를 없애주기 때문에 그 동아리에 가입하고 싶습니다. 동아리 회원들은 다른 모든 회원들과 함께 기타로 연주하고 싶은 새 노래를 각자 가져옵니다. 모두가 이 모든 새 노래들을 배운 후 기타로 연주합니다. 동아리는 매주 화요일 방과 후에 곧바로 음악실에서 모입니다. 빨리 동아리에 가입해서 재미있는 활동들을 하고 싶습니다.

08 Listening Test 정답 p. 80

01 ③	02 ②	03 ④	04 ⑤	05 ②
06 ①	07 ⑤	08 ③	09 ①	10 ①
11 ③	12 ③	13 ⑤	14 ④	15 ④
16 ⑤	17 ④	18 ⑤	19 ⑤	20 ②

01

M I was told you are a photo specialist.

W No, I'm not. I'm just fond of taking pictures.

M Do you have time to show me some of your photos?

W Sure. Just give me a minute. [pause] This is one of my photo albums.

M Let's see. Wow! I love this picture of a teacup with a saucer. The rose pattern in pink with green leaves looks like a real flower.

W Yes, and the white background makes the other colors look more vivid.

M Gold gilding on the rim and the handle of the cup also makes it look elegant. Where did you take this photo?

W After buying the teacup and saucer, I took the picture of them at home.

남 너 사진 전문가라고 하더라.

여 아니야. 나는 단지 사진 찍는 걸 좋아할 뿐이야.

남 나에게 너의 사진 일부를 보여줄 시간 있니?

여 물론이지. 잠깐만. 이게 내 사진첩 중 하나야.

남 어디 보자. 우와! 이 찻잔과 접시 사진 마음에 들어. 분홍색 장미 무늬와 녹색 잎은 생화처럼 보여.

여 맞아. 또 흰 배경 색은 다른 색깔들을 더 선명하게 보이게 만들지.

남 찻잔 테두리와 손잡이에 입힌 금박 때문에 찻잔이 우아해 보여. 어디서 이 사진을 찍었니?

여 찻잔과 접시를 구입한 후에 집에서 찍었어.

specialist 전문가 **be fond of** ~을 좋아하다 **saucer** 받침 접시 **vivid** 선명한 **rim** 테, 가장자리 **gilding** 도금, 금박 입히기 **elegant** 우아한

02

W May I help you?

M Yes, please. These days I often forget what I have to do. So I think I need to buy Post-it Notes. Do you have any?

W Of course we do. There are lots of styles and colors. What about these star shaped ones?

M They are cute, but I need some formal ones.

W How about these yellow rectangular ones?

M Do you have the original square ones?

W There you go. There are also lined square Post-it Notes.

M It looks easier to write things down when it has lines. I'll take those Post-it Notes in pink, please.

여 도와드릴까요?

남 네. 요즘 제가 해야 할 일들을 자주 잊어버려서요. 포스트잇을 사야 할 것 같아요. 그거 있나요?

여 물론 있지요. 많은 모양과 색깔들이 있어요. 이 별 모양의 포스트잇은 어떤가요?

남 귀엽긴 하지만 저는 좀 격식이 있는 것을 원해요.

여 이 노란색 직사각형은 어떠세요?

남 원래의 정사각형 포스트잇 있나요?

여 여기 있습니다. 줄이 있는 정사각형 포스트잇도 있어요.

남 줄이 있으면 필기하기가 더 쉬워 보이네요. 분홍색으로 된 저 포스트잇을 살게요.

formal 격식이 있는 **rectangular** 직사각형의 **original** 본래의, 원래의 **square** 정사각형(의) **lined** 줄을 그은

03

M I often take a nap during the day.

W You do? Where do you do it?

M Well, any place. Sometimes I sleep here.

W Right here? How do you do that?

M I find a quiet desk and just put my head on some books from the bookshelves and go to sleep.

W Are you serious? While others read books or study, you go to sleep? Do you wake up in time for class?

M Oh, yes. I have an alarm clock.

W An alarm clock? Here where people have to be quiet?

남 나는 종종 낮에 낮잠을 자.

여 낮잠을 잔다고? 어디서 그렇게 하니?

남 음, 어떤 곳에서도 자. 가끔은 여기서 자기도 해.

여 바로 여기서? 어떻게 그렇게 해?

남 조용한 책상을 찾아서 책장에서 가져온 몇몇 책에 머리를 대고 그냥 잠을 자.

여 정말이야? 다른 사람들이 책을 읽거나 공부하는 동안, 너는 잠을 잔다고? 수업시간에 늦지 않게 깨니?

남 응. 자명종 시계가 있거든.

여 자명종 시계라고? 조용해야 하는 여기에서?

take a nap 낮잠 자다 **in time** 늦지 않게

04

W I bought a ticket to Paris. I'm looking forward to seeing the city.

M Good for you! Traveling is so much fun. When are you leaving?

W Next week. I'm taking the red-eye because of the cheap price.

M How much is the airfare?

W I paid $300 for a round-trip ticket.

M No way! It was a steal. How did you find it?

W There is a website which lets you bid on any ticket they are selling. I'll show you the site later.

M Thanks. Anyway, I'm so jealous! I hope you have a great time there.

....

여 나 파리행 비행기표를 샀어. 그 도시를 보는 게 너무 기대가 돼.

남 잘됐다! 여행하는 것은 너무 재미있어. 언제 출발하니?

여 다음 주에. 싼 가격 때문에 야간비행기 탈 거야.

남 항공료는 얼마야?

여 왕복표 1매에 300달러를 지불했어.

남 설마! 횡재 했네. 어떻게 그 표를 찾았니?

여 판매자들이 판매하는 표에 사람들이 입찰하게 해주는 웹사이트가 있어. 나중에 그 사이트 보여줄게.

남 고마워. 아무튼, 너무 부러워! 거기서 즐거운 시간 보내길 바래.

① 부러워하는　　② 슬픔에 잠긴　　③ 짜증이 난
④ 긴장한　　　　⑤ 신이 난

●●
red-eye 야간 비행편　**airfare** 항공요금　**steal** 훔침; 횡재　**bid on** ~에 입찰하다

05

W What time is it? We're going to be late!

M It's a quarter to seven. We're on time. Don't panic.

W But we have to be at the restaurant by seven fifteen. We'll never make it there with all this evening traffic.

M Sure, we will. What time is Bill supposed to arrive for his surprise party?

W He is supposed to arrive at eight. But I promised Janie I would be there by seven fifteen. We will have many things to set up.

M We will get there by then. By the way, can you call the restaurant and ask them where we can park our car?

W All right.

....

여 몇 시예요? 우리 늦겠어요.

남 7시 15분 전이야. 우리 안 늦었어. 당황하지 마.

여 그렇지만 7시 15분까지 식당에 가야 해요. 이런 저녁 시간 교통

정체로는 도저히 제시간에 거기 도착할 수 없을 거예요.

남 제시간에 갈 수 있다니까. Bill은 자기 깜짝파티를 위해 언제 도착하기로 되어 있어?

여 8시에 도착하기로 되어 있어요. 하지만 나는 Janie에게 7시 15분까지 가겠다고 약속했어요. 준비해야 할 게 많이 있거든요.

남 그 때까지 도착할 거야. 그런데 음식점에 전화해서 어디에 주차하는지 물어봐 줄래?

여 네.

●●
quarter 1/4, 15분　**on time** 제시간에　**panic** 당황하다　**make it** 시간에 대다, 성공하다　**be supposed to-V** ~할 예정이다　**park** 주차하다

06

M Do you want me to drive your car when we go on a picnic tomorrow?

W No, I'll drive. Trust me! I promise not to drive too fast again!

M All right. But we also ran out of gas last time. Don't forget to put gas in the car before we depart!

W OK! Oh, I'll prepare some sandwiches and fruit. Could you bring your beach umbrella and chairs?

M Yes. And if you want, I'll call you in the morning and remind you about the gas.

W Don't worry! I'll fill up the car tonight. But can you call me at 7, anyways? You know I don't like getting up early.

M No problem. I'll call you then.

....

남 내일 소풍 갈 때 내가 네 차 운전할까?

여 아니, 내가 할게. 날 믿어. 다시는 과속운전 안 하기로 약속할게.

남 좋아. 하지만 지난번에 기름도 떨어졌었어. 출발하기 전에 차에 기름 넣는 것 잊지 말자.

여 알았어! 아, 나는 샌드위치와 과일을 준비할게. 너는 파라솔과 의자 가지고 올래?

남 좋아. 그리고 네가 원한다면, 너에게 아침에 전화해서 기름에 대해 상기시켜줄게.

여 걱정하지 마. 오늘밤에 차에 기름을 가득 채워 넣을 거야. 하지만 그래도 7시에 전화해주겠니? 너도 알다시피 내가 일찍 일어나는 걸 안 좋아하잖아.

남 물론이지. 그때 전화할게.

●●
trust 신뢰하다　**run out of** ~이 다 떨어지다　**depart** 출발하다

07

W   Excuse me. I'm looking for a <u>birthday gift</u> for my <u>14</u>-year-old daughter. Could you help me?

M   Sure. <u>How about</u> a hairpin?

W   I think she already has many of them. And she just cut her hair short last week.

M   If she likes to <u>listen to music</u>, how about a CD or other <u>school supplies</u> with her favorite pop star's pictures on it?

W   That's good. She's <u>a big fan of</u> the K-pop group, INFINITE. Can you show me something with the group's picture on it?

M   Here you are. We have <u>notebooks</u>, clear files and <u>pencil cases</u>.

W   I'll get the <u>last one</u>. She already has many nice <u>notebooks</u> and <u>clear files</u>.

여   실례합니다. 제 14살 된 딸의 생일 선물을 찾고 있습니다. 도와주시겠어요?

남   물론이죠. 머리핀은 어때요?

여   이미 많이 가지고 있어요. 그리고 지난주에 머리를 짧게 잘랐어요.

남   음악 듣는 것을 좋아한다면 CD나 그녀가 좋아하는 인기 가수들의 사진이 있는 다른 학용품은 어떨까요?

여   좋은 생각이에요. 제 딸은 INFINITE라는 K-pop 그룹의 광팬이거든요. 그 그룹의 사진이 있는 걸 좀 보여주시겠습니까?

남   여기 있습니다. 공책, 서류철, 그리고 필통이 있습니다.

여   마지막 것으로 할게요. 멋진 공책이랑 서류철을 이미 많이 가지고 있거든요.

① 머리핀   ② CD   ③ 공책
④ 연필   ⑤ 필통

••
school supplies 학용품

08

① W   The chart displays the <u>popularity</u> of different types of <u>volunteer work</u> among the students in <u>Tom's class</u>.

② W   According to the chart, <u>cleaning streets</u> is the most preferred type of volunteer work.

③ W   Mentoring children <u>in orphanages</u> is less preferred than <u>storytelling</u> to the elderly at nursing homes.

④ W   <u>Translating letters</u> for <u>charity organizations</u> is the least preferred type of volunteer work.

⑤ W   <u>Cleaning streets</u>, ranking first, accounted for <u>43</u>% of the students.

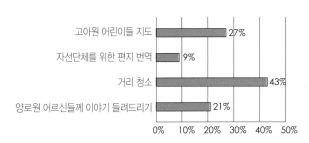

Tom의 반 친구들이 선호하는 봉사활동 유형

① 여   표는 각기 다른 봉사활동 유형에 대한 Tom의 학급 학생들 사이에서의 인기를 보여준다.

② 여   표에 의하면, 거리 청소가 가장 선호되는 유형의 봉사활동이다.

③ 여   고아원 어린이들에 대한 지도 상담은 양로원 어르신께 이야기해드리기보다 덜 선호된다.

④ 여   자선단체를 위해 편지를 번역하는 것은 가장 선호되지 않는 봉사활동 유형이다.

⑤ 여   1위에 오른 거리 청소는 43%를 차지했다.

••
popularity 인기   **volunteer** 자발적인   **orphanage** 고아원   **the elderly** 어르신들, 노인들   **nursing home** 양로원   **charity organization** 자선단체   **account for** ~을 차지하다

09

W   Hey, Robert. <u>Where are you going</u>?

M   I'm going to the library.

W   Why? The <u>midterm exams</u> are <u>over</u>. They were last week. Do you have any books to return?

M   No. I have to be ready for the <u>school festival</u>. I need to study.

W   What? What are you <u>talking about</u>?

M   I'll be competing in the Golden Bell Quiz Show <u>during the festival</u>. So I'm going to <u>check out some books</u> for that.

W   Now I understand. Good luck.

M   Thank you. Please come and <u>root for me</u>.

여 안녕. Robert. 어디 가니?

남 도서관에 가.

여 왜? 중간고사가 끝났잖아. 지난주에. 반납할 책이 있니?

남 아니. 학교 축제 준비를 해야 해. 공부를 해야 해서.

여 뭐라고? 무슨 말을 하는 거야?

남 축제 기간 동안 골든벨 퀴즈쇼에 나갈 거야. 그래서 그에 관한 책을 빌리려고.

여 이제 알겠네. 행운을 빌어.

남 고마워. 와서 나를 응원해줘.

●●
be over 끝나다 **be ready for** ~에 준비가 되다 **compete** 경쟁하다
festival 축제 **root for** ~을 응원하다

10

W What do you think about having a farewell party for our homeroom teacher?

M Sounds like a wonderful idea. Do you know when her last day is?

W As I know, this Friday is her last day at this school.

M Really? Then when can we have the party?

W How about this Wednesday?

M That would be good. I guess she will be busy packing up and saying goodbye to everyone on Thursday.

W You're right. We will be busy from now on.

M Yeah. We only have two days to prepare.

여 담임 선생님을 위한 송별회를 하는 거 어때?

남 좋은 생각이야. 선생님의 마지막 날이 언제인지 아니?

여 내가 알기로는 이번 주 금요일이 이 학교에서 마지막 날이야.

남 정말? 그러면 언제 파티를 하지?

여 이번 주 수요일 어때?

남 좋아. 내 생각에 목요일에는 짐을 싸고 모든 사람들에게 마지막 인사를 하느라 바쁘실 것 같아.

여 맞아. 우리가 이제부터 바빠지겠네.

남 응. 준비할 시간이 딱 이틀 남아 있어.

① 월요일　　　② 화요일　　　③ 수요일
④ 목요일　　　⑤ 금요일

●●
farewell party 송별회 **pack up** 짐을 꾸리다 **say goodbye** 작별을
고하다 **from now on** 이제부터

11

M Do you want to make your bones and teeth stronger? Do you think you need more calcium? Why don't you try our product? We have various kinds such as non-fat, low-fat, and regular. Besides plain, we have it in banana, strawberry, and melon. Each of those contains some real fruit juice. If you drink it every day, it will make your body healthier than ever. Please go to the market now and buy this Happy dairy product.

남 당신의 뼈와 치아를 더 튼튼하게 하고 싶습니까? 칼슘이 더 필요하다고 생각하십니까? 저희 제품을 드셔보시는 건 어떠세요? 저희는 무지방, 저지방, 그리고 일반 우유와 같은 다양한 종류를 갖추고 있습니다. 저희는 맛을 첨가하지 않은 것뿐 아니라 바나나, 딸기, 메론 맛의 세 가지 맛도 있습니다. 이 제품들에는 실제 과즙이 함유되어 있습니다. 매일 마시면, 그 어떤 때보다도 몸이 더 건강하게 될 것입니다. 가게에 가서서 이 Happy 유제품을 사세요.

① 생과일　　　② 유기농 식품　　　③ 우유
④ 다이어트 식품　　　⑤ 과일 주스

●●
bone 뼈 **calcium** 칼슘 **product** 제품 **various** 다양한 **non-fat**
무지방의 **low-fat** 저지방의 **plain** 평이한, 보통의 **dairy product**
유제품

12

W I really had a wonderful time on the field trip.

M Good for you. What did you do there?

W Well, I had a chance to plant seeds, bake a cake, ride a horse, swim in the river, and cook rice.

M Wow! How were they?

W Well, planting seeds was interesting. But baking a cake was the best activity I did there.

M What about the other activities?

W Horseback riding was interesting, too, but cooking rice wasn't. Actually it was the worst because I burnt the rice.

M Haha. How about swimming? Did you enjoy it?

W Not at all. It's really scary for me.

Susie의 견학 활동		
	지루했음	재미있었음
① 씨앗 심기	✓	
② 케이크 만들기	✓	
③ 말 타기		✓
④ 밥 짓기		✓
⑤ 수영		✓

여   나는 견학 가서 정말로 멋진 시간을 보냈어.

남   다행이네. 거기서 뭘 했는데?

여   응, 씨앗 심기, 케이크 만들기, 말 타기, 강에서 수영하기, 그리고 밥을 지을 기회가 있었어.

남   우와! 다 어땠어?

여   음, 씨앗 심기가 재미있었어. 하지만 케이크 만들기가 거기서 했던 활동 중 최고였어.

남   다른 활동들은 어땠어?

여   말 타기도 재미있었지만 밥 짓기는 재미없었어. 사실은 내가 밥을 태워서 제일 별로였어.

남   하하. 수영은? 재미있었어?

여   전혀. 난 수영이 정말 무서워.

•• **field trip** 견학   **seed** 씨앗   **bake** 굽다   **burn** 태우다   **scary** 겁먹은

13

M   Good morning. How many people are there in your party?

W   Four, two adults and two children.

M   Then, may I suggest the non-smoking area?

W   Sure. I want to have breakfast in a pleasant environment.

M   Please wait for a second. Let me check to see if there's a table available for you.

W   Thanks. Can I have a high chair for my baby?

M   Sure. We will bring it to you when you are seated.

W   Thank you.

남   안녕하세요. 일행이 몇 분이시죠?

여   4명입니다. 성인 2명, 아이 2명요.

남   그러면 비흡연 구역으로 드릴까요?

여   네. 쾌적한 환경에서 아침 식사를 하고 싶네요.

남   잠시만 기다리세요. 테이블이 있는지 알아보겠습니다.

여   감사합니다. 제 아기를 위한 높은 의자를 이용할 수 있을까요?

남   물론입니다. 자리에 앉으시면 가져다 드리겠습니다.

여   감사합니다.

•• **party** 일행   **adult** 성인   **suggest** 제안하다   **pleasant** 즐거운   **available** 이용 가능한   **be seated** 착석하다

14

M   My Goodness!

W   Why? What's the matter?

M   My computer just crashed while I was working on my English project.

W   I'm sure you saved the file, didn't you?

M   Unfortunately, no. I usually save it when I'm done with the work.

W   Uh-oh. Then you have lost all your work.

M   I know. It's terrible, but I have to finish this project by tomorrow. What should I do?

W   You'd better go to the teacher and explain what just happened. She will understand your situation.

M   Okay, I will.

남   세상에!

여   왜? 무슨 일이야?

남   영어 과제를 하고 있었는데 컴퓨터가 다운됐어.

여   파일은 저장해 놨지, 그렇지?

남   불행하게도, 아니야. 나는 보통 작업을 마친 후에 저장을 해.

여   이런. 그러면 네가 작업한 모든 것들을 잃어버린 거야.

남   알아. 끔찍하지만 내일까지 이 과제를 끝내야 하는데. 어떻게 하지?

여   선생님께 가서 일어난 일을 그대로 말씀 드려. 네 상황을 이해하실 거야.

남   그래. 그럴게.

•• **crash** (컴퓨터) 갑자기 멈추다   **explain** 설명하다

15

W   Attention, students! Due to the weather and road conditions, all after-school activities are canceled today. There will be no buses for after-school activities. All students should go home at the end of the school day on the regular school buses. These, however, may be delayed because of the traffic conditions. The school plans to be open tomorrow, Friday, with classes as normal. Any changes will be communicated by e-mail and they will be put on the school website.

여 학생 여러분, 주목해주세요. 날씨와 도로 상태 때문에, 오늘 모든 방과 후 활동은 취소됩니다. 방과 후 활동을 위한 버스는 운행하지 않습니다. 모든 학생들은 수업을 마친 후 정규 스쿨버스를 타고 집으로 가야 합니다. 하지만 이 버스들은 교통상황 때문에 지연될지도 모릅니다. 내일, 금요일은 학교가 문을 열고 수업이 정상적으로 진행되도록 할 계획입니다. 어떤 변화든 있으면 이메일로 알리고 학교 웹사이트에도 올리겠습니다.

due to ~ 때문에 **cancel** 취소하다 **after-school** 방과 후의 **delay** 지연시키다 **because of** ~ 때문에 **communicate** 의사소통을 하다

16

M The airport is filled with people today.

W Yeah. The lines are so long.

M Are you carrying any flammable materials?

W No. I don't have any of them.

M Did you put your cosmetics in your baggage? If you are carrying them now, liquids must be 100ml or less, and stored in a clear plastic bag.

W Don't worry about that.

M Then, don't forget to throw away your water bottle before you go through security.

W Oh, I almost forgot.

남 오늘 공항이 사람들로 꽉 찼네.

여 그러게. 줄이 정말 길다.

남 인화성 물질 혹시 지니고 있니?

여 아니. 그런 건 하나도 가지고 있지 않아.

남 화장품은 수하물에 넣었니? 만약 지금 가지고 있다면, 액체류는 100ml 미만이어야 하고, 반드시 투명 비닐봉투에 넣어야 해.

여 걱정 마.

남 그럼, 검색대를 통과하기 전에 생수병 버리는 거 잊지 마.

여 오, 깜빡할 뻔했어.

flammable 가연성의 **material** 물질 **cosmetics** 화장품 **liquid** 액체 **plastic bag** 비닐봉투 **go through** 통과하다 **security** (공항) 보안 검색대

17

① M How long will it take for the package to arrive?

W Let me see.

② M Can I give you a hand with the bookshelf?

W Sure. That's very kind of you.

③ M Did you buy anything for Parents' Day?

W Not yet, but I'm thinking about buying some clothes.

④ M Which do you prefer, horror or sci-fi movies?

W Yes, I prefer them.

⑤ M I really want to have that pair of oversized sunglasses.

W I guess they'll look nice on you.

---

① 남 소포가 도착하는 데 얼마나 걸릴까요?

여 어디 봅시다.

② 남 책장 일 좀 도와줄까?

여 그래. 정말 친절하구나.

③ 남 어버이날을 위해 뭔가를 샀니?

여 아니, 아직. 하지만 옷을 살까 생각 중이야.

④ 남 공포와 공상과학 영화 중, 너는 어는 것을 더 좋아하니?

여 응, 난 그것들을 선호해.

⑤ 남 난 정말 그 특대 사이즈 선글라스를 갖고 싶어.

여 그게 너한테 잘 어울릴 것 같아.

package 소포, 꾸러미 **bookshelf** 책장 **Parents' Day** 어버이날 **horror** 공포 **sci-fi** (science fiction) 공상과학 **oversized** 특대사이즈의

18

W Did you know that Gary has had a girlfriend since last year?

M Believe it or not, I heard it a few days ago.

W How come he didn't reveal this to you? You're his best friend.

M That's why I felt betrayed for a couple of days.

W Did he introduce her to you?

M Not yet, but we are going to have dinner this Friday.

W Oh, he's coming. [pause] Hello, Gary. What's up?

여 너 Gary가 작년부터 쭉 여자친구가 있었던 거 알았니?

남 믿거나 말거나, 들은 지 며칠 안 됐어.

여 어떻게 그가 네게 이 사실을 밝히지 않았을 수 있니? 넌 그의 단짝 친구인데.

남 그게 바로 내가 며칠 동안 배신감을 느꼈던 이유지.

여　그가 그녀를 네게 소개해줬니?

남　아니 아직, 하지만 이번 금요일에 함께 저녁을 먹을 거야.

여　오, 그가 온다. 안녕, Gary. 웬일이야?

① 식은 죽 먹기야.

② 호기를 놓치지 마라.

③ 아니 땐 굴뚝에 연기 나랴.

④ 어려울 때 친구가 참된 친구다.

⑤ 호랑이도 제 말하면 온다.

reveal 밝히다　**betray** 배신하다

19

W　Christine has a pet dog. Her name is Snoopy. She was an abandoned dog. Christine's parents brought home the dog to be their daughter's companion. Christine was happy because she always wanted to adopt a dog. Christine feeds, walks, and bathes the dog. This weekend, Christine's family is supposed to take a trip to Hong Kong. Christine has to find the right person who can take care of Snoopy. In this situation, what would Christine most likely say to her friend?

여　Christine은 애완견 한 마리가 있다. 이름은 Snoopy이다. Snoopy는 유기견이었다. Christine의 부모님이 그 개를 딸의 친구로 삼으려고 집으로 데려왔다. Christine은 항상 개 한 마리를 입양하고 싶어했기 때문에 행복했다. Christine은 개에게 먹이를 주고, 산책을 시키고, 목욕을 시킨다. 이번 주말에 Christine의 가족은 홍콩으로 여행 갈 것이다. Christine은 Snoopy를 돌봐 줄 적임자를 찾아야만 한다. 이 상황에서, Christine은 친구에게 뭐라고 말하겠는가?

① 네 애완견은 어떻게 생겼니?

② 개를 풀어줄 때는 조심해.

③ 하루에 몇 번씩 개에게 먹이를 줘야 되니?

④ 그 개는, 말하자면, 우리 식구나 마찬가지야.

⑤ 내가 외국에 나가 있는 동안 내 애완견을 돌봐줄 수 있니?

abandon 버리다　**companion** 반려, 친구　**adopt** 입양하다, 채택하다
feed 먹이를 주다　**bathe** 목욕시키다　**right person** 적임자

20

M　Does anything on the menu appeal to you?

W　How about tacos? It is one of the main dishes here.

M　Sounds good. I like meat-filled tacos with hot sauce.

W　Me too. What do you want to drink?

M　A mango smoothie for me. What about you?

W　I'll have lemonade. For dessert, let's try pineapple with cinnamon powder.

M　Okay. I hope the server comes soon. I'm really hungry.

W　So am I. I can't wait.

남　메뉴에 있는 것 중에서 끌리는 게 있니?

여　타코 어때? 이곳의 주 메뉴 중 하나야.

남　좋아. 나는 고기로 채워진 타코를 핫소스와 함께 먹는 게 좋아.

여　나도. 음료는 뭐로 할 거야?

남　난 망고 스무디. 넌?

여　난 레모네이드로 할래. 디저트로 계피가루 뿌려진 파인애플 한번 먹어보자!

남　좋아. 식당직원이 빨리 왔으면 좋겠어. 정말 배고프다.

여　나도 그래. 정말 기대가 돼.

① 그게 정말 맛있어.

② 나도 그래. 정말 기대가 돼.

③ 주문하시겠습니까?

④ 주문한 거 기다리는 중이야.

⑤ 무엇을 주문해야 할까?

appeal to ~의 마음에 들다　**meat-filled** 고기로 채워진　**cinnamon** 계피　**server** 식사 시중드는 사람

Further **S**tudy 정답 p. 84

1. He finds a quiet desk, puts his head on some books, and goes to sleep.

2. The reason is that it is cheap as it costs only $300 for a round trip.

3. He asks her to call the restaurant and ask them where they can park their car.

4. She is looking for a birthday gift for her 14-year-old daughter.

5. The reason is that she will have to pack up and say goodbye to everyone.

6. The reason is that she wants to have breakfast in a pleasant environment.

7. The reason is that Gary <u>didn't tell him that he had a girlfriend</u> until a few days ago.

8. They wanted the dog to <u>be Christine's companion</u>.

On Your Own 모범답안

p. 85

A

My School Festival	
(1) Events we have	talent show, quiz show, singing contest
(2) The most popular event	talent show
(3) Reason(s) it is popular	fun for the audience to see their friends performing
(4) An event I would add	talk concert with famous comedians
(5) Reason(s) I would add it	make us laugh a lot, and laughing would release all of our stress

I'm going to talk about the festival at my school. At the festival, we usually have (1)<u>a talent show, a quiz show, and a singing contest</u>. Students like (2)<u>the talent show</u> most. In my opinion, it is the most popular because (3)<u>it is so much fun for the audience to see their friends performing</u>. If I could add an event to our school festival, I would add (4)<u>a talk concert with famous comedians</u>. That is because (5)<u>this concert would make us laugh a lot, and laughing would release all of our stress</u>.

나의 학교 축제	
(1) 우리가 여는 행사	장기자랑, 퀴즈대회, 노래자랑
(2) 가장 인기 있는 행사	장기자랑
(3) 인기 있는 이유	관중들은 친구들이 공연하는 걸 보는 것이 재미있음
(4) 내가 추가하고 싶은 행사	유명 코미디언과 함께 하는 토크 콘서트
(5) 추가하고 싶은 이유	우리를 많이 웃게 만들어주고 웃는 것은 우리 모든 스트레스를 해소함

저희 학교 축제에 대하여 이야기하겠습니다. 축제에서 우리는 보통 장기자랑과 퀴즈대회, 노래자랑을 합니다. 학생들은 장기자랑을 가장 좋아합니다. 제 생각에 그 행사가 가장 인기 있는 이유는 관중들은 친구들이 공연하는 걸 보는 게 너무나 재미있기 때문입니다. 제가

만일 우리 학교 축제에 한 가지 행사를 추가할 수 있다면, 저는 유명 코미디언과의 토크 콘서트를 추가하고 싶습니다. 그 이유는 이 콘서트가 우리를 많이 웃게 해줄 것이고 웃음은 우리의 모든 스트레스를 해소해줄 것이기 때문입니다.

B

My Favorite Korean Dish	
(1) What the food is	bulgogi, which is grilled beef seasoned with spices
(2) Ingredients	thinly sliced beef, onions, and mushrooms; for the sauce, you need pear juice, garlic and soy sauce
(3) Tastes	sweet and savory
(4) Reason(s) I like it	it is not only tasty but also very healthy
(5) My favorite way to eat it	to wrap it with soybean paste in a lettuce leaf

I'm going to tell you about my favorite Korean dish. It is (1)<u>bulgogi, which is grilled beef seasoned with spices</u>. To make it, you need (2)<u>thinly sliced beef, onions, and mushrooms</u>. Also for the sauce, you need pear juice, garlic and soy sauce. It tastes (3)<u>sweet and savory</u>. I like it very much because (4)<u>it is not only tasty but also very healthy</u>. My favorite way to eat it is (5)<u>to wrap it with soybean paste in a lettuce leaf</u>. Try to make this delicious food and enjoy it.

내가 가장 좋아하는 한국 음식	
(1) 어떤 음식인지	불고기로서 양념으로 맛을 내어 불에 구운 쇠고기 요리
(2) 재료	얇게 썬 쇠고기, 양파, 버섯; 양념을 위해선 배즙, 마늘, 간장
(3) 맛	달고 풍미 있는 맛
(4) 좋아하는 이유	맛있을 뿐만 아니라 건강에도 매우 좋아서
(5) 먹는 방법으로 내가 좋아하는 것	된장과 함께 상추 잎에 싸 먹는 것

저는 제가 아주 좋아하는 한국 음식에 대해서 말하려고 합니다. 그것은 불고기로서 양념으로 맛을 내어 불에 구운 쇠고기 요리입니다. 그것을 만들기 위해서는, 얇게 썬 쇠고기, 양파 그리고 버섯이 필요합니다. 또한 양념을 만들기 위해서 배즙, 마늘, 그리고 간장이 필요합니다. 그것은 달고 풍미 있는 맛입니다. 그것은 맛있을 뿐만 아니라 건강에도 매우 좋아서 저는 그것을 아주 좋아합니다. 제가 좋아하는 먹는 법은 그것을 된장과 함께 상추 잎에 싸 먹는 것입니다. 이 맛있는 음식을 한번 만들어서 드셔 보세요.

01 ①	02 ⑤	03 ⑤	04 ②	05 ②
06 ①	07 ⑤	08 ④	09 ⑤	10 ①
11 ①	12 ②	13 ④	14 ③	15 ④
16 ②	17 ④	18 ③	19 ③	20 ④

01

W Hey, Thomas. What are you doing?

M I'm trying to buy a wine bottle holder on this website as a housewarming present for Junsu.

W Wow, this site has a good selection.

M Yes, but it's really difficult to choose one. Can you help me?

W Sure. What about this high heel shoe wine bottle holder? It looks very stylish and unique.

M Wine in a shoe. Well, not a good idea. I love this zombie one. Looks like the zombie is drinking wine.

W That's too scary. Then, how about this green alien one? Junsu is interested in extraterrestrial life.

M I like that design. I'll order it. Thanks for your help!

- -

여 안녕, Thomas. 뭐 하는 중이니?

남 준수의 집들이 선물로 이 웹사이트에서 와인병 홀더 사려고.

여 와, 이 사이트에는 구색이 잘 갖춰져 있네.

남 응. 그런데 하나를 고르기 너무 어려워. 나 좀 도와줄래?

여 물론이지. 이 하이힐 신발 와인병 홀더는 어때? 매우 멋지고 독특해 보여.

남 신발 안에 있는 와인이라. 글쎄, 좋은 생각 같지 않아. 나는 이 좀비 홀더가 마음에 들어. 좀비가 와인을 마시는 것처럼 보여.

여 그건 너무 무서워. 그럼, 이 녹색 외계인 홀더는 어때? 준수는 외계생명체에 관심이 있잖아.

남 그 디자인 맘에 든다. 이걸로 주문할게. 도와줘서 고마워.

• •
selection (같은 종류의) 구색 **unique** 독특한 **alien** 외계인 **extraterrestrial** 외계의, 지구 밖의

02

M Now, we have to arrange the contents of our club newspaper.

W Okay, why don't we put the title at the top of the paper and the issue date at the bottom of the paper?

M I think it looks a little distracting. So let's put the issue date below the title.

W That's good. Then, how can we position the two articles?

M What about dividing the newspaper into two columns?

W Well, not bad. We can put the first article in the left column and the other in the right.

M Yes. It will look balanced.

- -

남 이제 우리 동아리 신문의 내용을 배열해야 해.

여 그래, 제호를 신문의 위에 두고 발행일을 신문의 아래에 두는 게 어때?

남 내 생각에는 조금 산만하게 보일 것 같아. 그러니까 발행일을 제호 아래에 두자.

여 좋아. 그러면 두 개의 기사는 어떻게 위치시킬까?

남 신문을 두 개의 세로 단으로 나누는 것 어때?

여 글쎄, 나쁘지 않아. 첫 번째 기사는 왼편에, 다른 기사는 오른편에 두면 되겠네.

남 응. 균형 잡혀 보일 거야.

• •
arrange 배열하다 **issue** 발행 **distracting** 산만한 **position** 적당한 장소에 두다 **balanced** 균형 잡힌

03

W Minsu, why are you still awake?

M Mom, I'm having trouble sleeping.

W How come? The midterm exams start tomorrow. You need to get some sleep.

M I know, but the more I think about what I've studied, the more I can't sleep.

W You've studied hard enough this month. So what's the matter?

M Even though I studied hard for the last exams, I made lots of mistakes and got poor scores.

W Let bygones be bygones. You have to double check each answer before submitting the answer sheet this time, OK?

M Yes, Mom. Now I'll try to get some sleep. Good night, Mom.

여 민수야, 왜 아직 안 자고 있니?

남 엄마, 잠이 안 와요.

여 왜? 중간고사가 내일부터 시작이잖아. 잠을 좀 자야 해.

남 알아요. 하지만 공부한 걸 생각하면 생각할수록, 점점 더 잠을 잘 수가 없어요.

여 이번 달에 충분히 열심히 공부했잖아. 뭐가 문제이니?

남 지난번 시험을 위해 열심히 공부했지만, 실수를 많이 했고 점수가 안 좋았잖아요.

여 지나간 일은 잊어버리렴. 이번에는 답안지를 제출하기 전에 꼭 모든 답을 다시 한 번 확인해야 해, 알겠니?

남 네, 엄마. 이제 잠 자볼게요. 안녕히 주무세요, 엄마.

① 희망에 찬   ② 확고한   ③ 자랑스러운
④ 즐거운   ⑤ 긴장한

have trouble -ing ~하는 데 어려움을 겪다   **midterm exam** 중간고사
bygone 지난 일, 과거사   **double check** 다시 검토하다

04

W What can I help you with?

M It's about my dog. He is vomiting yellow liquid continually.

W Sounds like food poisoning.

M He ate some eggs. They fell and broke on the floor. I couldn't pick them up fast enough.

W When did he have the eggs?

M This morning, around 10 o'clock.

W Eggs can cause food poisoning. But I think he will be okay. Bring him here as fast as possible.

M Yes, I'll do that right now.

여 무엇을 도와드릴까요?

남 제 개 때문에요. 계속 노란색 액체를 토해내고 있어요.

여 식중독 같군요.

남 달걀을 좀 먹었어요. 달걀이 바닥에 떨어져 깨졌어요. 제가 충분히 빨리 집어 올리지를 못했습니다.

여 언제 달걀을 먹었다고요?

남 오늘 아침, 10시쯤에요.

여 달걀이 식중독을 일으킬 수도 있어요. 하지만 개는 괜찮을 거예요. 가급적 빨리 개를 여기에 데리고 오세요.

남 네, 지금 당장 그렇게 할게요.

① 내과의사   ② 수의사   ③ 농부
④ 사육사   ⑤ 요리사

vomit 토하다   **continually** 계속해서   **food poisoning** 식중독

05

W These sea animal squirts are soft enough to hold and squeeze.

M Yes, they are popular bath toys with little children.

W Good. My little boy seems to be bored while bathing. I'm looking for some bath toys that can amuse and entertain him. How much are these?

M The regular price for a set of five squirts is 10 dollars, but now it's on sale. It's 40% off.

W Oh, really? I'll take one set. Can I use this 10% off coupon?

M I'm sorry, but you can't use it on sale items.

W Okay. Here is my credit card.

여 이 바다동물 물총은 쥐고 짜기에 충분히 부드럽네요.

남 네, 그것들은 어린 아이들에게 인기 있는 목욕용 장난감이에요.

여 잘됐네요. 제 어린 아들이 목욕하는 동안 지루해 하는 것 같아요. 아이를 신나고 재미있게 해줄 목욕용 장난감을 좀 사고 싶어요. 이것들은 얼마인가요?

남 다섯 개 물총 한 세트의 정상 가격은 10달러인데 지금 세일 중이에요. 40퍼센트 할인합니다.

여 오, 정말요? 한 세트 살게요. 이 10퍼센트 할인 쿠폰을 사용할 수 있나요?

남 죄송하지만 세일 품목에는 쿠폰을 사용하실 수 없습니다.

여 네. 여기 신용카드 있습니다.

squirt 물총   **squeeze** 꽉 쥐다   **amuse** 재미있게 하다   **entertain** 즐겁게 하다

06

M Hi, Minhee. Long time no see.

W Hi, Jim. What a coincidence! I haven't seen you since we graduated from university. What are you doing here?

M I just got a new job in this city, so I'm shopping for some clothes. How about you?

W I'm looking for a shirt for my brother's birthday present. What do you think of this shirt?

M Well, you know how much I love blue. See? I've

got <u>the same</u> shirt!

W You always did have <u>good taste</u>. I'll take this. <u>After buying</u> this stuff, how about eating dinner together?

M Why not?

- -

남 안녕, 민희야. 오랜만이야.

여 안녕, Jim. 어쩌면 이런 우연의 일치가 있담! 대학교 졸업 후에 처음 보는 거잖아. 여기서 뭐 하는 중이야?

남 이 도시에서 새 직장을 구해서, 옷을 좀 사려고 쇼핑 중이야. 너는 어쩐 일이니?

여 내 동생 생일 선물로 셔츠를 고르는 중이야. 이 셔츠 어떠니?

남 내가 얼마나 파란색을 좋아하는지 알잖아. 보이니? 이미 같은 셔츠를 골랐어.

여 넌 항상 정말 훌륭한 취향을 가지고 있었어. 이걸로 해야겠다. 이것 산 후에 저녁 같이 먹는 것 어떠니?

남 좋아.

coincidence 우연의 일치 **graduate from** ~을 졸업하다 **taste** 취향

07

W Welcome to Brent <u>International High School</u>. I'm Laura, a <u>second year student</u>.

M Hello. Thank you for <u>welcoming me</u>. I'm Ben.

W How do you <u>feel about becoming</u> a high school student?

M I'm very <u>nervous</u> and everything is so <u>confusing</u>.

W Don't worry. You will be fine soon. Just <u>be fully aware of</u> and <u>follow</u> the basic <u>school rules</u>.

M School rules? What are they? <u>Could you please</u> tell me them?

W Okay. They are the following: speak in English only, always <u>wear</u> your name tag, and <u>be on time for</u> your classes.

M I will <u>keep them in mind</u> and try to follow them. Thank you.

W If you have any questions later on, just <u>ask me anytime</u>.

- -

여 Brent 국제고등학교에 온 것을 환영해. 나는 2학년생 Laura야.

남 안녕하세요. 반겨줘서 고마워요. 나는 Ben입니다.

여 고등학생이 되니 어떤 느낌이 드니?

남 불안하고 모든 것이 혼란스러워요.

여 걱정하지 마. 곧 괜찮아질 거야. 교칙들만 잘 알고 따르면 돼.

남 교칙요? 어떤 것들인데요? 그것들에 대해 이야기해 줄래요?

여 그래. 이런 것들이야. 영어로만 말하기, 항상 명찰 착용하기, 수업 시간에 늦지 않기.

남 머릿속에 새겨서 따르도록 할게요. 고마워요.

여 나중에도 궁금한 것이 있으면, 언제든지 물어봐.

confuse 혼란스럽게 하다 **be aware of** ~을 알다 **basic** 기초적인 **on time** 제시간에 **anytime** 아무 때나

08

M The next one we can see is at 4:30.

W <u>What time is it</u> now?

M It's <u>a quarter to four</u>.

W We only have to wait for 45 minutes. That's fine with me.

M Okay. I will <u>keep standing in line</u> to buy tickets. Why don't you <u>go and get</u> some snacks and drinks?

W Alright. I will <u>get something light</u> because we will <u>have dinner</u> after the movie.

M I'm <u>kind of starving</u> now, but something light will be okay, I guess.

W I'll be <u>right back</u>.

- -

남 우리가 볼 수 있는 다음 건 4시 30분이야.

여 지금 몇 시인데?

남 4시 15분 전.

여 45분만 기다리면 되네. 나는 괜찮아.

남 좋아. 영화표 사게 계속 줄 서 있을게. 너는 가서 간식이랑 음료수를 사오는 게 어때?

여 알았어. 영화 끝나고 저녁 먹어야 하니 간단한 것으로 사올게.

남 지금 굉장히 배가 고프지만 간단한 것도 괜찮은 것 같아.

여 금방 갔다 올게.

stand in line 줄을 서다 **kind of** 다소, 좀 **starve** 굶주리다

09

① M I want to <u>show you</u> my <u>new car</u>.

W You <u>bought</u> a new car?

② M Do you know why I <u>pulled you over</u>?

W I don't know. All of a sudden I heard your siren.

③ M <u>What happened</u> to your car?

W I got this dent in the parking lot.

④ **M** How long do we have to wait for the bus?

W It will come here in 5 minutes.

⑤ **M** Loot at that! The car just ran a red light and hit that truck!

W Is anyone hurt?

---

① 남 나 너에게 내 새 차를 보여주고 싶어.

여 너 새 차 샀니?

② 남 내가 왜 당신을 갓길로 세운지 아세요?

여 모르겠어요. 저는 갑자기 사이렌 소리를 들었어요.

③ 남 네 차에 무슨 일이 있었던 거야?

여 주차장에 세워뒀는데 여기 움푹 들어갔어.

④ 남 버스는 얼마 기다려야 와요?

여 5분 후에 올 거예요.

⑤ 남 저것 좀 봐! 차가 빨간 불에 지나가서 저 트럭에 부딪혔어.

여 다친 사람 있을까?

pull over ~에게 차를 대게 하다 **all of a sudden** 갑자기 **dent** 움푹 팬 곳 **run a red light** 정지신호에 달리다

10

M With busy lives, it can be hard to find time to volunteer. However, the benefits of volunteering are enormous not only to you but also your family and your community. It can help you make friends, reach out to the community, learn new skills, and even advance your career. Volunteering can also help protect your mental and physical health. Today, let's learn more about the many benefits of volunteering and find tips on getting started as a volunteer.

남 바쁜 생활로 인해 자원봉사를 할 시간을 찾는 것은 어려울 수 있습니다. 하지만, 자원봉사는 여러분뿐만 아니라 여러분의 가족과 여러분의 지역사회에도 엄청난 이점이 있습니다. 그것은 여러분이 친구를 만드는 것, 지역사회와 접촉하는 것, 새로운 기술을 배우는 것, 그리고 심지어는 여러분의 경력을 향상시키는 데도 도움을 줄 수 있습니다. 자원봉사는 또한 여러분의 정신적, 육체적 건강을 지키는 데 도움을 줄 수 있습니다. 오늘 자원봉사의 많은 장점들에 대해서 더 배우고 자원봉사자로서 시작하는 것에 대한 방법들을 찾아봅시다.

benefit 이점, 장점 **enormous** 막대한 **reach out to** ~와 접촉하려 하다 **advance** 향상시키다 **mental** 정신의 **physical** 육체의, 물리적인

11

M Oh, no! What should I do?

W Calm down. What's wrong with you?

M It's eight thirty already. School starts at eight fifty. I will be late for school.

W No, you won't. This clock has stopped. Anyway, it looks like it's 40 minutes faster than the real time.

M Forty minutes faster? Good. There's enough time to have breakfast.

W But hurry. Don't forget to pack up all the things you have to bring.

M I will. Could you please set the table for me, mom? I will be back in 15 minutes after washing up.

W Okay.

남 오, 이런! 어떻게 하죠?

여 진정해. 무슨 문제인데?

남 벌써 8시 30분이에요. 학교는 8시 50분에 시작하는데요. 학교에 늦겠어요.

여 아니야. 이 시계는 멈춘 거라고. 어쨌든 실제보다 40분 더 빠른 것 같네.

남 40분 더 빠르다고요? 잘됐다. 아침 먹을 시간이 충분하네요.

여 그래도 서둘러. 가져가야 할 물건들 잘 챙기는 것 잊지 말고.

남 그럴게요. 다 씻고 15분 후에 올 테니 식사 준비 좀 해줘 주실래요?

여 알았어.

calm down 진정하다 **pack up** 짐을 꾸리다 **set the table** 식탁을 차리다

12

W Hello, shoppers! Thank you for shopping at Big Mart. You can buy fresh fruit and vegetables like apples, oranges, and cucumbers. We have a special low price on mushrooms today. If you buy one pack of mushrooms, you can get the second pack free. As we said in our advertisement, our fruit and vegetables are delivered directly from local producers. So, walk over to our fruit and vegetable section on the first floor and take a look at them.

여 　쇼핑하시는 손님 여러분 안녕하십니까! Big Mart를 애용해주셔서 감사 드립니다. 여러분들은 사과, 오렌지, 오이 같은 신선한 과일과 채소들을 구입하실 수 있습니다. 오늘은 버섯을 특별히 저렴한 가격으로 드립니다. 만일 한 팩을 구입하시면, 다른 한 팩을 무료로 드립니다. 광고에서 언급했듯이 저희의 과일과 채소는 산지에서 직접 배송됩니다. 그러니 1층에 있는 과일과 채소 구역에 오셔서 둘러보시기 바랍니다.

•• **mushroom** 버섯 **advertise** 광고하다 **deliver** 배달하다 **local** 현지의 **producer** 생산자 **take a look at** ~을 보다

13

M　Hi, Judy. You look really healthy and thin. What is your secret?

W　Actually, I've been working out every day for a month or so.

M　Really? What kind of exercise do you do?

W　I jump rope for about half an hour in the morning. It was hard at first, but I feel better now.

M　That's really a good habit. How much weight have you lost?

W　I've lost three kilograms.

M　Wow, I'll go buy a jump rope, too. Do you have anything to buy at the YJ Mart? They're having a sale on this weekend.

W　Oh, I want to buy light running shoes. Let's go together.

남　안녕, Judy. 너 아주 건강하고 날씬해 보인다. 비법이 뭐니?
여　사실은, 한 달여 정도 매일 운동하고 있어.
남　정말? 어떤 종류의 운동을 하니?
여　아침에 30분 정도 줄넘기 해. 처음엔 힘들었는데, 이젠 훨씬 나은 것 같아.
남　정말 좋은 습관이다. 살을 얼마나 뺐니?
여　3킬로그램 뺐어.
남　와, 나도 줄넘기 사러 가야겠어. 너 YJ 마트에서 뭐 살 거 없니? 이번 주말에 세일을 할 거거든.
여　오, 나 가벼운 러닝화를 사고 싶어. 같이 가자.

•• **thin** 날씬한, 얇은 **secret** 비밀 **jump rope** 줄넘기하다; 줄넘기 **light** 가벼운

14

M　Hello. How may I help you?

W　Can you recommend either an action or an animation movie?

M　Sure. Have you seen *Iron Man* or *Frozen*?

W　No, I haven't seen either of them. I've missed all my chances to see them.

M　They are awesome. You should watch them.

W　Then, I'd like to rent those two movies. How much are they?

M　Two thousand won each. What's your phone number?

W　736-9842. When is the due date?

M　By Saturday or there will be a late fee.

남　안녕하세요. 무엇을 도와 드릴까요?
여　액션이나 애니메이션 영화 중에 하나를 추천해 주시겠습니까?
남　물론이죠. 〈아이언 맨〉이나 〈겨울왕국〉 보셨나요?
여　아니요, 둘 다 못 봤습니다. 볼 기회를 모두 놓쳤지요.
남　아주 재미있어요. 보셔야 해요.
여　그러면 그 두 개를 빌릴게요. 얼마인가요?
남　각각 2,000원입니다. 전화번호가 어떻게 되세요?
여　736-9842번입니다. 기한은 언제예요?
남　토요일까지입니다. 그렇지 않으면 연체료가 있습니다.

•• **recommend** 추천하다 **either A or B** A나 B 둘 중 하나 **due date** 기한일, 마감일 **late fee** 연체료

15

W　Best Eastern Real Estate. How may I help you?

M　Yes. Is the house you advertised still available?

W　Do you mean the one with three bedrooms fully furnished?

M　Yes, that's the one. Could you please tell me more about it?

W　My pleasure. It's five minutes' walk from a subway station, line number two.

M　How much is the rent?

W　It's 515 dollars a month and has a deposit of 3,000 dollars.

M　What's included in the rent?

W All utilities are included except for the electric bill.

주택 임대	
① 방 :	3개
② 가구 :	완비
③ 위치 :	치하철역 도보 5분 거리
④ 임대료 :	매월 $550 / 보증금 $3,000
⑤ 공과금 :	전기요금을 제외한 모두 포함

여 Best Eastern 부동산입니다. 무엇을 도와드릴까요?
남 네, 광고하신 집이 아직 있습니까?
여 가구가 완비된 방 3개짜리 집 말씀이신가요?
남 네, 바로 그것입니다. 좀더 자세히 말씀해주시겠습니까?
여 물론이지요. 지하철 2호선 역에서 도보 5분 거리에 위치해 있습니다.
남 집세는요?
여 한 달에 515달러이며 보증금은 3,000달러입니다.
남 집세에는 무엇이 포함되어 있나요?
여 전기 요금을 제외한 모든 공과금이 포함되어 있습니다.

•• real estate 부동산 advertise 광고하다 furnish (가구를) 비치하다 ~ minutes' walk 걸어서 ~분 거리 deposit 보증금 utilities (수도, 가스 등) 공익 설비, 공공 요금 electric bill 전기요금 고지서

16

① M Can you tell me why you like rice noodles?
   W Because they are very delicious.
② M Do you need help getting to the park?
   W Yes. I know how to get there myself.
③ M Why don't you get Tom a cell phone case?
   W That's a good idea.
④ M Please take this box and sign here.
   W I wonder who sent this. There is no name and address.
⑤ M Did you enjoy the movie?
   W Not much. I prefer sci-fi movies.

① 남 년 왜 쌀국수를 좋아하는지 말해 줄래?
   여 맛있기 때문이야.
② 남 공원까지 가는 데 도움이 필요한가요?
   여 예. 저는 거기 가는 방법을 알아요.
③ 남 Tom에게 휴대전화 케이스를 사 주는 것은 어때?
   여 그거 좋은 생각이다.
④ 남 이 상자 받으시고 여기 서명하세요.
   여 누가 이걸 보냈는지 궁금하네요. 이름과 주소가 없어요.

⑤ 남 영화 재미있었니?
   여 별로. 나는 공상과학 영화가 더 좋아.

•• rice noodle 쌀국수 get to ~에 도착하다 cell phone 휴대전화

17

W I'm going to buy a bottle of sunscreen for this Friday.
M Okay. Then, are you going to be outside on that day?
W Don't you remember? Our field trip to the amusement park is this Friday. Aren't you coming?
M Oh, I completely forgot about that. Could you let me know when and where we will meet?
W Yes. We're going to meet at the front gate of the school at 9 a.m. to get on the bus.
M As I remember, our teacher has not mentioned a detailed schedule yet.
W Yes, that's right. But I think in the morning we're going to learn about the working mechanisms for the rides.
M Oh, that's interesting.
W Right. The afternoon is leisure time. After we have lunch at the cafeteria, we have free time until 4 o'clock.

여 나 이번 금요일을 위해 자외선차단제 한 병을 살 거야.
남 좋아. 그런데, 그날 너 야외에 있을 거니?
여 기억 안 나? 놀이공원으로 현장학습 가는 것이 이번 금요일이잖아. 넌 안 갈 거니?
남 오, 완전 깜빡했어. 언제 어디서 만나는지 알려줄래?
여 그래. 우린 버스에 타기 위해 학교 정문 앞에서 아침 9시에 만날 거야.
남 내가 기억하는 한, 우리 선생님은 상세한 일정에 대해서 아직 말씀하신 적이 없어.
여 맞아. 하지만 오전엔 놀이기구들의 작동 장치에 대해 배울 것 같아.
남 오, 그거 재미있겠다.
여 맞아. 오후 시간은 노는 시간이야. 구내식당에서 점심을 먹은 후에 4시까지 자유시간을 즐길 거야.

•• amusement park 놀이공원 mention 언급하다 mechanism 장치, 구조 ride 탈것 leisure 놀이, 여가

18

M Jim's friend, Cathy, spends too much time on the Internet because she enjoys online shopping. She especially likes to collect the latest, most popular fashion items. Buying things in online shops is usually cheaper than buying them in offline shops. But the problem is she spends almost all her allowance on buying clothes. After she spends all of her allowance shopping online, she sometimes borrows money from her friends. In this situation, what would Jim likely say to Cathy?

남 Jim의 친구인 Cathy는 온라인쇼핑을 즐기기 때문에 너무 많은 시간을 인터넷을 하며 보낸다. 그녀는 특히 최신의, 가장 인기 있는 패션 품목들을 수집하는 것을 좋아한다. 온라인 상점에서 물건을 사는 것은 오프라인 상점에서 사는 것보다 대개 더 저렴하다. 하지만 문제는 그녀가 옷을 사는 데 그녀의 용돈 대부분을 쓴다는 것이다. 온라인쇼핑을 하느라 용돈을 다 쓴 후에, 그녀는 가끔 친구들로부터 돈을 빌리기도 한다. 이 상황에서 Jim은 Cathy에게 뭐라고 말하겠는가?

① 가장 새롭게 유행하는 옷은 어떤 거야?
② 죄송합니다. 저흰 그 물건이 없습니다.
③ 넌 인터넷에서 옷을 사는 걸 그만둬야 해.
④ 그 멋진 옷과 신발을 모두 어디서 샀니?
⑤ 유행에 뒤떨어지지 말고 온라인쇼핑을 즐겨.

•• **collect** 수집하다　**latest** 최신의　**allowance** 용돈

19

W Hi, Jack. I need your advice.

M Sure. What is it?

W I promised to sell things with my friends at a charity bazaar the day after tomorrow.

M That will be fun! Then, what's the problem?

W This morning, my mom said I have to attend my grandfather's 10th memorial service on the same day.

M You mean it's hard to tell your friends that you can't go?

W Exactly.

M I think you should tell them as soon as possible. Your friends will understand you 100%.

W I guess you're right. Thank you for your advice.

··

여 안녕, Jack. 네 충고가 필요해.
남 그래. 뭐니?
여 내일모레 친구들과 한 자선 바자회에서 물건을 팔기로 약속했었어.
남 재미있겠다. 그런데 문제가 뭐니?
여 오늘 아침, 엄마가 말씀하시길 같은 날 할아버지의 10주기 추도식에 참석해야 한대.
남 친구들에게 못 간다고 말하는 게 힘들다는 거니?
여 맞아.
남 내 생각엔 가능한 한 빨리 말해야 할 것 같아. 네 친구들이 100% 널 이해해줄 거야.
여 네 말이 맞는 것 같아. 충고 고마워.

① 너 뭐 팔 물건 있니?
② 바자회에서 너를 돕고 싶구나.
③ 네 말이 맞는 것 같아. 충고 고마워.
④ 이 재미있는 바자회에 초대해줘서 고마워.
⑤ 참여해주세요. 이번 행사에도 뵐 수 있기를 바랍니다.

•• **charity bazaar** 자선 바자회　**attend** 참석하다　**memorial service** 추도식

20

W Good afternoon. Welcome to the Grand Hotel. How may I help you?

M I have a reservation for today. It's under the name of John Smith. Here's my ID.

W Thank you. We've reserved a twin bed room for you for three nights. Is that correct?

M Yes, it is.

W Excellent. Could you just sign along the bottom, please?

M Whoa! 350 dollars a night! Hmm. OK, so what room am I in?

W You are in Room 487. Here is your key. If you have any questions or requests, please dial '0' from your room.

M Oh, when is the swimming pool available?

W Its opening hours are from 5 a.m to 1 a.m.

여　안녕하세요. 그랜드 호텔에 오신 것을 환영합니다. 무엇을
　　도와드릴까요?

남　오늘 예약되어 있어요. John Smith라는 이름으로요. 여기 제 신분증
　　있습니다.

여　감사합니다. 트윈베드룸 3박을 예약해드렸네요. 맞습니까?

남　네, 맞습니다.

여　좋습니다. 하단에 사인 좀 부탁 드릴까요?

남　세상에! 1박에 350달러라니! 음. 네, 저는 몇 호실에 묵나요?

여　487호입니다. 여기 열쇠 있습니다. 질문이나 요청 사항이 있으시면,
　　방에서 0번을 누르세요.

남　오, 수영장은 언제 이용 가능한가요?

여　<u>개장시간은 오전 5시에서 오전 1시까지입니다.</u>

① 제가 준비해 드리겠습니다.
② 이것은 호텔 숙박요금에 추가될 것입니다.
③ 저녁 6시에 호텔로 당신을 데리러 갈게요.
④ 개장 시간은 오전 5시에서 오전 1시까지입니다.
⑤ 인터넷은 로비에서 24시간 이용 가능합니다.

reserve 예약하다　**bottom** 밑바닥　**request** 요청

Further Study 정답
p. 94

1. She wants to buy <u>bath toys</u> that can <u>amuse and entertain her son</u>.

2. He likes it because he <u>loves its color, blue</u>.

3. She is explaining <u>the basic school rules that students must follow</u>.

4. ① To help you make <u>friends</u>
　 ② To help you reach out to <u>the community</u>
　 ③ To help you learn <u>new skills</u> and advance <u>your career</u>
　 ④ To protect <u>your mental and physical health</u>

5. You can get <u>two packs of mushrooms</u> for the price of one pack.

6. She has <u>been jumping rope for about half an hour in the morning</u> for a month or so.

7. She has to <u>pay a late fee</u>.

8. She was supposed to <u>sell things with her friends at a charity bazaar</u> the day after tomorrow.

On Your Own 모범답안
p. 95

A

Why Should Students Volunteer?	
(1) First reason	learn about how our society works, which is hard to achieve by only studying at school
(2) Second reason	learn about our future job while we make some meaningful contributions to our community
(3) Third reason	get to know people we don't usually interact with and thus gain various perspectives on our own life

I'd like to tell you about why volunteering is important for young students like us. First, it is important because (1)<u>we can learn about how our society works, which is hard to achieve by only studying at school</u>. Second, (2)<u>we can learn about our future job while we make some meaningful contributions to our community</u>. Finally, it is a valuable chance (3)<u>for us to get to know people we don't usually interact with and thus to gain various perspectives on our own life</u>. So, let's not hesitate to volunteer in our community.

왜 학생들은 자원봉사를 해야 하는가?	
(1) 첫 번째 이유	우리 사회가 어떻게 작동하는지에 관해 배울 수 있는데, 이런 점은 학교에서 공부하는 것만으로는 얻기 힘듦
(2) 두 번째 이유	공동체 사회에 의미 있는 공헌을 하면서 미래 직업에 대해서 배울 수 있음
(3) 세 번째 이유	평소에 잘 접촉하지 않는 사람들을 알고, 그로 인해 우리 자신의 인생에 대한 다양한 시각을 얻을 수 있음

우리처럼 어린 학생들에게 봉사활동이 왜 중요한지에 관해 말하고자 합니다. 첫 번째로, 우리 사회가 어떻게 작동하는지에 관해 배울 수 있기 때문에 중요한데, 이런 점은 학교에서 공부하는 것만으로는 얻기 힘든 것입니다. 두 번째로, 공동체 사회에 의미 있는 공헌을 하면서 미래 직업에 대해서도 배울 수 있습니다. 마지막으로, 봉사활동은 우리가 평소에 잘 접촉하지 않는 사람들을 알고, 그로 인해 우리 자신의 인생에 다양한 시각을 얻을 수 있는 좋은 기회입니다. 따라서 우리 공동체 사회에서 자원 봉사하는 일을 주저하지 맙시다.

B

My Most Memorable School Field Trip	
Where	(1) Lotte World
When	(2) this spring
What I did	(3) learned about the working mechanisms of the rides (4) had lunch with my classmates (5) enjoyed riding my favorite rides such as the Flume Ride
What was impressive	(6) an exciting time with my friends, a chance to understand how the rides work

My most memorable school field trip was a trip to (1)Lotte World. I went there (2)this spring. I did many things there. First, (3)I learned about the working mechanisms of the rides. Second, (4)I had lunch with my classmates. Finally, (5)I enjoyed riding my favorite rides such as the Flume Ride. The reason this field trip is the most memorable for me is that (6)I had an exciting time with my friends and a chance to understand how the rides work.

나의 가장 추억할 만한 학교 현장학습	
장소	(1) 롯데월드
때	(2) 올 봄
한 일	(3) 놀이기구들의 작동 원리를 배움 (4) 반 친구들과 점심을 먹음 (5) 내가 좋아하는 놀이기구인 후룸 라이드 같은 것을 타며 즐김
인상적이었던 점	(6) 친구들과 신났던 시간임, 놀이기구가 어떻게 작동하는지를 이해할 수 있는 기회였음

나의 가장 기억에 남는 학교 현장학습은 롯데월드로 간 여행이었습니다. 올 봄에 거기 갔지요. 저는 거기서 많은 것을 했습니다. 첫째, 놀이기구들이 작동하는 원리를 배웠습니다. 둘째, 반 친구들과 점심을 먹었습니다. 마지막으로, 제가 좋아하는 놀이기구인 후룸 라이드 같은 것을 타며 즐겼습니다. 이 여행이 가장 기억에 남는 이유는 친구들과 신나는 시간을 보냈고 놀이기구가 어떻게 작동하는지를 이해할 수 있는 기회였기 때문입니다.

---

01 ①	02 ①	03 ②	04 ①	05 ③
06 ③	07 ④	08 ②	09 ④	10 ③
11 ②	12 ⑤	13 ④	14 ⑤	15 ⑤
16 ⑤	17 ①	18 ④	19 ④	20 ③

01

M Mom, I want to buy Jane a cell phone case for her birthday present. Can you help me?

W Of course. There are lots of covers and cases for any cell phone here.

M Yes. Do you think she will like this case with golden studs?

W It doesn't look attractive. What about this one with flower stickers or that one with polka dots?

M I dislike the patterns on both of them.

W Come on, Mike! It's not for you but for Jane.

M That's right. Okay then I'll buy that one with polka dots.

남 엄마, Jane에게 생일 선물로 휴대전화 케이스를 선물하고 싶은데 저 좀 도와주시겠어요?

여 물론이지. 여기에 휴대전화 케이스와 덮개가 많구나.

남 네. 금색 징을 박아놓은 이 케이스 좋아할까요?

여 좋아 보이지는 않구나. 꽃무늬 스티커가 있는 이 케이스나 물방울 무늬가 있는 저 케이스 어떠니?

남 전 두 가지 무늬가 다 싫어요.

여 얘, Mike. 그건 널 위한 게 아니라 Jane을 위한 거잖아.

남 맞아요. 그러면 물방울 무늬가 있는 것을 살게요.

stud 장식 징, 장식 단추 **attractive** 매력적인 **polka dot** 물방울 무늬 **pattern** 무늬, 도안

02

W Excuse me, sir. Do you know how to get to the women's clothing department?

M Yes. Take the escalator up to the fourth floor, then go through the furnishings department and it's right past the toy department.

W Thank you. Escalator to the <u>fourth</u> floor, <u>straight</u> <u>ahead through</u> the furnishings department and then the toy department.

M Yes, that's right.

W And <u>where</u> <u>is the escalator</u>?

M Can you see the <u>cosmetics shop</u> over there? Go around the shop and the escalator is <u>opposite of</u> it.

W Okay, I see. Thank you so much.

- -

여 실례합니다. 여성복 매장에 어떻게 가는지 아세요?

남 네. 에스컬레이터를 타고 4층까지 올라가셔서 가구 매장을 지나시면, 장난감 매장 바로 지나서 여성복 매장이 있습니다.

여 감사합니다. 에스컬레이터를 타서 4층에 내리고, 앞으로 곧장 가서 가구 매장을 지나면 장난감 매장이 있는 거죠.

남 맞습니다.

여 그리고 에스컬레이터는 어디에 있나요?

남 저기 화장품 가게 보이십니까? 그 가게를 돌아가면 맞은편에 에스컬레이터가 있습니다.

여 네, 알겠습니다. 대단히 감사합니다.

department 부, 과, (상품별) 매장 **furnishings** 가구, 비품 **past** ~를 지나서 **cosmetics** 화장품 **opposite of** ~의 맞은편에

03

M <u>How did you like</u> the movie?

W Well, <u>to tell you the truth</u>, I was a little <u>disappointed</u>.

M Disappointed? Why? It got <u>great reviews</u>, didn't it?

W It wasn't <u>as exciting as</u> I thought it would be.

M Really? All my friends told me it was <u>the most exciting movie</u> they had ever seen.

W I really <u>expected</u> it to be a lot <u>more interesting</u>. By the way, what time do we have to <u>leave for</u> tonight's family get-together?

M We <u>must leave</u> at seven with the kids.

- -

남 영화 어땠어요?

여 글쎄, 사실대로 말하자면, 약간 실망했어요.

남 실망했다고? 왜요? 그 영화는 좋은 감상평들을 받았잖아, 그렇지 않아요?

여 내가 생각했던 것만큼 흥미진진하지 않았어요.

남 정말? 내 친구들은 모두 그 영화가 자기들이 본 영화 중 가장 재미있는 영화라고 말했는데.

여 나도 그것이 훨씬 더 재미있을 거라고 기대했었어요. 그런데, 오늘 저녁 가족모임을 위해 몇 시에 출발해야 하죠?

남 아이들과 함께 7시에 출발해야 해요.

① 영화감독 – 여배우   ② 남편 – 아내
③ 비평가 – 기자   ④ 직원 – 고객
⑤ 교사 – 학부모

disappointed 실망한 **review** 감상평 **expect** 기대하다 **get-together** 모임, 친목회

04

W Hey, Jim. What's wrong with <u>your eyes</u>? Did you get in a <u>fight</u> with your roommate?

M No. I just <u>sat up all night</u> doing research for my term paper, so they look <u>terrible</u>.

W Look at those <u>dark circles</u> under your eyes. You look like a <u>panda</u> with them.

M Stop <u>making fun of me</u>. It's not a laughing matter.

W You look really <u>cute</u> like a panda, though.

M Just <u>stop it</u>! Please leave me alone.

W Sorry. I <u>didn't mean</u> to upset you.

- -

여 안녕, Jim. 네 눈에 무슨 문제라도 있니? 너 룸메이트와 싸웠니?

남 아니. 학기말 보고서를 위한 조사를 하느라 밤을 세워서 눈이 엉망이야.

여 네 눈 밑의 다크서클 좀 봐. 판다처럼 보여.

남 그만 놀려. 웃을 일이 아니잖아.

여 하지만 너 판다처럼 정말 귀여워 보여.

남 제발 그만 좀 해! 부탁이니까 혼자 있게 좀 해줘.

여 미안해. 네 기분을 상하게 할 생각은 없었어.

① 기분 나쁜   ② 흥미 있는   ③ 신이 난
④ 실망한   ⑤ 안도한

get in a fight with ~와 싸우다 **sit up** 자지 않고 일어나 있다 **research** 조사 **term paper** 학기말 논문[숙제] **make fun of** ~를 놀리다

05

[Telephone rings.]

W Hello?

M Is Jane there? This is Max speaking.

W Hi, Max! It's me. How are you?

M I'm fine. I was wondering if you'd like to go to a movie tonight with me.

W Sure, I'd love to. What's playing?

M I was thinking about *Love in Paris*. What do you think?

W Sounds great!

M Okay. The movie starts at eight thirty so I'll pick you up at eight o'clock.

W Well, how about meeting an hour and a half early before the movie to get dinner? I'll treat you to dinner tonight.

M Great. See you then. Bye!

. . . .

[전화벨이 울린다.]

여 여보세요?

남 Jane 거기 있나요? 전 Max입니다.

여 안녕. Max. 나야. 어떻게 지내니?

남 잘 지내. 오늘밤에 나랑 영화 보러 갈 건가 해서.

여 좋아, 그러자. 어떤 게 상영되고 있지?

남 〈파리에서의 사랑〉을 볼까 생각 중이야. 네 생각은 어떠니?

여 아주 좋아.

남 그래. 영화가 8시 30분에 시작하니까 8시에 너를 데리러 갈게.

여 음. 영화 시작 전 1시간 30분 더 일찍 만나서 저녁 먹는 거 어때? 오늘 저녁은 내가 살게.

남 좋아. 그럼 그때 보자. 안녕!

••
play 상영되다   **treat** 대접하다, 한턱 내다

06

W Hello, everyone. Last class, I told you about the pop art movement in the United States. Today, we're going to be taking a look at the art movement called impressionism. This art movement originated with a group of Paris based artists in the 1800s. Their independent artistic expressions brought them to prominence, in spite of the hard opposition from the conventional art community in France.

. . . .

여 안녕하세요, 여러분. 지난 시간에 미국 대중미술 운동에 대해서 말했어요. 오늘은 인상주의라고 불리는 미술 운동에 대해 살펴 볼 겁니다. 이 미술 운동은 1800년대에 파리를 기반으로 하는 화가들의

그룹에 의해서 유래되었습니다. 그들의 독립적인 미술 표현은 프랑스의 전통 미술계로부터 거센 저항을 받았음에도 불구하고 그들에게 큰 명성을 가져다 주었습니다.

••
impressionism 인상주의   **originate** 유래하다   **independent** 독립적인   **prominence** 탁월, 명성   **in spite of** ~에도 불구하고
opposition 반대   **conventional** 전통의, 재래의

07

W Paul, let's give mom a day off and do some household chores for her.

M That's a good idea. What do you want me to do?

W Would you vacuum the carpet?

M Sure. What should I do after that?

W Well, you can change the water in the fish tank.

M Okay. But what are you going to do?

W I'm going to wash the dishes, and after that I have to do the laundry.

M Do you think we can switch jobs? Yours seem easier.

W All right, all right.

. . . .

여 Paul, 엄마에게 하루 휴가 드리고 엄마를 위해 우리가 집안일 좀 하자.

남 좋은 생각이야. 내가 뭘 하길 원해?

여 진공청소기로 카펫 청소해 줄래?

남 그래. 그 다음엔 뭘 하지?

여 그럼, 어항에 물을 갈아줘.

남 좋아. 그런데 누난 뭘 할 거야?

여 난 설거지를 할 거고, 그 후엔 빨래를 해야 해.

남 바꿔서 할 수 있을까? 누나 일이 더 쉬워 보여.

여 알았어, 알았다구.

••
give[get] a day off 하루 휴가를 주다[받다]   **household** 가족의, 가사의
vacuum 진공청소기로 청소하다   **fish tank** 어항   **do the laundry**
빨래하다   **switch** 바꾸다

08

M Have a look at this Techno Mart sale advertisement. The laptop costs less than $400.

W Awesome. Until when can we buy the listed items at the reduced prices?

M It says prices are valid until Black Friday, November

28. There's only a week left. I'm planning to buy a 3D TV.

W Umm. The 3D TV costs $679 and that price includes four pairs of 3D glasses.

M Are you interested in an E-reader? We can buy a second E-reader at half the price if we buy one.

W I'm in. Let's buy them together and get the second one 50% off. Oh, there is no delivery charge on all the items. Cool.

```
                   테크노 마트
                   파격 제안

    전자책 단말기               $149
    3D 스마트 LED HDTV          $679
  ① 노트북 컴퓨터              $395

  ② 할인 기간 : 가격은 11월 28일, 블랙 프라이데이에 한해 유효함.
  ③ 3D TV를 사면 4벌의 3D 안경 드림.
  ④ 전자책 단말기 2개를 구입하면 1개는 50% 할인.
  ⑤ 모든 품목 무료 배송.
```

남 이 테크노 마트 할인 광고 좀 봐. 노트북 컴퓨터가 400달러도 안 하네.

여 굉장한 걸. 할인품목들을 언제까지 할인가로 구매할 수 있는 거야?

남 가격은 11월 28일, 블랙 프라이데이까지 유효하대. 딱 일주일 남았다. 난 3D TV를 살 계획이야.

여 음. 3D TV는 가격이 679달러인데 이 가격은 3D 안경 4벌을 포함한 거야.

남 너 전자책 단말기에 관심 있니? 하나를 사면 두 번째 단말기를 반 값에 살 수 있어.

여 나 할게. 우리 함께 사고 두 번째 것은 50% 할인 받자. 오, 모든 제품들에 배달료가 없어. 좋은데.

advertisement 광고 **reduce** 줄이다 **valid** 유효한 **E-reader** 전자책 단말기 **delivery** 배달 **charge** 요금

09

W Sangyoon, do you know when the library opens and closes?

M It opens at 8:30 in the morning and closes at 7 in the evening.

W What about on weekends?

M I'm not sure. I've never been on weekends.

W I see. If it is okay with you, please check it for me.

M No problem. But then why do you want to know?

W That is because I need more reference books for my report. Next Monday is the due date.

M I see. I will let you know in 10 minutes.

여 상윤아. 너 도서관이 언제 문 열고 닫는지 아니?

남 아침 8시 30분에 열어서 저녁 7시에 닫아.

여 주말에는?

남 잘 모르겠네. 주말에는 안 가봐서.

여 알았어. 괜찮다면, 확인 좀 해줘.

남 알았어. 그런데 왜 알려고 해?

여 리포트에 참고도서가 더 필요해서. 다음 주 월요일이 마감일이거든.

남 그렇구나. 10분 후에 알려줄게.

reference book 참고도서

10

M What are you doing here, Haena?

W I'm waiting for Daeun. We made an appointment to meet here at seven o'clock.

M Then why are you here so early? You have to wait more than thirty minutes.

W What? According to my watch, it's five to seven. Is that wrong?

M Yes. It's exactly twenty five after six.

W I see. Then my watch must be fast. Thank you for letting me know.

M You're welcome. What are you going to do until seven?

W Well. I'll just sit here and wait for her.

남 해나야, 여기서 뭐 하니?

여 대은이 기다려. 7시에 여기서 만나기로 약속했거든.

남 그런데 왜 이렇게 일찍 왔어? 30분도 더 기다려야 하잖아.

여 뭐라고? 내 시계는 7시 5분 전인데. 잘못됐어?

남 응. 지금 정확히 6시 25분이야.

여 그렇구나. 내 시계가 빠른가 봐. 알려주어 고마워.

남 천만에. 7시까지 뭐 할 거야?

여 음. 그냥 여기 앉아서 기다리지 뭐.

make an appointment 약속하다 **according to** ~에 따르면 **exactly** 정확하게

11

M   Look at the poster on the board.

W   What's it about? I can't see it well. I have poor eyesight and too many people are in front of me.

M   It says there will be a party for all students who were born in April. It will be held in Room 101 at 3:00 p.m.

W   Really? What else?

M   They will prepare a large cake, pizza, fried chicken and several different kinds of drinks.

W   I'm going. I was born in April! Can I bring a friend who wasn't born in April?

M   Yes, you can bring a friend but only one.

W   Any other information?

M   All the teachers and the staff members of the school will be at the party too. And the party is free.

⸱⸱⸱⸱⸱⸱⸱⸱⸱⸱⸱⸱⸱⸱⸱⸱⸱⸱⸱⸱⸱⸱⸱⸱⸱⸱⸱⸱⸱⸱⸱⸱

남   게시판의 포스터를 봐.

여   뭐에 관한 거야? 잘 안 보여. 난 눈도 안 좋은 데다 내 앞에 너무 많은 사람들이 있어.

남   4월에 태어난 모든 학생들을 위한 생일파티가 있을 예정이래. 오후 3시에 101호에서 열린대.

여   정말? 다른 것은?

남   큰 케이크와 피자, 프라이드 치킨, 그리고 여러 다른 종류의 음료를 준비할 거래.

여   나 갈래. 나 4월에 태어났거든! 4월생이 아닌 친구도 데려갈 수 있어?

남   친구를 데려갈 수 있는데 한 명만 돼.

여   다른 정보는?

남   학교의 모든 선생님들과 직원들도 오실 거야. 그리고 파티는 무료야.

⸱⸱
board 판자, 게시판   **be born** 태어나다   **be held** 열리다   **staff** 직원

12

① W *Miracle in Cell No.7* is on only in the morning.

② W *Iron Man 3* is on in Theater 3.

③ W *Les Miserables* is on both in the morning and in the afternoon.

④ W *Frozen* is on only once a day in Theater 4.

⑤ W *Lion King and Iron Man 3* are on at the same time.

영화	시간	상영관
7번방의 선물	오전 10:00, 오후 04:00	1
아이언맨 3	오전 11:30, 오후 05:00	2
레미제라블	오후 03:00, 오후 06:00	3
겨울왕국	오후 04:30, 오후 07:30	4
라이온 킹	오전 11:30, 오후 05:00	5

① 여 〈7번방의 선물〉은 오전에만 상영한다.

② 여 〈아이언맨 3〉는 3번 상영관에서 상영한다.

③ 여 〈레미제라블〉은 오전과 오후 모두 상영한다.

④ 여 〈겨울왕국〉은 4번 상영관에서 하루 한 번만 상영한다.

⑤ 여 〈라이온 킹〉과 〈아이언맨 3〉는 같은 시간에 상영한다.

⸱⸱
once 한 번   **at the same time** 동시에

13

M   Mom, I'm starving. I want fried rice for dinner.

W   Let's buy the ingredients for it.

M   What are they?

W   I don't think we have any carrots, potatoes, and onions.

M   Okay. They are in the vegetable section. What else do we need to buy?

W   If we add ground beef, it will taste better.

M   My mouth is watering already. Thank you, mom.

W   You're welcome. I'll get some oranges for dessert.

⸱⸱⸱⸱⸱⸱⸱⸱⸱⸱⸱⸱⸱⸱⸱⸱⸱⸱⸱⸱⸱⸱⸱⸱⸱⸱⸱⸱⸱⸱⸱⸱

남   엄마, 너무 배고파요. 저녁에 볶음밥 먹고 싶어요.

여   그럼 재료들을 사자꾸나.

남   뭔데요?

여   집에 당근, 감자, 그리고 양파가 없는 것 같아.

남   네. 그것들은 채소 구역에 있어요. 그리고 또 뭐가 필요해요?

여   소고기 간 것을 넣으면 더 맛있을 거야.

남   벌써 군침이 도는데요. 고마워요, 엄마.

여   천만에. 나는 디저트로 먹을 오렌지를 사야겠구나.

① 꽃가게   ② 식당   ③ 커피숍
④ 식료품점   ⑤ 부엌

⸱⸱
carrot 당근   **section** 구역   **grind** 갈다   **water** 침 흘리다

14

M Ladies and gentlemen, I am here to swear in
front of you that I will keep my election pledges.
Are you satisfied with where you are living now?
Don't you want a safer and merrier city? Here is
the answer. Vote for me on mayoral election day.
Please remember my name, Gyomoon Kang. The
future of our city depends on your vote. One thing
I can promise you is that I won't disappoint you. I
won't make you regret voting for me. Please vote
for Number 1. Thank you.

남 신사숙녀 여러분, 저는 여러분 앞에서 저의 선거 공략을 지키겠다는
맹세를 하기 위해 여기에 나왔습니다. 지금 살고 계신 곳에
만족하십니까? 더 안전하고 즐거운 도시를 원하지 않으십니까?
여기에 그 답이 있습니다. 시장 선거일에 저를 뽑아주십시오. 제 이름
강교문을 기억해 주십시오. 우리 도시의 미래는 여러분의 투표에 달려
있습니다. 제가 약속드릴 수 있는 한 가지는 여러분들을 실망시키지
않을 것이란 점입니다. 여러분이 저를 뽑아주신 것을 후회하지 않게 할
것입니다. 기호 1번을 뽑아 주십시오. 감사합니다.

swear 맹세하다 **election** 선거 **pledge** 서약 **be satisfied with**
~에 만족하다 **mayoral** 시장의 **vote for** ~에 찬성 투표하다 **depend
on** ~에 달려 있다

15

[Telephone rings.]

M Hello?

W Hello. Is this Namgyu? This is Minji.

M Hi, Minji. What's up?

W You left your English textbook in my house.

M Thank you for calling. I was wondering where I had
left it. I thought it was in my school locker.

W You do have English homework tonight, don't you?

M I do. I have to memorize the words, the
conversation part and the main text.

W Do you want me to take it to your house?

M Wonderful. I will make a sandwich for you.

[전화벨이 울린다.]

남 여보세요?

여 여보세요. 남규니? 나 민지야.

남 안녕, 민지야. 무슨 일이야?

여 네가 우리 집에 네 영어 교과서를 놓고 갔어.

남 전화해줘서 고마워. 어디에 두었는지 걱정하고 있었어. 학교 사물함에
있다고 생각했는데.

여 오늘밤에 영어 숙제를 꼭 해야 하잖아, 그렇지?

남 응. 단어, 대화문, 그리고 본문을 외워야 해.

여 너희 집으로 가져다 줄까?

남 좋아. 너를 위해 샌드위치를 만들게.

locker 사물함 **memorize** 암기하다

16

M Wow. What a beautiful view!

W Look at that! We can see the N Seoul Tower.

M The view here is breathtaking! I'm happy that we
came up here on a clear day.

W Yes. But I feel a little exhausted.

M I think you need to get into better shape, so we'd
better climb mountains more often.

W Hey, what about this? Why don't you teach me
how to swim?

M That's a great idea.

남 와! 전망이 너무 아름답다!

여 저것 좀 봐. N서울타워가 보여.

남 여기 전망은 숨이 막힐 정도야. 화장한 날씨에 여기에 올라오니 기뻐.

여 응, 하지만 난 조금 피곤해.

남 내 생각에 너는 몸이 더 단련되어야 할 것 같아. 그래서 더 자주
등산하는 게 좋을 것 같아.

여 이건 어때? 네가 나에게 수영하는 방법을 가르쳐 주는 거?

남 좋은 생각이야.

breathtaking 깜짝 놀랄 만한 **clear** 화창한 **shape** 상태, 컨디션

17

① M I won first prize in a vocabulary contest.

　 W You must be disappointed.

② M What do you think of your meal?

　 W Good. Especially, the side dishes were very
delicious.

③ M Excuse me, can I park here?

w Sorry, this section is only for the handicapped.

④ M Can I help you?

　 w Yes, please. I want to buy a ticket to Busan.

⑤ M Excuse me. Is this seat taken?

　 w Yes. My friend will be back soon.

---

① 남 나 단어대회에서 1등을 했어.

　 여 실망했겠구나.

② 남 식사 어땠어요?

　 여 좋았어요. 특히 곁들임 요리들이 아주 맛있었어요.

③ 남 실례합니다만, 여기에 주차할 수 있나요?

　 여 죄송하지만, 이 구역은 장애인 전용입니다.

④ 남 도와드릴까요?

　 여 네, 부산행 표를 사고 싶어요.

⑤ 남 실례합니다. 이 자리 임자 있나요?

　 여 네, 제 친구가 곧 올 거예요.

side dish 반찬, 곁들임 요리　**the handicapped** 장애인들

18

w Excuse me. Could you tell me how I can check some books out? I am a freshman.

M It's very simple. Just give me your student ID card and the books you want.

w OK. How long can I keep the books?

M You can actually keep them for a week. But if you make an extension, you can keep them for another week. It is allowed once.

w Then, can I make an extension online?

M Sure. Just log into your library account on the school library website. Any other questions?

w Oh, how many books can I borrow at a time?

M Five is the maximum for a freshman.

w Thank you. You were very helpful.

여 실례합니다. 책을 어떻게 대출할 수 있는지 말씀해주실 수 있습니까? 제가 신입생이어서요.

남 아주 간단해요. 학생증과 원하는 책을 주시면 돼요.

여 네. 얼마 동안 책을 가지고 있을 수 있나요?

남 일주일 동안 가지고 있을 수 있습니다. 하지만 연장을 하면 일주일을 더 가지고 있을 수 있습니다. 연장은 1회만 허용됩니다.

여 그럼 온라인으로 연장할 수 있나요?

남 물론이죠. 학교 도서관 웹사이트에서 학생의 도서관 계정에 로그인

하면 됩니다. 다른 질문 있으세요?

여 아, 책은 한 번에 몇 권을 빌릴 수 있나요?

남 1학년은 최대 5권입니다.

여 감사합니다. 정말 도움이 되었어요.

check out (절차를 밟고) 빌리다　**ID card** 신분증　**extension** 연장
account 계정, 계좌

19

w Judy is planning to have her elementary school class reunion at 6 p.m. next Saturday. She decides to reserve a good restaurant first. Even though the number of students in her class was 40, the number attending will be much smaller. So she decides to make a reservation for 10 people. She searches for a good restaurant and calls it to make a reservation. In this situation, what would Judy likely say to the person on the phone?

여 Judy는 다음 주 토요일 오후 6시에 초등학교 반 동창회를 열 계획이다. 그녀는 먼저 멋진 레스토랑을 예약하기로 결심한다. 비록 그녀의 반 학생 수는 40명이었지만, 참석자 수는 훨씬 더 적을 것이다. 그래서 그녀는 10명 자리를 예약하기로 결정한다. 그녀는 좋은 레스토랑을 검색하고 예약을 위해 전화한다. 이 상황에서 Judy는 전화상의 사람에게 뭐라고 말하겠는가?

① 내가 그 식당에 우리 자리를 예약할게.

② 누구 이름으로 예약하시고 싶습니까?

③ 우리는 이미 저녁파티 예약을 했어요.

④ 다음 토요일 10명 테이블을 예약하고 싶습니다.

⑤ 며칠 전 예약한 테이블을 확정하려고 전화 드려요.

reunion 재회, 친목회　**even though** 비록 ~이지만　**search** 검색하다, 찾다

20

w Is it my imagination or have you lost a lot of weight?

M Well, I'm on a special diet.

w What's that?

M I try to stick to a low-carbohydrate and high-protein diet these days and I try to eat lots of fruit and vegetables, too.

W I see. I'll try the same diet from now on.

M Go for it. And don't forget to exercise for half an hour in the morning. You can stay fit like me.

W Well, you like to exercise, don't you?

M Yes, I try to exercise as often as I can.

- -

여 내가 망상인 거니 아니면 네가 살이 많이 빠진 거니?

남 응, 나 특별한 식이요법 중이야.

여 그게 뭔데?

남 난 요즘 저탄수화물 고단백 식단을 고수하려고 노력 중인데 과일과 채소를 많이 먹으려는 노력도 하고 있어.

여 그렇구나. 나도 지금부터 똑같은 식이요법을 해볼 거야.

남 그렇게 해. 그리고 아침에 30분 동안 운동하는 거 잊지 말고. 너도 나처럼 건강한 상태를 유지할 수 있어.

여 그런데, 너 운동을 좋아하지, 그렇지 않니?

남 응, 난 가능한 한 자주 운동하려고 노력해.

① 얼마나 자주 운동 하세요?

② 운동을 좀 해 보는 거 어때?

③ 응, 난 가능한 한 자주 운동하려고 노력해.

④ 아니, 너무 과한 운동은 금물이야.

⑤ 운동하기 싫어하는 사람들이 많아.

●●
imagination 상상, 망상 **stick to** ~을 고수하다 **diet** 식이요법 **low-carbohydrate** 저탄수화물의 **high-protein** 고단백의 **fit** 건강한

Further **S**tudy 정답   p. 104

1. She wants to go to the women's clothing department.

2. The reason is that he sat up all night doing research for his term paper.

3. She will treat him to dinner before the movie starts.

4. They want to give their mom a day off.

5. It is for all students who were born in April.

6. He wants fried rice.

7. It is a mayoral election.

8. She is planning to have her elementary school class reunion at a good restaurant.

On **Y**our **O**wn 모범답안   p. 105

A

Hello, my name is Jungmin Han, and I'm running for student council president. As president of the student council, I would fight for better school meals, more after-school activities, and more field trip programs. I would always be open to your ideas on how the school can be improved and be more fun. Vote for me!

- -

안녕하십니까. 저는 한정민이며 학생회장에 출마했습니다. 학생회장으로서 저는 더 나은 학교급식, 더 많은 방과 후 활동, 그리고 더 많은 견학 프로그램을 위해 분투할 것입니다. 저는 학교가 어떻게 더 발전되고 더 즐거워질 수 있는지에 대한 여러분의 생각에 항상 귀를 기울일 것입니다. 저를 뽑아주세요!

B

I Did...	
For whom & When?	(1) my mom, last Parents' Day
What did you do?	(2) did some household chores for her such as doing the dishes, doing the laundry, etc.
Why did you do it?	(3) she seemed to be exhausted and had no free time to rest
What did you feel?	(4) realized doing household chores is really hard and not fun at all (5) was amazed at how she could do so many exhausting things every day

I would like to tell you about the special things that I did for my (1)mom last Parents' Day. I (2)did some household chores for her such as doing the dishes, doing the laundry, etc. I did it because (3)she seemed to be exhausted and had no free time to rest. After doing them, I felt two things. First, (4)I realized doing household chores is really hard and not fun at all. Second, (5)I was amazed at how she could do so many exhausting things every day. Anyway, it always seems awesome to help someone else.

나는 …을 했습니다	
누구를 위해 언제?	(1) 엄마, 작년 어버이날
한 일은?	(2) 엄마를 위해 설거지, 빨래 등과 같은 집안일을 좀 해드림
그 일을 한 이유는?	(3) 엄마가 지쳐 보였고 쉴 시간이 없어서
뭘 느꼈나요?	(4) 집안일을 하는 것은 정말 힘들고 결코 간단한 일이 아니란 점을 깨달음 (5) 매일 그 많은 힘든 일을 엄마가 어떻게 하실 수 있었는지 놀라웠음

저는 작년 어버이날 엄마를 위해 한 특별한 일에 대해 말하고 싶습니다. 저는 엄마를 위해 설거지, 빨래 등과 같은 집안일을 좀 해드렸습니다. 제가 그 일을 한 이유는 엄마가 지쳐 보였고 쉴 시간이 없으셨기 때문입니다. 그 일을 한 후, 저는 두 가지를 느꼈습니다. 먼저 집안일을 하는 것은 정말 힘들고 결코 간단한 일이 아니란 점을 깨달았습니다. 둘째, 매일 그 많은 힘든 일을 엄마가 어떻게 하실 수 있었는지 놀라웠습니다. 어쨌든 다른 누군가를 돕는 것은 언제나 멋진 일인 것 같습니다.

---

11 Listening Test 정답

p. 110

01 ③	02 ①	03 ①	04 ③	05 ④
06 ②	07 ⑤	08 ⑤	09 ⑤	10 ①
11 ④	12 ②	13 ②	14 ①	15 ①
16 ④	17 ⑤	18 ③	19 ④	20 ④

01

W What are you doing?

M I'm looking for a swimsuit for our son, John, on this website. How about these swim shorts with fish?

W They look cute, but he needs a swim shirt, too.

M Those shorts match this green swim shirt with sharks.

W Hmmmm… I think we'd better buy him a long-sleeved shirt. Let's look at another swim set.

M Okay. This set includes a long-sleeved shirt and shark printed shorts. I like it.

W So do I. Especially, I love the printed message on the shirt, CUTE BOY. That can make him cuter.

M Great! Let's go with that set.

여 뭐 하고 있어요?

남 이 웹사이트에서 우리 아들, John에게 줄 수영복을 고르는 중이야. 이 물고기 그림이 있는 수영 반바지 어때?

여 귀여워 보이긴 하지만, 수영복 상의도 필요해요.

남 그 반바지는 이 상어 그림이 있는 녹색 셔츠와 잘 어울려.

여 음… 소매가 긴 셔츠를 사주는 게 좋을 것 같아요. 다른 수영복 세트 좀 봐요.

남 그래. 이 세트는 긴 소매 셔츠와 상어 그림이 인쇄된 반바지로 구성되어 있네. 마음에 들어.

여 나도 그래요. 특히 셔츠에 '귀여운 소년'이라고 인쇄된 문구가 마음에 들어요. 그것은 그를 더 귀엽게 보이게 할 거예요.

남 좋아! 이 세트로 사자.

••
swimsuit 수영복 **match** ~에 어울리다 **long-sleeved** 소매가 긴 **shorts** 반바지

02

M Yoomi! Thank you for coming to the exhibition.

W I'm glad to be invited. Which one is yours, Namsoo? There are still-lifes, portraits, and landscapes.

M Mine is a portrait of my dad.

W I see. Is it a half-length portrait?

M No, it's not. It's a full-length portrait.

W OK. I think I have to find it. The man in this painting has a generous and kind look. Your dad is like that.

M Oh, thank you for saying so. My dad will be happy to hear that.

W Is he the one wearing glasses?

M Well, he usually wears glasses but I painted him without them.

남 유미야! 전시회에 와줘서 고마워.

여 나는 초대되어 기뻐. 남수야, 어느 것이 네 그림이니? 정물화, 초상화, 그리고 풍경화가 있네.

남 내 그림은 우리 아버지 초상화야.

여 그렇구나. 반신 초상화니?

남 아니. 전신 초상화야.

여 그렇구나. 내가 찾아봐야겠어. 이 그림의 남자는 관대하고 친절한 모습이야. 너네 아버지가 그러시잖아.

남 오, 그렇게 말해줘서 고마워. 아버지가 그 말을 들으시면 기뻐하실 거야.

여 안경 쓰고 있는 사람이니?

남 음, 대개 쓰시는데 그림에는 안 그렸어.

••
exhibition 전시회 **still-life** 정물화 **portrait** 초상화 **landscape** 풍경, 풍경화 **half-length** 반신의 **full-length** 전신의

03

W It's a shame the boss is in such a bad mood.

M I agree. I wish she were in a better mood.

W Actually, I was hoping I could ask her for a couple of days off.

M It looks like that's out of the question.

W I have to go to Busan. My niece is getting married there. I want to attend her wedding ceremony.

M The boss is under a lot of stress right now.

W I know. What shall I do?

여 사장님이 저렇게 우울해 하시다니 안타까워요.

남 맞아요. 기분이 더 좋으시면 좋을 텐데요.

여 사실은 사장님께 이틀 휴가를 부탁 드릴 수 있길 바랐어요.

남 불가능한 것 같아요.

여 부산에 가야 하는데. 조카딸이 거기서 결혼을 하거든요. 결혼식에 참석하고 싶어요.

남 사장님이 지금 스트레스를 많이 받고 계신 것 같아요.

여 알아요. 어떻게 하죠?

① 답답한   ② 기쁜   ③ 슬픔에 찬
④ 부끄러운   ⑤ 비참한

••
It's a shame that ~해서 유감이다 **ask for a day off** 하루 휴가를 요청하다 **niece** 조카딸, 질녀 **out of the question** 불가능한 **ceremony** 기념식

04

[Telephone rings.]

M Hello, this is Brian. I'm sorry I'm not in right now. Please leave a message. I'll call you back.

[Beep]

W Hey Brian. This is Becky. I'm calling to let you know that I can't go to Tim's surprise birthday party tonight. My mom told me to take care of my younger brother because she will be late home from work tonight. I'm very sorry for not being able to go. Anyway, I'll call you again. Have fun. Bye.

[전화벨이 울린다.]

남 안녕하세요, Brian입니다. 제가 지금 집에 없습니다. 메시지를 남겨주세요. 전화 드리겠습니다.

여 Brian, 나 Becky야. 나 오늘 밤 Tim의 깜짝 생일파티에 못 간다고 알려주려고 전화했어. 엄마가 오늘 밤에 회사에서 늦으신다고 내 남동생을 돌보라고 하셨어. 못 가서 정말 미안해. 어쨌든, 다시 전화할게. 즐거운 시간 보내. 안녕.

••
take care of ~을 돌보다

05

W Can I help you?

M Yes, please. I want to order some pens to give away as a promotional gift for the opening of my store.

W How many do you want to order?

M I'm thinking of 400 pens. I want ones that cost one dollar each.

W Okay. These are the options that you can choose from.

M I love this pen. Do you have any discount policy if I buy a larger amount? And is there a fee for printing the logo?

W Logo printing is 5 cents per pen. And we can give you a 5% discount if you order 500 pens or more.

M That's good.

W And if you order 700 pens or more, there is a 10% discount and free logo printing.

M Oh, that's really cheap. I'll order 700 pens.

여 도와드릴까요?

남 네. 제 가게를 개업하게 되어서 판촉 선물로 돌릴 펜을 좀 주문하려고 해요.

여 얼마나 주문하실 건가요?

남 400개를 생각 중입니다. 개당 1달러짜리를 원합니다.

여 네. 이 펜들이 당신이 선택하실 수 있는 것들이에요.

남 이 펜이 좋군요. 더 많은 양을 사면 할인해주는 규정 있습니까? 그리고 로고 인쇄하는 데 요금이 듭니까?

여 로고 인쇄는 펜당 5센트입니다. 그리고 손님이 500개 이상 주문하시면 5% 할인을 해드릴 수 있습니다.

남 괜찮네요.

여 700개 이상 주문하시면 10% 할인에 로고를 무료로 인쇄해드립니다.

남 아, 아주 싸군요. 700개 펜을 주문하겠습니다.

give away 나누어 주다 **promotional** 판촉의 **option** 선택할 수 있는 것 **policy** 규정, 정책 **fee** 요금

06

M This is an announcement from your Fire Safety Administrator. I'm sorry to interrupt your working day by shouting over the building's intercom like this. However, this test is essential to your well-being in case of an emergency. We urge you to be patient during this test so we can ensure your safety in the future. Since this is only a test of the system, not a fire drill, there will be no need to leave the building at this time. Thank you again for your patience.

남 여러분의 화재안전 관리자가 드리는 안내방송입니다. 구내방송으로 이렇게 큰소리를 내어 여러분의 근무시간을 방해해 죄송합니다. 하지만, 이 시험은 비상사태 발생시 여러분의 안녕을 위해서 필수적인 것입니다. 미래에 여러분의 안전을 보장하기 위해서 이 시험을 하는 동안 양해해 주시길 바랍니다. 이것은 화재대피 훈련이 아니라 시스템을 시험하는 것이기 때문에 이번엔 건물 밖으로 나가실 필요는 없습니다. 양해해주셔서 다시 한 번 감사 드립니다.

administrator 관리자 **interrupt** 방해하다 **essential** 필수적인 **in case of** ~의 경우에 **emergency** 비상 사태 **urge** 촉구하다 **ensure** 보장하다 **fire drill** 화재대피 훈련

07

W Hey, Peter! Where are you going?

M I'm going home. Oh, that is a very lovely bouquet of flowers. Who is it for?

W It is for my sister, Jessica. Today is her graduation day.

M It must have cost you a fortune.

W I paid $60 for it but it is worth it. Today is a very important day for my sister and I want to make it special for her.

M That is very nice of you. If you want, I can drive you to her school.

W Can you? I appreciate your kindness.

여 안녕, Peter! 어디 가는 중이니?

남 집에 가는 중이야. 오, 아주 예쁜 꽃다발이구나. 누구한테 줄 거니?

여 내 여동생, Jessica에게 줄 거야. 오늘이 그녀의 졸업식이거든.

남 돈 많이 썼겠구나.

여 60달러 지불했지만 그만한 가치가 있어. 오늘은 내 여동생에게 아주 중요한 날이고, 나는 그녀를 위해서 오늘을 특별하게 만들어주고 싶어.

남 너 참 착하다. 원한다면, 내가 동생 학교까지 태워다 줄까?

여 그럴래? 친절을 베풀어줘서 고마워.

graduation 졸업 **must have p.p.** ~였음에 틀림없다 **fortune** 큰 돈, 운수 **worth** ~의 가치가 있는

08

W Donghee, do you have any special plans tomorrow?

M Yes. Tomorrow is my grandma's 80th birthday. All the members of my family will gather together and have lunch with her.

W I see. What time will you come back?

M Around 5 p.m., I guess.

W What will you do when you come home?

M I have many things to do tomorrow in the evening.

W I see. I was wondering if we can study math together.

M I'm sorry. I have to have my hair trimmed and finish writing a report in the evening.

- -

여 동희야, 너 내일 특별한 계획 있니?

남 응. 내일은 할머니 80번째 생신이셔. 모든 가족들이 같이 모여서 점심 식사를 할 거야.

여 그렇구나. 몇 시에 돌아와?

남 아마도 오후 5시쯤일 것 같아.

여 돌아오면 뭐 할 거야?

남 내일 저녁에 해야 할 일들이 많아.

여 알았어. 난 같이 수학공부 할 수 있을까 했지.

남 미안해. 저녁에 머리를 자르고 리포트 쓰는 것을 끝내야 해.

gather 모이다 **trim** 정리하다, 자르다

09

① M Hi, do you have any wall-mounted flower pots?
   W I'm sorry but we don't have that kind of pot.

② M How much are these roses?
   W They are $10 for a dozen.

③ M What are you doing with that basket?
   W I'm cleaning it for a flower arrangement.

④ M What is your favorite flower?
   W I do love tulips since they look elegant.

⑤ M Where can I put this flower basket?
   W Oh! It's beautiful. You can put it here next to my computer.

- -

① 남 안녕하세요, 벽걸이형 화분 있나요?
   여 죄송하지만 그런 종류의 화분은 없습니다.
② 남 이 장미들은 얼마인가요?
   여 12송이 한 묶음에 10달러예요.
③ 남 그 바구니로 뭘 하고 있는 중이니?
   여 꽃꽂이 하려고 청소하는 중이야.
④ 남 네가 가장 좋아하는 꽃은 뭐니?
   여 우아해 보여서 튤립을 정말 좋아해.

⑤ 남 이 꽃바구니 어디에 둘까요?
   여 오, 예뻐요. 여기 제 컴퓨터 옆에 두면 돼요.

mount 붙박다 **pot** 항아리 **flower arrangement** 꽃꽂이

10

M Hey, Dorothy. Did you buy the biology textbook?

W Of course. I bought it with all my other textbooks last week. You didn't buy it yet?

M No, I didn't. I bought all the textbooks except it. How much is it?

W I bought a used one for $10.

M Wow! That's a real bargain. Where did you get it?

W At the secondhand bookstore near the dormitory.

M Oh, I didn't know there is a used bookstore near the campus. Here comes the history professor. Let's talk more about it after this.

- -

남 안녕, Dorothy. 생물 교재 샀니?

여 물론이지. 지난주에 다른 교재들과 함께 샀어. 너 아직 안 샀니?

남 응, 안 샀어. 그것만 빼고 다른 책들은 다 샀어. 책 값 얼마니?

여 10달러에 헌 책 샀어.

남 와! 진짜 싸다. 어디서 샀니?

여 기숙사 근처에 있는 헌책방에서 샀어.

남 오, 학교 근처에 헌책방이 있는 줄 몰랐어. 역사 교수님 오신다. 이 수업 마치고 더 이야기하자.

① 교실   ② 기숙사   ③ 사무실
④ 서점   ⑤ 도서관

biology 생물학 **except** ~를 제외하고 **used** 중고의 **secondhand** 중고의 **professor** 교수

11

M Hooray! I can't believe this!

W What's up, Donggyoon?

M Please pinch my cheek. I have grown a lot since last year.

W Congratulations! How much have you grown?

M Thirteen centimeters. I guess I'm two centimeters taller than Jisung.

W How tall is he?

M He said he is 164cm.

W Nice to hear that. I hope you will grow more until you reach your ideal height.

남 야호! 믿을 수가 없어!

여 동균아, 무슨 일이니?

남 내 볼을 꼬집어봐. 나 작년 이후로 키가 많이 컸어.

여 축하해! 얼마나 자랐어?

남 13센티미터. 나 지성이보다 2센티미터 더 큰 것 같아.

여 그 애는 키가 얼만데?

남 164cm라고 했어.

여 잘됐네. 네가 원하는 키가 될 때까지 더 키가 자라길 바래.

pinch 꼬집다 **ideal** 이상적인 **height** 키

12

W This Saturday and Sunday, Bing Bing Toy Store is having a big sale. For two days, many children's toys are 70% off. Each morning, we will serve free hot chocolate to the children and coffee to all adults. Also, we will give balloons to all young customers. Lastly, there will be a "Buy 2, get 1 for free" sale. If you buy two toy sets, you will get a third one for free. So stop by the Bing Bing Toy Store on 3rd Street and be ready for the upcoming Children's Day.

여 이번 토요일과 일요일에, Bing Bing 장난감 가게에서는 대대적인 할인 행사를 합니다. 이틀 동안 많은 어린이 장난감이 70% 할인됩니다. 매일 오전에는 어린이들에게는 핫초콜릿을, 모든 어른에게는 커피를 무료로 제공할 것입니다. 또한 모든 어린이 고객에게 풍선을 줄 것입니다. 마지막으로, "두 개를 사면 한 개는 공짜" 세일이 있을 것입니다. 만일 장난감 두 벌을 사신다면, 세 번째 장난감은 무료입니다. 3번가에 있는 Bing Bing 장난감 가게에 들르셔서 다가오는 어린이 날을 준비하세요.

customer 고객 **stop by** ~에 들르다 **upcoming** 다가오는

13

M Lisa, what do you want to be in the future?

W When I was young, I wanted to be a teacher.

M A teacher? Then why are you majoring in science?

W My parents recommended I choose it, but I think it does not suit me. So I decided to change my major.

M Obviously to the education department?

W No. I'm thinking of entering the social welfare department. I'd like to help people who need a hand.

M That sounds great. That was what I wanted to do when I was young. But now I think flying all over the world will be more fun.

W I see. You'll be a great pilot.

Lisa의 직업 계획	
① 원래의 꿈	선생님
② 현재 전공	교육학
③ 현재 전공에 대한 동기	부모님의 추천
④ 생각 중인 새 전공	사회복지
⑤ 새 전공에 대한 동기	사람들을 돕고 싶어서

남 Lisa, 너는 장래에 무엇이 되고 싶니?

여 어렸을 때는 선생님이 되고 싶었어.

남 선생님? 그러면 왜 과학을 전공하는 거야?

여 부모님이 선택하라고 권해 주셨는데, 내겐 안 맞는 것 같아. 그래서 전공을 바꾸기로 결심했어.

남 그러면 당연히 교육학과로 가겠네?

여 아니. 사회복지학과 들어가는 것을 생각하고 있어. 도움을 필요로 하는 사람들을 돕고 싶거든.

남 멋진 생각이네. 그게 내가 어렸을 때 하고 싶었던 거야. 그런데 이젠 비행기를 타고 세계를 다니는 게 더 재미있을 것이란 생각이 들어.

여 그렇구나. 너는 훌륭한 비행기 조종사가 될 거야.

major in ~을 전공하다 **recommend** 추천하다 **suit** ~에 어울리다 **obviously** 명백하게 **social welfare** 사회복지

14

W How was your Sunday? Did you have fun?

M Yes, very much.

W What did you do?

M I rode several rides. I also ate a bulbogi burger and churros.

W Rides?

M Yes. I rode a roller coaster, the Viking, and a train

with my friends. I also enjoyed a <u>water slide</u> and the <u>bumper cars</u>.

W Sounds great. <u>What else</u> did you do?

M I saw a <u>parade</u> and <u>fireworks</u> at night. I had a <u>fantastic</u> Sunday.

....

여 일요일 어땠니? 재미있게 보냈니?

남 응, 아주 많이.

여 뭐 했는데?

남 나는 여러 가지 탈것들을 탔어. 불고기 버거랑 츄러스도 먹었어.

여 탈것들?

남 응. 친구들이랑 롤러코스터랑, 바이킹, 그리고 기차를 탔어. 또 수중 미끄럼틀이랑 범퍼카도 탔어.

여 재밌었겠다. 또 뭘 했니?

남 밤에 퍼레이드와 불꽃놀이를 봤어. 나는 환상적인 일요일을 보냈어.

① 놀이공원   ② 패스트푸드 레스토랑   ③ 기차역
④ 박물관   ⑤ 극장

••
have fun 재미있게 놀다 **ride** 탈것 **fireworks** 불꽃놀이 **fantastic** 환상적인

15

W When are you leaving <u>Sydney</u>?

M I'm leaving <u>the</u> day <u>after</u> <u>tomorrow</u>.

W Is there <u>anything</u> <u>you</u> <u>want</u> <u>to</u> <u>do</u> before you leave Sydney?

M I'd like to visit Australia Square. I heard that the view from <u>the</u> <u>revolving</u> <u>restaurant</u> on top of the building is <u>really</u> <u>beautiful</u>.

W It really is. You can see <u>the</u> <u>Opera</u> <u>House</u> and the Harbor Bridge there. You shouldn't miss it.

M Yeah. I also heard that the building has been described as <u>the</u> <u>most</u> <u>beautiful</u> building <u>in</u> <u>Australia</u>.

W Why don't we <u>have</u> <u>dessert</u> <u>there</u> after this lunch? I'll <u>book</u> <u>a</u> <u>table</u> for us.

M That sounds <u>wonderful</u>!

....

여 너 언제 시드니를 떠나니?

남 내일모레 떠나.

여 시드니 떠나기 전에 뭐 하고 싶은 거 없니?

남 Australia Square에 가보고 싶어. 그 빌딩 꼭대기의 회전

레스토랑에서 보는 풍경이 정말 아름답다고 들었어.

여 정말 그래. 거기에서 오페라 하우스와 하버 브리지를 볼 수 있어. 너 거기 꼭 가봐야 돼.

남 응, 그 건물이 호주에서 가장 아름다운 건물로 불려진다는 것도 들었어.

여 우리 이 점심 먹고 후식을 거기서 먹는 거 어때? 내가 우리 테이블 예약할게.

남 훌륭해!

••
square 광장, 정사각형 **revolve** 회전하다 **describe** 묘사하다 **book** 예약하다

16

① **M** I'd like <u>two tickets</u> for <u>the three o'clock show</u>.

  W I'm sorry. The tickets are <u>all sold out</u>.

② **M** I <u>lost</u> the tennis match. It <u>makes me sad</u>.

  W I know how you feel. But don't <u>take it so hard</u>.

③ **M** It's nice weather, <u>isn't it</u>?

  W Yeah, it's perfect weather <u>for a picnic</u>.

④ **M** Where's Cindy? Didn't you <u>invite her</u>?

  W She invited us <u>to her party</u>.

⑤ **M** Can't you stay <u>a little longer</u>?

  W That's very <u>nice of you</u>, but I really can't.

....

① 남 3시 영화로 표 두 장 주세요.

  여 죄송합니다. 표가 전부 매진입니다.

② 남 나 테니스 경기에서 졌어. 그래서 슬퍼.

  여 네 기분 알겠어. 하지만 너무 심각하게 받아들이지는 마.

③ 남 날씨 참 좋다, 그렇지 않니?

  여 응, 소풍 가기에 완벽한 날씨야.

④ 남 Cindy는 어디 있어? 그녀를 초대하지 않았니?

  여 그녀는 우리를 파티에 초대했어.

⑤ 남 좀 더 있으면 안 돼?

  여 고맙지만, 정말 그럴 수 없어.

••
be sold out 매진되다 **match** 경기 **perfect** 완벽한 **invite** 초대하다

17

W Can you guess how many people <u>die</u> by getting <u>struck</u> <u>by</u> <u>lightning</u> in the U.S. every year?

M Well...maybe around 10 people?

W No, more than <u>100</u> die as a result of lightning strikes.

M What a surprise! Is there any way we can protect ourselves in a lightning strike?

W If you get caught in an open field during a lightning storm, find a ditch to lie in if possible.

M What if I can't find a ditch?

W Put your feet close together and crouch down with your head lowered and don't lie flat.

M Any other ways to protect ourselves?

W Find a car and get in it. Even though it is metal, the electricity will travel around the surface of the vehicle and then go into ground.

....

여 미국에서 매년 몇 명이 번개에 맞아 사망하는지 짐작할 수 있겠니?

남 글쎄…아마 약 10명쯤?

여 아니, 100명 이상이 번개에 맞아 사망해.

남 놀랍다! 번개가 칠 때 우리를 보호할 수 있는 방법이 있을까?

여 천둥 번개가 치는 동안 뻥 뚫린 들판에 있게 된다면, 가능하다면 들어가 누울 수 있는 도랑을 찾아.

남 도랑을 못 찾는다면 어떻게 해야 돼?

여 두 발을 가까이 모으고 머리를 낮게 숙인 채로 몸을 웅크려. 하지만 납작 눕지는 마.

남 우리를 보호할 또 다른 방법은?

여 차를 찾아서 안에 들어가. 차가 금속이긴 하지만 전기가 차량 표면을 타고 이동한 후 땅으로 갈 거야.

lightning 번개 **protect** 보호하다 **ditch** 도랑, 개천 **crouch** 웅크리다
electricity 전기 **surface** 표면 **vehicle** 탈것, 차량

18

M Minho is traveling in England. He thinks he has to see the Eiffel Tower in Paris while he is traveling in Europe. So he takes the Eurostar from London to Paris. When he arrives at the station in Paris, he finds out he has lost his wallet. He doesn't have any euros now. Fortunately, he has some Korean won in his backpack. To buy a metro ticket to the Eiffel Tower, he needs to exchange the money. He goes to a bank. In this situation, what would Minho likely say to the teller at the bank?

....

남 민호는 영국을 여행 중이다. 그는 유럽에서 여행을 하는 동안 파리의 에펠탑을 봐야 한다고 생각한다. 그래서 그는 런던발 파리행 Eurostar를 탄다. 그는 파리역에 도착해서, 지갑을 잃어버린 것을

발견한다. 그는 지금 유로가 하나도 없다. 다행스럽게도, 그는 배낭에 한국 돈을 좀 가지고 있다. 에펠탑까지 가는 지하철 표를 사려면, 그는 돈을 바꿔야 한다. 그는 은행에 간다. 이 상황에서 민호는 은행직원에게 뭐라고 말하겠는가?

① 계좌를 개설하고 싶습니다.

② 이 여행자 수표를 현금으로 바꾸고 싶습니다.

③ 한국 돈을 유로로 바꾸고 싶습니다.

④ 오늘 제 계좌를 해지하려고 해요.

⑤ 오늘의 환율은 유로당 1,400원입니다.

fortunately 다행스럽게도 **backpack** 배낭 **metro** 지하철
exchange 교환하다

19

W Hey, David! I saw you going somewhere with your friends yesterday. Where did you go?

M My friends and I visited an orphanage in my neighborhood.

W What did you do there?

M We played basketball with the children and then taught them computing and English.

W You're like a big brother to them.

M That's right. We visit the kids every Sunday and try hard to be good role models for them.

W I'm sure you're helping them a lot.

....

여 야, David! 나 어제 너랑 네 친구들이 어디론가 가는 걸 봤어. 어디 갔었니?

남 친구들과 나는 우리 지역에 있는 고아원을 방문했어.

여 거기서 뭘 했니?

남 아이들과 농구하고 나서 컴퓨터 사용하는 거랑 영어를 가르쳐줬어.

여 네가 그들에게 큰형 같구나.

남 맞아. 우리는 매주 일요일 그 어린이들을 찾아가서 좋은 역할 모델이 되기 위해 열심히 노력해.

여 네가 그들에게 많은 도움이 되고 있다는 것을 확신해.

① 난 내가 한 일이 자랑스러워.

② 난 패션 모델이 되고 싶어.

③ 저 모델 꽤 멋져 보인다.

④ 네가 그들에게 많은 도움이 되고 있다는 것을 확신해.

⑤ 너 그들에 대해 걱정하는 것처럼 보여.

orphanage 고아원 **neighborhood** 이웃, 인근 지역 **computing**
컴퓨터 사용

20

M I can't believe the vacation is over already.

W Me neither! Time really flies. I regret spending last year without having any outstanding achievements.

M You can say that again.

W By the way, do you have any special plans for this year?

M Actually, I want to try something new. I've decided to learn the drums.

W Wow! That sounds exciting!

M Yeah, I can't wait! I'll try out for the school band next week.

W Wow! I'll keep my fingers crossed for you.

남 방학이 벌써 끝나다니 믿어지지가 않아.

여 나도 안 믿겨! 시간 참 빨라. 뚜렷한 성과 하나 못 내고 작년을 보낸 걸 후회해.

남 동감해.

여 그건 그렇고, 올해 특별한 계획 있니?

남 사실은, 나 새로운 것에 도전해 보고 싶어. 드럼을 배워보기로 결심했어.

여 와! 그거 재미있겠다!

남 응, 무척 기대돼! 다음 주에 학교밴드에 지원해 보려고.

여 와! 행운을 빌어.

① 걱정 마. 약속 꼭 지킬게.
② 사실, 난 그런 영화를 못 참겠어.
③ 나는 공상소설 읽는 것에 푹 빠져 있어.
④ 와! 행운을 빌어.
⑤ 괜찮아. 그냥 재미 삼아 치고 싶어.

regret 후회하다 **outstanding** 두드러진, 뚜렷한 **achievement** 성과 **try out for** ~가 되기 위해 겨루다 **keep one's fingers crossed for** ~에 행운을 빌다

Further Study 정답

p. 114

1. The reason is that she wants to go to Busan to attend her niece's wedding ceremony.

2. The reason is that he can get a 10% discount and free logo printing.

3. She bought a bouquet of flowers because today is her sister's graduation day.

4. They are going to gather together and have lunch in celebration of her grandma's 80th birthday.

5. The reason is that he has grown 13 centimeters since last year.

6. It will be on this Saturday and Sunday.

7. The electricity travels around the surface of the vehicle and goes into ground.

8. I guess it is Monday because yesterday was Sunday.

On Your Own 모범답안

p. 115

A

My Schedule for Tomorrow	
In the morning	(1) watch TV for the news and weather while I have breakfast (2) go to school by 8:30
In the afternoon	(3) go to my school club room after school; draw cartoons there (4) go to my English academy; go there every Monday, Wednesday and Friday
In the evening	(5) do my homework and review and preview school lessons after dinner (6) play online games for an hour before I go to bed

I'm going to talk about what I am going to do tomorrow. In the morning, I will (1)watch TV for the news and weather while I have breakfast. Then I will (2)go to school by 8:30. In the afternoon, I will (3)go to my school club room after school. I will draw cartoons there. After that, I will (4)go to my English academy. I go there every Monday, Wednesday and Friday. Finally, in the evening, I will (5)do my homework and review and preview school lessons after dinner. And then, I will (6)play online games for an hour before I go to bed.

나의 내일 일정	
아침	(1) 아침식사 하며 TV로 뉴스와 날씨를 봄
	(2) 8시 30분까지 학교에 가기
오후	(3) 방과 후 학교 동아리 방 가기; 거기서 만화 그리기
	(4) 영어학원 가기; 매주 월, 수, 금 거기 감
저녁	(5) 저녁 식사 후 숙제와 교과 내용을 복습, 예습함
	(6) 잠자리에 들기 전 한 시간 동안 온라인 게임 하기

제가 내일 무엇을 할 것인지에 대해 이야기해 드리겠습니다. 아침에는 아침 식사를 하며 TV로 뉴스와 날씨를 볼 것입니다. 그 다음엔 8시30분까지 학교에 갈 것입니다. 오후에는 방과 후에 학교 동아리 방에 갈 것입니다. 저는 거기서 만화를 그릴 것입니다. 그리고 나서는 영어학원에 갈 것입니다. 저는 매주 월요일, 수요일, 그리고 금요일에 거기에 갑니다. 마지막으로 저녁에는 저녁 식사를 한 후 숙제와 교과내용을 복습과 예습 할 것입니다. 그 다음엔 잠자리에 들기 전 한 시간 동안 온라인 게임을 할 것입니다.

B

My Favorite Foreign Tourist Attraction	
Name & Location of the place	(1) Australia Square; Sydney, Australia
Nearby attractions	(2) Sydney Opera House, Harbor Bridge, Royal Botanic Garden
Reasons to recommend it	(3) very beautiful
	(4) the view from the revolving restaurant on top of the building is breathtaking; can see the Opera House and the Harbor Bridge from there

I'd like to tell you about my favorite foreign tourist attraction that I have been to. It is (1)Australia Square and is located in Sydney, Australia. Famous tourist attractions you can visit nearby are (2)the Sydney Opera House, the Harbor Bridge, and the Royal Botanic Garden. I'd like to recommend this place because (3)I think the building is very beautiful. Second, (4)the view from the revolving restaurant on top of the building is breathtaking. You can see the Opera House and the Harbor Bridge from there. I really want to visit this place again sometime.

내가 좋아하는 외국의 관광명소	
장소명과 위치	(1) Australia Square; 호주의 시드니
근처 가볼 만한 곳	(2) 시드니 오페라하우스, 하버 브리지, 왕립식물원
추천 이유	(3) 매우 아름다움
	(4) 빌딩 꼭대기에 위치한 회전 레스토랑에서 보는 풍경이 정말 놀라움; 거기서 오페라 하우스와 하버 브리지도 볼 수 있음

제가 방문한 적이 있는, 제가 아주 좋아하는 외국의 관광명소에 대해 말씀 드리겠습니다. 그곳은 Australia Square이며 호주의 시드니에 위치해 있습니다. 근처에서 여러분이 가볼 수 있는 유명 관광명소로는 시드니 오페라 하우스, 하버 브리지, 왕립식물원이 있습니다. 저는 그 건물이 매우 아름답기 때문에 이곳을 추천하고 싶습니다. 둘째, 빌딩 꼭대기에 위치한 회전 레스토랑에서 보는 풍경이 정말 놀랍습니다. 거기서 오페라 하우스와 하버 브리지도 볼 수 있습니다. 저는 언젠가 이곳에 다시 가보고 싶습니다.

12 Listening Test 정답
중학영어듣기 모의고사 1?회

p. 120

01 ④	02 ①	03 ①	04 ③	05 ②
06 ③	07 ②	08 ③	09 ⑤	10 ④
11 ①	12 ③	13 ⑤	14 ①	15 ⑤
16 ④	17 ⑤	18 ②	19 ②	20 ③

01

M Darling, we only have two months left before our wedding ceremony.

W Yes. I think it's time to send out the wedding invitation cards. Why don't we choose the design of the card from the ones on this website?

M Good. Do you have a card style in mind?

W Not really. What about this tri-fold card?

M It's good but as you know I do love simple things. I like this bi-fold one. It's simple as the card is only folded in half.

W Okay, then which is better on the front? A floral pattern or a photo?

M How about using one of the studio wedding photos?

W Great idea! Now, let's think about the wording on the card.

··

남 자기야, 우리 결혼식이 두 달밖에 남지 않았어.

여 응. 이제 청첩장을 보낼 때인 것 같아. 같이 이 웹사이트에 있는 것 중에서 청첩장 디자인 선택하는 거 어때?

남 좋아. 염두에 두고 있는 카드 스타일 있니?

여 아니. 이 삼단으로 접은 카드 어때?

남 좋긴 한데. 너도 알다시피, 나는 단순한 걸 좋아하잖아. 이 이단 카드가 마음에 들어. 반으로만 접어서 단순해.

여 좋아. 그럼 앞에는 어떤 게 좋아? 꽃무늬 또는 사진?

남 사진관에서 촬영한 결혼 사진 중에서 하나 사용하는 거 어떨까?

여 좋은 생각이야. 그럼 이제 카드에 쓸 문구에 대해 생각해보자.

wedding invitation card 청첩장 **tri-fold** 삼중으로 접은 **bi-fold** 이중으로 접은 **floral** 꽃의, 꽃무늬의 **wording** 말로 나타내기

02

W May I help you?

M Yes. I'd like to buy something to help organize my son's toys.

W How about this wooden toy box? If he has a lot of large toys, you can also choose the bigger one here.

M Hmm. I want something to hold the toys according to their size.

W Okay. What about this multi-bin organizer? There are two big bins, three medium bins, and four small bins.

M Well, the big bins are not large enough to hold his big toys.

W I think this toy box with two drawers is perfect for you then. You can put big toys in this roomy box and small ones in the removable drawers at the bottom.

M Looks good. I'll take this one.

··

여 도와드릴까요?

남 네. 제 아들 장난감을 정리하는 데 도움이 되는 것을 사고 싶어요.

여 이 나무로 된 장난감 함 어떠세요? 아드님이 큰 장난감이 많다면 여기 더 큰 함도 있어요.

남 음. 저는 크기별로 장난감을 담을 수 있는 것이 필요해요.

여 네. 이 다양한 용기로 된 정리함은 어떠세요? 큰 용기 2개, 중간 용기 3개, 작은 용기 4개가 있어요.

남 음. 큰 용기가 큰 장난감을 담기에 충분히 크지 않네요.

여 그럼 이 서랍이 두 개 있는 장난감함이 적당할 것 같네요. 큰 장난감들은 이 넓은 함에 넣으시고 작은 장난감들은 밑에 있는 떼어낼 수 있는 서랍에다 두실 수 있습니다.

남 좋네요. 이것으로 할게요.

organize 정리하다 **according to** ~에 따라서 **organizer** 정리함 **bin** 용기, 통 **drawer** 서랍 **roomy** 널찍한 **at the bottom** 바닥에

03

M Good morning! How can I help you?

W I have some time off from work next month and I was thinking of going to Denmark.

M That sounds great. How long is your vacation?

W Just 10 days. My last day of work is July 21st and I'll go back on August 1st.

M Okay. This is a brochure about Denmark. Have a look at it. Denmark has many beautiful spots to visit.

W Yeah, I really want to see Tivoli Gardens in Copenhagen, the National Museum, and Legoland.

M I understand. Where do you want to stay while you're in Denmark?

W Copenhagen, of course.

M Great. The city has many nice hotels. OK, now I'll help you to plan a great time in Denmark.

··

남 안녕하세요. 어떻게 도와드릴까요?

여 다음 달에 직장 휴가가 있어서, 덴마크로 여행을 갈까 생각 중이에요.

남 잘 됐네요. 휴가 기간은 어떻게 되나요?

여 10일이에요. 마지막 근무일은 7월 21일이고 8월 1일에 복귀할 겁니다.

남 네. 이것은 덴마크에 관한 안내책자입니다. 한번 보세요. 덴마크는 방문할 만한 멋진 장소가 많이 있습니다.

여 맞아요. 난 코펜하겐에 있는 Tivoli 정원과 국립 박물관, 레고랜드를 정말 보고 싶어요.

남 이해합니다. 덴마크에 있는 동안 어디서 묵으실 건가요?

여 물론 코펜하겐입니다.

남 좋습니다. 그 도시에는 괜찮은 호텔이 많이 있습니다. 네, 이제 고객님이 덴마크에서의 멋진 시간을 계획할 수 있도록 도와드리겠습니다.

work 일, 직장 **brochure** 소책자 **spot** 장소, 점

04

[Telephone rings.]

M Hello?

W Hello, is this Tim?

M Yes. Who is this?

W This is Amy. I'm afraid I can't come to the office today as I fell down the stairs and I hurt my ankle. The doctor told me to rest in bed all day.

M You should have been more careful! Listen, I can't do all this work alone.

W I feel really sorry, Tim. I will try to be in tomorrow.

M Well, you should be. There is a pile of things to do and I cannot cover your part.

W Don't worry! I will take care of it when I come in.

⋯⋯⋯⋯⋯⋯⋯⋯⋯⋯⋯⋯⋯⋯⋯⋯⋯⋯⋯⋯⋯⋯⋯⋯

[전화벨이 울린다.]

남 여보세요?

여 여보세요, Tim인가요?

남 네. 누구세요?

여 Amy예요. 계단에서 넘어져서 복사뼈를 다쳐서 오늘 사무실에 못 갈 것 같아요. 의사가 하루 종일 누워서 쉬라고 했어요.

남 조심했어야죠. 그런데 나 혼자 이 모든 일들을 다 못해요.

여 정말 죄송해요, Tim. 내일은 출근하도록 해볼게요.

남 음, 그래야지요. 일이 산더미처럼 쌓여있고 나는 당신이 해야 할 부분까지 다 할 수 없어요.

여 걱정하지 마세요! 제가 출근하면 다 처리할게요.

① 사려 깊은   ② 관대한   ③ 배려심 없는
④ 건성의   ⑤ 책임감 있는

fall down 넘어지다 **stairs** 계단 **alone** 혼자

05

W Do you make these?

M Yes, I do. That's my job.

W When do you work?

M I work from 11 in the morning to 9 in the evening.

W What is your job like?

M It's hard work but also fun. I start with the dough. I spin the dough to make it thin and big. Then, I put beef, bacon, cheese, onions, and more on top.

W Do you like your job?

M Yes, I really love what I am doing and I am proud of my job.

⋯⋯⋯⋯⋯⋯⋯⋯⋯⋯⋯⋯⋯⋯⋯⋯⋯⋯⋯⋯⋯⋯⋯⋯

여 이런 걸 만드십니까?

남 네, 제 일입니다.

여 언제 일하시죠?

남 저는 아침 11시부터 밤 9시까지 일합니다.

여 당신의 직업은 어떤 일인가요?

남 힘든 일이지만 재미있습니다. 저는 밀가루 반죽 덩어리를 가지고 시작합니다. 반죽을 얇고 크게 만들기 위해 돌립니다. 그런 다음 쇠고기, 베이컨, 치즈, 양파 등을 위에 올립니다.

여 직업이 마음에 드세요?

남 네. 저는 제가 하는 일이 정말 좋고 제 직업에 자부심도 느낍니다.

① 식료품 상인   ② 요리사   ③ 선생님
④ 농부   ⑤ 의사

from A to B A부터 B까지 **dough** 반죽 덩어리 **spin** 돌리다 **be proud of** ~을 자랑스러워 하다

06

W Sir, have you seen the catalog for our in-flight shop? Would you like to order any duty free goods?

M Yes, can I pay by credit card?

W Of course, all major credit cards are accepted but you can't spend more than 500 dollars.

M Okay, I'd like this perfume for my wife. It costs 58 dollars.

W Is there anything else you'd like, sir?

M Yes, I'd also like this bottle of whisky which is 215 dollars.

W Will that be all, sir?

M I've changed my mind. Instead of the perfume, I want to get this electric toothbrush which is 65 dollars. Here is my credit card.

⋯⋯⋯⋯⋯⋯⋯⋯⋯⋯⋯⋯⋯⋯⋯⋯⋯⋯⋯⋯⋯⋯⋯⋯

여 승객님, 기내 상품 목록 보셨나요? 면세품 주문하고 싶으신 것

있습니까?

남 네, 신용카드로 계산할 수 있나요?

여 물론이죠. 주요 신용카드는 모두 이용 가능하지만. 500달러 이상은 쓸 수 없습니다.

남 네, 제 아내에게 줄 이 향수를 사겠습니다. 58달러이군요.

여 그 밖에 더 사실 것 있습니까?

남 네, 215달러짜리 이 위스키 한 병도 사고 싶어요.

여 그게 다입니까, 승객님?

남 마음이 바뀌었어요. 향수 대신에 65달러짜리 이 전동칫솔을 사고 싶어요. 제 신용카드 여기 있습니다.

•• **in-flight** 기내의 **duty free goods** 면세품 **accept** 받아들이다 **perfume** 향수 **instead of** ~ 대신에 **electric toothbrush** 전동 칫솔

07

M Can you give me a hand, Kate?

W Sure. What can I do for you?

M I don't know what to wear to my job interview tomorrow. Can you give me some tips?

W You'd better wear a formal suit and not casual clothing.

M Okay. What about the color of the suit? Which color will make me look more intelligent and responsible?

W I think a dark gray one would be great. By the way, did you return the books I asked you to in the morning?

M Yes, I did. As soon as I came to the campus, I headed to the library.

W Thanks. Now, what about your tie and shoes?

··

남 Kate, 나 좀 도와줄래?

여 그래. 뭘 도와줄까?

남 내일 취업 면접에 뭘 입고 가야 할지 모르겠어. 조언 좀 해줄래?

여 정장을 입고 가는 게 낫고 평상복은 입지 마.

남 응. 정장 색깔은 어때? 어떤 색깔이 나를 더 지적이고 책임감 있게 보이게 할까?

여 내 생각에는 짙은 회색이 좋을 것 같아. 그런데, 내가 아침에 부탁했던 책 반납했니?

남 응, 했어. 학교에 도착하자마자 도서관으로 향했지.

여 고마워. 이제 넥타이와 신발은?

•• **formal suit** 정장 **casual** 격식을 차리지 않은 **intelligent** 지적인 **head** 향하다

08

W Jinho, can you open the door for me? As you can see, I can't open it by myself.

M Sure. What's the box you're carrying? Do you want me to help you?

W It's okay. It's not heavy. My cousin gave me her winter clothes. And I have to put them in my closet and arrange them.

M Oh, really? Why did she give them to you anyway?

W They don't fit her anymore because she has grown a lot since last year.

M I wish I had a cousin like that. I think handing old clothes on to someone else who can use them is a good habit.

W Well, it is not always good, though. My parents hardly ever buy me clothes. I sometimes would like to wear new clothes.

M Hmm, I guess I would too.

··

여 진호야, 문 좀 열어 줄래? 보다시피 나 스스로 문을 열 수가 없어.

남 물론이지. 네가 나르고 있는 박스는 무엇이니? 내가 도와줄까?

여 괜찮아. 별로 무겁지 않아. 사촌 언니가 겨울 옷을 줬어. 그 옷들을 장롱 안에 넣고 정리해야 돼.

남 오, 그래? 근데 그녀가 왜 너한테 그 옷들을 준 거야?

여 사촌 언니가 작년 이후로 많이 자라서 더 이상 맞지 않는대.

남 나도 그런 사촌이 있으면 좋겠다. 헌 옷을 입을 수 있는 누군가에게 물려주는 것은 좋은 습관인 것 같아.

여 응, 그런데 나쁜 점도 있어. 부모님이 나에겐 옷을 거의 안 사주시거든. 나는 가끔은 새 옷을 입고 싶어.

남 음, 나도 그럴 것 같아.

•• **by oneself** 혼자서 **carry** 나르다 **closet** 옷장 **arrange** 정리하다 **fit** ~에게 맞다 **hand on** 양도하다 **hardly** 거의 ~ 아니다

09

W Hi, Tom. Are you still looking for a job?

M Yes. Is there a good position you know of?

W Hotel Korea is looking for a chef.

M What are the <u>requirements</u>?

W A <u>chef's certificate</u> is required, with a minimum of <u>two years' experience</u>.

M What <u>documents</u> should I submit?

W You need to submit a <u>curriculum vitae</u> and a <u>letter of application</u>.

M I see. Anything else?

W You should include the <u>names</u> and <u>contact details</u> of <u>three references</u> in your <u>curriculum vitae</u>.

M How should I send in the documents?

W Your documents should be sent in <u>by post</u>.

```
                        모집 공고
                       Korea 호텔

   ① 직위 : 주방장
   ② 자격 : 요리사 자격증
   ③ 경력 : 2년
   ④ 서류 : – 이력서 (추천인 3명의 이름과 상세한 연락처)
            – 지원서
   ⑤ 송부 : 매니저 Ivan Donovan, manager@hotelkorea.com
```

여 안녕, Tom. 너 아직 구직 중이니?

남 응. 네가 아는 좋은 자리 있니?

여 응. Korea 호텔이 주방장을 구하고 있어.

남 자격 조건들은 뭐니?

여 최소 2년의 경력과 함께 요리사 자격증이 요구돼.

남 무슨 서류들을 제출해야 하니?

여 이력서와 지원서를 제출해야 해.

남 알겠어. 다른 건?

여 이력서에는 추천인 3명의 이름과 상세한 연락처를 포함시켜야 하고.

남 서류를 어떻게 보내야 해?

여 서류는 우편으로 보내야 해.

••
chef 요리사, 주방장 **certificate** 증명서, 인가증 **requirement** 자격 **document** 서류 **curriculum vitae** 이력서 **application** 지원, 지원서 **reference** 신원보증인, 참고 **by post** 우편으로

10

M Shall we <u>play tennis</u> after school?

W <u>Sounds like fun</u>. But I have to <u>stop by the</u> cafeteria. I will meet Jessica and give her notebook back to her.

M <u>What time</u> will you meet her?

W At 2:45. But it <u>won't take long</u>.

M When should I meet you then?

W <u>How about</u> 30 minutes after that?

M Good. Let's meet <u>in front of</u> the school gate.

W Okay. <u>See you then</u>.

남 방과 후에 테니스 할까?

여 재미있겠다. 그런데 구내식당에 들러야 해. Jessica를 만나서 공책을 돌려줘야 하거든.

남 몇 시에 만날 거야?

여 2시 45분. 그렇지만 오래 걸리진 않을 거야.

남 그러면 언제 널 만나야 하는 거야?

여 그 후 30분 후는 어때?

남 좋아. 학교 정문 앞에서 만나자.

여 좋아. 그때 봐.

••
cafeteria 구내식당, 셀프서비스 식당

11

W This is a game <u>played by</u> two or four players <u>on a court</u>. It has been an <u>Olympic sport since</u> 1992. There is a high net <u>in the middle of</u> the court. The players try to <u>score points</u> by hitting a <u>shuttlecock</u> across the net using a racket. The player or team winning the previous point always <u>serves</u>. A <u>point is scored</u> once the <u>shuttlecock strikes the floor</u>. A player or team must score 21 points first <u>to win a game</u>. The match ends when one team wins two games.

여 이것은 코트에서 두 사람 혹은 네 사람이 하는 게임입니다. 1992년 이후로 올림픽 스포츠 종목이 되었습니다. 코트의 중간에 높은 네트가 있습니다. 선수들은 라켓을 사용하여 셔틀콕을 쳐서 네트를 넘김으로써 점수를 내려고 합니다. 이전에 점수를 낸 선수나 팀이 항상 서브를 넣습니다. 셔틀콕이 바닥을 치면 점수가 납니다. 선수나 팀이 게임을 이기기 위해서는 21점을 먼저 내야 합니다. 한 팀이 두 게임(세트)를 이기면 경기가 끝납니다.

① 배드민턴　　　② 테니스　　　③ 배구
④ 탁구　　　　　⑤ 농구

••
court 뜰, 코트 **since** ~ 이후로 **shuttlecock** 셔틀콕 **previous** 이전의

12

M Where are you going?

W I'm going to Changdeokgung to get some information to write a report for history class.

M Is it about the history of Changdeokgung?

W No, it's about how I felt after looking around that World Heritage Site.

M Sounds interesting. Aren't they closed today?

W I don't think so. According to the website, they will close at 5 today.

M I see. I actually went there last Monday after school, and they closed at six thirty on that day.

W Thanks for the information.

창덕궁		
요일	개장	폐장
월, 화, 목	오전 9:30	오후 6:30
수	폐장	
금	오전 9:30	오후 5:00
토	오전 10:00	오후 4:00
일	오전 10:00	오후 2:00

남 너 어디 가니?

여 역사 수업 보고서를 쓰는 데 필요한 정보를 좀 얻으려고 창덕궁에 가.

남 창덕궁 역사에 관한 거야?

여 아니, 그 세계문화유산을 둘러보고 난 후 내가 어떻게 느꼈는지에 대한 거야.

남 재미있겠다. 오늘 문 안 열지 않나?

여 아닌 것 같아. 웹사이트에 보니까 오늘 5시에 폐관한대.

남 그렇구나. 나는 사실 지난주 월요일 방과 후에 갔었는데 그 날은 6시 30분에 문을 닫더라고.

여 정보 고마워.

heritage 유산 **look around** 둘러보다 **information** 정보

13

W How about taking a break for a while?

M I'd love to. Shall we go out for lunch?

W Where do you want to go?

M How about a fast food restaurant near the bus station?

W I want to go to the Japanese restaurant across the street from here.

M Okay. Let's fill up our stomachs first and then keep looking for reference materials for our project.

W Alright. Let's leave a note on the table so that no one will take our seats.

M I'll do it.

여 잠시 휴식시간을 가질까?

남 그러고 싶어. 점심 먹으러 나갈까?

여 어디 가고 싶니?

남 버스 정류장 근처의 패스트푸드 레스토랑 어때?

여 여기서 길 건너편에 있는 일식점에 가고 싶어.

남 좋아. 배 먼저 채우고, 우리 과제에 필요한 참고 자료들을 계속 찾아보자.

여 좋아. 책상에 메모를 남겨서 다른 사람이 자리에 못 앉게 하자.

남 내가 할게.

take a break 짧은 휴식을 취하다 **for a while** 잠시 동안 **Shall we ~?** ~하는 것 어때? **fill up** 채우다 **stomach** 배, 위 **reference** 참고, 참고 문헌

14

M Do you want to make your car look brand new? Bring your car, taxi or van into Clean Car Wash today! We will clean and polish your car for an extremely reasonable price. It's four dollars for a car or taxi and six dollars for a van. Your car will look brand new again! Drive your car into our workshop located on Walnut Street. If you want to make an appointment, please call us at 474-1100. Thank you.

남 당신 차를 금방 뽑은 새 차처럼 보이게 하고 싶으신가요? 당신의 차, 택시 또는 밴을 Clean 세차장으로 오늘 가지고 오세요! 당신의 차를 지극히 적정한 가격에 세차하고 광을 내드릴 겁니다. 승용차나 택시는 4달러이고 밴은 6달러입니다. 당신의 차는 다시 금방 뽑은 새 차로 보이게 될 것입니다. Walnut 가에 있는 저희 세차장으로 차를 몰고 오세요. 예약하길 원하신다면 474-1100번으로 전화주세요. 감사합니다.

brand new 아주 새로운 **polish** 윤을 내다 **extremely** 극단적으로 **reasonable** (가격이) 적정한

15

W Are you good at computers?

M Yes. I majored in computer engineering. Why?

W My friend in the U.S. sent me an e-mail with an attached file, but I can't open it.

M Let me see. Oh, it's a PDF file.

W Oh, really? What should I do then?

M You need to download Acrobat Reader to open this file, first.

W Where and how can I download it?

M I will show you how to do it.

여 너 컴퓨터 잘하니?

남 응. 컴퓨터공학을 전공했어. 왜?

여 미국에 있는 내 친구가 첨부 파일과 함께 이메일을 보냈는데 열 수가 없어.

남 내가 볼게. 아, PDF파일이네.

여 오, 정말? 그러면 어떻게 해야 해?

남 이 파일을 열기 위해서는 먼저 Acrobat Reader라는 프로그램을 다운로드 해야 해.

여 어디서 어떻게 다운로드 받는 거야?

남 어떻게 하는지 내가 보여줄게.

be good at ~을 잘하다 **major in** ~을 전공하다 **engineering** 공학
attach 첨부하다 **PDF** 이동 가능한 문서형식(Portable Document Format)

16

W I like using the subway because it is easy to catch up on some sleep while I'm on the train.

M Good. By the way, don't you think the girl over there is talking on her cell phone too loudly? This is a public place.

W Yeah, I agree with you.

M I think she's so rude to talk so loudly on her cell phone.

W It's really annoying! Let's keep good manners all the time.

M Anyway, how many more subway stations do we have to go?

W Oh, we have to transfer to the bus at this station.

여 난 기차에 타고 있는 동안 부족한 잠을 보충하기가 쉬워서 지하철 타는 게 좋아.

남 잘됐네. 그런데 저기에서 휴대전화로 통화하는 저 여자 너무 큰소리로 떠든다고 생각하지 않니? 여긴 공공장소인데.

여 응. 동의해.

남 휴대전화로 저렇게 크게 얘기하다니 너무 무례한 것 같아.

여 정말 짜증난다! 우린 항상 예의를 잘 지키도록 하자.

남 어쨌든, 우리 몇 정거장 더 가야 하니?

여 오, 우리 이 역에서 버스로 환승해야 해.

catch up on ~을 따라잡다, 만회하다 **public place** 공공장소
annoying 거슬리는 **transfer** 옮기다, 갈아타다

17

① **M** I'd like to send this parcel to Sydney.

　W Would you like to send it by airmail or surface mail?

② **M** That was a hard test, wasn't it?

　W It was terrible! I don't think I did very well.

③ **M** Can you tell me how to get to the community center?

　W Sorry, but I don't know either. You'd better ask someone else.

④ **M** Look at this sign. You must not walk on the lawn.

　W Sorry, I didn't see the sign.

⑤ **M** How do I look in this shirt?

　W I'm looking for a striped shirt.

---

① 남 이 소포를 Sydney로 보내고 싶어요.

　여 항공우편으로 보내시겠습니까, 육상우편으로 보내시겠습니까?

② 남 어려운 시험이었어, 그렇지 않니?

　여 끔찍했어! 시험을 잘 본 것 같지 않아.

③ 남 지역센터에 가는 길 좀 알려주실래요?

　여 죄송하지만, 저도 모릅니다. 다른 사람에게 물어보시는 게 좋겠네요.

④ 남 이 표지판 좀 보세요. 잔디 위를 걸으면 안 됩니다.

　여 죄송해요, 표지판을 못 봤습니다.

⑤ 남 나 이 셔츠 입은 거 어때 보여?

　여 저는 줄무늬 셔츠를 찾고 있어요.

by airmail 항공우편으로 **by surface mail** 육상우편으로 **lawn** 잔디
striped 줄무늬의

18

[Telephone rings.]

W Thank you for calling ABC Printing Services. How may I help you?

M Hi, I've just uploaded my final draft of a research report on your website under the name of Jeff. I need 200 copies printed.

W OK, we'll check it out.

M When will they be ready? I can't wait to see how they look.

W They'll be done by this Friday. If you want to see the complete design before it is sent to the printer, you can get it via email for six dollars.

M Oh, that'll be great. Well, can I make any changes after I see the design?

W Of course. Any mistake of ours, we'll fix for free. Otherwise, we'll charge you three dollars and 50 cents per change.

M All right.

W Oh, please also remember that we'll do minor text changes free of charge.

[전화벨이 울린다.]

여 ABC 인쇄 서비스에 전화 주셔서 감사합니다. 무엇을 도와드릴까요?

남 안녕하세요. 제가 방금 Jeff라는 이름으로 귀사의 웹사이트에 제 연구 보고서 최종본을 보냈습니다. 200부를 인쇄해주십시오.

여 네, 확인하겠습니다.

남 언제 다 될까요? 어떤 모습일지 빨리 보고 싶습니다.

여 이번 금요일까지는 완료됩니다. 만약 인쇄기로 보내지기 전에 완제품 디자인을 보시고 싶으면, 6달러에 이메일로 받아보실 수 있습니다.

남 오, 그거 좋을 것 같은데요. 혹시 그 디자인을 본 후에라도 수정할 수 있나요?

여 물론이죠. 저희 실수에 대해서는 무료로 수정해드립니다. 그렇지 않으면 수정 건당 3달러 50센트를 청구할 것입니다.

남 알겠습니다.

여 아, 사소한 본문 수정은 무료로 해드린다는 점도 기억하세요.

draft 초안, 문안 **complete** 완전한 **via** ~을 통해 **fix** 고치다 **per** ~당
free of charge 무료로

19

M While surfing the Internet, Sue finds that there's a Pompeii exhibition at the Arts Center by this weekend. The exhibition is said to be very popular and it is expected to be sold out on the weekend. So she thinks if she would like to go to the exhibition on the weekend, she'd better book the tickets in advance. Since Sue knows John is interested in Pompeii, she calls John to see if he wants to join her. However, his brother says he's out now. Sue wants John to call her back. In this situation, what would Sue likely say to John's brother?

남 인터넷 검색을 하던 중 Sue는 이번 주말까지 예술의전당에서 폼페이 전시회가 있다는 것을 발견한다. 그 전시회는 매우 인기가 있는 것으로 알려져 있어서 주말에는 매진이 예상된다. 그래서 만약 주말에 그 전시회에 가려면, 미리 표를 예매해야 한다고 그녀는 생각한다. Sue는 John이 폼페이에 관심이 있다는 것을 알기 때문에 그녀는 John이 함께 가려는지 알아보러 전화한다. 하지만 그의 남동생은 그는 지금 외출 중이라고 한다. Sue는 John이 자신에게 전화해주기를 바란다. 이 상황에서 Sue는 John의 남동생에게 뭐라고 말하겠는가?

① 내일 아침 제일 먼저 전화부터 할게.
② 그에게 357-9864로 나한테 전화해달라고 전해줄래?
③ 좀 더 편한 시간에 다시 전화할까?
④ 다 준비되면 나한테 전화 좀 해줄래?
⑤ 내일 오후에 내가 다시 전화하겠다고 그에게 말해줄래?

exhibition 전시회 **in advance** 미리

20

M Surprise!

W Tom! What a surprise!

M I just wanted to stop by and thank you for driving me to the airport last week.

W No. It was my pleasure to do it. But, what's this?

M It's just a small gift.

W Wow, it's lovely, but you didn't have to bring a gift.

M It's nothing really. I just wanted to say thank you.

남 놀랐지!

여 Tom! 깜짝 놀랐어!

남 그냥 들러서 지난주에 나를 공항에 태워 준 것에 대해 고마움을 표시하고 싶었어.

여 아니야. 그건 내가 좋아서 한 일이야. 그런데 이게 뭐야?

남　그냥 작은 선물이야.

여　와, 예쁘다. 그런데 선물은 안 가지고 와도 됐는데.

남　<u>정말 별거 아니야. 그냥 고맙다는 말을 하려고 한 거야.</u>

① 맞아. 선물로 그걸 사진 않을 거야.
② 걱정하지 마. 이제 와서 어쩔 수 없지.
③ 정말 별거 아니야. 그냥 고맙다는 말을 하려고 한 거야.
④ 선물 정말 고마워. 어디서 산 거야?
⑤ 내가 받은 것 중에 가장 좋은 선물이었어. 정말 고마워.

••
pleasure 기쁨　**lovely** 멋진, 사랑스러운

Further Study 정답

p. 124

1. The reason is that he thinks the big bins are <u>not large enough</u> to hold his son's <u>big toys</u>.
2. It starts on <u>July 22nd</u> and ends on <u>July 31st</u>.
3. The reason is that she <u>fell down the stairs</u> and <u>hurt her ankle</u>.
4. He spins the dough <u>to make it thin and big</u>.
5. They are going to meet <u>in front of the school gate</u>.
6. It was <u>computer engineering</u>.
7. The reason is that she is <u>talking on her cell phone too loudly</u> in a public place.
8. She <u>drove him to the airport</u>.

On Your Own 모범답안

p. 125

A

My Favorite Places in My City	
Places	Reasons I choose them
(1) Insadong	(2) home to Korea's traditional arts and culture, there are many antique shops and art galleries
(3) N Seoul Tower	(4) Namsan is Seoul's landmark peak and the tower has a fantastic view when you go there at night

I live in <u>Seoul</u> and there are lots of beautiful places in the city I'd recommend foreigners visit. Now I'll tell you about two of them. Firstly, I recommend (1)<u>Insadong</u> because (2)<u>it's home to Korea's traditional arts and culture and there are many antique shops and art galleries</u>. Secondly, I recommend (3)<u>N Seoul Tower</u> because (4)<u>Namsan is Seoul's landmark peak and the tower has a fantastic view when you go there at night</u>. I'm sure foreigners will have a great time in the two places I recommend.

우리 시에서 내가 아주 좋아하는 장소	
장소	선정 이유
(1) 인사동	(2) 한국 전통예술과 문화의 중심지임. 많은 골동품 가게와 미술관이 있음
(3) N서울타워	(4) 남산은 서울의 경계표가 되는 봉우리이고 그 타워는 밤에 가면 환상적인 야경을 볼 수 있음

저는 서울에서 사는데 서울에는 외국인들에게 방문하도록 추천하고 싶은 많은 멋진 장소가 있습니다. 지금은 그중 두 곳을 여러분들에게 말씀드리겠습니다. 첫 번째로, 인사동을 추천합니다. 왜냐하면 인사동은 한국 전통예술과 문화의 중심지이고 많은 골동품 가게와 미술관이 있기 때문입니다. 두 번째로, N서울타워를 추천합니다. 왜냐하면 남산은 서울의 경계표가 되는 봉우리이고 그 타워는 밤에 가면 환상적인 야경을 볼 수 있기 때문입니다. 저는 제가 추천한 그 두 곳에서 외국인들이 즐거운 시간을 보내리라 확신합니다.

B

Help from Somebody Unknown	
(1) When and where?	near the school gate on the first day of my midterm exams this spring
(2) What was the problem?	that morning I took a taxi, but when I arrived at school I found that I had left my wallet at home
(3) Who helped you and how?	saw a female student of my school and helplessly asked her to lend me 10,000 won; surprisingly, she gave me the amount
(4) Your feelings	felt I should also help people who desperately need somebody else's help

I would like to talk about a time I got help from someone I didn't know. It happened (1)<u>near the school gate on the first day of my midterm exams this spring</u>. The problem I had was this. (2)<u>That morning I took a taxi, but when I arrived at school I found that I had left my wallet at home</u>. Then (3)<u>I saw a female student</u>

of my school and helplessly asked her to lend me 10,000 won. Surprisingly, she gave me the amount. I felt (4)I should also help people who desperately need somebody else's help. Still I can't forget the person who was willing to help me even though we didn't know each other.

모르는 사람으로부터의 도움	
(1) 언제 어디서?	올 봄 중간고사 첫날 학교 정문 근처에서
(2) 어떤 문제였나요?	그날 아침 택시를 탔음, 하지만 학교에 도착했을 때 지갑을 집에 놓고 온 것을 알게 되었음
(3) 누가 어떻게 두와 주었나요?	우리 학교 여학생을 보아서 힘없이 만원을 빌려 달라고 말함; 놀랍게도 그 액수를 내게 줌
(4) 느낌	나도 누군가 다른 사람의 도움을 절실하게 필요로 하는 사람을 도와야겠다고 느낌

저는 제가 모르던 누군가로부터 도움을 받았던 때에 대해 말씀드리고 싶습니다. 그 일은 올 봄 중간고사 첫날 학교 정문 근처에서 일어났습니다. 제가 처했던 문제는 이런 것이었습니다. 그날 아침 택시를 탔는데 학교에 도착했을 때 지갑을 집에 놓고 온 것을 알았습니다. 그때 우리 학교 여학생을 보아서 힘없이 만원을 빌려 달라고 말했습니다. 놀랍게도 그녀는 그 액수를 내게 주었습니다. 저는 나도 누군가 다른 사람의 도움을 절실하게 필요로 하는 사람을 도와야겠다고도 느꼈습니다. 저는 아직도 우리가 서로 알지도 못했지만 기꺼이 저를 도와준 그 사람을 잊을 수가 없습니다.

01 Actual Test 정답   p. 132

01 ①	02 ③	03 ①	04 ②	05 ④
06 ⑤	07 ⑤	08 ①	09 ④	10 ③
11 ②	12 ①	13 ③	14 ⑤	15 ⑤
16 ④	17 ②	18 ②	19 ④	20 ⑤

01

w Hello. I'm looking for a toy computer for my three-year-old son.

m Hello, ma'am! How about this penguin-shaped one? It is the bestselling toy computer for kids. You can practice spelling and adding numbers with it.

w Oh, but he already has too many toys with the same character.

m I see. Then how about this train-shaped one with a microphone? He can record his voice with this microphone.

w Not bad. Can I see that bird-shaped one?

m Yes, this is also a popular item for kids. It has a piano and drum playing function.

w Hmm... I like the functions on the first one you recommended to me. And while I'm sick and tired of that penguin, he is not.

여 안녕하세요. 세 살 된 제 아들에게 줄 장난감 컴퓨터를 사려고 해요.
남 안녕하세요. 이 펭귄 모양의 컴퓨터는 어떠세요? 아이들에게 가장 많이 팔리는 장난감 컴퓨터예요. 그것으로 철자와 덧셈을 연습할 수 있습니다.
여 오, 하지만 이미 똑같은 캐릭터의 장난감이 너무 많아요.
남 네, 알겠습니다. 그럼 마이크가 있는 이 기차 모양 컴퓨터는 어떠세요? 이 마이크로 목소리를 녹음할 수 있어요.
여 나쁘진 않네요. 저 새 모양의 컴퓨터 볼 수 있을까요?
남 네, 이것 또한 아이들에게 인기 있는 제품이에요. 피아노와 드럼을 연주하는 기능이 있답니다.
여 흠. 당신이 제게 제일 먼저 권해준 것에 있는 기능이 맘에 드네요. 그리고 저는 펭귄에 아주 질려버렸지만 제 아들은 아니거든요.

bestselling 가장 잘 팔리는 **function** 기능 **be sick of** ~에 질리다

02

m What are you working on?

w I'm trying to design a logo for my club.

m What's the purpose of the club?

w We volunteer to help poor people such as elderly people living alone.

m Then why don't you use a heart as your logo?

w That's good. And I want to put two hands holding each other in the heart.

m Okay. And why don't you put some words below the heart? Do you have any words in mind?

W Yes, I'm thinking of 'Volunteer Today' and V and T are meant to be capitalized.

M That looks good. I'm sure it'll be a nice logo.

W I hope so. Thank you for your suggestions.

. . . .

남 뭐 하는 거니?

여 동아리에서 사용할 의장을 만들려고 하는 중이야.

남 뭐 하는 동아리야?

여 우리는 독거노인과 같은 어려운 사람들을 돕기 위해서 자원봉사를 해.

남 그러면 하트를 의장으로 사용하는 거 어때?

여 좋아. 그리고 나는 서로 마주 잡은 두 손을 하트 안에 넣고 싶어.

남 좋아. 그리고 하트 아래에 말을 좀 넣는 건 어때? 생각해둔 말이라도 있니?

여 응, Volunteer Today라는 말을 생각 중인데, V와 T는 대문자로 표시하고 싶어.

남 좋아 보여. 틀림없이 멋진 의장이 될 거야.

여 그랬으면 좋겠어. 제안해줘서 고마워.

purpose 목적 **volunteer** 자원 봉사하다 **elderly** 나이든 **capitalize** 대문자로 쓰다 **suggestion** 제안

03

M You look so tired. Are you alright?

W No. All this housework makes me exhausted.

M You'd better take a rest. Go and lie on the bed.

W But I still have lots of things to do.

M Don't worry. I'll take care of everything. Trust me.

W Are you sure? Are you really going to do the rest of the housework?

M I'm not joking, Mom. I'll do my best to help you as you're not feeling well.

W Oh, my little angel. I am so touched. Thank you.

. . . .

남 너무 피곤해 보이세요. 괜찮으세요?

여 아니. 이 많은 집안일들이 나를 지치게 만드는구나.

남 쉬시는 게 나을 것 같아요. 가서 좀 누우세요.

여 하지만 아직 할 일이 많아.

남 걱정하지 마세요. 제가 다 할게요. 저를 믿으세요.

여 정말? 너 진짜 나머지 집안일을 할 거야?

남 농담 아니에요. 엄마. 엄마가 기분이 안 좋아 보여서 엄마를 돕기 위해 최선을 다할 거예요.

여 오, 내 작은 천사. 나 정말 감동받았어. 고마워.

trust 믿다 **rest** 휴식, 나머지 **do one's best** 최선을 다하다 **touched** 감동한

04

M You don't look good. How was your interview?

W It was the worst ever. I think I'd better stop looking for a job and try something different.

M Huh? With this current economic downturn, you should strive to get a job! What else can you do?

W What about running a coffee shop? It looks easy to do.

M But have you prepared yourself financially?

W I can start it by getting a loan from the bank. Once I open the coffee shop, I think I can manage it.

M You must research it carefully.

W Oh, there won't be any problems. It's easy to run a coffee shop.

. . . .

남 안 좋아 보이네. 면접은 어땠어?

여 최악의 면접이었어. 내 생각에는 나는 구직활동을 그만 하고 다른 것을 해보는 게 좋을 것 같아.

남 뭐? 요즘 같은 경기침체기에는 직장을 구하려고 노력해야 해! 그밖에 어떤 일을 하겠어?

여 커피숍을 운영하는 건 어떨까? 쉬워 보이던데.

남 하지만 경제적으로 준비되어 있어?

여 은행에서 대출받아서 시작하면 되지. 일단 커피숍을 열면, 내가 어떻게든 꾸려나갈 수 있을 것 같아.

남 너는 주의 깊게 조사해봐야 해.

여 오, 문제 없을 거야. 커피숍을 경영하는 건 쉬워.

① 분별 있는 ② 되는 대로의 ③ 신중한
④ 수동적인 ⑤ 부지런한

current 현재의 **economic** 경제의 **downturn** 침체 **strive** 노력하다 **run** 경영하다 **financially** 제정적으로 **loan** 대출

05

W Hi, Daniel. What are those flowers?

M I'm going to plant flowers to make a small garden.

W How many kinds of flowers did you buy?

M I bought four kinds of them: daisies, tulips, roses, and orchids. And I've got six of each kind.

W It seems that you spent lots of money. How much are they?

M Six dollars for each flower. They're giving a special

discount and selling all the different plants for the same price.

W What a bargain! Do you need my help? I'm also interested in gardening.

M Really? Thank you. Then can you dig some holes in the ground here?

....

여 안녕, Daniel. 저 꽃들은 뭐야?

남 작은 정원을 만들기 위해서 꽃들을 심을 거야.

여 몇 가지 꽃들을 산 거야?

남 네 가지 꽃들을 샀어. 데이지, 튤립, 장미, 그리고 난초. 각 종류마다 6송이를 샀지.

여 돈 많이 쓴 것 같다. 얼마야?

남 각각 6달러야. 특별할인을 하고 있는데 각기 다른 식물들을 모두 균일가로 팔고 있어.

여 정말 싸게 샀구나! 좀 도와줄까? 나도 원예에 흥미가 있거든.

남 정말? 고마워. 그러면 여기 땅에 구멍 몇 개 파주겠어?

●●
orchid 난초 **bargain** 염가 판매 **gardening** 원예

06

M Ladies and gentlemen, this is your captain speaking. I'm afraid we are having some engine troubles, so we'll have to make an emergency landing. Please make sure your seatbacks and tray tables are in their full upright position. Make sure your seat belt is securely fastened and turn off all electronic devices, as well. There is no cause for alarm as we can land quite safely. I apologize for the inconvenience.

....

남 신사 숙녀 여러분, 기장입니다. 엔진에 문제가 발생해서 비상착륙을 해야 할 것 같습니다. 반드시 여러분들의 등받이와 테이블이 완전히 똑바로 선 위치가 되도록 해주십시오. 또한 안전벨트를 확실하게 매주시고 모든 전자장치도 꺼주시기 바랍니다. 아주 안전하게 착륙할 수 있으므로 불안해 하실 필요 없습니다. 불편을 끼쳐드려 죄송합니다.

●●
emergency landing 비상착륙 **seatback** 등받이 **tray table** 접이식 테이블 **upright** 똑바로 선 **securely** 안전하게, 튼튼하게 **fasten** 매다 **alarm** 불안, 공포 **apologize** 사과하다

07

W Jake, can you give me a hand?

M Sure.

W I need to assemble this toy robot for my little brother. While I was putting it away, I accidentally dropped it and it broke into many pieces.

M How clumsy you are! Does he know that?

W Yes. And I told him that I would assemble it again even though I don't know how to do it.

M I'm sorry, I'm not good at putting things together. My brother is good at it, instead. Can I take the pieces to my house?

W Of course. Thank you! One moment, please. I'll go get a plastic bag to put them in.

....

여 Jake, 나 좀 도와줄래?

남 물론이지.

여 내 남동생을 위해서 이 장난감 로봇을 조립해야 해. 내가 이걸 치우던 중에 잘못해서 떨어뜨렸고, 산산조각이 나버렸어.

남 덤벙대긴! 동생이 알고 있니?

여 응. 그리고 어떻게 조립하는지도 모르지만, 다시 조립해준다고 말했어.

남 미안하지만 나도 조립하는 건 잘 못해. 대신에 우리 형이 잘 해. 부품들 우리 집으로 가져가도 되니?

여 물론이지. 고마워. 잠깐만. 부품들을 담을 비닐봉지 가서 가져올게.

●●
assemble 조립하다 **put away** 치우다 **break into pieces** 산산조각 나다 **clumsy** 솜씨 없는, 서투른 **put together** 합치다 **instead** 대신에 **plastic bag** 비닐봉지

08

W Would you like a newspaper to read, sir?

M Yes, please. I'll take that one.

W Here you go, sir. By the way, you look a little uncomfortable. Are you okay?

M Not so good. I'm always nervous before flying.

W Don't worry too much, sir. This is the safest form of travel.

M I know that. I'm sure I'll be better after we take off.

W You know we have some in-flight entertainment for you. You can find the movie guide in the pocket in front of you.

M Oh, good. A nice film will help me relaxed.

여 신문 읽으시겠어요?

남 네. 저것으로 주세요.

여 여기 있습니다. 그런데, 약간 불편해 보이시네요. 괜찮으세요?

남 그렇게 좋진 않습니다. 저는 항상 비행 전에 긴장하죠.

여 너무 걱정하지 마세요. 이것은 가장 안전한 형태의 여행이니까요.

남 알고 있습니다. 이륙 후에는 분명 더 나아질 겁니다.

여 승객님을 위한 기내 오락물이 있습니다. 앞에 있는 주머니 안에 영화 안내지가 있습니다.

남 오, 좋아요. 좋은 영화는 제가 편안해지는 데 도움이 되겠네요.

① 비행기   ② 극장   ③ 기차
④ 거리   ⑤ 서점

• •
uncomfortable 불편한 **nervous** 긴장한 **take off** 이륙하다
entertainment 오락, 오락물 **in front of** ~의 앞에

09

① M May I help you?

W I'd like to send this package to San Francisco.

② M How much is the entrance fee?

W It's $3 for adults, $1 for children from seven to sixteen years old and free for children under seven.

③ M Where can I find monthly magazines?

W They're in aisle seven.

④ M What's the purpose of your visit?

W I'm here on vacation.

⑤ M How often should I take this?

W Three times a day 30 minutes before meals.

---

① 남 무엇을 도와드릴까요?
   여 이 소포를 San Francisco에 보내고 싶습니다.
② 남 입장료 얼마인가요?
   여 성인은 3달러이고 7세에서 16세 미만 어린이는 1달러, 7살 이하 어린이는 무료입니다.
③ 남 월간 잡지는 어디서 찾을 수 있을까요?
   여 7번 통로에 있습니다.
④ 남 방문 목적이 무엇입니까?
   여 휴가차 왔습니다.
⑤ 남 이것을 얼마나 자주 먹어야 하나요?
   여 하루에 세 번, 식사 30분 전에 드세요.

• •
entrance fee 입장료 **monthly magazine** 월간 잡지 **on vacation** 휴가차

10

W Tom, hurry up! If not, you will be late for school.

M But Mom, I think I have a fever.

W Really? I will get the thermometer. [pause] Let's check your body temperature.

M What's my temperature?

W Yours is 39 degrees.

M Should I go to school?

W It's probably not a good idea. I'll call your teacher and then find a fever reducer. I don't think the clinic is open yet.

M Alright. I will go back to bed.

여 Tom, 서둘러! 안 그러면 학교에 늦을 거야.

남 그런데 엄마, 저 열이 있는 것 같아요.

여 정말? 체온계 가져올게. 체온을 재보자.

남 체온이 얼마예요?

여 39도야.

남 학교에 가요?

여 좋은 생각이 분명 아닌 것 같다. 선생님께 전화하고 해열제를 찾아볼게. 병원은 아직 열지 않았을 것 같아.

남 알았어요. 다시 누울게요.

• •
have a fever 열이 있다 **thermometer** 온도계 **body temperature** 체온 **fever reducer** 해열제

11

M Hi, Sarah! What are you doing now?

W I'm making invitation cards for a birthday party.

M Isn't your birthday in May?

W Right. This is for Timothy. I want to have a surprise party for him.

M That will be exciting. When is his birthday?

W It's next Wednesday, March 10th. But the party will be three days later, on Saturday.

M Okay. Is there anything I can help you with?

W Please put these cards into the red envelopes one

by one.

남 안녕, Sarah. 지금 뭐 하고 있어?
여 생일 초대장 만들고 있어.
남 네 생일은 5월 아니니?
여 맞아. 이건 Timothy를 위한 거야. 나는 그를 위한 깜짝 파티를 열고 싶어.
남 재미있겠다. 생일이 언제인데?
여 다음 주 수요일, 3월 10일이야. 그런데 파티는 3일 후 토요일에 열 거야.
남 알았어. 내가 도와줄 일 있니?
여 이 카드들을 빨간 봉투에 하나씩 넣어줘.

① 3월 10일   ② 3월 13일   ③ 4월 10일
④ 4월 13일   ⑤ 5월 10일

●●
invitation card 초대장 **envelope** 봉투 **one by one** 하나씩 차례로

12

W This is a traditional Korean sport. Two people kneel on the sand inside a circle. They have a piece of cloth, either red or blue, around their waists and thighs. During the match, if one contestant forces the other contestant to touch the ground with any part of his body, then he will be the winner. We call the winner Chunha-Jangsa or Baekdu-Jangsa in Korean. What is this?

여 이것은 한국 전통 운동입니다. 두 사람이 원 안에서 모래 위에 무릎을 꿇습니다. 그들은 그들의 허리와 허벅지에 빨간 색이나 파란색 천 조각 중 하나를 묶습니다. 경기 중에 만일 한 참가자가 다른 참가자의 신체 일부분이 땅에 닿도록 하면 승자가 됩니다. 우리는 그 승자를 한국말로 천하장사 혹은 백두장사라고 합니다. 이것은 무엇입니까?

●●
traditional 전통의 **kneel** 무릎을 꿇다 **waist** 허리 **thigh** 허벅지
contestant 경쟁자, 참가자

13

[Telephone rings.]
W Happy Airlines. How can I help you?
M I'd like to book a flight for this Saturday to Tokyo.
W Which city are you going to fly from, Seoul or Busan?

M From Seoul.
W Would you like to reserve a one-way or a round-trip ticket?
M A round-trip ticket, please.
W Would you like business class or economy class?
M I prefer business class.

	출발	구분	요일	등급
①	서울	편도	금요일	일반석
②	서울	편도	토요일	비즈니석
③	서울	왕복	토요일	비즈니석
④	부산	편도	일요일	일반석
⑤	부산	왕복	토요일	비즈니석

[전화벨이 울린다.]
여 Happy 항공사입니다. 무엇을 도와드릴까요?
남 이번 토요일에 도쿄로 가는 비행기를 예약하고 싶습니다.
여 어느 도시에서 탑승하실 건가요, 서울인가요, 부산인가요?
남 서울에서요.
여 편도를 원하세요, 왕복을 원하세요?
남 왕복으로 해주세요.
여 비즈니스석을 원하십니까, 일반석을 원하십니까?
남 비즈니스석이 더 좋습니다.

●●
reserve 예약하다 **economy class** 일반석

14

M Is this Jessica? What a surprise! I didn't expect to see you here. What are you doing?
W Hi, Denny. I'm waiting for my dad. He's coming back from Washington today. How about you?
M I'm waiting for my dad, too. He left on a business trip to England last week and he is returning today too.
W I see. Did his plane land?
M No, not yet. I have to wait for him for at least an hour more I guess. How about your dad?
W According to the arrivals board, his plane landed a few minutes ago. I can see him soon.
M That's good.

남 Jessica니? 정말 놀랍다. 이 곳에서 너를 만날 것이라고 생각 못 했어.

뭐 하고 있어?

여 안녕, Denny. 아빠 기다려. Washington에서 오늘 돌아오시거든.
너는?

남 나도 아빠를 기다려. 아빠도 지난 주에 영국으로 출장 가셨다가 오늘
돌아오시거든.

여 그렇구나. 아빠가 타신 비행기는 도착했니?

남 아니 아직. 내 생각에는 최소한 한 시간은 더 기다려야 하는 것 같아.
네 아빠는?

여 도착안내판에 의하면 비행기가 몇 분 전에 착륙했어. 곧 만날 수 있을
것 같아.

남 잘됐다.

••
land 착륙하다 **at least** 최소한 **arrivals board** (공항) 도착안내판

15

M Kate, what will be a good present for my grandma?
Her birthday is this Friday.

W What about a scarf?

M That was what I thought, but my mom bought one
for her last week.

W Oh, that's too bad. How about comfortable shoes
or health food?

M They are too common, aren't they? Is there
anything better?

W Let me think… Oh, what do you think of a famous
singer's dinner and concert ticket?

M Wow! That would be great. She can enjoy the
concert while having dinner.

W Right. Hurry to make a booking.

남 Kate, 할머니께 드릴 좋은 선물이 뭘까? 할머니 생신이 이번
금요일이야.

여 스카프 어때?

남 그게 내가 생각했던 것이었는데, 엄마가 이미 지난주에 할머니를 위해
사셨어.

여 오, 안됐다. 편안한 신발이나 건강식품은 어때?

남 그것들은 너무 흔해, 그렇지 않니? 좀 더 나은 게 없을까?

여 어디 좀 생각해 보자… 오, 유명 가수의 디너쇼 티켓은 어떻게 생각해?

남 왜! 그거 괜찮겠다. 할머니께서 저녁만찬을 드시면서 콘서트도 즐기실
수 있겠어.

여 맞아. 예약 서둘러.

••
comfortable 편안한 **common** 평범한 **make a booking** 예약하다

16

① M Did you hear that Bill made it to the finals?

W Yes, I did. It's incredible, isn't it?

② M Do you prefer online shopping to shopping at
stores?

W Yes, I do. Online shopping is more convenient.

③ M Oz Air Travel. How may I help you?

W I'd like to book tickets to Singapore for two
adults.

④ M Would you mind telling me what's wrong with
this alarm?

W I don't remember where I put it.

⑤ M You're late by an hour!

W I'm really sorry. The traffic jam was terrible.

① 남 Bill이 결승전까지 진출했다는 소식 들었니?

여 응, 들었어. 그거 믿을 수 없지, 안 그래?

② 남 너는 상점에서 쇼핑하는 것보다 온라인에서 쇼핑하는 것을 더 좋아
하니?

여 응, 그래. 온라인 쇼핑이 더 편리해.

③ 남 Oz 항공사입니다. 어떻게 도와드릴까요?

여 성인 2명 싱가폴행 표를 예약하고 싶습니다.

④ 남 이 자명종이 뭐가 잘못된 건지 말해줄래?

여 그걸 어디에 뒀는지 기억이 안 나요.

⑤ 남 한 시간이나 늦었구나!

여 정말 죄송해요. 교통체증이 끔찍했어요.

••
make it to ~에 이르다 **final** 결승전 **incredible** 믿을 수 없는
convenient 편리한 **traffic jam** 교통체증

17

W Hi, I'm into singing songs so I'm interested in this
club. Could you tell me about it?

M Welcome. We are a community choir for men and
women over 15 years old. We enjoy singing songs
from pop to classical, in unison, and in harmony.

W Great. To become a member, do I have to audition?

M You don't have to audition to join us nor do you
need to be able to read music. We will only
audition someone if they want a solo part.

W Are there any special things about this club?

M We are taught by a professional mezzo-soprano, Mary Johnson. Under her expert guidance you can improve your musicality.

W Sounds really interesting. Do you give concerts, too?

M Yes. We put on two concerts per year.

· ·

여 안녕하세요, 저는 노래 부르기에 푹 빠져있어서 이 동아리에 관심이 있습니다. 동아리에 대해서 말씀해주실 수 있나요?

남 반갑습니다. 우리는 15세 이상 남녀로 구성된 지역 합창단이죠. 우리는 팝에서 클래식, 제창, 화음에 이르기까지 어떤 노래든 부르는 걸 좋아합니다.

여 아주 좋군요. 회원이 되려면 오디션을 받아야 하나요?

남 가입을 위해 오디션을 받을 필요도 없고 악보를 읽는 능력도 필요 없습니다. 솔로 파트를 원하는 사람만 오디션을 할 것입니다.

여 이 동아리의 특별한 점이 있나요?

남 우리는 전문 메조소프라노인 Mary Johnson 씨의 지도를 받습니다. 그녀의 전문적인 지도하에 음악성을 향상시킬 수 있지요.

여 아주 흥미로워요. 콘서트도 여나요?

남 네. 1년에 두 번 콘서트를 엽니다.

· ·
choir 합창단 in unison 제창으로 audition 음성 테스트를 하다[받다]
expert 전문가(의) improve 향상시키다 musicality 음악성 put on 공연하다

18

W Josh decides to buy a denim shirt. He enters a shop and chooses the shirt he would like to buy. But he realizes that he left his wallet at home. He doesn't have enough money to buy the shirt at the moment. So, he decides to try it on and just keep looking around. A clerk, named Nancy, comes to him and asks if she can help him. In this situation, what would Josh most likely say to Nancy?

· ·

여 Josh는 데님 셔츠를 사기로 결심한다. 그는 가게로 들어가 그가 사고 싶은 셔츠를 고른다. 그러나 그는 지갑을 집에 두고 나왔다는 것을 깨닫는다. 그는 지금 그 셔츠를 살 만큼 돈이 충분하지 않다. 그래서 그는 한번 입어보고 그냥 계속 둘러보기만 하기로 한다. Nancy라는 이름의 점원이 그에게 다가와서 도움이 필요한지 묻는다. 이 상황에서 Josh는 Nancy에게 뭐라고 말하겠는가?

① 도와드릴까요?
② 그냥 둘러보는 중이에요.

③ 전 이 바지는 원치 않습니다.
④ 죄송합니다. 제가 지금 바쁩니다.
⑤ 다른 거 보여주시겠습니까?

· ·
realize 깨닫다 at the moment 지금은 try on 입어보다 clerk 점원

19

[Telephone rings.]

W BF Dental Clinic. How may I help you?

M Hi there. I want to make an appointment with Dr. Smith as soon as possible. I have a terrible toothache.

W I see. Please hold for a moment while I check his schedule for any openings. [pause] Can you come in tomorrow at 2 p.m.?

M No, I can't. I have an important business meeting. Do you have anything in the morning?

W No, we don't have any openings in the morning. How about Wednesday at 11 a.m.?

M I have to send off my client at the airport at 10 so I won't be able to make it to your office by 11. Can I come in at eleven thirty instead?

W Sure, eleven thirty in the morning sounds good. Would you like a reminder call tomorrow?

M No, that's fine. I will remember the date and time.

· ·

[전화벨이 울린다.]

여 BF 치과입니다. 어떻게 도와드릴까요?

남 안녕하세요. Smith 선생님과 가능한 한 빨리 약속을 잡고 싶습니다. 이가 많이 아픕니다.

여 알겠습니다. 빈 시간이 있는지 스케줄을 확인하는 동안 잠시만 기다리세요. 내일 오후 2시에 오실 수 있나요?

남 아뇨, 안 됩니다. 중요한 업무상 회의가 있어서요. 오전에는 하나도 없을까요?

여 네, 오전에는 비는 시간이 없습니다. 수요일 오전 11시는 어때요?

남 공항에서 10시에 고객을 배웅해야 해서 거기 치과까지 11시까지는 못 갈 것 같습니다. 대신 11시 30분에 가도 될까요?

여 네, 오전 11시 30분 괜찮네요. 내일 알림 전화 드릴까요?

남 아니요. 괜찮습니다. 제가 날짜와 시간을 기억하겠습니다.

① 다음 주로 일정을 재조정할 수 있습니다.
② 아침에 전화로 깨워주셨으면 합니다.
③ 좀 더 이른 시간으로 재조정하시겠습니까?

④ 아니요, 괜찮습니다. 제가 날짜와 시간을 기억하겠습니다.

⑤ 네. 여기 내 전자수첩에 메모를 해 놓을게요.

make an appointment 약속하다 **send off** 배웅하다 **reminder call** 전화 알림 서비스

20

W　Hi, Ben. How was your weekend?

M　Hey, Jenny. I was pretty busy. How about you?

W　Nothing special for me. What did you do?

M　My club had a flea market to help the orphans at the community center.

W　That sounds great! Did you raise a lot of money?

M　Because of the heavy rain, not many people showed up. We raised 1,500 dollars, but we wanted to raise 1,000 dollars more.

W　Sorry to hear that. When do you plan to have another flea market? I'd like to help.

M　It is supposed to be next month.

여　안녕, Ben. 주말 어땠니?

남　안녕, Jenny. 꽤 바빴어. 너는 어땠어?

여　난 특별한 건 없었어. 넌 뭐 했어?

남　우리 동아리가 지역 문화센터에서 고아들을 돕기 위해 벼룩시장을 열었어.

여　멋진데! 돈은 많이 모금했니?

남　비가 많이 와서, 사람들이 많이 안 왔어. 1,500달러를 모금했지만 우린 1,000달러를 더 모금하고 싶었거든.

여　그 말을 들으니 유감이구나. 다음 벼룩시장은 언제 할 계획이니? 나도 돕고 싶어.

남　다음 달로 예정돼 있어.

① 우린 두 주 전에 했어.

② 그건 원래 계획이 아니었어.

③ 이 일을 앞으로 2년 동안 할 계획이야.

④ 날 많이 도와준 거 정말 고마워.

⑤ 다음 달로 예정돼 있어.

flea market 벼룩시장 **orphan** 고아 **raise money** 돈을 모금하다

p. 140

02 Actual Test 정답

01 ③	02 ①	03 ①	04 ②	05 ⑤
06 ②	07 ④	08 ⑤	09 ①	10 ⑤
11 ④	12 ②	13 ③	14 ④	15 ③
16 ④	17 ③	18 ③	19 ①	20 ⑤

01

M　Hey, Angela. I have a surprise for you.

W　What is it this time?

M　I'm setting you up on a blind date with my classmate, Jake. I think you two would make a really good couple.

W　Thanks, but I don't even know what he looks like.

M　I know you put a big value on appearance. He will meet your expectation. Look at this photo. He is right next to me.

W　Where are you? Oh, here you are, with long, curly hair. Which guy is he?

M　The guy with very short hair and a bright smile. He is almost a head taller than me. You will like him.

W　Oh, he's tall and handsome.

남　안녕, Angela. 너를 깜짝 놀라게 할 일이 있지.

여　이번에는 뭐야?

남　내 반친구, Jake와 소개팅을 시켜줄게. 내 생각에 너희 둘은 정말 잘 어울릴 것 같아.

여　고맙지만 나는 그가 어떻게 생겼는지도 몰라.

남　난 네가 외모를 중요하게 여긴다는 걸 알아. 그는 네 기대에 부응할 거야. 이 사진 좀 봐. 그는 내 바로 옆에 있어.

여　네가 어디에 있지? 오, 긴 곱슬머리를 하고 여기에 있구나. 그는 어느 남자니?

남　아주 짧은 머리에 밝게 웃고 있는 남자야. 그는 나보다 거의 머리 하나 만큼 더 커. 너는 그가 마음에 들 거야.

여　오, 키도 크고 잘생겼네.

blind date 서로 모르는 남녀간의 데이트 **value** 가치 **appearance** 외모 **meet** 충족시키다 **expectation** 기대

02

W We have only one week left before Christmas. Why don't we buy a floral wreath for the front door?

M That's a good idea. Look at this website. What about this pair of white mittens with green leaves?

W I don't know, but I think a more colorful one would be better.

M How about this wreath that has red berries, gold leaves, pine leaves, and red and gold ribbons?

W That's good. But it would be so much better if there were a bell.

M Here you go! This is exactly what you want. A colorful wreath with a bell.

W Yes, it looks amazing. Let's order this one.

여 크리스마스가 일주일밖에 안 남았어. 대문에 달 리스를 사는 거 어때?

남 좋은 생각이야. 이 웹사이트 좀 봐. 초록색 잎이 있는 이 하얀색 벙어리 장갑 한 켤레 어때?

여 잘 모르겠지만 좀더 다채로운 색깔의 리스면 더 좋을 것 같아.

남 빨간 열매, 금색 나뭇잎, 소나무 잎, 그리고 빨간색과 황금색 리본이 있는 이 리스는 어때?

여 좋아. 하지만 종이 있으면 훨씬 더 좋을 것 같아.

남 여기 있다! 딱 네가 원하는 거야. 종이 있는 다채로운 색상의 리스 말이야.

여 그래, 너무 멋지게 보인다. 이것으로 주문하자.

wreath 화환, 리스 **mittens** 벙어리 장갑

03

M Why the long face?

W Haven't you heard the news about Roy?

M No, I haven't. What happened to him?

W He got in a car accident on the way to school. I was told a van ran into him while he was crossing the street.

M Is he all right? Where is he now?

W He's in the hospital now and he has fallen into a coma.

M Oh my God! How could such a thing happen to him? What a pity.

남 왜 그런 우울한 얼굴을 하고 있니?

여 Roy에 관한 소식 못 들었니?

남 응, 못 들었어. 그에게 무슨 일 생겼어?

여 학교에 오는 길에 차 사고를 당했어. 건널목을 건너던 중에 밴에 치였다고 들었어.

남 그는 괜찮아? 지금 어디에 있어?

여 지금 병원에 있고 혼수상태에 빠졌대.

남 오, 세상에! 어떻게 그런 일이 그에게 일어날 수가 있지? 정말 안됐다.

① 걱정하는   ② 안도하는   ③ 무관심한

④ 짜증 난   ⑤ 증오하는

long face 우울한 표정 **run into** ~와 충돌하다 **coma** 혼수상태 **What a pity**. 안됐다.

04

W Is this your first visit here?

M Yes, it is.

W Please fill out this form. Do you have any allergies?

M No, I don't.

W Please tell me what your problem is.

M Well, recently I have been feeling tired, and sometimes I have really bad headaches and an upset stomach.

W When did you start having those symptoms?

M I started feeling tired about one month ago and after that the headaches came.

W OK. Please wait till it's your turn.

여 여기에 처음 오셨나요?

남 네, 그렇습니다.

여 이 양식 좀 작성해주세요. 혹시 알레르기 있으세요?

남 아뇨.

여 증상이 뭔지 말씀해주세요.

남 음, 최근에 계속 피곤하고 가끔 머리가 정말 아프고 배가 아프기도 합니다.

여 그런 증상이 언제부터 시작됐나요?

남 피곤한 건 한 달 전부터 시작되었고 그리고 나서 두통이 왔습니다.

여 알겠습니다. 순서가 될 때까지 기다려주세요.

fill out 작성하다 **headache** 두통 **upset stomach** 배탈

05

M Hey, Susan. Let's go work out later today.

W Sure. <u>What parts of our body</u> are we going to work on today?

M How about working on our <u>legs and back</u>?

W I <u>wonder</u> if we can work on our arms and stomach today. As I <u>have taken the stairs</u> six or seven times today, <u>my legs</u> are <u>killing me</u>.

M No problem. <u>What time</u> do you want to go?

W How about at <u>three thirty</u>?

M That sounds <u>a little bit early</u>. Can we meet an <u>hour later</u>?

W Okay. Then, let's meet in front of the gym.

....

남 Susan. 오늘 이따가 운동하러 가자.

여 좋아. 오늘 우리 몸 어디를 운동할 거야?

남 다리랑 등을 운동할까?

여 오늘 팔과 배 운동을 할 수 있을지 모르겠네. 오늘 계단 오르기를 예닐곱 번 했더니 다리가 아파 죽을 지경이야.

남 좋아. 몇 시에 가고 싶어?

여 3시 30분 어때?

남 조금 이른 것 같아. 한 시간 더 늦게 만날 수 있을까?

여 좋아. 그럼 체육관 앞에서 만나자.

work out 운동하다 **My legs are killing me**. 다리 아파 죽겠어.

06

M Welcome to my house! Come on in!

W This present is for you, Sean. Thank you for <u>inviting me</u> to <u>your housewarming party</u>. Are the others here yet?

M Oh, thank you. Nobody has come here yet. So just <u>make yourself at home</u>.

W Thanks. This is a great apartment! Do you mind if I <u>look around</u>?

M No, go ahead.

W Oh, everything here is neat. Especially I like this <u>antique sofa</u> and <u>table</u>. How awesome!

M Jina, I hate to ask this, but would you mind helping me <u>chop the vegetables</u>? I haven't cooked all the dishes yet.

W <u>Not at all</u>. I'm happy to help you.

....

남 우리 집에 온 걸 환영합니다! 어서 들어와요!

여 당신을 위한 선물이에요. Sean. 집들이에 초대해줘서 고마워요. 다른 사람들은 왔나요?

남 고마워요. 아직 아무도 안 왔어요. 그러니 편히 있어요.

여 고마워요. 멋진 아파트네요. 둘러봐도 될까요?

남 네, 그럼요.

여 오, 여기에 있는 모든 것이 다 깔끔하네요. 특히 이 고풍스러운 소파와 탁자가 마음에 들어요. 너무 멋져요.

남 Jina, 이런 부탁 하기 싫지만 혹시 채소 잘게 써는 거 도와줄 수 있나요? 내가 아직 요리를 다 못했거든요.

여 그럼요. 돕게 돼서 기뻐요.

housewarming party 집들이 **chop** 잘게 썰다

07

W When is the County Cup <u>final match</u>?

M It's <u>already over</u>. It was on July 28.

W Oh, really? Where was it played? At Donald <u>Stadium</u>?

M Yes. Mars <u>played against</u> Venus.

W <u>Who won the match</u>?

M Mars! They <u>won by two points</u>. The score was <u>three to one</u>.

W Hmm. Who was the MVP?

M Jake Johnson.

....

카운티컵 결승전	
① 날짜	7월 28일
② 장소	Donald 구장
③ 팀	Mars 대 Venus
④ 점수	3대 2
⑤ MVP	Jake Johnson

여 카운티컵 결선이 언제야?

남 이미 끝났어. 7월 28일이었어.

여 오, 정말? 경기가 어디서 열렸어? Donald 구장에서?

남 응. Mars가 Venus를 상대로 경기를 했어.

여 누가 이겼어?

남 Mars가! 2점 차이로 이겼어. 점수가 3대 1이었어.

여 음. 누가 최고의 선수였어?

남 Jake Johnson이야.

08

M   What are you going to do tomorrow?

W   Well, tomorrow will be a really busy day from morning till evening.

M   What are you going to do?

W   First, I have to help my mom clean the house in the morning, and then I have a math class at 11.

M   And then?

W   I will meet Sumi at one to have lunch together. Then I have to practice the violin in the afternoon.

M   Well, do you think you'll have time in the evening to have dinner with me?

W   I'm afraid I can't. I have to finish writing a report. It's due the day after tomorrow.

M   Oh, no! That's too bad.

남   너 내일 뭐 할 거니?

여   음. 내일은 아침부터 저녁까지 정말 바쁜 날이 될 거야.

남   뭐 할 건데?

여   먼저, 아침에는 엄마가 집 청소하시는 것을 도와드려야 하고 그 다음 11시에는 수학 수업이 있어.

남   그 다음엔?

여   1시에 수미를 만나서 점심을 같이 먹을 거야. 그 다음 오후에는 바이올린 연습을 해야 해.

남   음, 저녁에 나랑 같이 저녁 먹을 시간이 있을 것 같니?

여   안 될 것 같아. 리포트 작성을 끝내야 해. 내일모레까지가 기한이거든.

남   저런! 안됐구나.

09

M   Hello, may I get a refund for this beanie?

W   No problem. Can I have the receipt?

M   Thanks. Here it is.

W   Oh, you bought this over a month ago.

M   Yes. I bought this when it was on sale. Is there a problem?

W   I'm sorry, but yes. We don't give refunds on sale items. And we only give refunds within two weeks.

M   But I've never worn it and didn't remove the price tag.

W   I'm sorry, that's our refund policy. There's nothing I can do.

남   안녕하세요. 이 비니 환불을 받을 수 있을까요?

여   문제없습니다. 영수증 가지고 계세요?

남   고맙습니다. 여기 있습니다.

여   어, 사신 지 한 달이 더 지났네요.

남   네. 세일할 때 샀어요. 무슨 문제라도 있나요?

여   죄송하지만 그렇습니다. 세일품목은 환불이 되지 않습니다. 그리고 2주 안에 오셔야 환불해드립니다.

남   그렇지만 아직 써보지도 않았고 가격표도 안 떼었어요.

여   죄송하지만 환불규정이 그렇습니다. 제가 해드릴 수 있는 것이 없습니다.

10

W   Are you enjoying staying here in Korea?

M   Yes, very much. It's a beautiful country.

W   When did you come to Korea?

M   I came here on the first day of April.

W   What is your impression of Korea?

M   The people are really kind and I love to see the cherry blossoms at this time of year.

W   How long are you going to stay?

M   My original plan was to stay for two weeks, but yesterday I decided to stay a week longer.

W   I see. I hope you will have a great time.

여   한국에서 즐겁게 지내고 계세요?

남   네, 무척요. 한국은 아름다운 나라입니다.

여   한국에 언제 오셨습니까?

남   4월 1일에 왔습니다.

여   한국에 대한 인상이 어떠세요?

남   사람들이 정말 친절한 데다 저는 연중 이 시기에 벚꽃을 보는 것을 무척 좋아합니다.

여   얼마 동안 머무실 건가요?

남   원래는 2주 머물 계획이었는데 어제 한 주 더 머물기로 결심했습니다.

여   그렇군요. 즐거운 시간 보내시기 바랍니다.

● ●
impression 인상   **blossom** 꽃, 개화   **decide** 결심하다

11

M   You can easily find this in the kitchen. Its body is usually made of metal while the grip is made of plastic or wood. This is used for cutting meat, vegetables, fruit, etc. This is a very useful and necessary tool but you have to be really careful. That is because the metal part is sharp and has a keen edge. If you are careless, you might get hurt or wounded.

....

남   여러분은 이것을 주방에서 쉽게 찾을 수 있습니다. 그것의 몸통은 대개 금속으로 만들어졌지만 손잡이는 플라스틱이나 나무로 만들어져 있습니다. 이것은 고기, 채소, 과일 등을 자르는 데 사용됩니다. 이것은 매우 유용하고 필요한 도구이지만 정말 조심해야 합니다. 그 이유는 금속 부분은 날카롭고 날이 뾰족하기 때문입니다. 당신이 부주의하면, 다치거나 상처를 입을 수도 있습니다.

● ●
be made of ～으로 만들어지다   **metal** 금속   **grip** 손잡이   **keen** 날카로운   **edge** 테두리, 날   **careless** 부주의한   **wound** 상처를 입히다

12

W   Good afternoon, everyone. I'm pleased to introduce Mr. Mike Brown. He majored in business administration and has fifteen years of experience in increasingly responsible roles within marketing at several companies. He's going to be the new manager of our marketing department. I believe that his experience and knowledge will help this company greatly. So please give a warm welcome to Mr. Mike Brown.

....

여   안녕하세요, 여러분. Mike Brown 씨를 소개하게 되어 기쁩니다. 그는 경영학을 전공했으며 여러 회사의 마케팅 분야에서 점점 더 책임 있는 역할로 15년을 근무한 경력이 있습니다. 그는 우리 마케팅부의 새로운 부장이 될 것입니다. 저는 그의 경험과 지식이 이 회사에 굉장히 도움이 될 것이라고 믿습니다. 그러니 Mike Brown 씨를 따뜻하게 환영해 주세요.

● ●
be pleased to-V ～하게 되어 기쁘다   **administration** 경영, 관리   **increasingly** 더욱 더   **knowledge** 지식

13

W   Hey, Taemin. Are you still here in Korea? I thought you had already left for Taiwan.

M   Hi, Yuna. Not yet. I'm leaving this Thursday. Are you on your way home now?

W   No, I'm going to the bookstore. I want to look at newly released books about the economy.

M   Do you always buy that kind of book?

W   Of course not. If there is an interesting one, that's the one I'll get. But I buy other kinds of books, too. Where are you going?

M   I'm going to the department store to buy a birthday gift for my mom.

W   Oh, I have to get off at the next stop. I have to press the bell. Why don't you take my seat?

M   Thanks. Have a nice day!

....

여   태민아. 너 아직 한국에 있는 거야? 대만으로 벌써 간 줄 알았어.

남   안녕, 연아야. 아니 아직. 이번 목요일에 떠나. 지금 집에 가는 길이니?

여   아니, 서점에 가. 경제에 관한 신간도서를 보고 싶어서.

남   너는 항상 그런 종류의 책을 사니?

여   당연히 아니지. 흥미로운 게 있다면 그걸 사는 거지. 하지만 다른 종류의 책들도 사. 너는 어디 가?

남   엄마 생신 선물 사러 백화점에 가.

여   오, 나 다음 정류장에서 내려야 해. 벨을 눌러야 하는데. 내 자리에 앉지 그래?

남   고마워. 잘 가.

● ●
newly 새롭게   **release** 방출하다, 발매하다   **economy** 경제   **get off** 내리다

14

W   Mingyu, do you know any good ways to save natural resources?

M   Well, it is helpful to take buses, subways, or trains instead of cars.

W   Definitely, it is. Carpooling can also be a good way

but not many people do it because they don't feel safe.

M They don't feel safe?

W Yes. Some people don't feel it's safe to drive with someone they don't know well.

M Oh, I got it. I think unplugging electronic devices when we aren't using them is helpful.

W How smart! What do you think of using paper cups?

M I guess we can save a lot of trees if we don't use them.

W You're right.

....

여 민규야, 자연자원 절약을 위한 좋은 방법을 알고 있니?

남 음. 자동차 대신에 버스, 지하철 혹은 기차를 타는 것이 도움이 돼요.

여 맞아. 카풀도 좋은 방법이긴 한데 안전하다고 느끼질 않기 때문에 많은 사람들이 하지는 않아.

남 안전하지 못하다고 느낀다고요?

여 응. 어떤 사람들은 잘 모르는 사람과 함께 차를 운전하고 가는 것에 대해 안전하지 않다고 느껴.

남 아, 알겠어요. 전기기구들을 사용하지 않을 때는 플러그를 뽑아두는 것도 도움이 될 것 같아요.

여 똑똑하구나! 종이컵을 사용하는 것은 어떨 것 같니?

남 사용하지 않는다면 많은 나무들을 아낄 수 있을 것 같아요.

여 맞아.

natural resources 자연자원 **instead of** ~ 대신에 **definitely** 분명히, 확실히 **carpooling** 자용차 합승, 카풀 **unplug** 플러그를 뽑다 **electronic device** 전자기기

15

① W The most popular free-time activity among the students in George's class is playing computer games.

② W Twenty-two percent said that they enjoy listening to music when they are free.

③ W The number of students who answered playing sports was less than half of the number who answered playing computer games.

④ W More students enjoy watching movies than reading books.

⑤ W Except for other activities, the least number of

---

students in George's class want to read books in their free time.

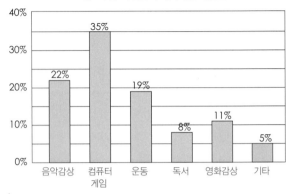

George의 반 학생들의 여가시간 사용법

음악감상	컴퓨터 게임	운동	독서	영화감상	기타
22%	35%	19%	8%	11%	5%

① 여 George의 반 학생들 사이에 가장 인기 있는 여가 활동은 컴퓨터 게임을 하는 것이다.

② 여 22%는 여가시간에 음악감상을 즐긴다고 대답했다.

③ 여 운동하기에 답한 학생 수는 컴퓨터 게임 하기에 답한 학생 수의 절반에도 못 미쳤다.

④ 여 책을 읽는 것보다 영화 보는 것을 즐기는 학생들이 더 많다.

⑤ 여 기타 활동들을 제외하면 George의 반에서 가장 적은 수의 학생들이 여가시간에 책을 읽고 싶어한다.

activity 활동 **except for** ~을 제외하고

16

W Ben, here is something that will make you happy. Have a look at this ad.

M Let me see. Oh, I have long been looking for a sign that says, "Pets are welcome!"

W Congratulations! From now on, you have a restaurant to go to with your puppy.

M Thanks. Why don't we go have lunch there today? They have a lunch special even on the weekend.

W What do they have for a lunch special today?

M Mexican food. The lunch special today is tacos.

W Oh, that's cool. Let's go!

....

여 Ben, 너를 기쁘게 해줄 뭔가가 여기 있어. 이 광고 좀 봐.

남 어디 보자. 오, 나 오랫동안 "애완동물 입장 가능"이라고 말하는 표지판을 찾아왔었어.

여 축하해! 이제부터 네 강아지와 함께 갈 음식점이 생겼네.

남 고마워. 오늘 거기에서 점심 먹는 거 어때? 주말에도 점심특선이 있어.

여　오늘 점심특선으로 뭐가 있니?
남　멕시코음식. 오늘의 점심특선은 타코야.
여　오, 그거 괜찮은데. 가자!

•• **ad** 광고　**lunch special** 점심 특가메뉴

17

① M　Excuse me, I think you're sitting in my seat.
　W　Oh, really? Let me check my ticket. I'm sorry.
② M　Does this bus go to City Hall?
　W　No, you should take bus number 602.
③ M　I'd like to buy some mouthwash for my teeth.
　W　How about this pair of goggles?
④ M　Didn't you talk with her about how you feel?
　W　Well, I tried to, but she didn't want to discuss the matter.
⑤ M　What time should I get to the theater?
　W　Ten minutes before the play starts.

① 남　실례합니다만, 제 자리에 앉으신 것 같은데요.
　여　아, 정말요? 제 표를 확인해 볼게요. 죄송합니다.
② 남　이 버스가 시청으로 가나요?
　여　아니오, 602번 버스를 타세요.
③ 남　제 이를 위한 양치약을 좀 사고 싶습니다.
　여　이 고글 안경 어때요?
④ 남　네가 어떤 기분인지 그녀와 얘기해 보지 않니?
　여　음, 시도는 해봤지만, 그녀는 그 일을 얘기하고 싶어하지 않아.
⑤ 남　몇 시에 극장에 도착해야 하나요?
　여　연극이 시작하기 10분 전에요.

•• **mouthwash** 양치약　**goggles** 보안경, 고글　**theater** 극장　**play** 연극

18

M　Jane, do you know who Jeff is?
W　Do you mean the biggest troublemaker in our school?
M　Yeah, that's him. He gets into lots of fights and the teachers always seemed to be angry about his behavior.
W　Why are you talking about him all of a sudden? You aren't close to him.
M　Are you ready for this?

W　Okay. What is it?
M　He was accepted into Harvard University.
W　Wow, what a surprise!

남　Jane, 너 Jeff가 누구인지 알지?
여　우리 학교에서 제일가는 문제아 말이니?
남　응, 바로 걔야. 그 앤 싸움을 많이 하고 선생님들은 항상 그의 행동에 화가 나셨던 것 같아.
여　그런데 갑자기 왜 걔 이야길 하는 거니? 넌 그와 친하지 않잖아.
남　준비됐니?
여　그래. 뭔데?
남　그가 하버드 대학에 합격했대.
여　와, 정말 놀라운데!

① 쉽게 번 돈은 쉽게 나간다.
② 돌다리도 두들겨 보고 건너라.
③ 겉을 보고 속을 판단하지 마라.
④ 눈에는 눈, 이에는 이.
⑤ 한 가지 일에 전부를 걸지 마라.

•• **troublemaker** 문제아, 말썽꾼　**behavior** 행동　**all of a sudden** 갑자기

19

W　Jessica arrives at a fast food restaurant to meet her friends. Because it's Saturday, almost every table is filled with people. Fortunately, she sees a table available for four people. But there are only three chairs. She sees an empty chair by a man sitting alone at another table. Since he is writing something on his laptop, Jessica thinks that he came alone. So she would like to ask him if she can take the chair. In this situation, what would Jessica most likely say to the man sitting alone at the table?

여　Jessica는 친구들을 만나기 위해 패스트푸드 식당에 도착한다. 토요일이라, 거의 모든 테이블이 사람들로 꽉 찼다. 운 좋게도, 그녀는 4명이 앉을 테이블 하나를 발견한다. 하지만 의자는 3개뿐이다. 그녀는 다른 테이블에서 혼자 앉아있는 남자 옆에서 빈 의자 하나를 발견한다. 그 남자는 노트북컴퓨터에 뭔가를 쓰고 있기 때문에 Jessica는 그가 혼자 왔다고 생각한다. 그래서 그녀는 그에게 그 의자를 가지고 와도 되는지 묻고 싶어한다. 이 상황에서 Jessica는 테이블에 혼자 앉아있는 남자에게 뭐라고 말하겠는가?

① 이 의자 임자 있나요?
② 4명이 앉을 테이블을 주세요.
③ 이 의자 어디다 두면 될까요?
④ 이 의자 좀 치워 주시겠어요?
⑤ 빈 테이블 어디 없을까요?

be filled with ~로 가득 차다   **empty** 텅 빈

20

M   Thank you for visiting. Please have a seat.

W   Thank you. May I ask why you wanted to see me?

M   Kate has always been a good student when it comes to her studies. But these days I think one of her friends is bullying her.

W   Oh, I didn't know that. Her behavior at home is the same.

M   Well, she isn't talkative and happy at school anymore. She is afraid to talk these days.

W   I wasn't aware of the problem. Thank you for letting me know.

M   Please talk to her about it, so we can solve the problem.

남   방문해주셔서 감사합니다. 앉으세요.
여   감사합니다. 왜 저를 보자고 하신 건지 여쭤도 될까요?
남   Kate는 학업 면에서 항상 우수한 학생입니다. 하지만 요즘 친구 중 한 명으로부터 괴롭힘을 당하고 있는 것 같습니다.
여   오, 전 몰랐습니다. 집에서는 행동이 똑같거든요.
남   저, 그녀는 학교에서 더 이상 수다스럽거나 즐거워하지 않습니다. 요즘에는 말하는 것을 두려워합니다.
여   전 그 문제를 몰랐습니다. 알려주셔서 감사합니다.
남   그 문제를 해결할 수 있도록 그녀와 얘기해보세요.

① 저도 그러길 바래요.
② 제 생각을 바꾸지 않을 거예요.
③ 조언 고맙습니다. 감사합니다.
④ 여기서 즐겁게 머무시길 바랍니다. 마음껏 드십시오.
⑤ 그 문제를 해결할 수 있도록 그녀와 얘기해보세요.

when it comes to ~에 관해서라면   **bully** (약한 자를) 괴롭히다
talkative 수다스러운   **be aware of** ~을 알다

MEMO

MEMO

MEMO

MEMO

MEMO

MEMO